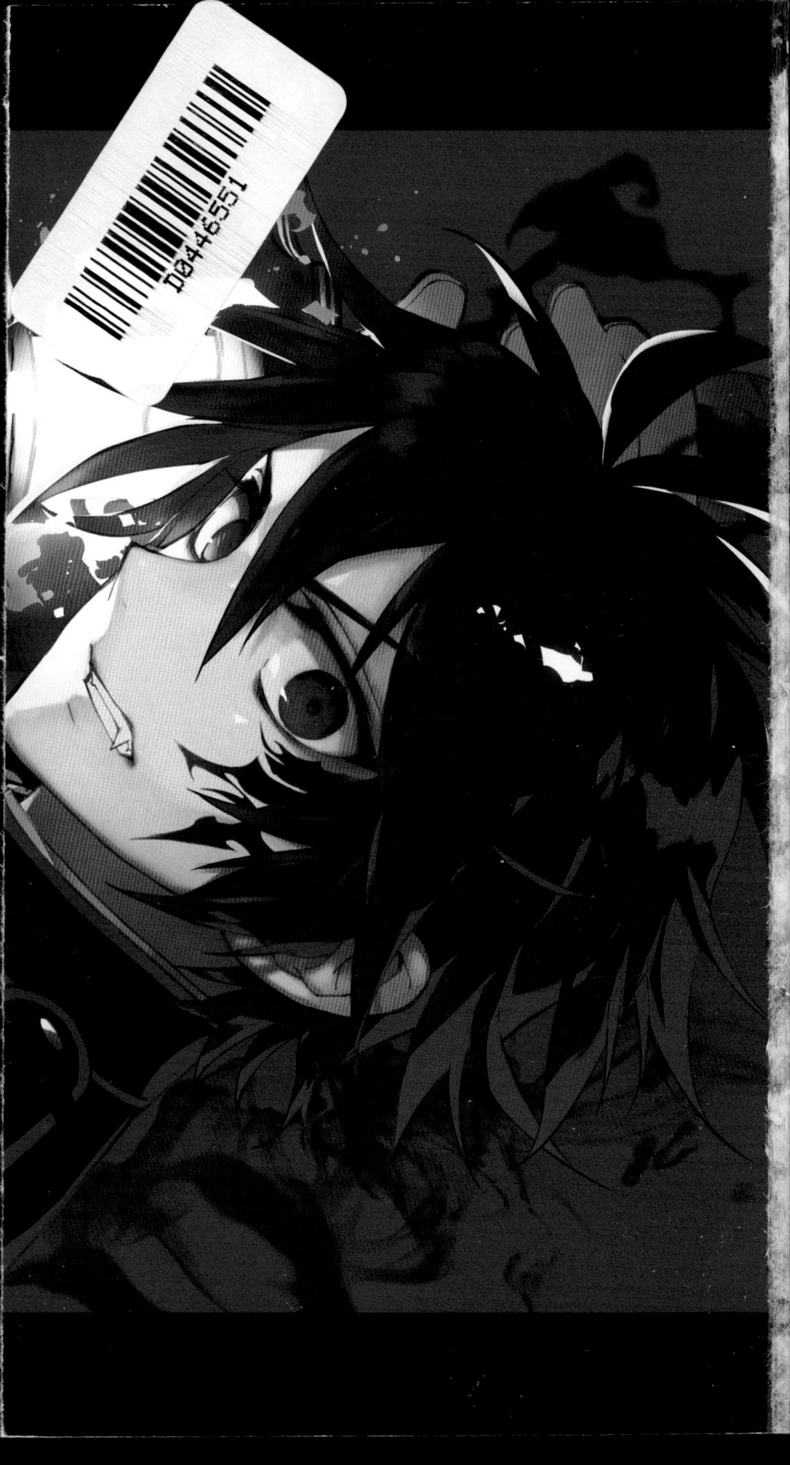

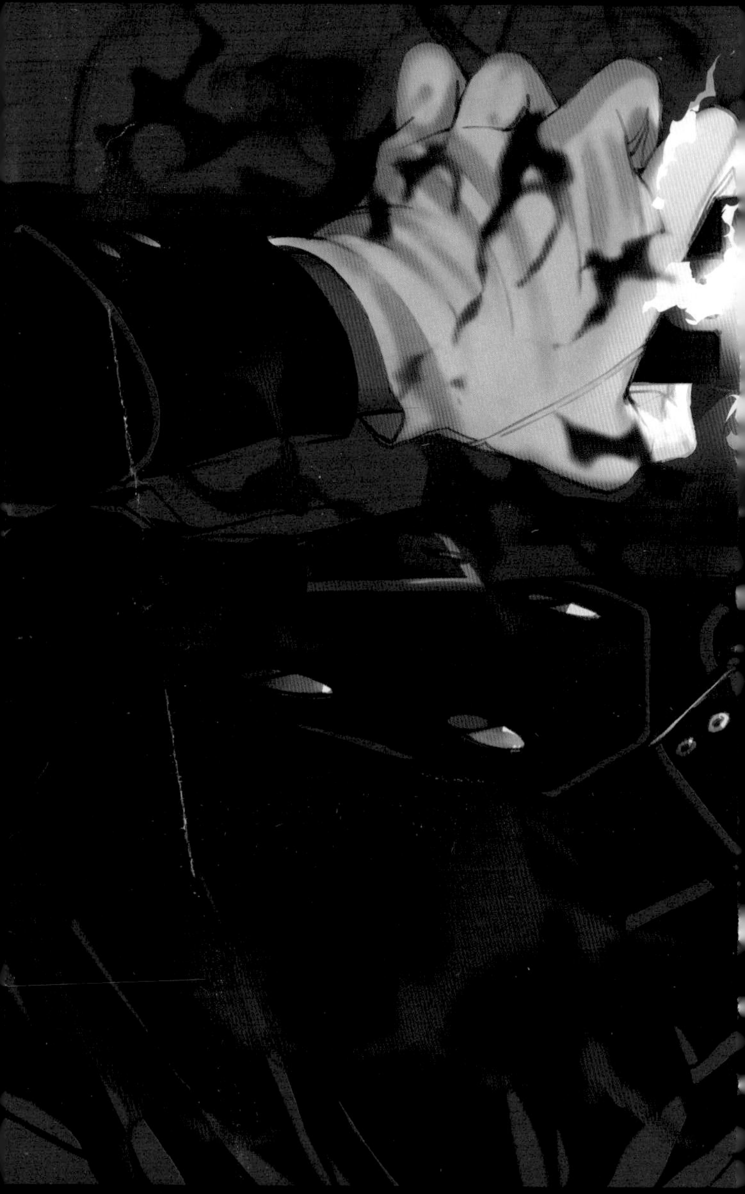

Seraph of the End

─VAMPIRE REIGN─

15

STORY BY **Takaya Kagami**

ART BY **Yamato Yamamoto**

STORYBOARDS BY **Daisuke Furuya**

CHARACTERS

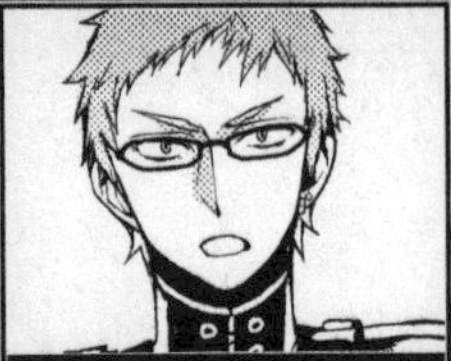

SHIHO KIMIZUKI

Yuichiro's friend. Smart but abrasive. His Cursed Gear is Kiseki-o, twin blades.

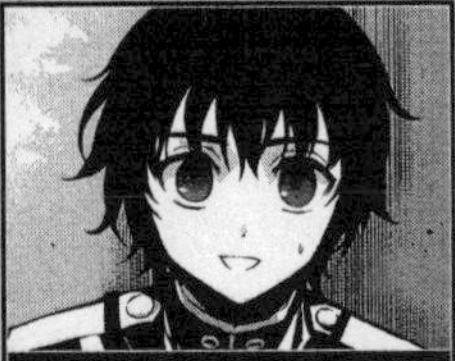

YOICHI SAOTOME

Yuichiro's friend. His sister was killed by a vampire. His Cursed Gear is Gekkouin, a bow.

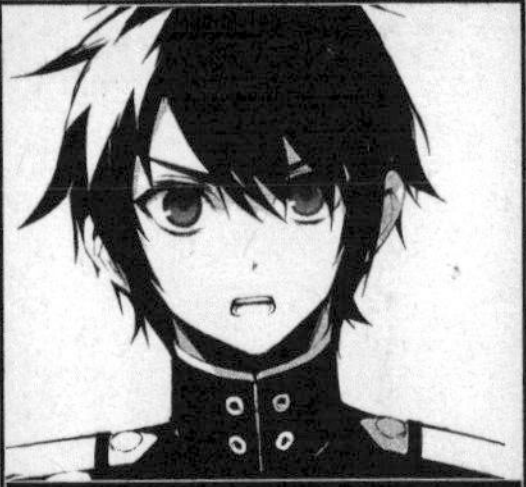

YUICHIRO HYAKUYA

A boy who escaped from the vampire capital, he has both great kindness and a great desire for revenge. Lone wolf. His Cursed Gear is Asuramaru, a katana.

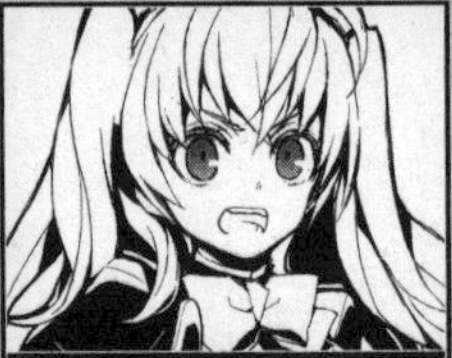

MITSUBA SANGU

An elite soldier who has been part of the Moon Demon Company since age 13. Bossy. Her Cursed Gear is Tenjiryu, a giant axe.

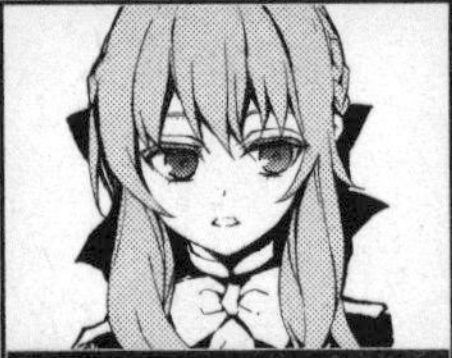

SHINOA HIRAGI

Guren's subordinate and Yuichiro's surveillance officer. Member of the illustrious Hiragi family. Her Cursed Gear is Shikama Doji, a scythe.

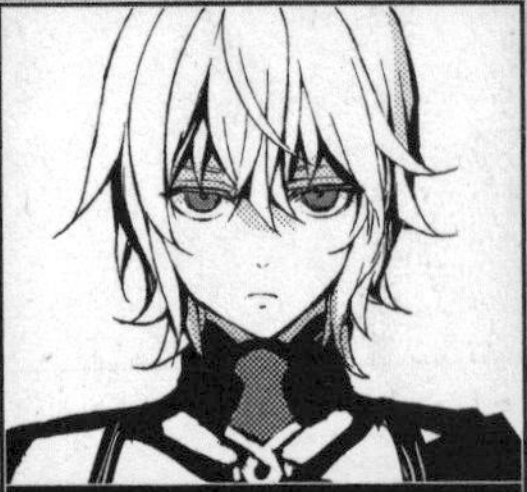

MIKAELA HYAKUYA

Yuichiro's best friend. He was supposedly killed but has come back to life as a vampire. Currently working with Shinoa Squad.

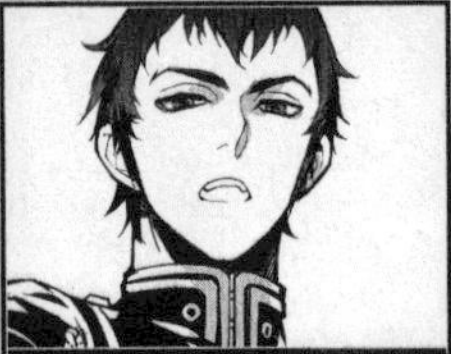

KURETO HIRAGI

A Lieutenant General in the Demon Army. Heir apparent to the Hiragi family, he is cold, cruel and ruthless.

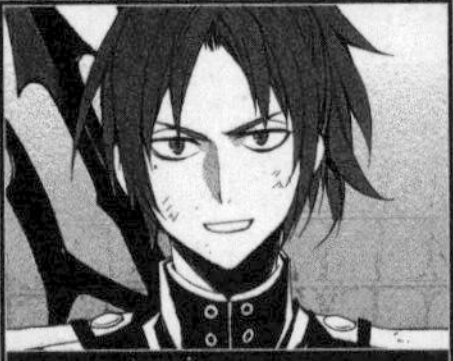

MAKOTO NARUMI

Former leader of Narumi Squad. After his entire squad died during the battle of Nagoya, he deserted the Demon Army with Shinoa Squad.

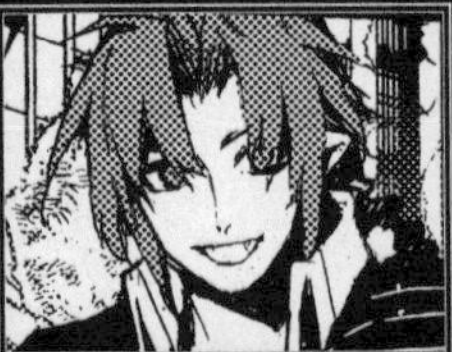

CROWLEY EUSFORD

A Thirteenth Progenitor vampire. Part of Ferid's faction.

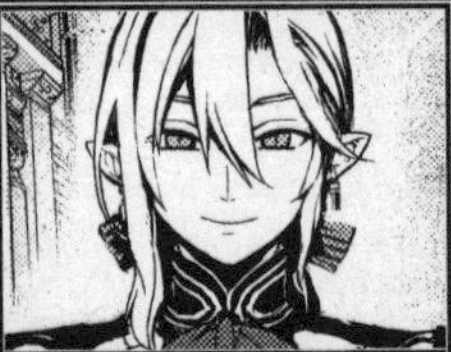

FERID BATHORY

A Seventh Progenitor vampire, he killed Mikaela.

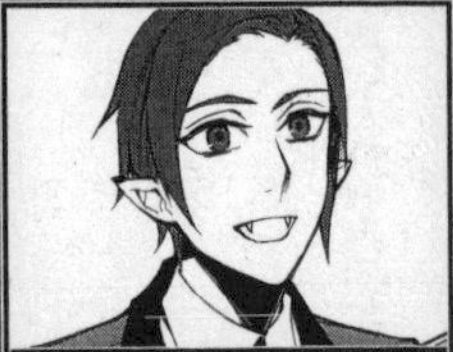

KY LUC

A Fifth Progenitor vampire under Second Progenitor Urd Geales. Currently guarding the two vampires undergoing exposure torture.

SHIGURE YUKIMI

A 2nd Lieutenant and Guren's subordinate along with Sayuri. Very calm and collected.

SAYURI HANAYORI

A 2nd Lieutenant and Guren's subordinate. She's devoted to Guren.

GUREN ICHINOSE

Lieutenant Colonel of the Moon Demon Company, a Vampire Extermination Unit. He recruited Yuichiro into the Japanese Imperial Demon Army. He's been acting strange ever since the battle in Nagoya... His Cursed Gear is Mahiru-no-yo, a katana.

SHINYA HIRAGI

A Major General and an adopted member of the Hiragi Family. He was Mahiru Hiragi's fiancé.

NORITO GOSHI

A Colonel and a member of the Goshi family. He has been friends with Guren since high school.

MITO JUJO

A Colonel and a member of the Jujo family. She has been friends with Guren since high school.

STORY

A mysterious virus decimates the human population, and vampires claim dominion over the world. Yuichiro and his adopted family of orphans are kept as vampire fodder in an underground city until the day Mikaela, Yuichiro's best friend, plots an ill-fated escape for the orphans. Only Yuichiro survives and reaches the surface.

Four years later, Yuichiro enters into the Moon Demon Company, a Vampire Extermination Unit in the Japanese Imperial Demon Army, to enact his revenge. There he gains Asuramaru, a demon-possessed weapon capable of killing vampires. Along with his squad mates Yoichi, Shinoa, Kimizuki and Mitsuba, Yuichiro deploys to Shinjuku with orders to thwart a vampire attack.

In a battle against the vampires, Yuichiro discovers that not only is his friend Mikaela alive, but he also has been turned into a vampire. After misunderstandings and near-misses, Yuichiro and Mikaela finally meet each other in Nagoya.

Kureto Hiragi begins an experiment on the Seraph of the End at Nagoya Airport. Caught up in the cruel procedure, the Moon Demon Company suffers extreme losses. Even worse, Guren appears to betray his friends, participating in the experiment and gravely wounding Yuichiro. To further complicate things, vampires appear to stop the experiment and Ferid stages a coup, capturing the Vampire Queen and throwing everything into chaos.

Declaring enough is enough, Shinoa Squad deserts the Demon Army and escapes Nagoya to hide away in a small seaside town. Ferid tracks them down and tells them that Guren was the one who caused the Catastrophe eight years ago, and that all the answers are in Osaka. The group arrives just in time to meet up with Second Progenitor Urd Geales and a horde of vampire nobles. They're all captured, and Ferid and Krul are sentenced to torture by exposure. Yu decides to rescue the two vampires, but to defeat their guard, the hugely powerful Fifth Progenitor Ky Luc, Yu needs to control the immense power within himself. Right then, the supposedly traitorous Guren arrives in Osaka...

Seraph of the End
—VAMPIRE REIGN—

15

CONTENTS

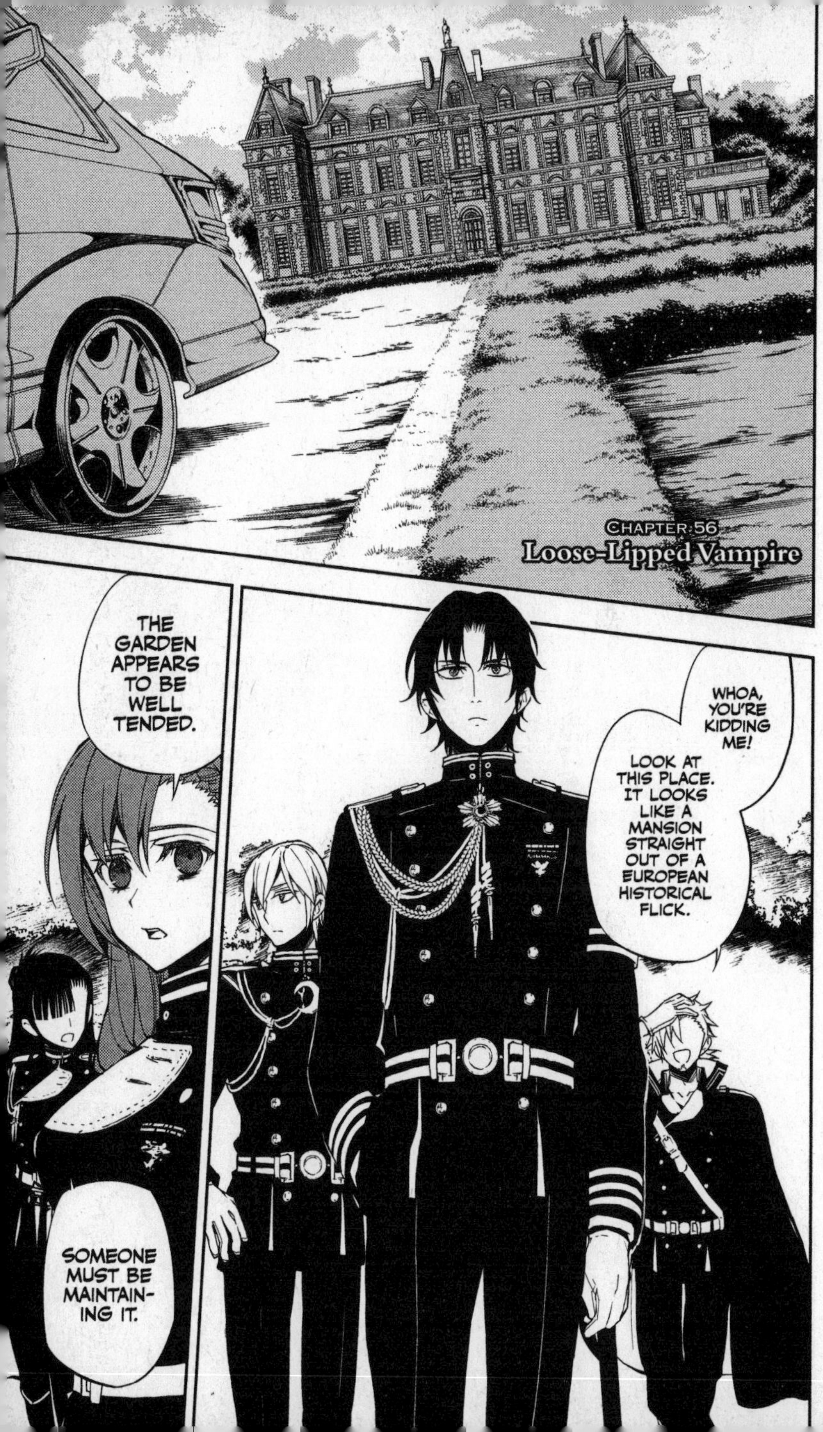
CHAPTER 56
Loose-Lipped Vampire
WHOA, YOU'RE KIDDING ME!
LOOK AT THIS PLACE. IT LOOKS LIKE A MANSION STRAIGHT OUT OF A EUROPEAN HISTORICAL FLICK.
THE GARDEN APPEARS TO BE WELL TENDED.
SOMEONE MUST BE MAINTAIN-ING IT.

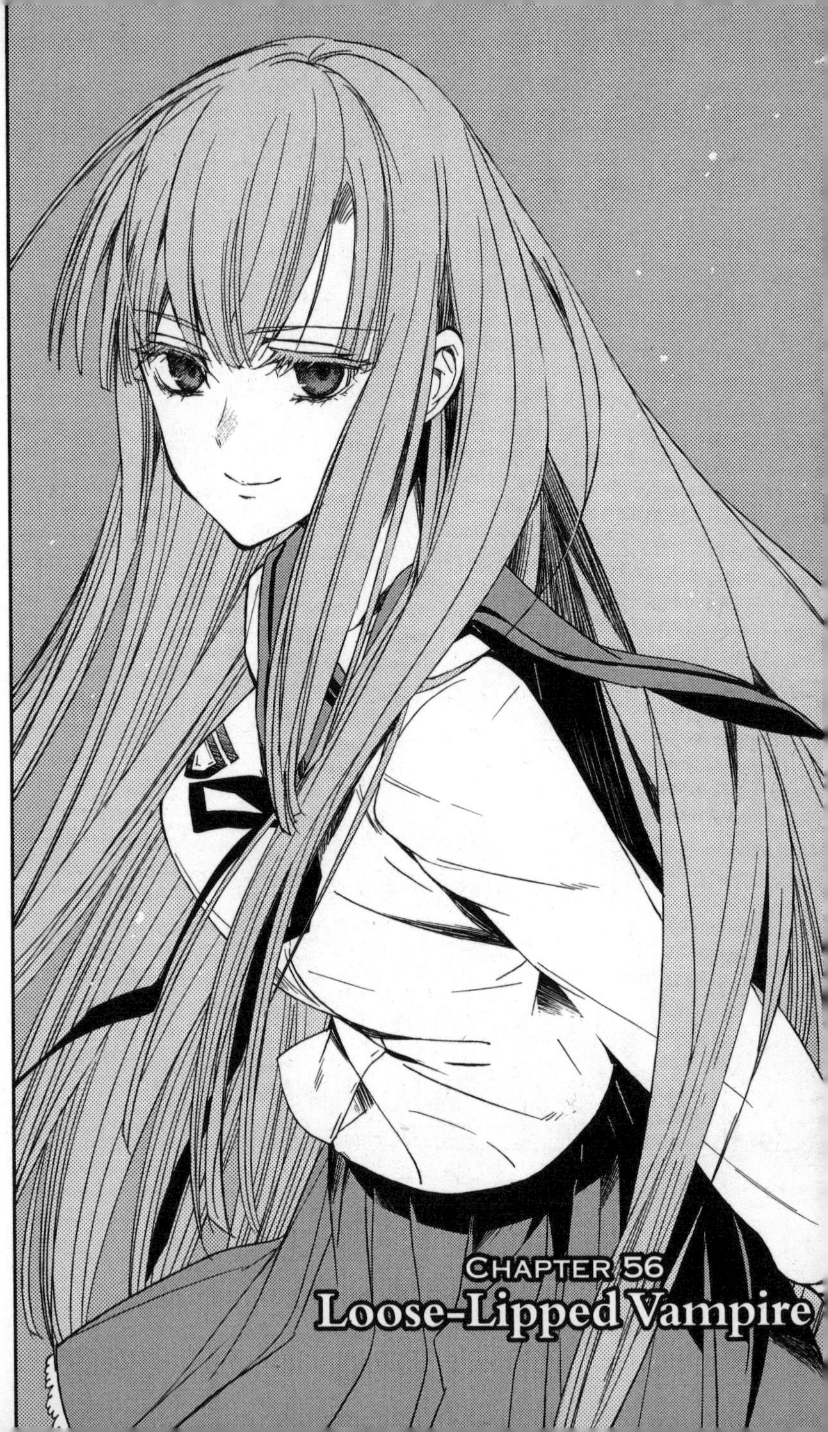
CHAPTER 56
Loose-Lipped Vampire

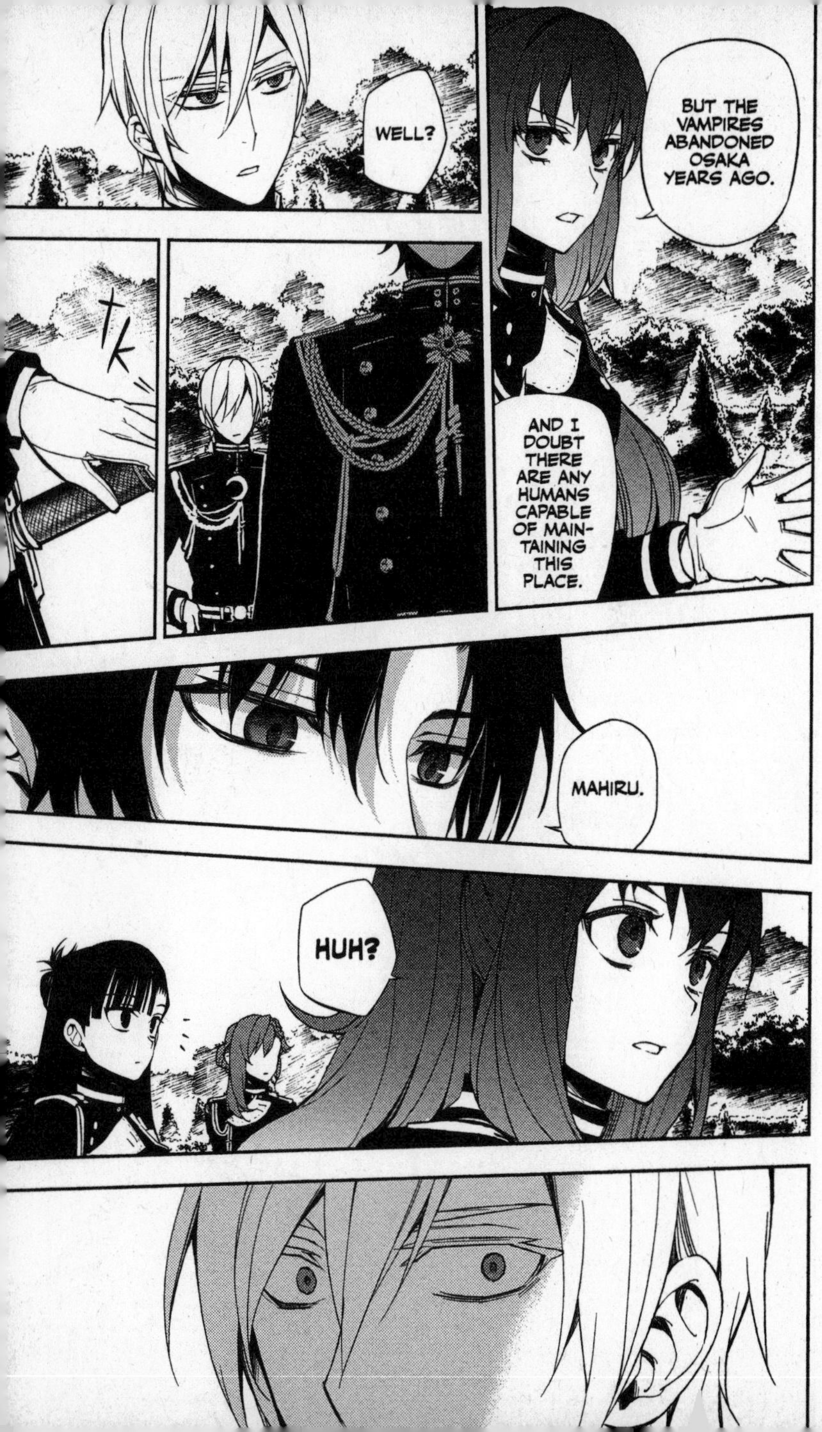
BUT THE VAMPIRES ABANDONED OSAKA YEARS AGO.
AND I DOUBT THERE ARE ANY HUMANS CAPABLE OF MAIN-TAINING THIS PLACE.
WELL?
TK
MAHIRU.
HUH?

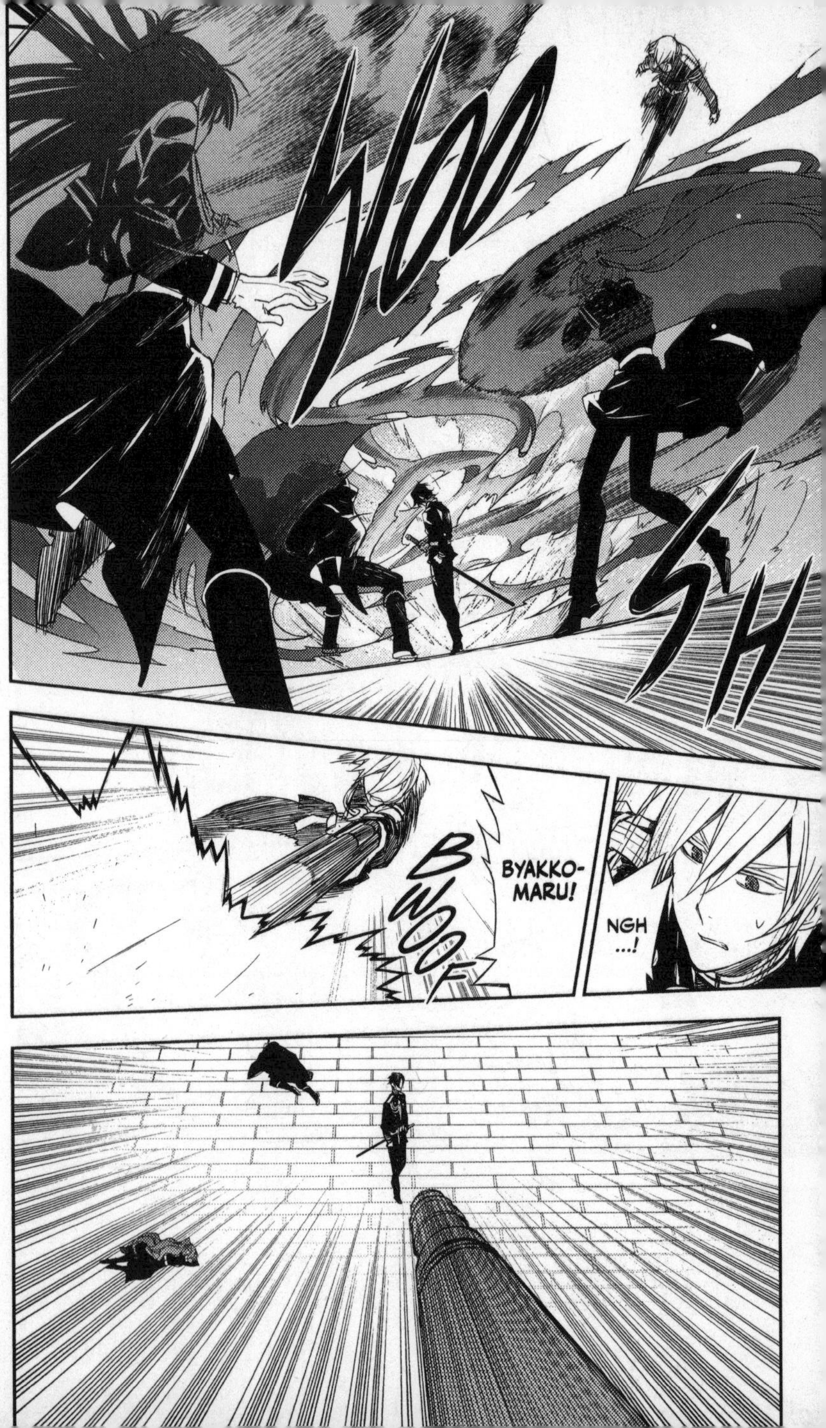
WHOO
SHH
NGH ...!
BYAKKO-MARU!
BWOOF

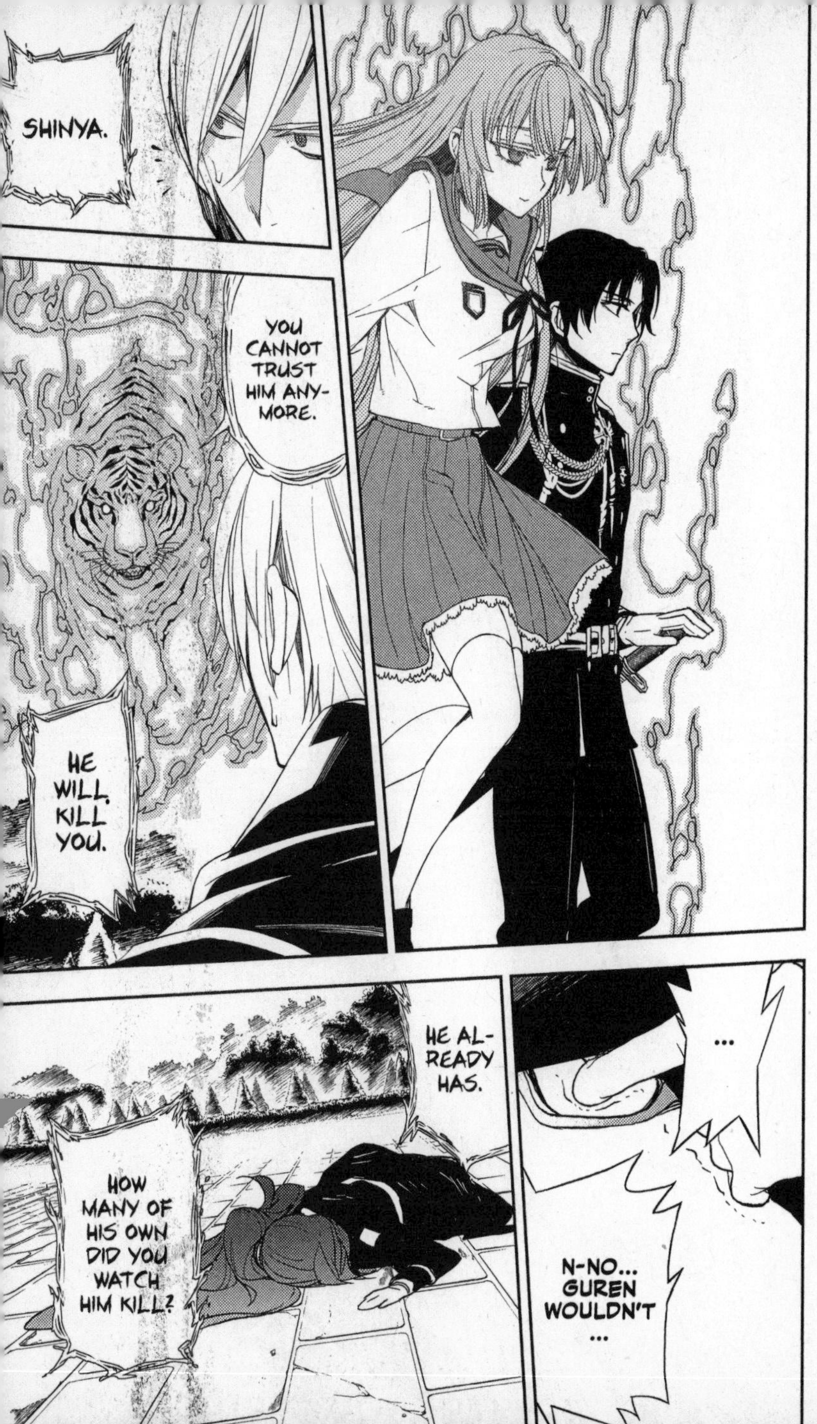
SHINYA.
YOU CANNOT TRUST HIM ANY-MORE.
HE WILL. KILL YOU.
...
N-NO... GUREN WOULDN'T ...
HE AL-READY HAS.
HOW MANY OF HIS OWN DID YOU WATCH HIM KILL?

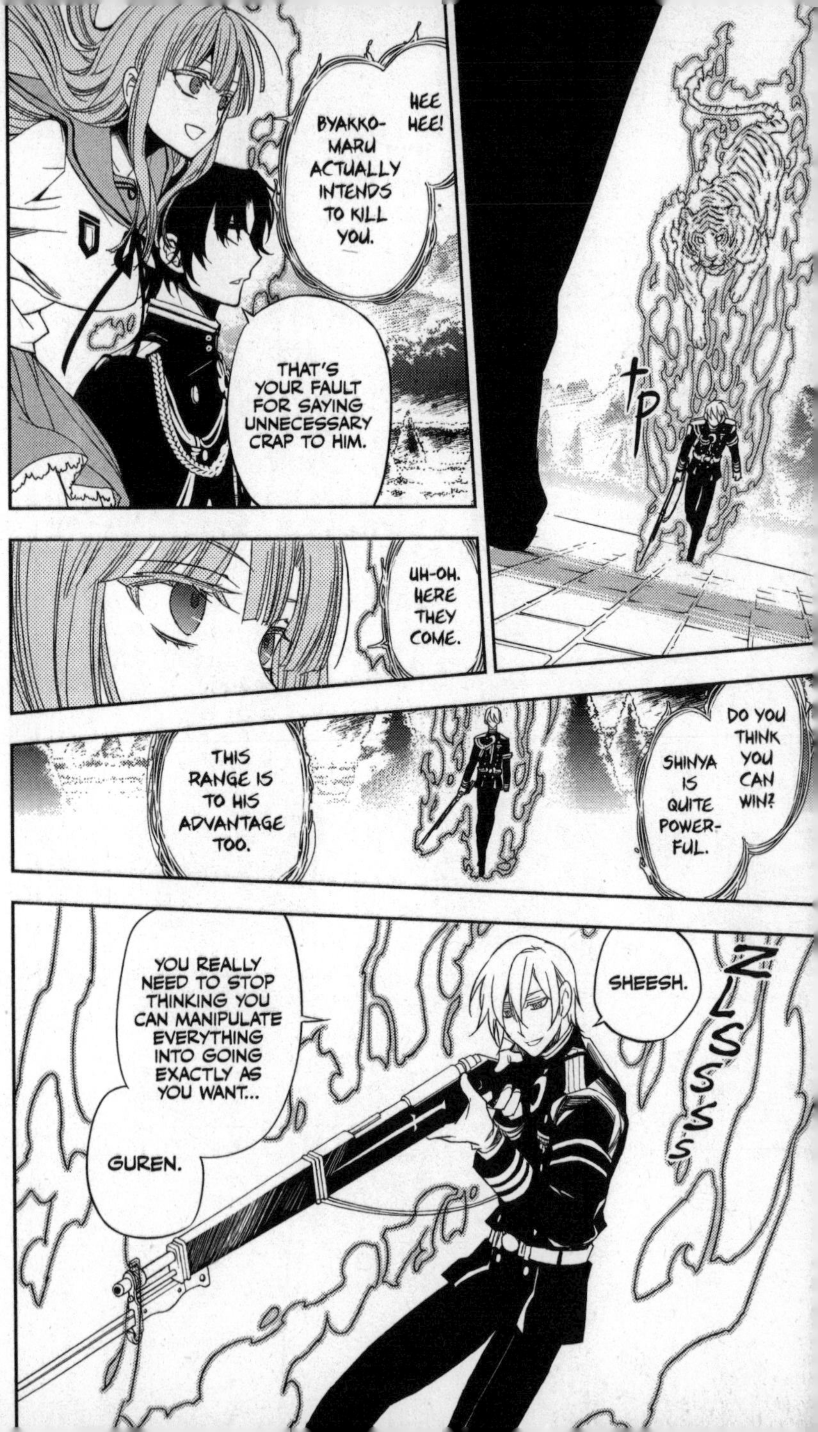
TP
HEE HEE! BYAKKO-MARU ACTUALLY INTENDS TO KILL YOU.
THAT'S YOUR FAULT FOR SAYING UNNECESSARY CRAP TO HIM.
UH-OH. HERE THEY COME.
DO YOU THINK YOU CAN WIN? SHINYA IS QUITE POWER-FUL.
THIS RANGE IS TO HIS ADVANTAGE TOO.
ZLSSSSS
SHEESH.
YOU REALLY NEED TO STOP THINKING YOU CAN MANIPULATE EVERYTHING INTO GOING EXACTLY AS YOU WANT...
GUREN.

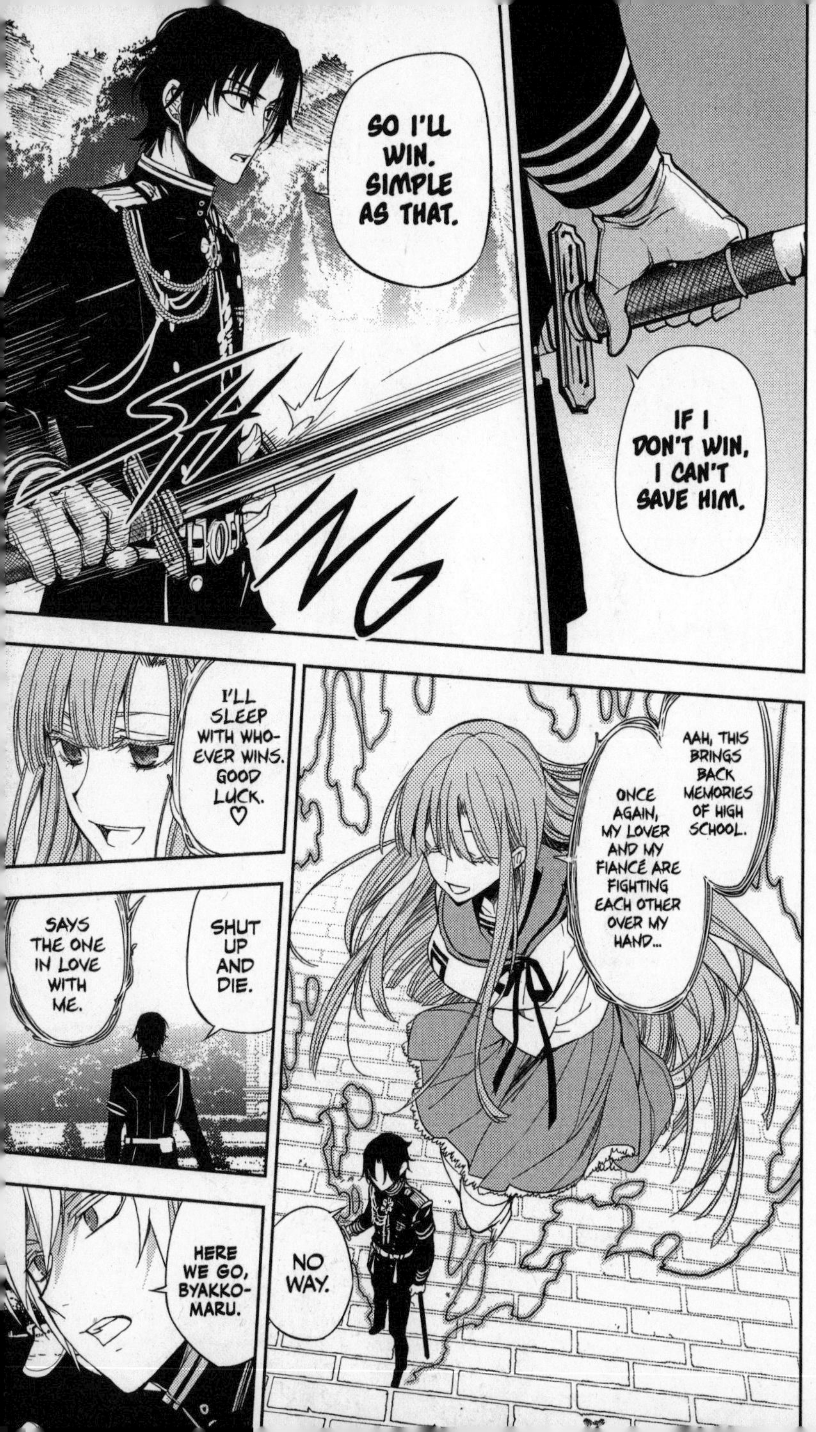
IF I DON'T WIN, I CAN'T SAVE HIM.
SO I'LL WIN. SIMPLE AS THAT.
SHING
AAH, THIS BRINGS BACK MEMORIES OF HIGH SCHOOL.
ONCE AGAIN, MY LOVER AND MY FIANCÉ ARE FIGHTING EACH OTHER OVER MY HAND...
NO WAY.
I'LL SLEEP WITH WHO-EVER WINS. GOOD LUCK. ♡
SHUT UP AND DIE.
SAYS THE ONE IN LOVE WITH ME.
HERE WE GO, BYAKKO-MARU.

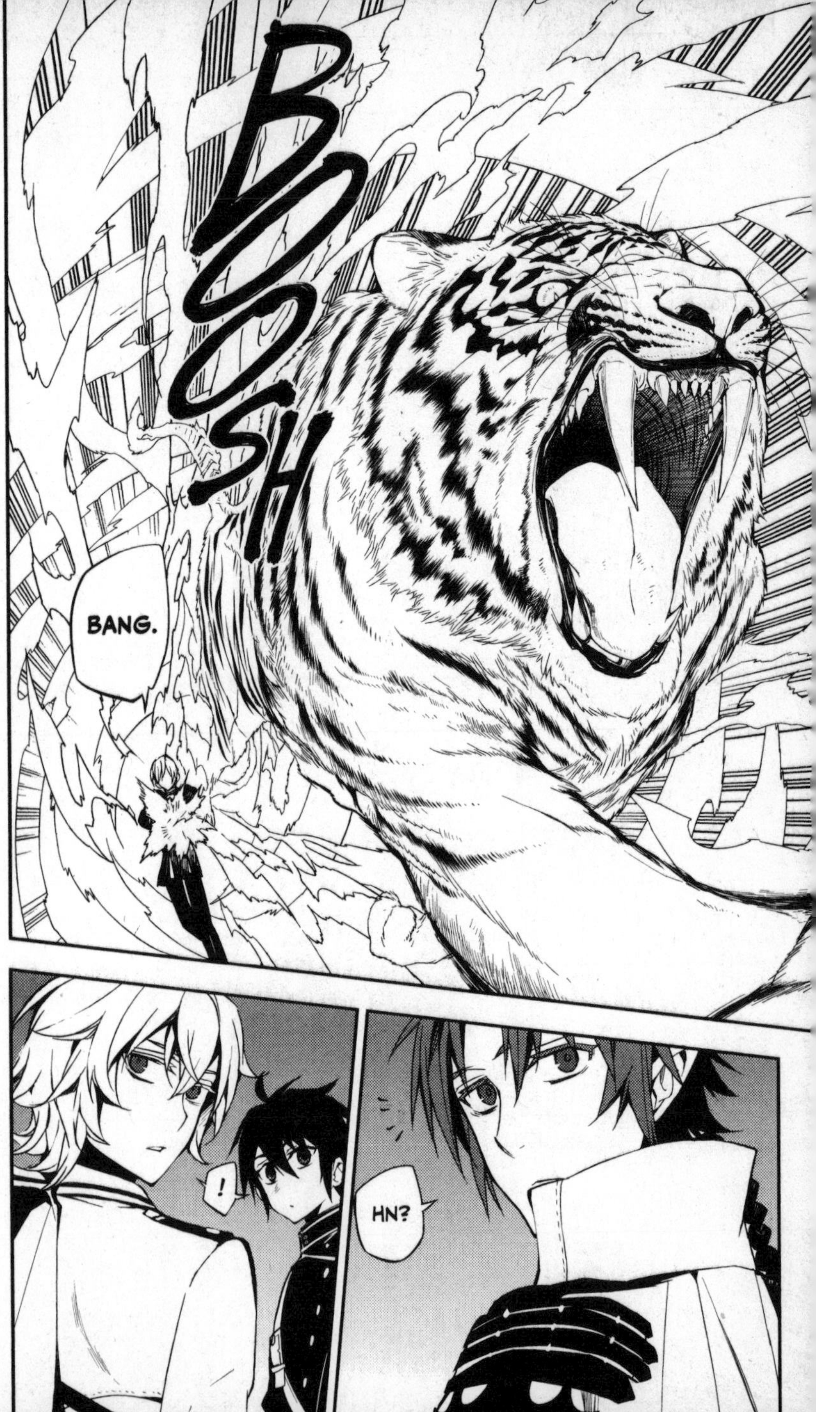
BOSH
BANG.
HN?
!

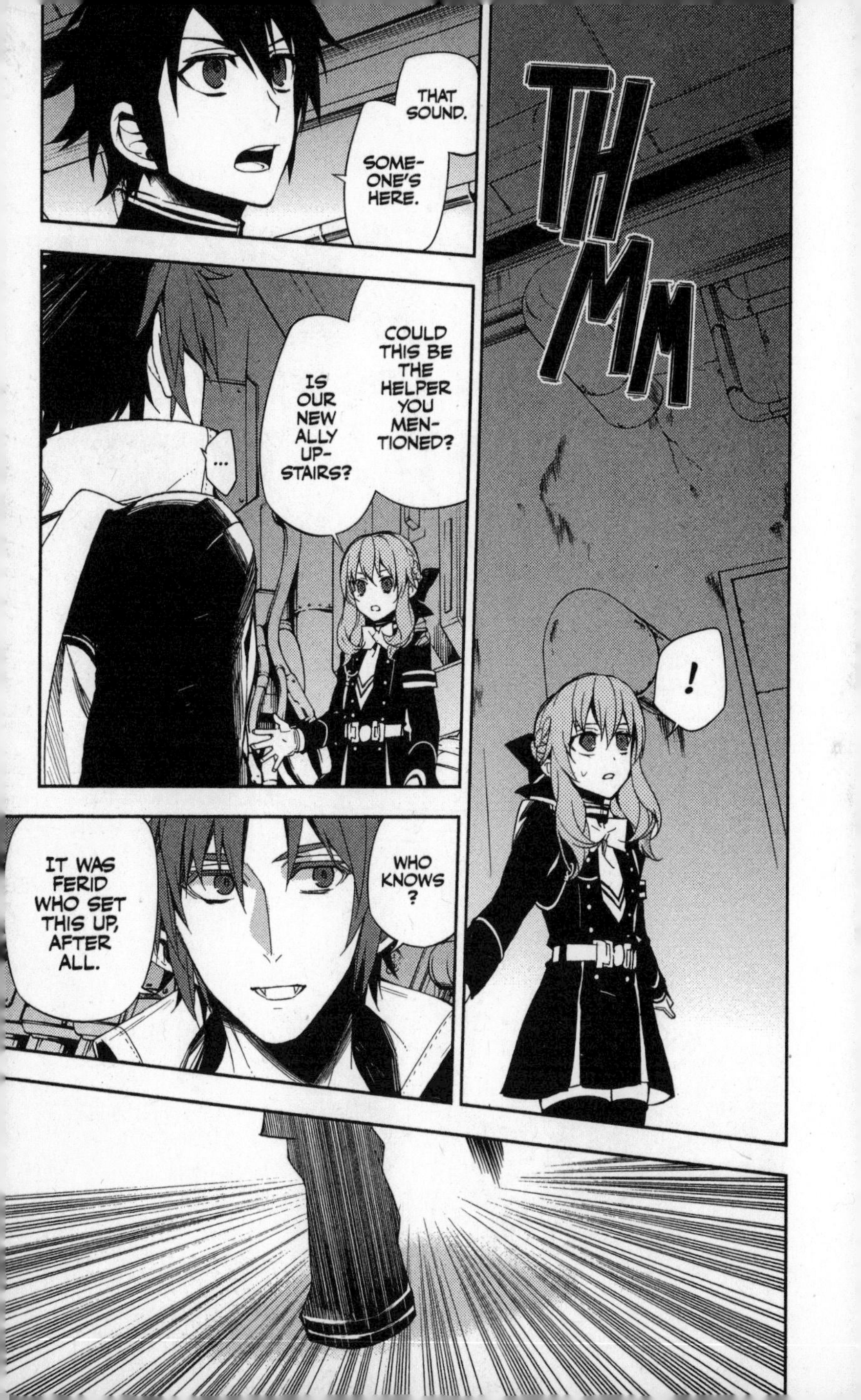
THMM
!
THAT SOUND.
SOME-ONE'S HERE.
COULD THIS BE THE HELPER YOU MEN-TIONED?
IS OUR NEW ALLY UP-STAIRS?
...
WHO KNOWS?
IT WAS FERID WHO SET THIS UP, AFTER ALL.

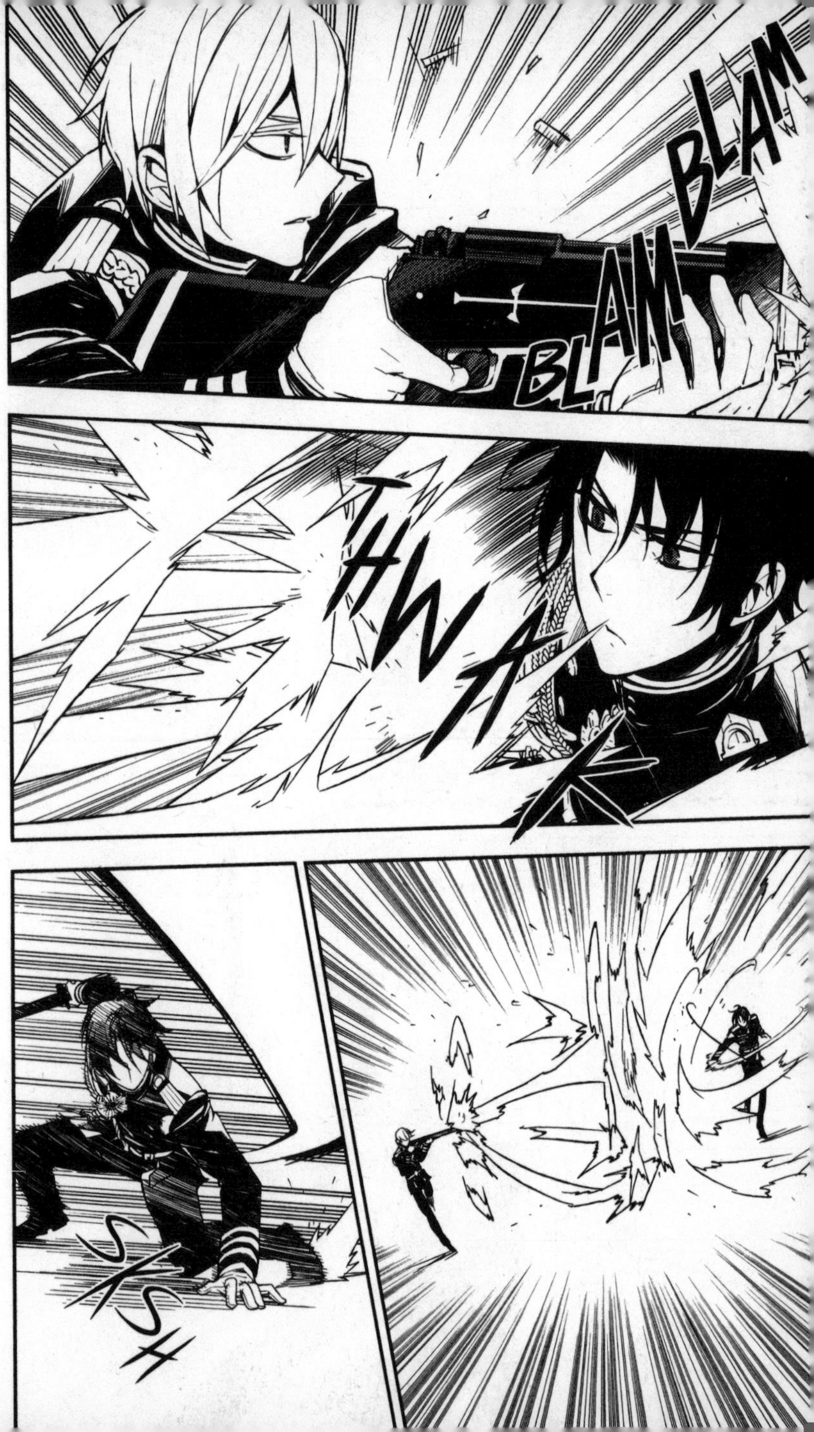
BLAM BLAM BLAM
THWAK
SKSH

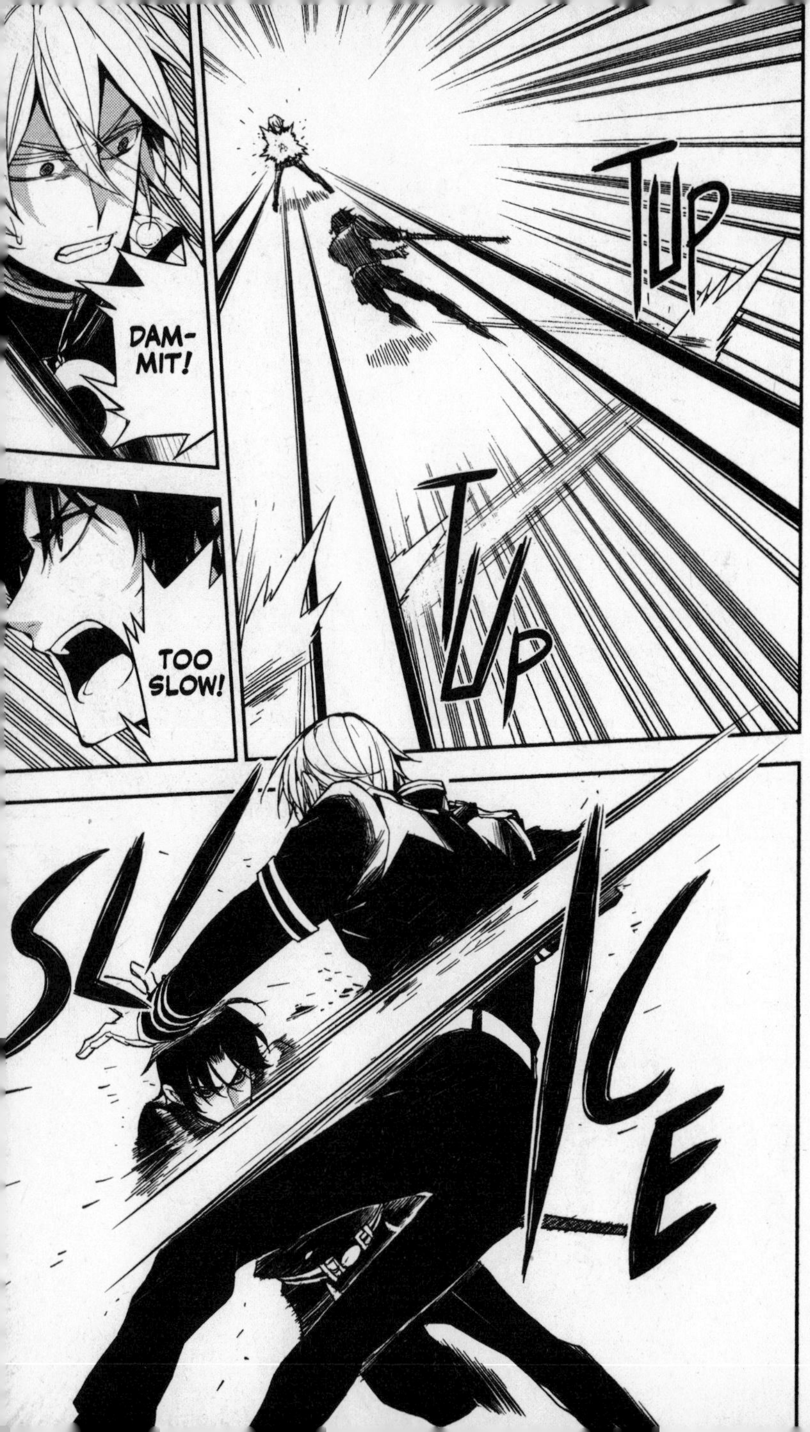
TUP
TUP
DAM-
MIT!
TOO
SLOW!
SLICE

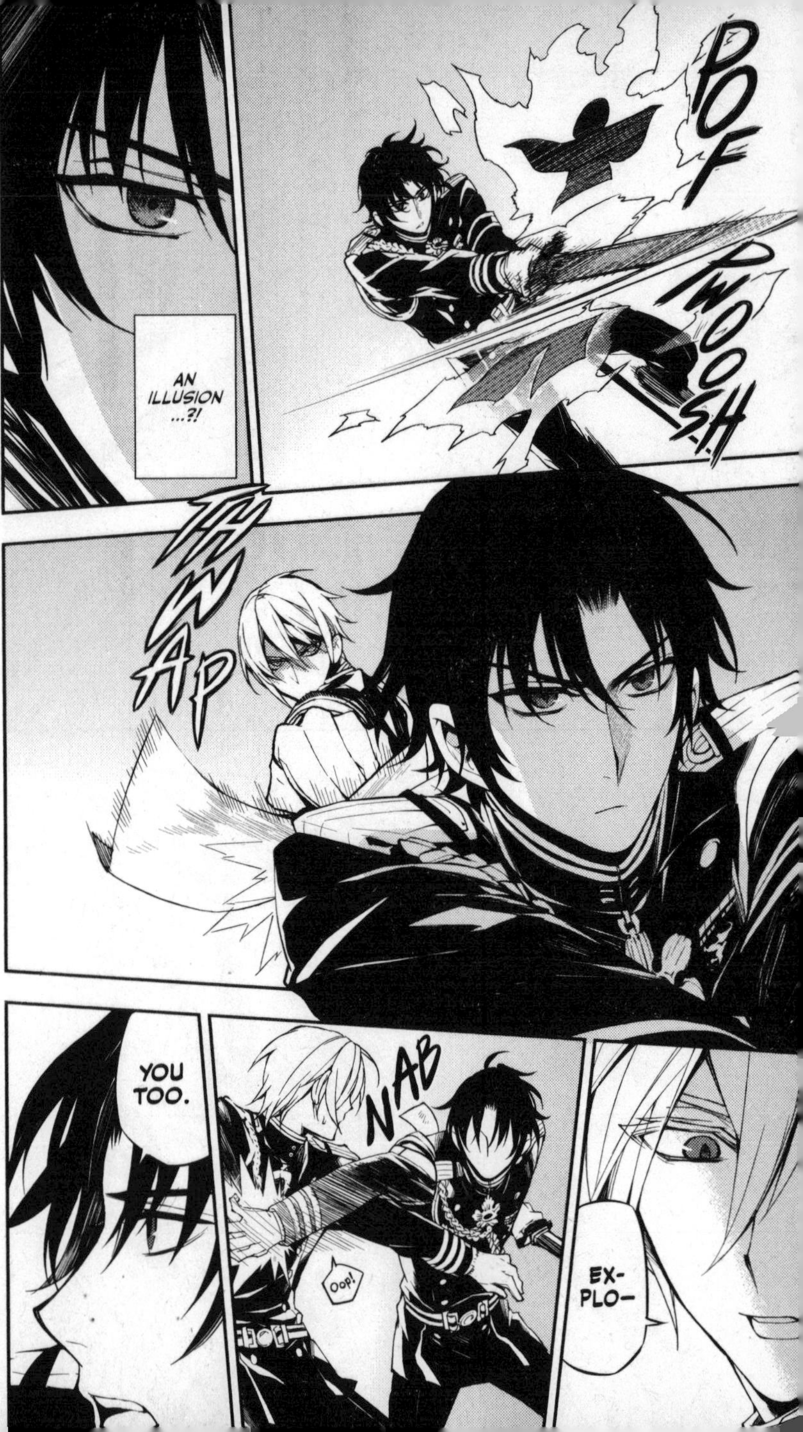
POOF
PWOOSH
AN ILLUSION ...?!
THWAP
EX-PLO—
NAB
Oop!
YOU TOO.

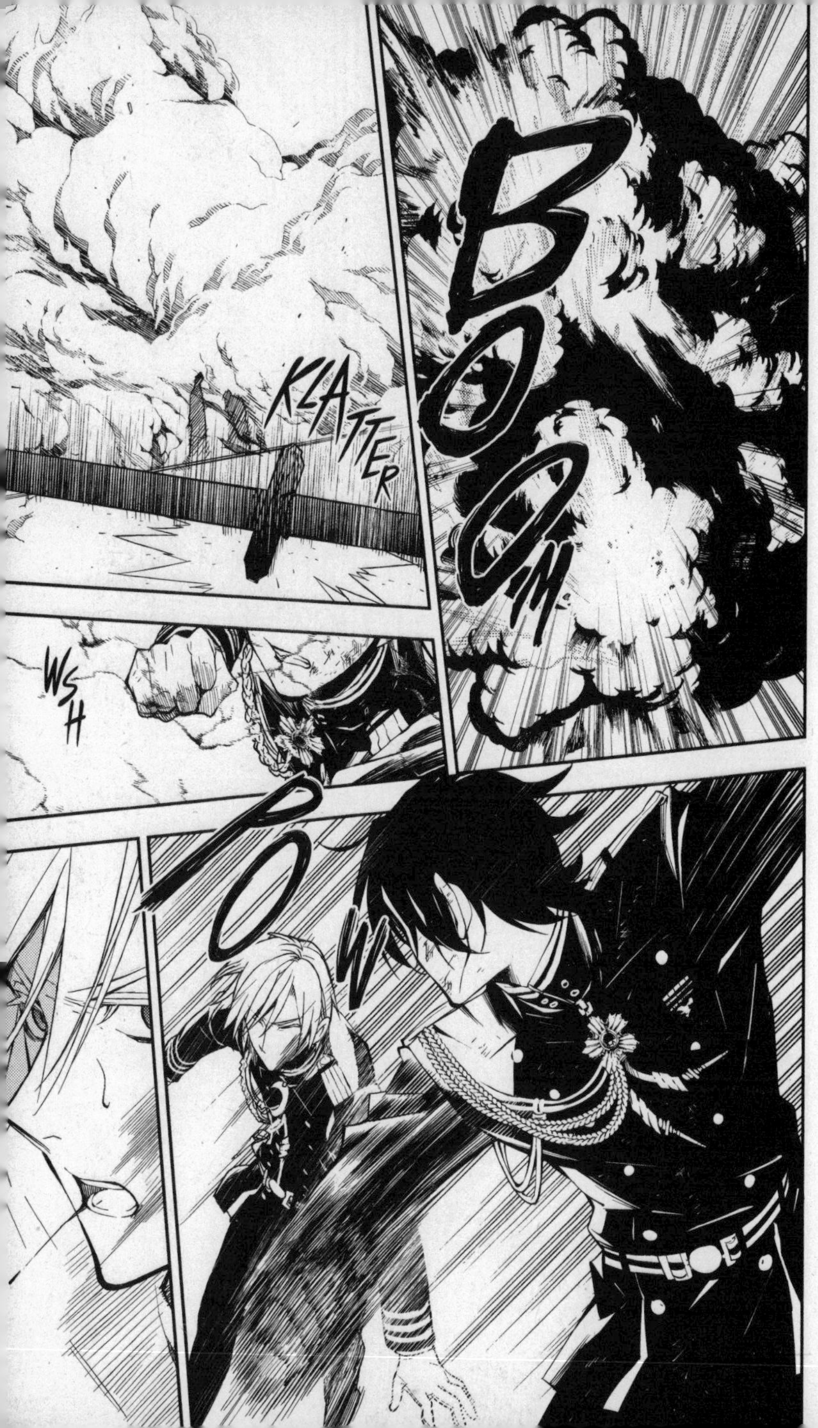
BOOOM
KLATTER
WSH
POW

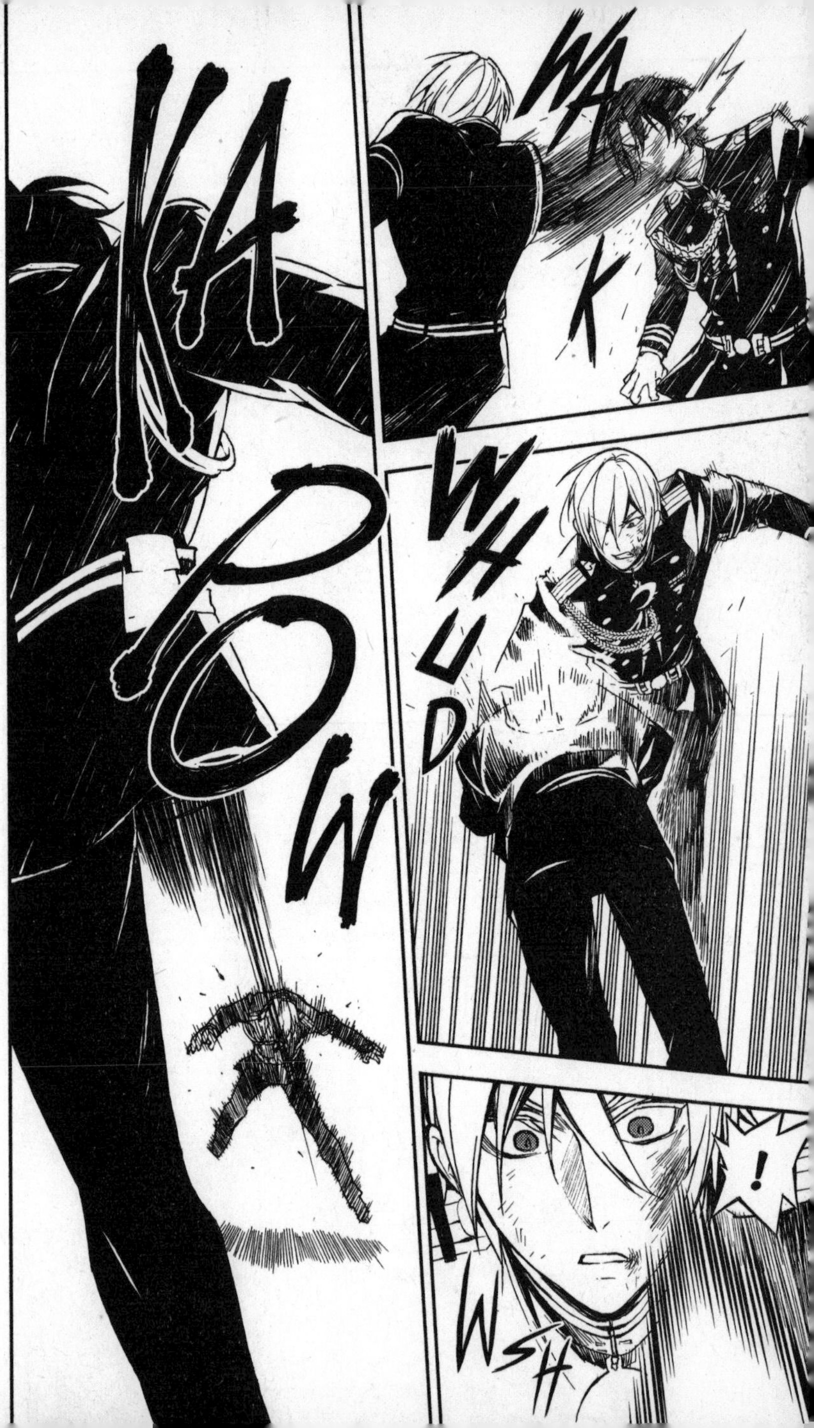
WHAK
WHUD
!
WSH
KAPOW

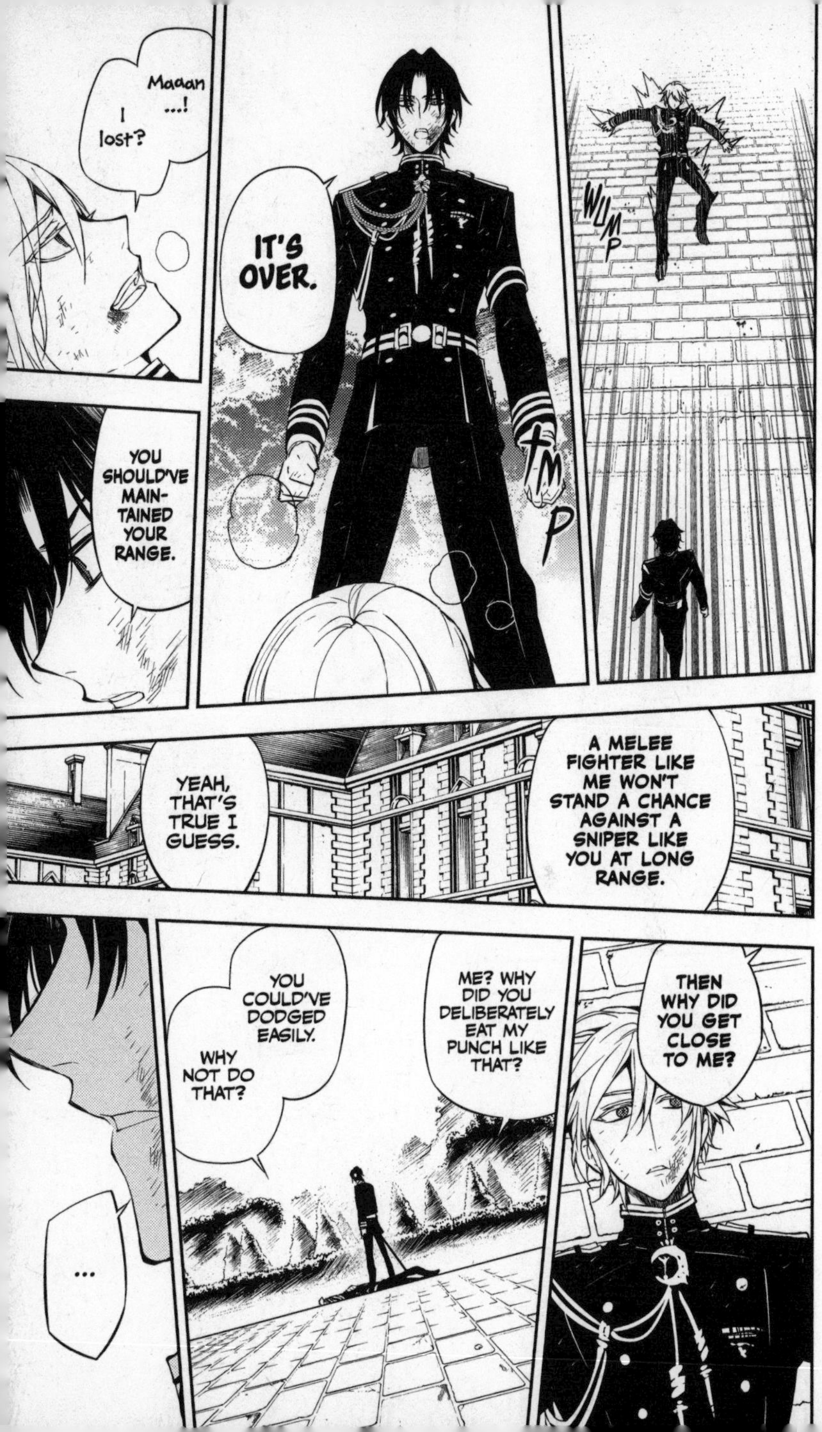
WUMP
IT'S OVER.
TMP
Maaan ...! I lost?
YOU SHOULD'VE MAIN-TAINED YOUR RANGE.
A MELEE FIGHTER LIKE ME WON'T STAND A CHANCE AGAINST A SNIPER LIKE YOU AT LONG RANGE.
YEAH, THAT'S TRUE I GUESS.
THEN WHY DID YOU GET CLOSE TO ME?
ME? WHY DID YOU DELIBERATELY EAT MY PUNCH LIKE THAT?
YOU COULD'VE DODGED EASILY.
WHY NOT DO THAT?
...

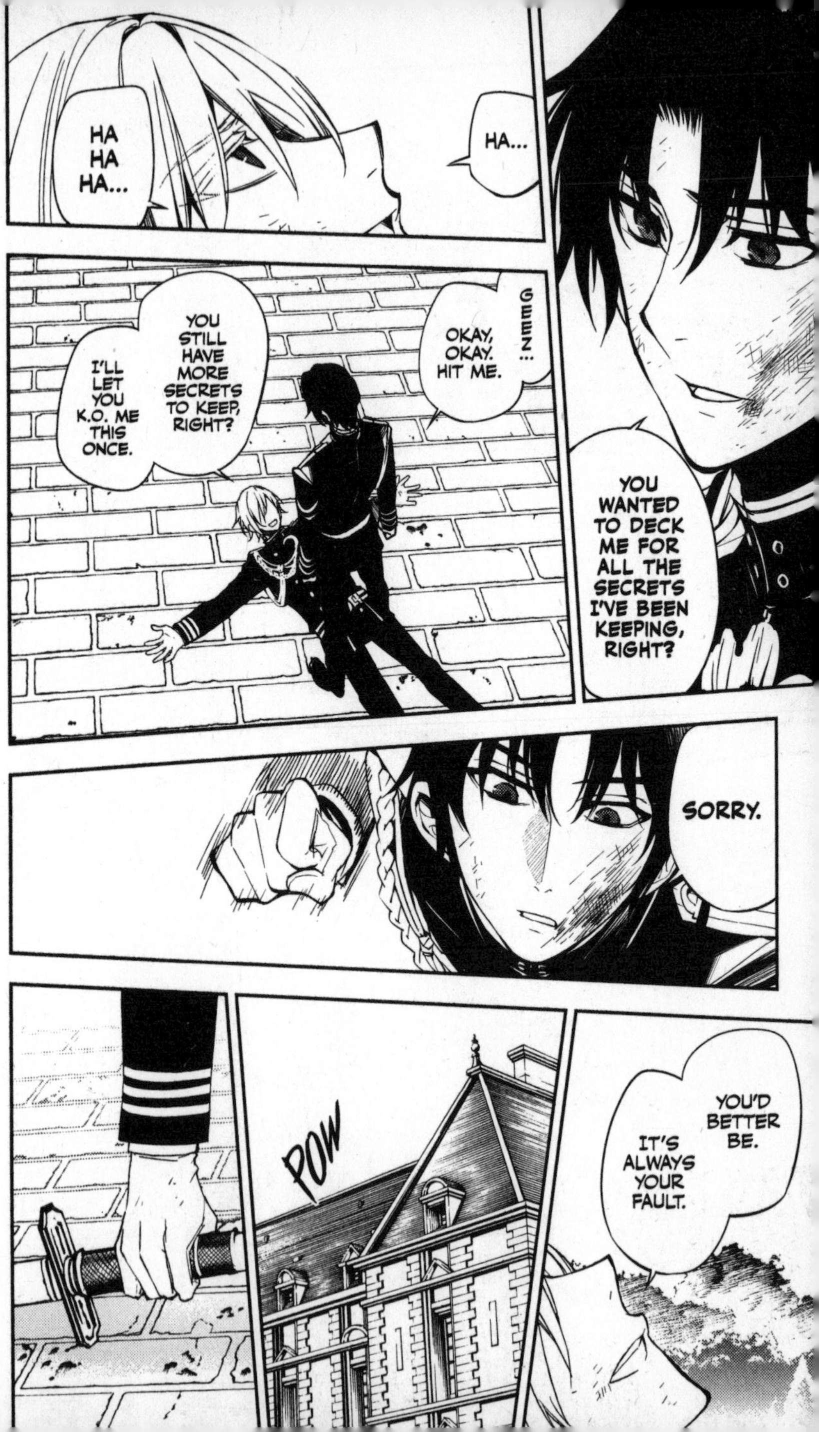
YOU WANTED TO DECK ME FOR ALL THE SECRETS I'VE BEEN KEEPING, RIGHT?
HA...
HA HA HA...
GEEZ...
OKAY, OKAY. HIT ME.
YOU STILL HAVE MORE SECRETS TO KEEP, RIGHT?
I'LL LET YOU K.O. ME THIS ONCE.
SORRY.
YOU'D BETTER BE.
IT'S ALWAYS YOUR FAULT.
POW

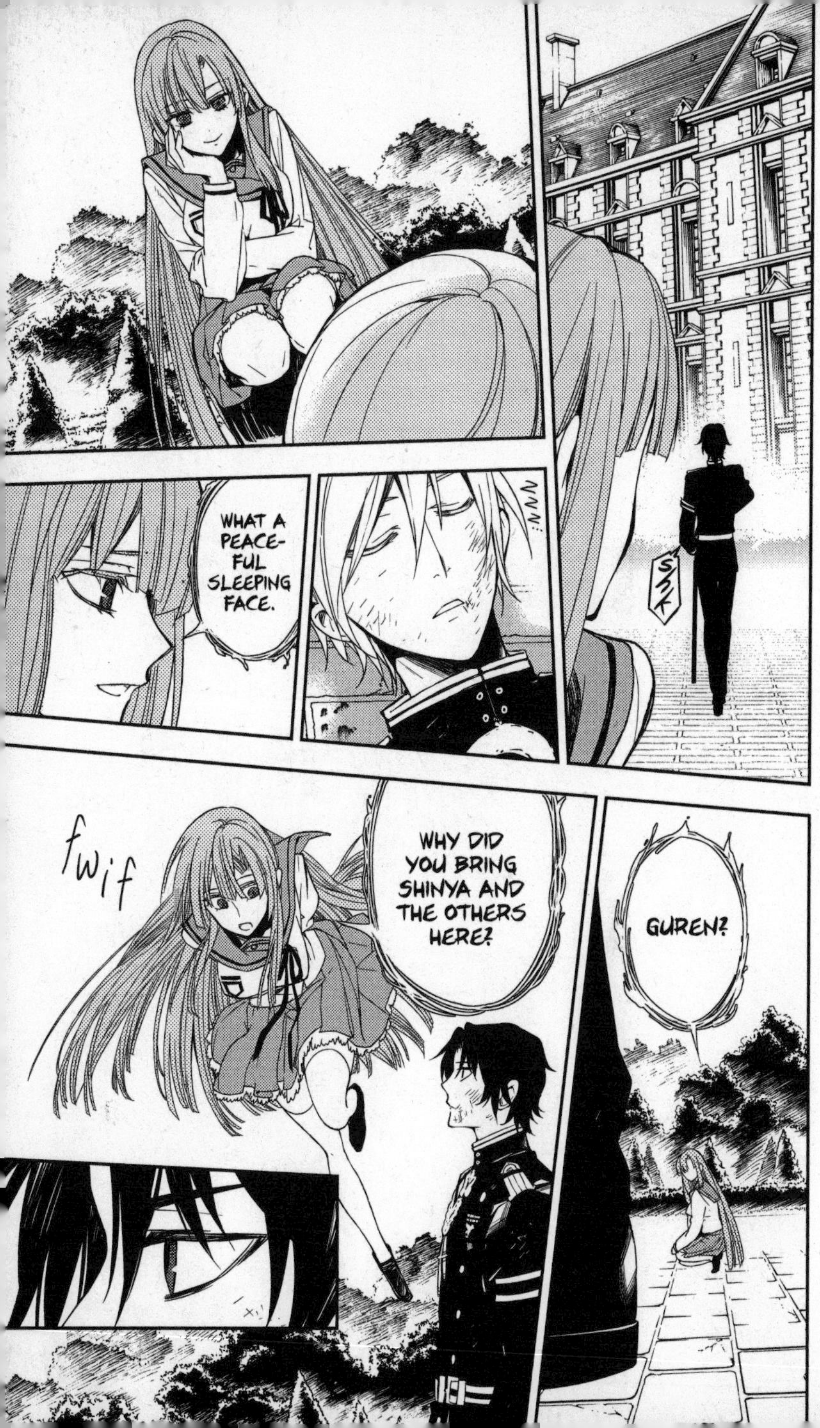
SHK
ZZZ
WHAT A PEACE-FUL SLEEPING FACE.
GUREN?
WHY DID YOU BRING SHINYA AND THE OTHERS HERE?
fwif

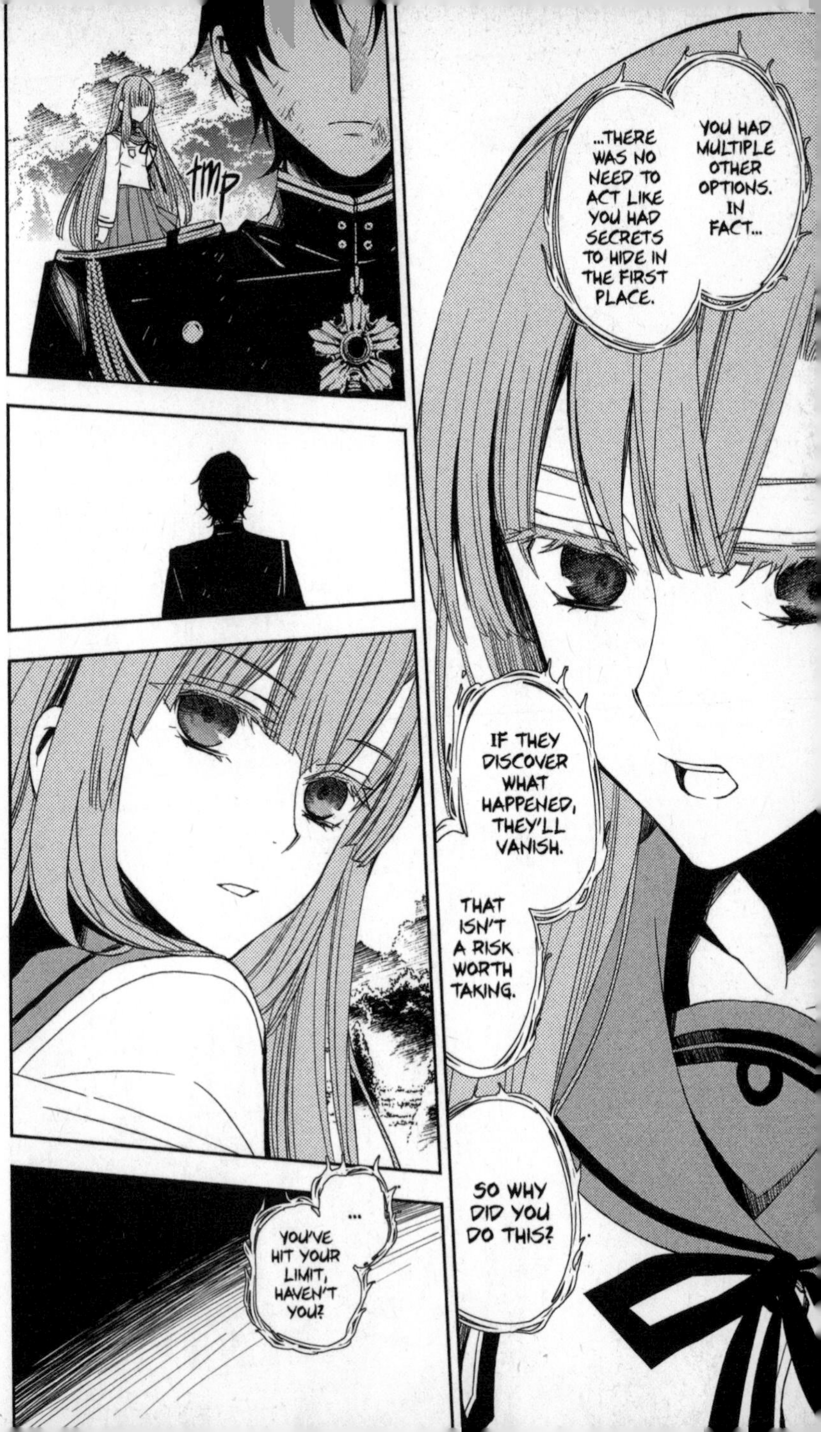
YOU HAD MULTIPLE OTHER OPTIONS. IN FACT...
...THERE WAS NO NEED TO ACT LIKE YOU HAD SECRETS TO HIDE IN THE FIRST PLACE.
IF THEY DISCOVER WHAT HAPPENED, THEY'LL VANISH.
THAT ISN'T A RISK WORTH TAKING.
SO WHY DID YOU DO THIS?
tmp
...
YOU'VE HIT YOUR LIMIT, HAVEN'T YOU?

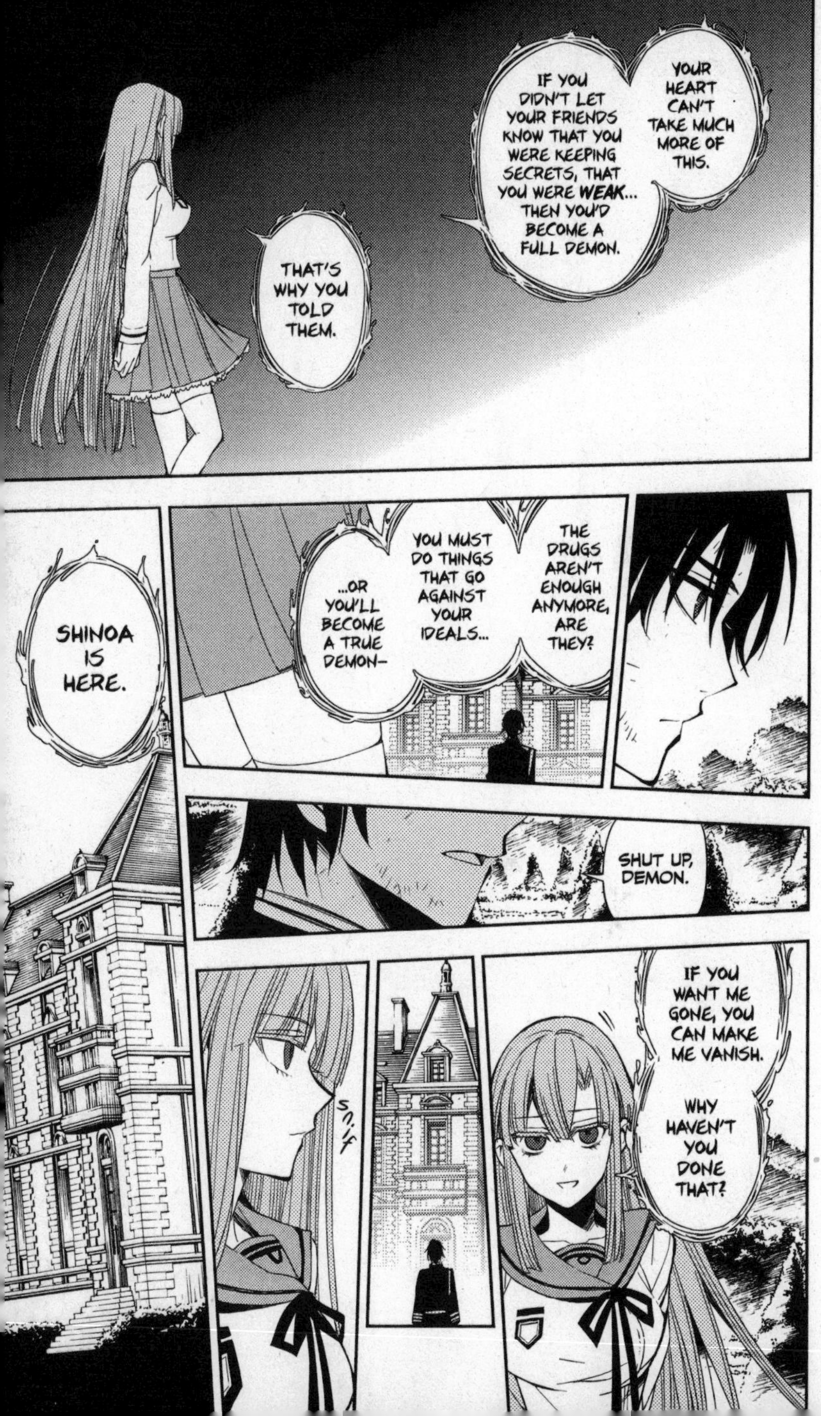
YOUR HEART CAN'T TAKE MUCH MORE OF THIS.
IF YOU DIDN'T LET YOUR FRIENDS KNOW THAT YOU WERE KEEPING SECRETS, THAT YOU WERE **WEAK**... THEN YOU'D BECOME A FULL DEMON.
THAT'S WHY YOU TOLD THEM.
THE DRUGS AREN'T ENOUGH ANYMORE, ARE THEY?
YOU MUST DO THINGS THAT GO AGAINST YOUR IDEALS...
...OR YOU'LL BECOME A TRUE DEMON–
SHUT UP, DEMON.
IF YOU WANT ME GONE, YOU CAN MAKE ME VANISH.
WHY HAVEN'T YOU DONE THAT?
SNIFF
SHINOA IS HERE.

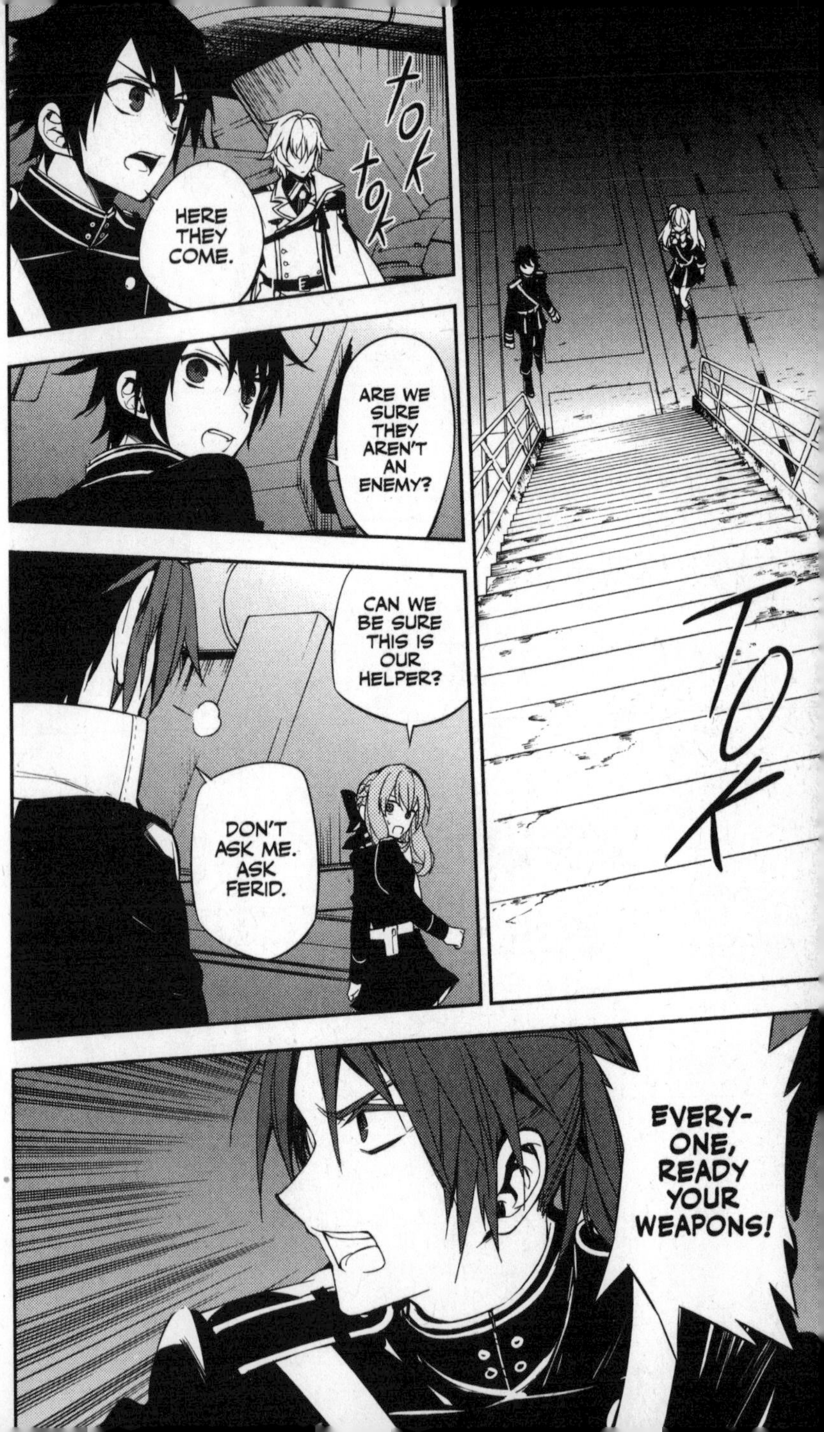
TOK
TOK TOK
HERE THEY COME.
ARE WE SURE THEY AREN'T AN ENEMY?
CAN WE BE SURE THIS IS OUR HELPER?
DON'T ASK ME. ASK FERID.
EVERY-ONE, READY YOUR WEAPONS!

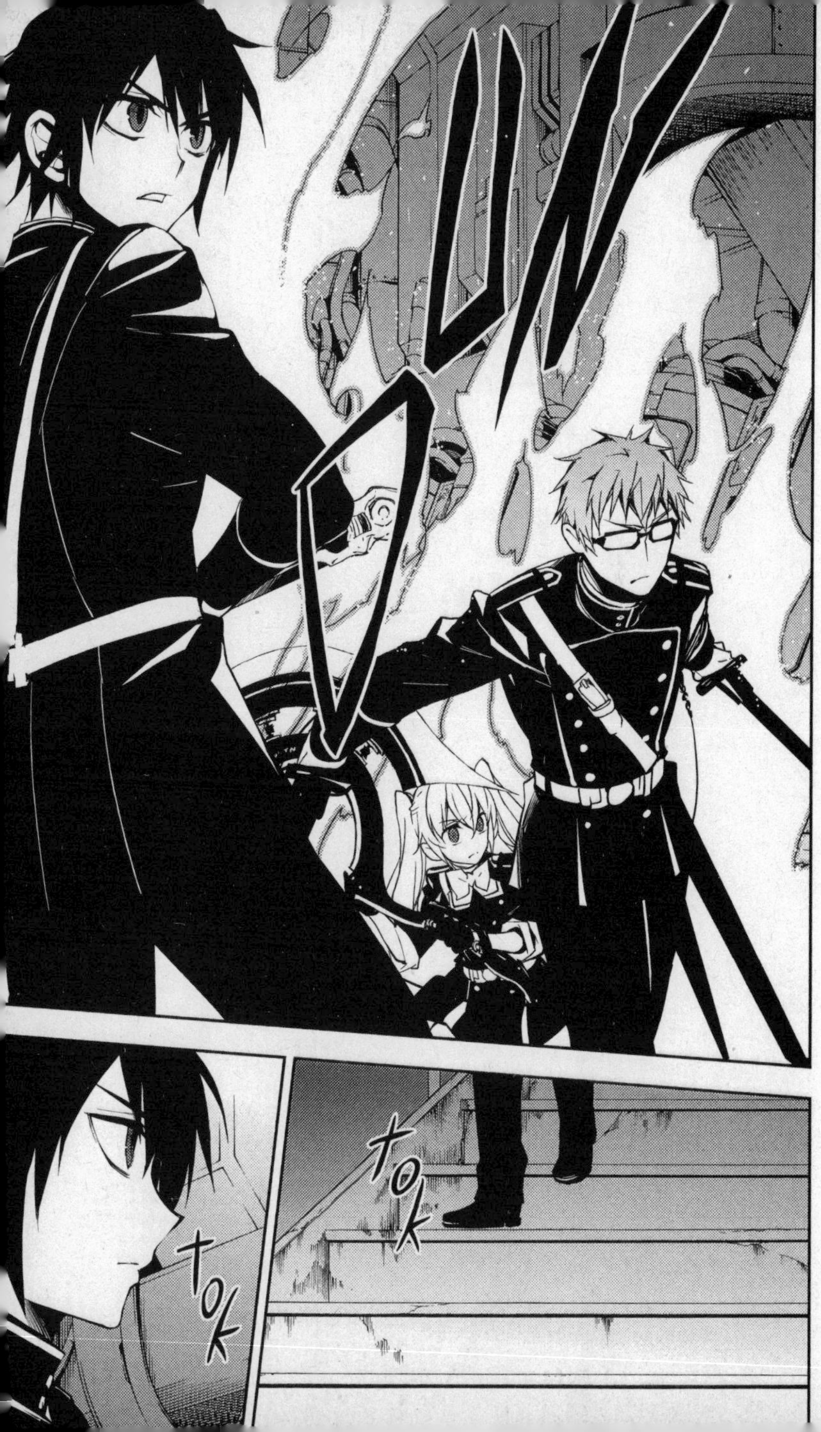
tok
tok

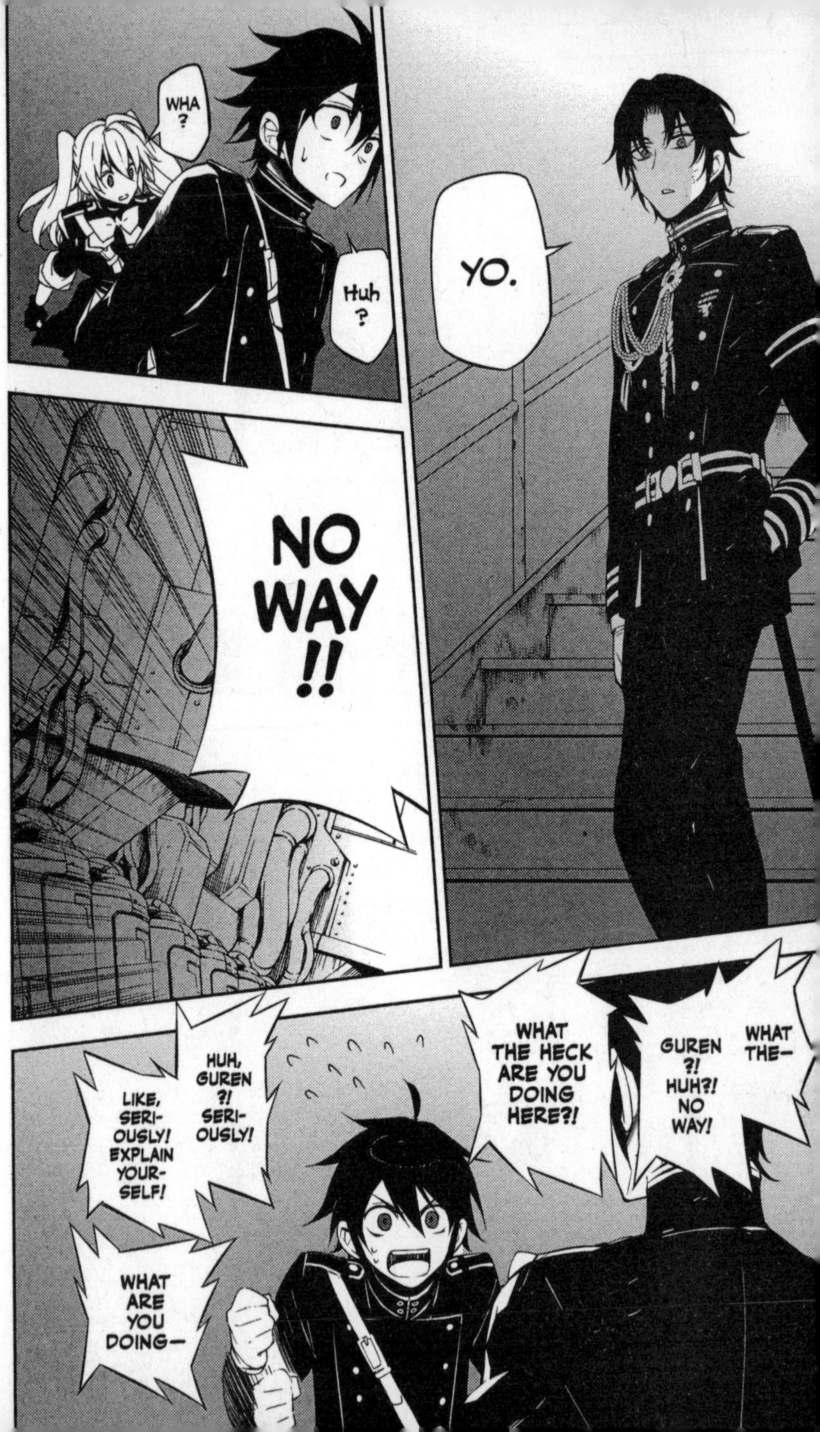
YO.
Huh?
WHA?
NO WAY!!
WHAT THE—
GUREN?! HUH?! NO WAY!
WHAT THE HECK ARE YOU DOING HERE?!
HUH, GUREN?! SERIOUSLY!
LIKE, SERIOUSLY! EXPLAIN YOURSELF!
WHAT ARE YOU DOING—

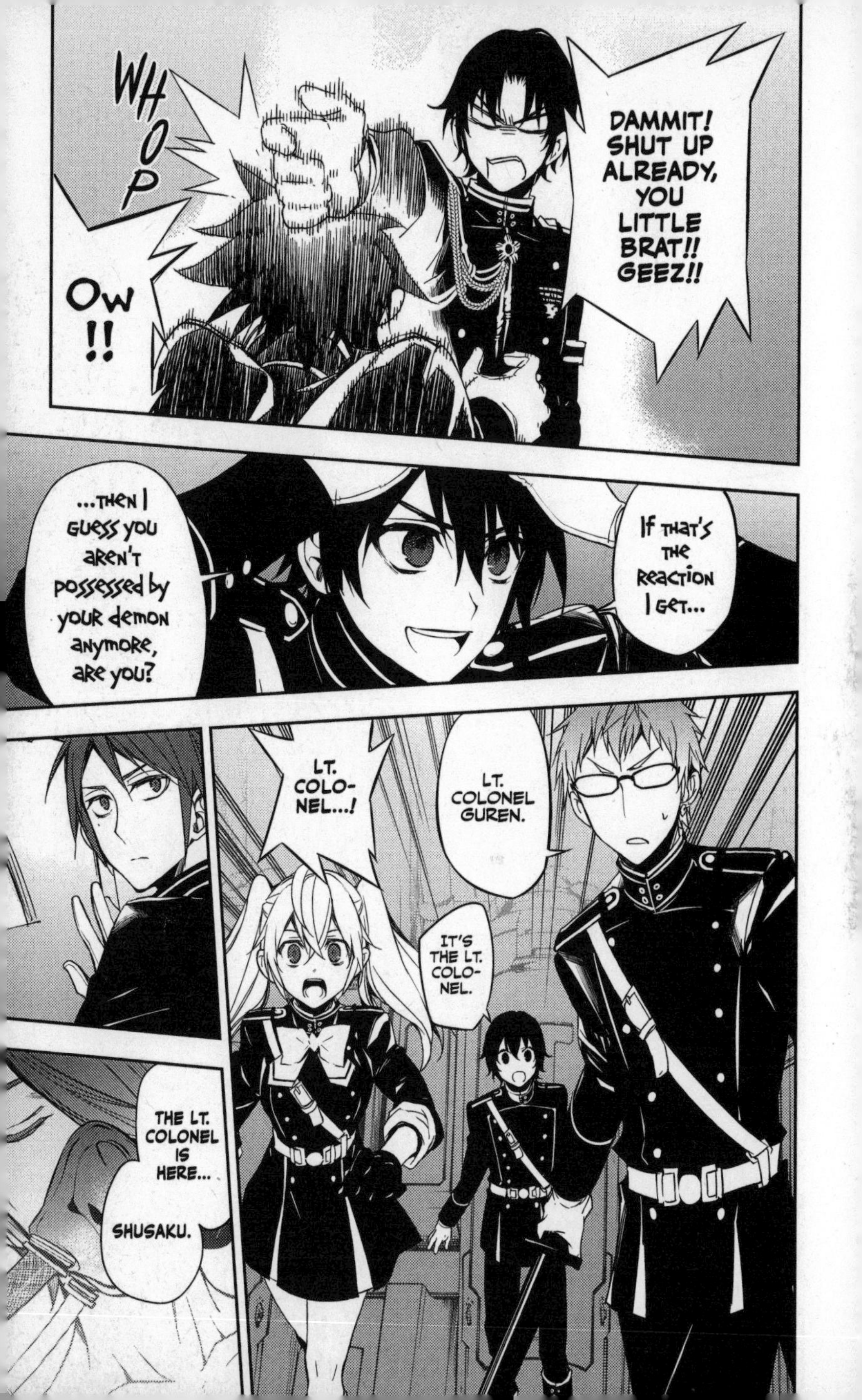
DAMMIT! SHUT UP ALREADY, YOU LITTLE BRAT!! GEEZ!!
WHOP
Ow !!
If that's the reaction I get...
...then I guess you aren't possessed by your demon anymore, are you?
LT. COLONEL GUREN.
LT. COLO-NEL...!
IT'S THE LT. COLO-NEL.
THE LT. COLONEL IS HERE...
SHUSAKU.

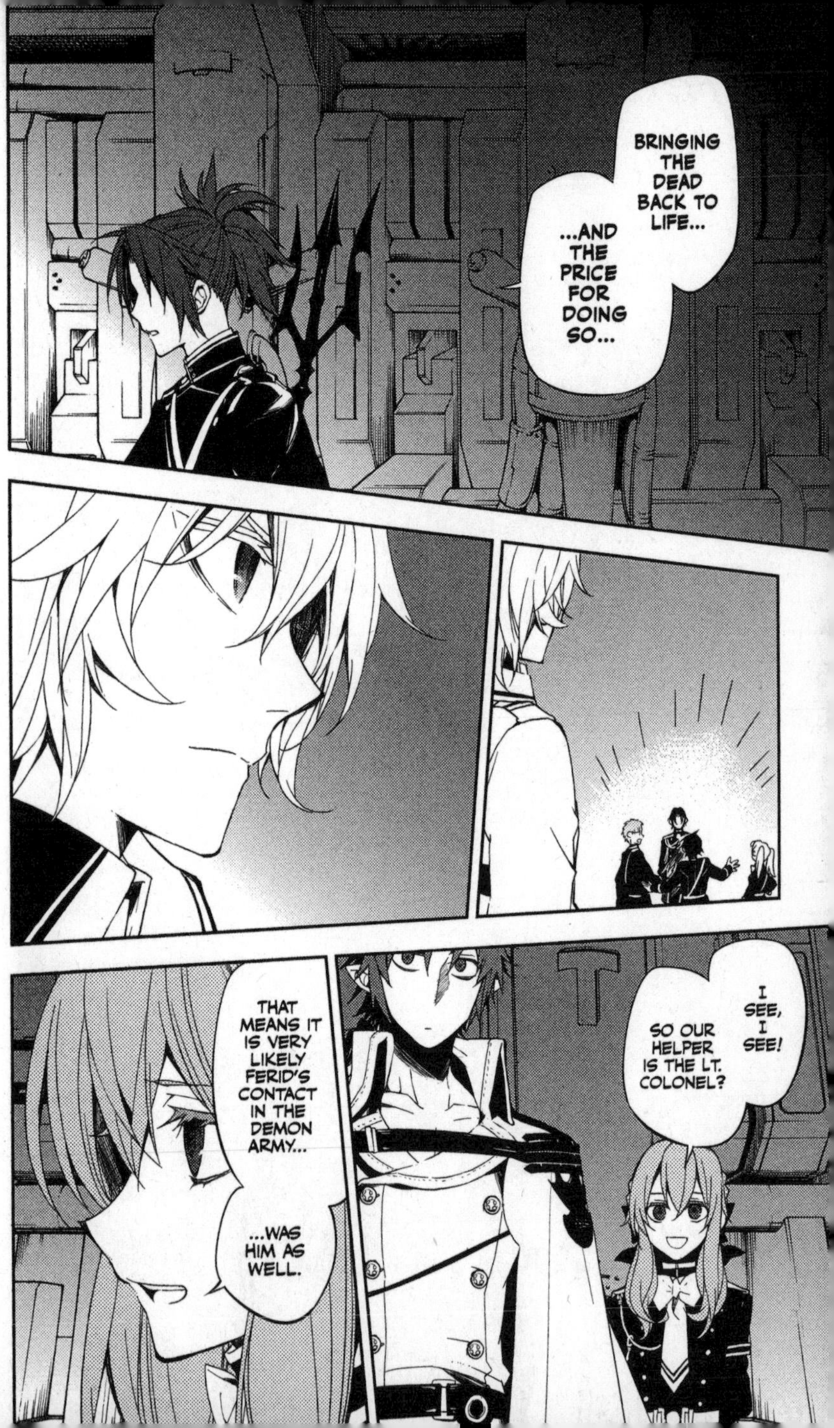
BRINGING THE DEAD BACK TO LIFE...
...AND THE PRICE FOR DOING SO...
I SEE, I SEE!
SO OUR HELPER IS THE LT. COLONEL?
THAT MEANS IT IS VERY LIKELY FERID'S CONTACT IN THE DEMON ARMY...
...WAS HIM AS WELL.

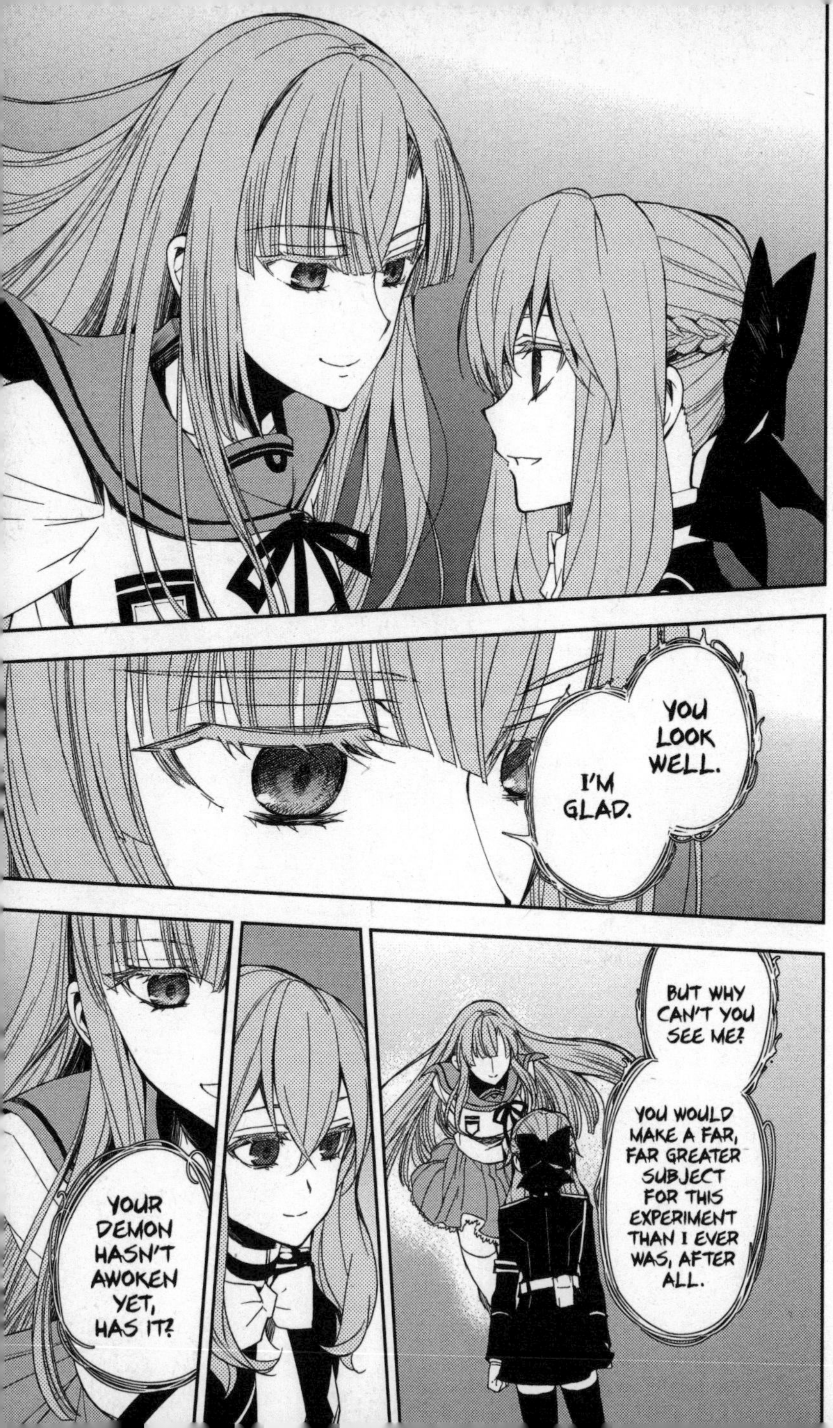
YOU LOOK WELL.
I'M GLAD.
BUT WHY CAN'T YOU SEE ME?
YOU WOULD MAKE A FAR, FAR GREATER SUBJECT FOR THIS EXPERIMENT THAN I EVER WAS, AFTER ALL.
YOUR DEMON HASN'T AWOKEN YET, HAS IT?

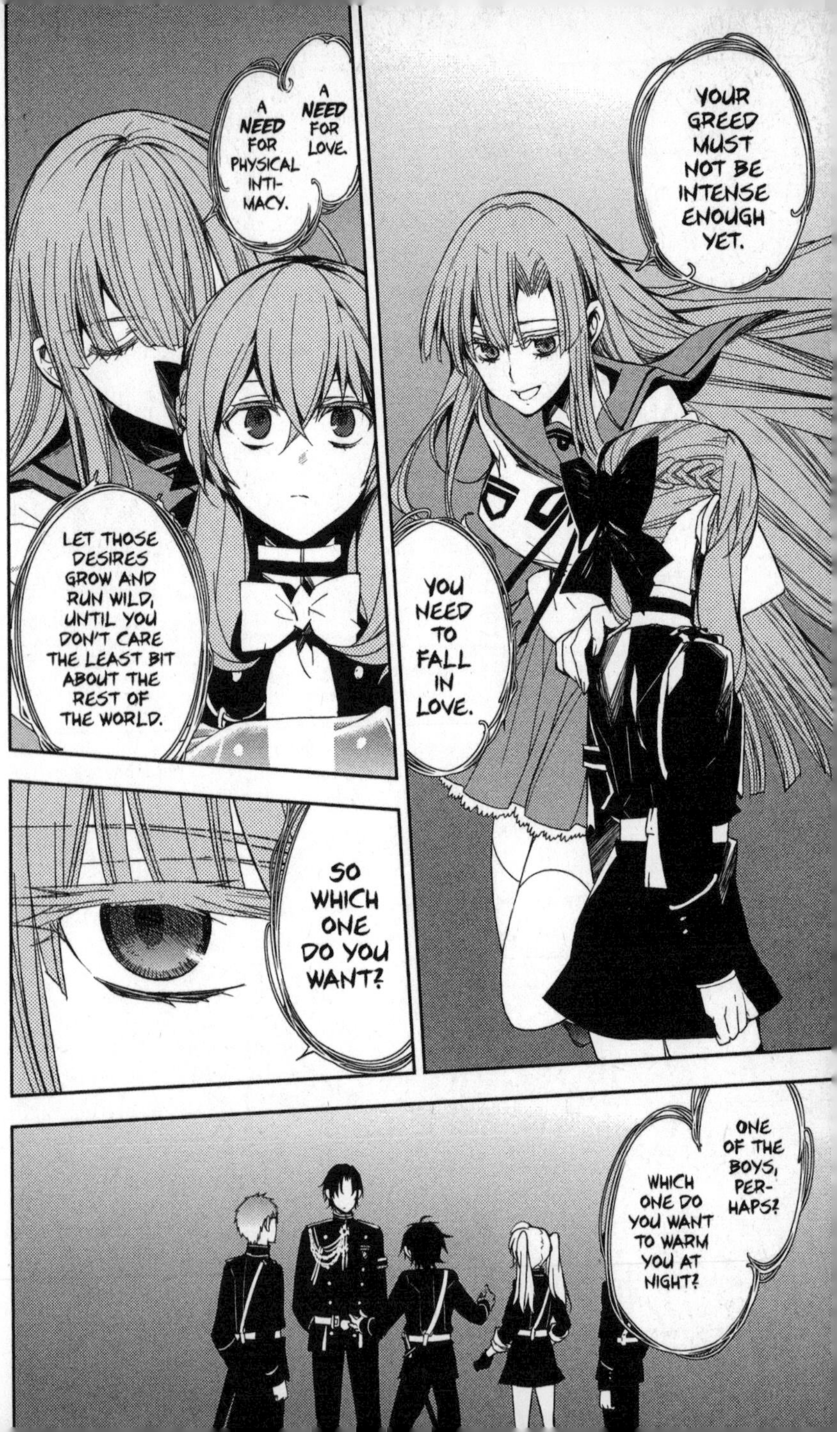
YOUR GREED MUST NOT BE INTENSE ENOUGH YET.
YOU NEED TO FALL IN LOVE.
A NEED FOR LOVE.
A NEED FOR PHYSICAL INTI-MACY.
LET THOSE DESIRES GROW AND RUN WILD, UNTIL YOU DON'T CARE THE LEAST BIT ABOUT THE REST OF THE WORLD.
SO WHICH ONE DO YOU WANT?
ONE OF THE BOYS, PER-HAPS?
WHICH ONE DO YOU WANT TO WARM YOU AT NIGHT?

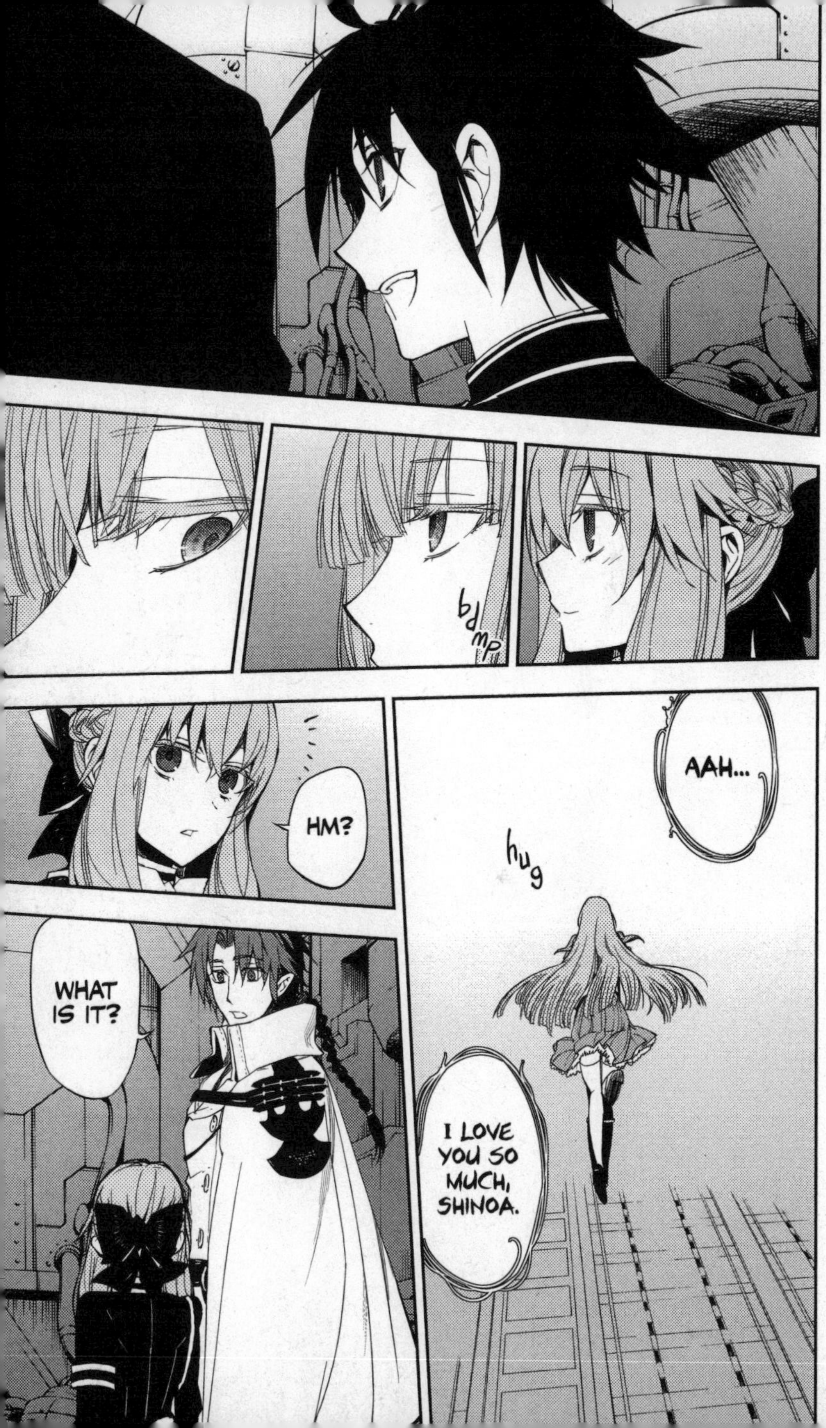
bdmp
AAH...
hug
I LOVE YOU SO MUCH, SHINOA.
HM?
WHAT IS IT?

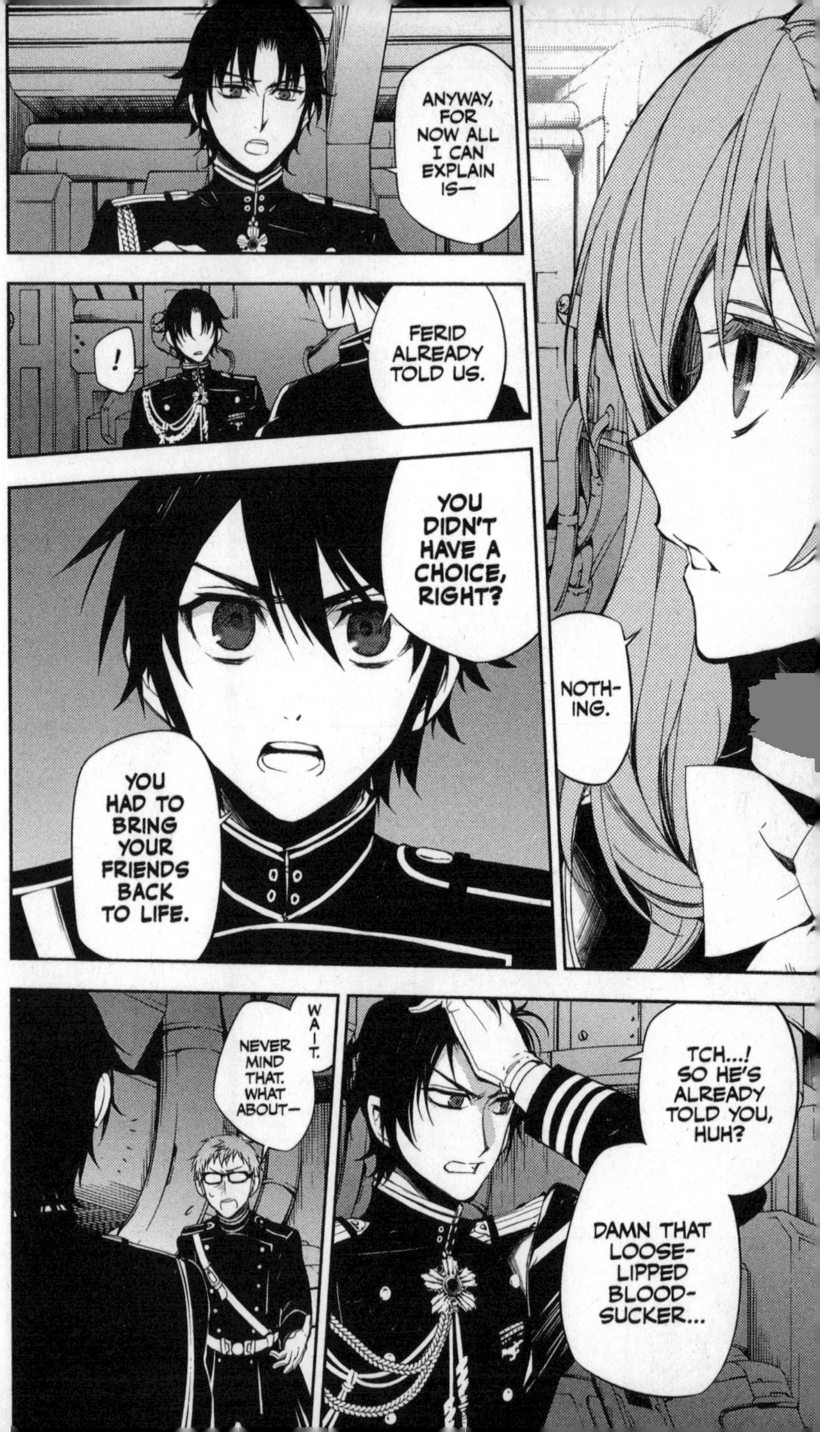
NOTH-ING.
ANYWAY, FOR NOW ALL I CAN EXPLAIN IS—
FERID ALREADY TOLD US.
!
YOU DIDN'T HAVE A CHOICE, RIGHT?
YOU HAD TO BRING YOUR FRIENDS BACK TO LIFE.
TCH...! SO HE'S ALREADY TOLD YOU, HUH?
DAMN THAT LOOSE-LIPPED BLOOD-SUCKER...
WAIT.
NEVER MIND THAT. WHAT ABOUT—

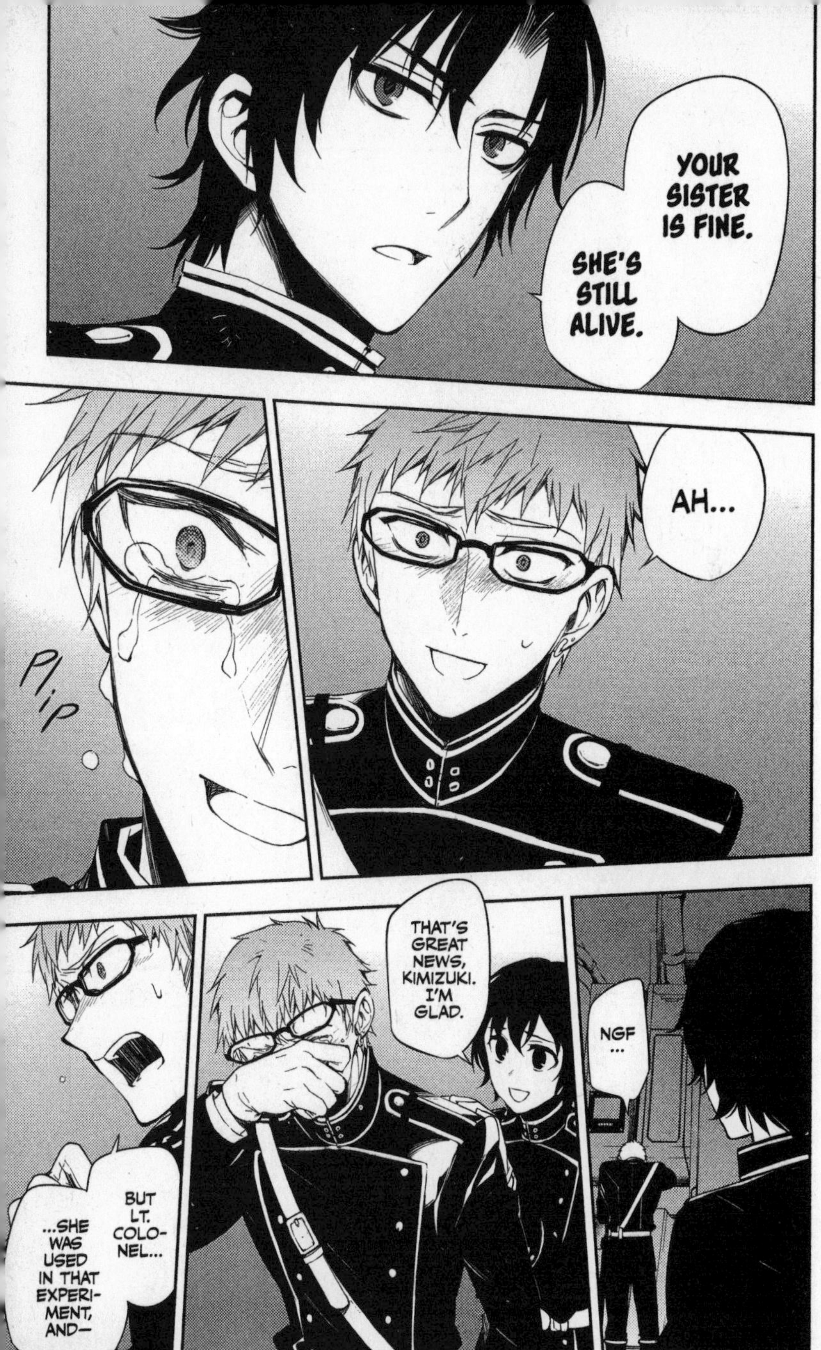
YOUR SISTER IS FINE.
SHE'S STILL ALIVE.
AH...
Plip
NGF...
THAT'S GREAT NEWS, KIMIZUKI. I'M GLAD.
BUT LT. COLONEL...
...SHE WAS USED IN THAT EXPERIMENT, AND—

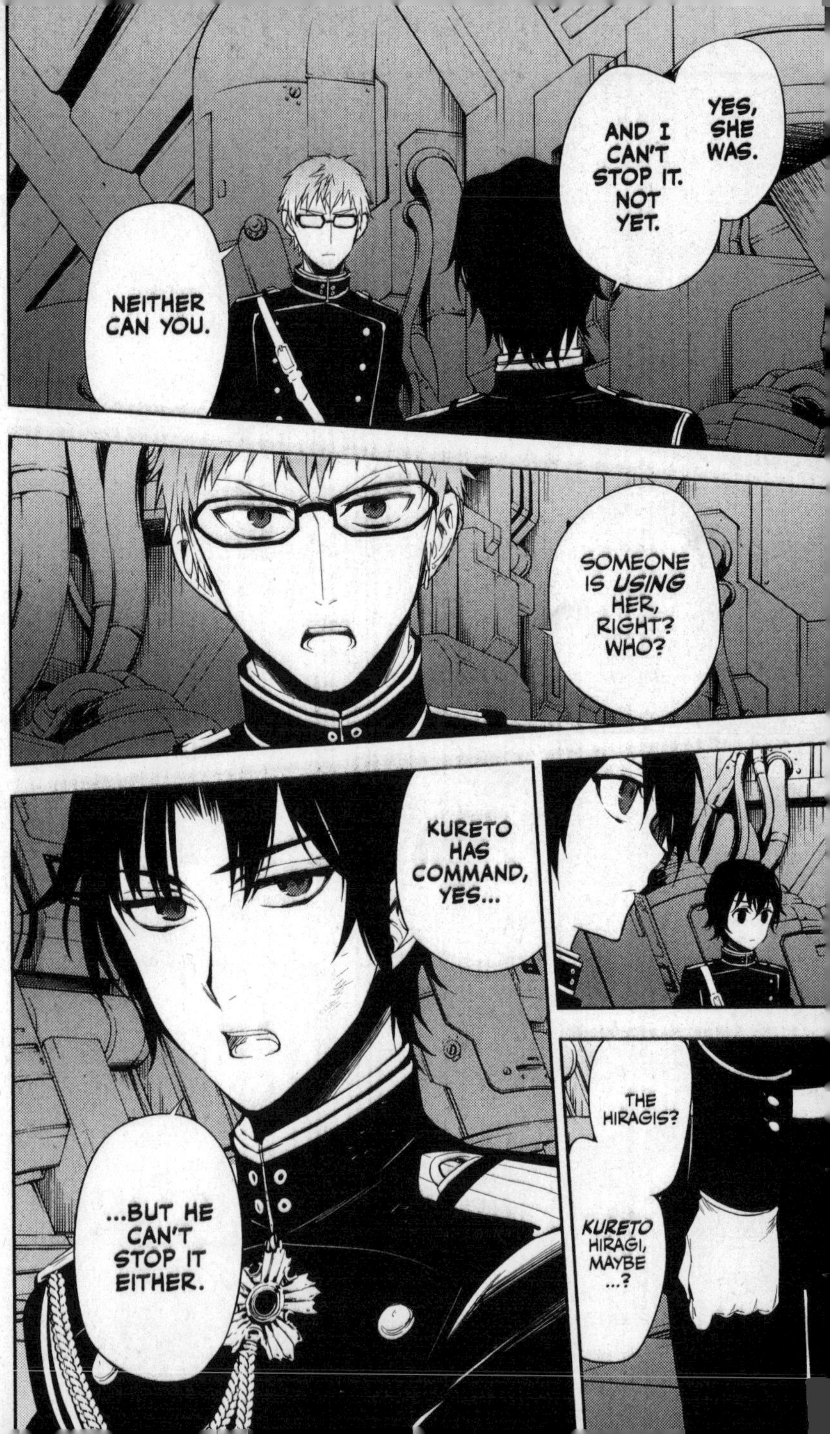
YES, SHE WAS.
AND I CAN'T STOP IT. NOT YET.
NEITHER CAN YOU.
SOMEONE IS *USING* HER, RIGHT? WHO?
THE HIRAGIS?
KURETO HIRAGI, MAYBE ...?
KURETO HAS COMMAND, YES...
...BUT HE CAN'T STOP IT EITHER.

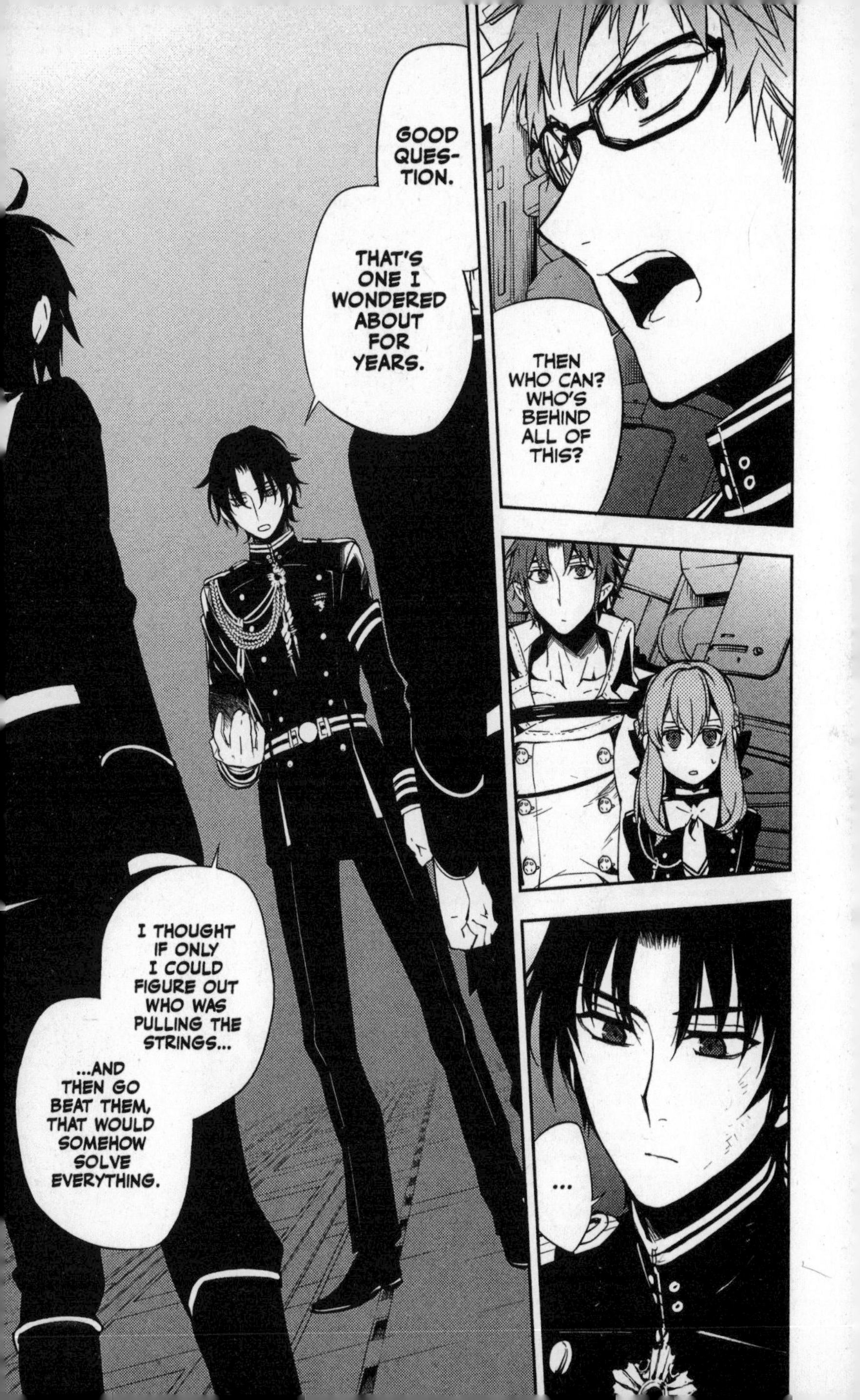
THEN WHO CAN? WHO'S BEHIND ALL OF THIS?
...
GOOD QUES-TION.
THAT'S ONE I WONDERED ABOUT FOR YEARS.
I THOUGHT IF ONLY I COULD FIGURE OUT WHO WAS PULLING THE STRINGS...
...AND THEN GO BEAT THEM, THAT WOULD SOMEHOW SOLVE EVERYTHING.

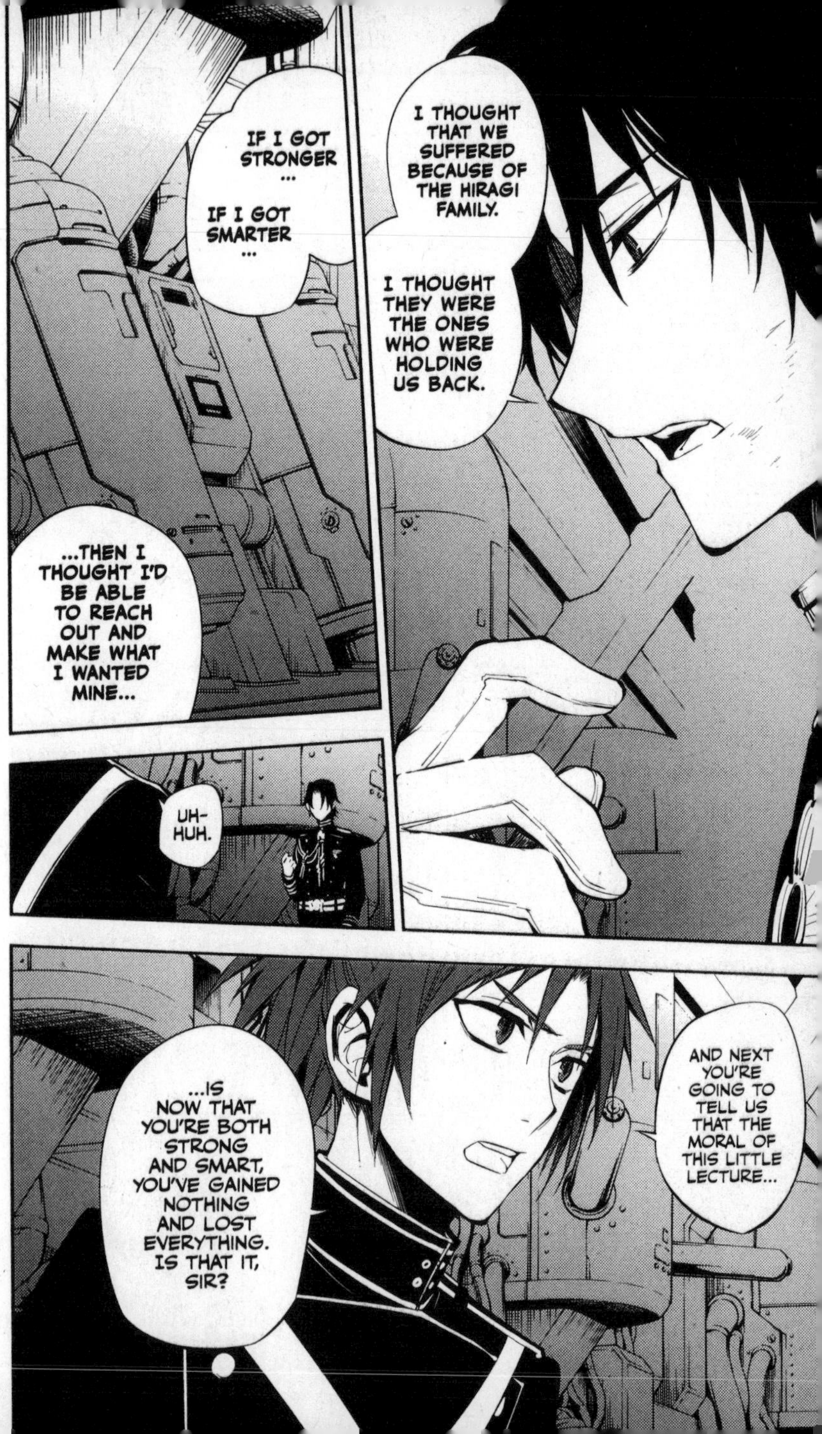
I THOUGHT THAT WE SUFFERED BECAUSE OF THE HIRAGI FAMILY.
I THOUGHT THEY WERE THE ONES WHO WERE HOLDING US BACK.
IF I GOT STRONGER ...
IF I GOT SMARTER ...
...THEN I THOUGHT I'D BE ABLE TO REACH OUT AND MAKE WHAT I WANTED MINE...
UH-HUH.
AND NEXT YOU'RE GOING TO TELL US THAT THE MORAL OF THIS LITTLE LECTURE...
...IS NOW THAT YOU'RE BOTH STRONG AND SMART, YOU'VE GAINED NOTHING AND LOST EVERYTHING. IS THAT IT, SIR?

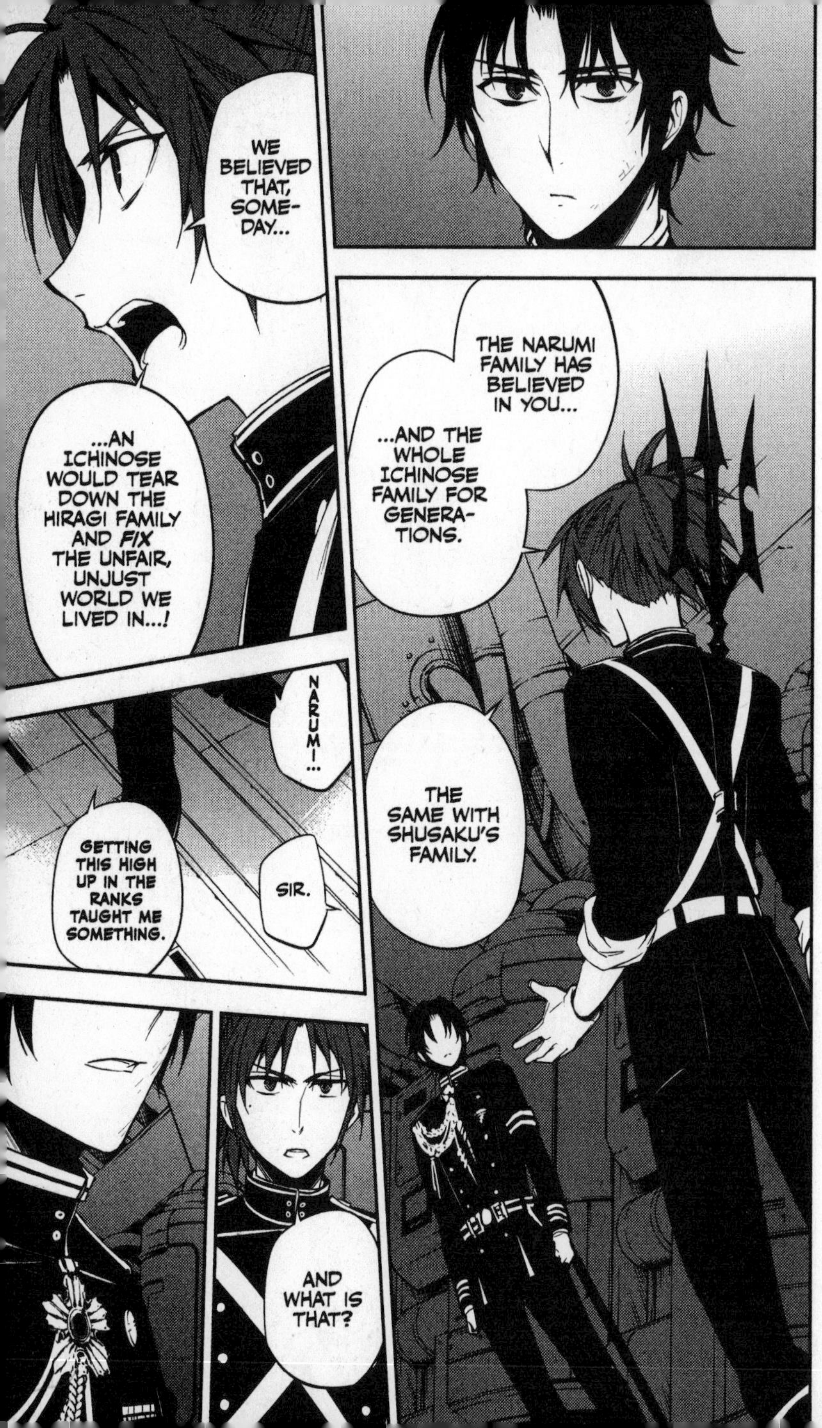
THE NARUMI FAMILY HAS BELIEVED IN YOU...
...AND THE WHOLE ICHINOSE FAMILY FOR GENERATIONS.
THE SAME WITH SHUSAKU'S FAMILY.
WE BELIEVED THAT, SOMEDAY...
...AN ICHINOSE WOULD TEAR DOWN THE HIRAGI FAMILY AND *FIX* THE UNFAIR, UNJUST WORLD WE LIVED IN...!
NARUMI!...
SIR.
GETTING THIS HIGH UP IN THE RANKS TAUGHT ME SOMETHING.
AND WHAT IS THAT?

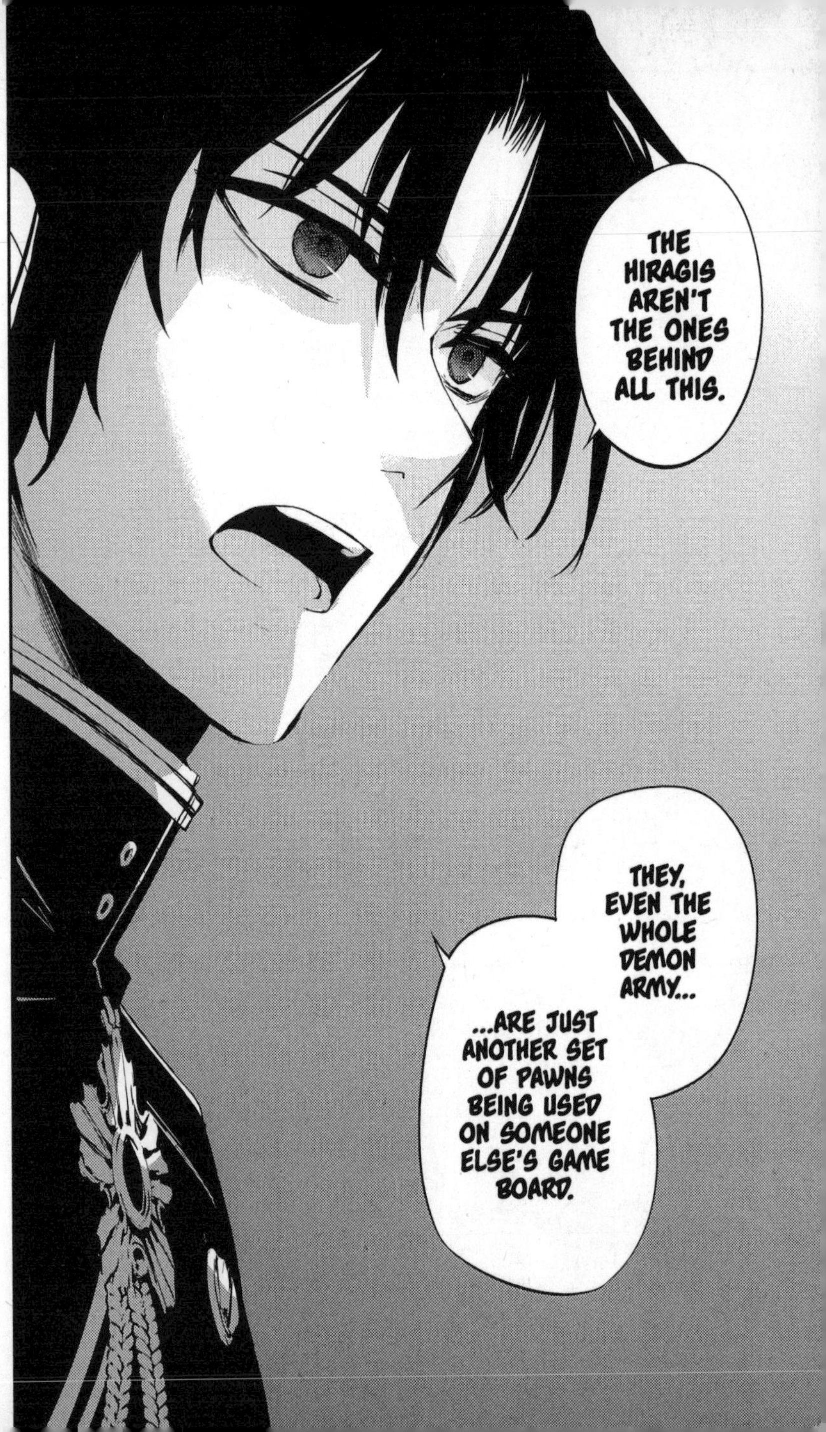
THE HIRAGIS AREN'T THE ONES BEHIND ALL THIS.
THEY, EVEN THE WHOLE DEMON ARMY...
...ARE JUST ANOTHER SET OF PAWNS BEING USED ON SOMEONE ELSE'S GAME BOARD.

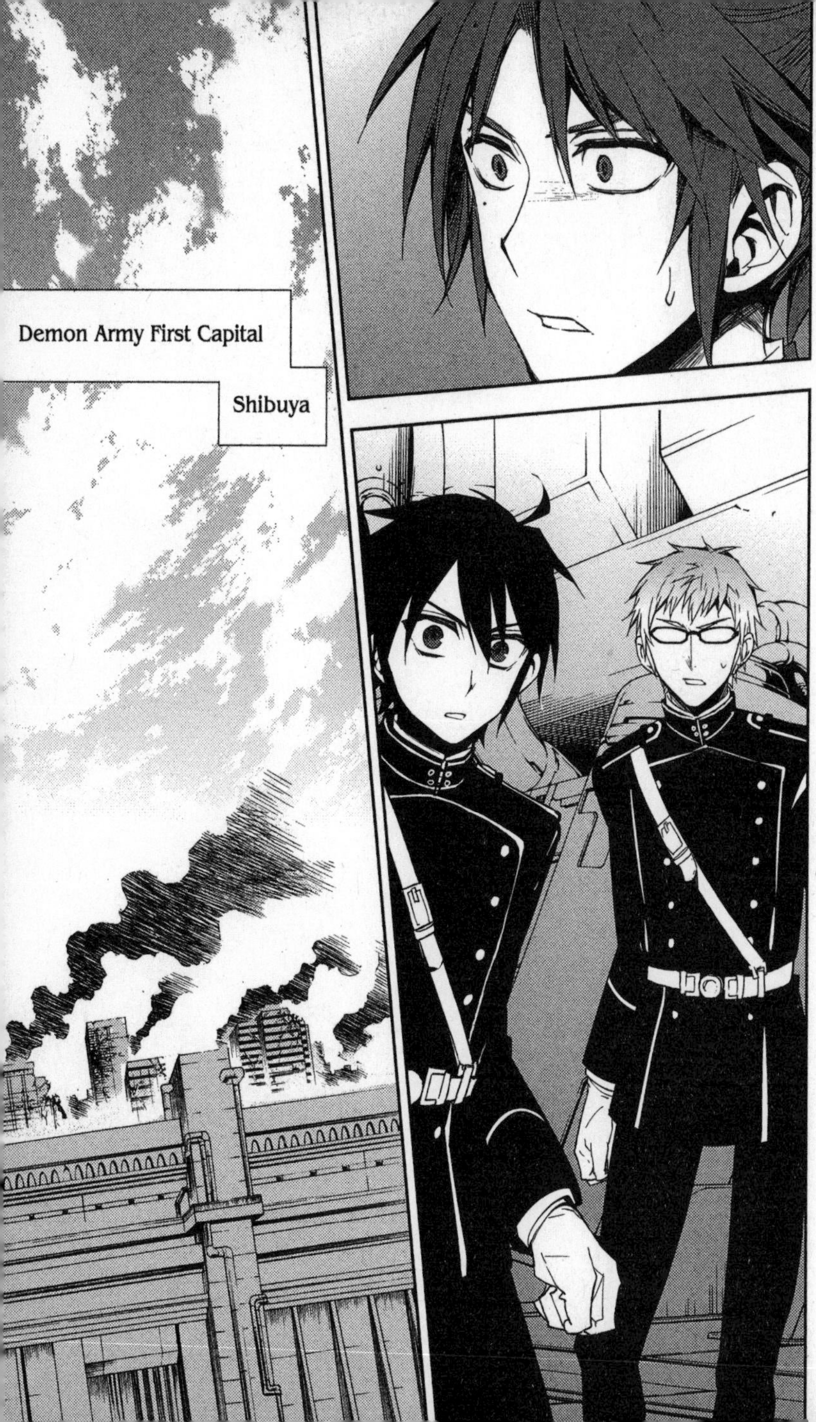
Demon Army First Capital
Shibuya

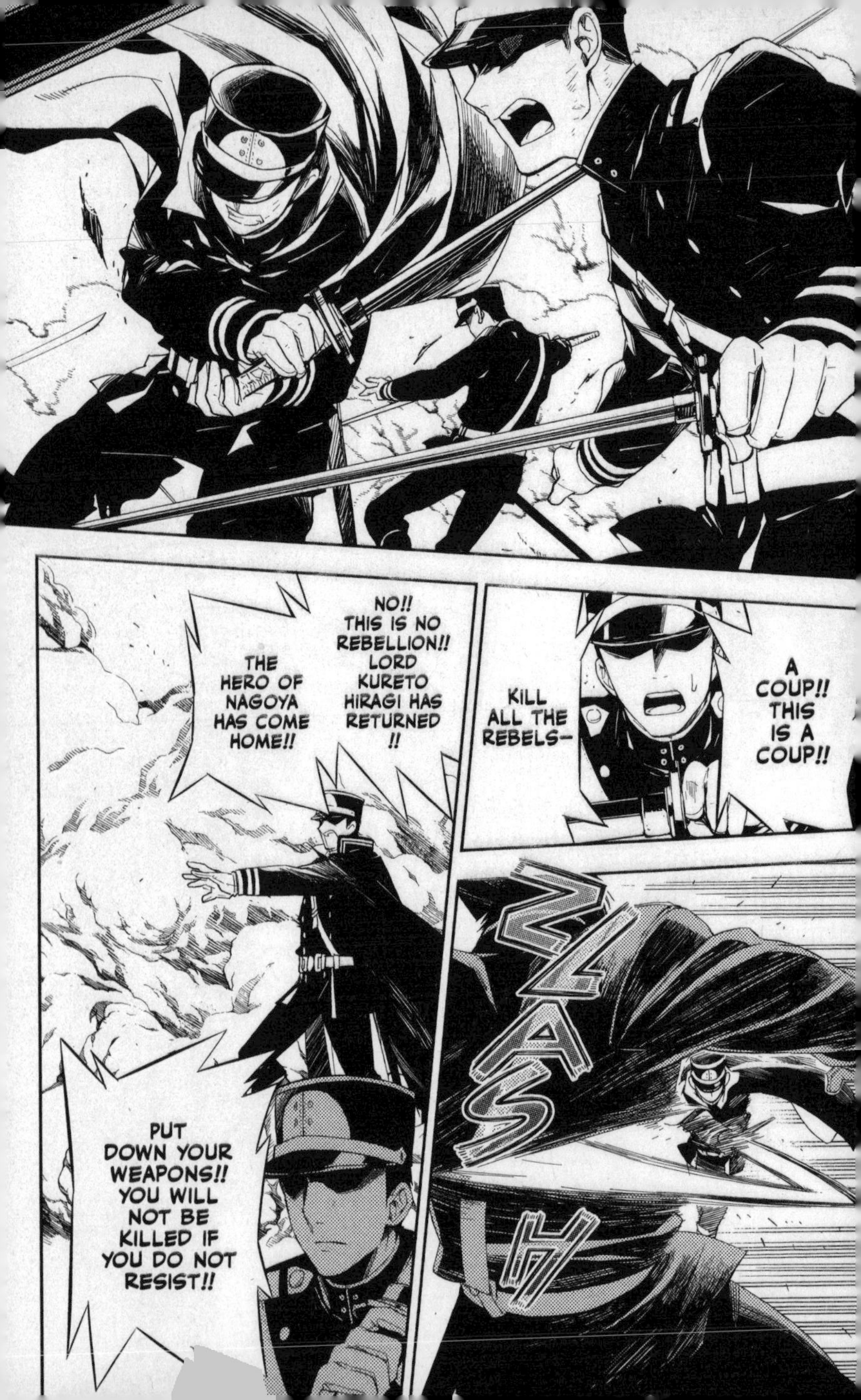
A COUP!! THIS IS A COUP!!
KILL ALL THE REBELS—
SLASH
NO!! THIS IS NO REBELLION!! LORD KURETO HIRAGI HAS RETURNED!!
THE HERO OF NAGOYA HAS COME HOME!!
PUT DOWN YOUR WEAPONS!! YOU WILL NOT BE KILLED IF YOU DO NOT RESIST!!

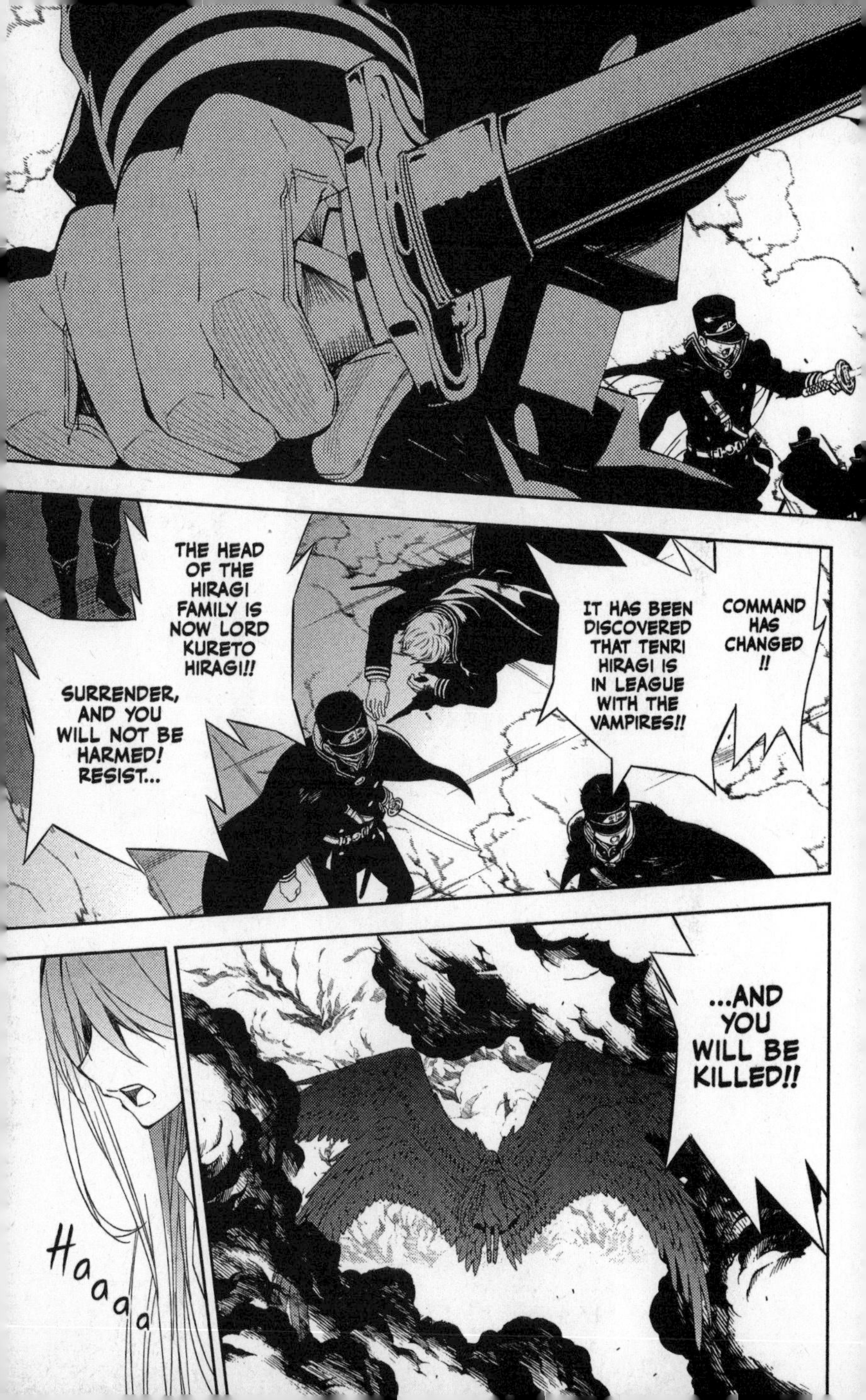
COMMAND HAS CHANGED!!
IT HAS BEEN DISCOVERED THAT TENRI HIRAGI IS IN LEAGUE WITH THE VAMPIRES!!
THE HEAD OF THE HIRAGI FAMILY IS NOW LORD KURETO HIRAGI!!
SURRENDER, AND YOU WILL NOT BE HARMED! RESIST...
...AND YOU WILL BE KILLED!!
Haaaa

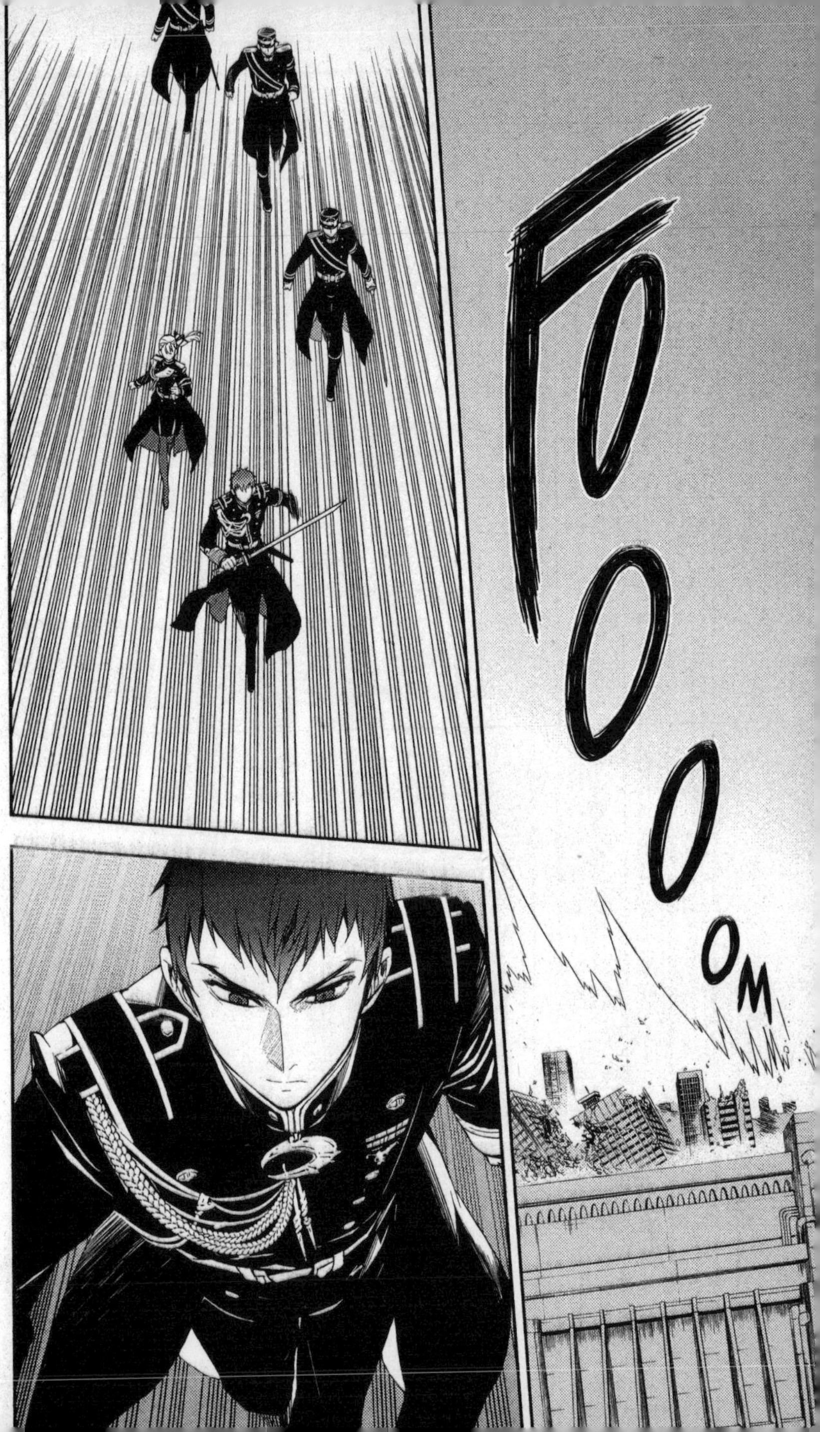
FOOOOOM

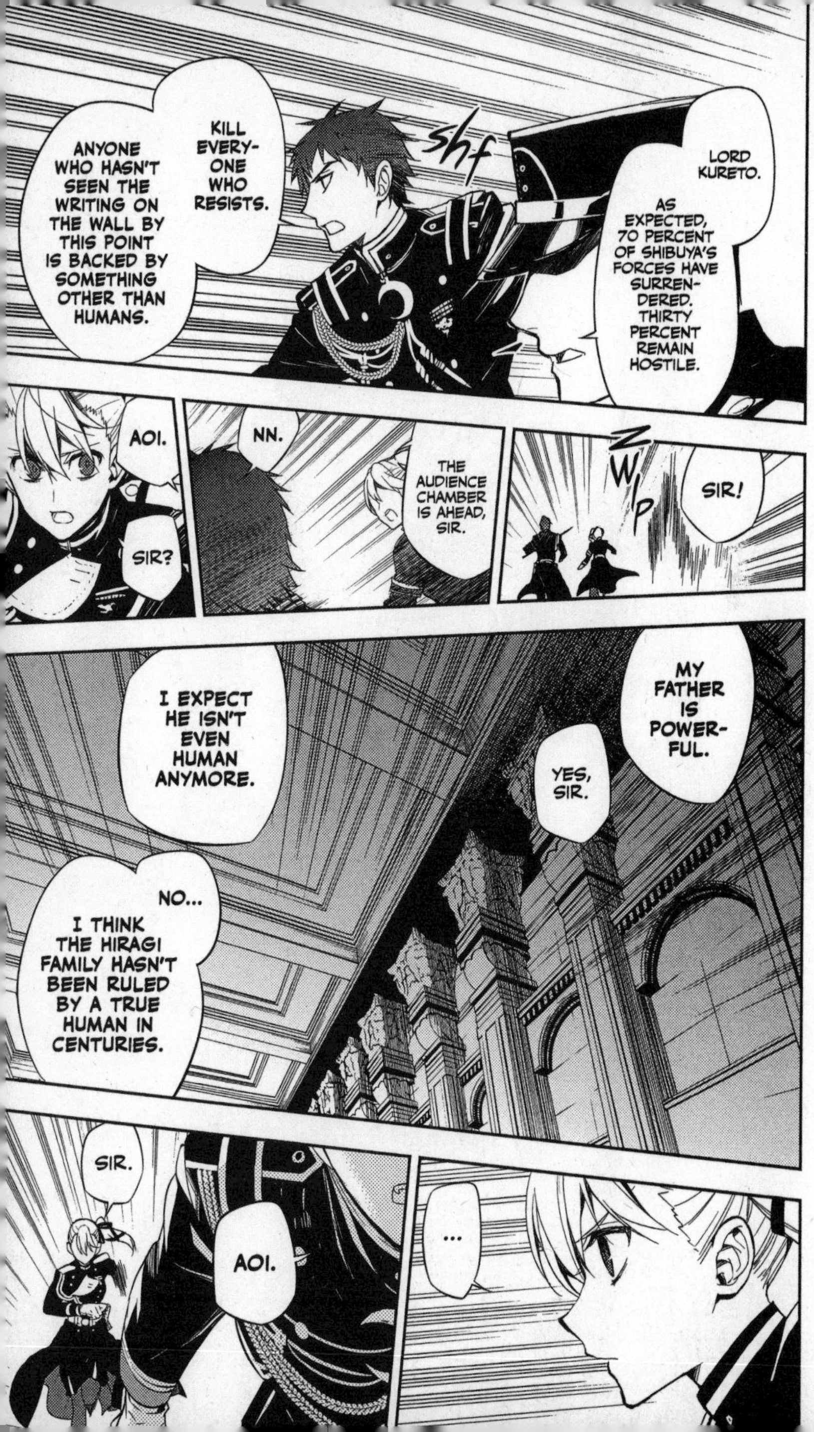
LORD KURETO.
AS EXPECTED, 70 PERCENT OF SHIBUYA'S FORCES HAVE SURRENDERED. THIRTY PERCENT REMAIN HOSTILE.
shf
KILL EVERYONE WHO RESISTS.
ANYONE WHO HASN'T SEEN THE WRITING ON THE WALL BY THIS POINT IS BACKED BY SOMETHING OTHER THAN HUMANS.
ZWIP
SIR!
THE AUDIENCE CHAMBER IS AHEAD, SIR.
NN.
AOI.
SIR?
MY FATHER IS POWERFUL.
YES, SIR.
I EXPECT HE ISN'T EVEN HUMAN ANYMORE.
NO... I THINK THE HIRAGI FAMILY HASN'T BEEN RULED BY A TRUE HUMAN IN CENTURIES.
...
SIR.
AOI.

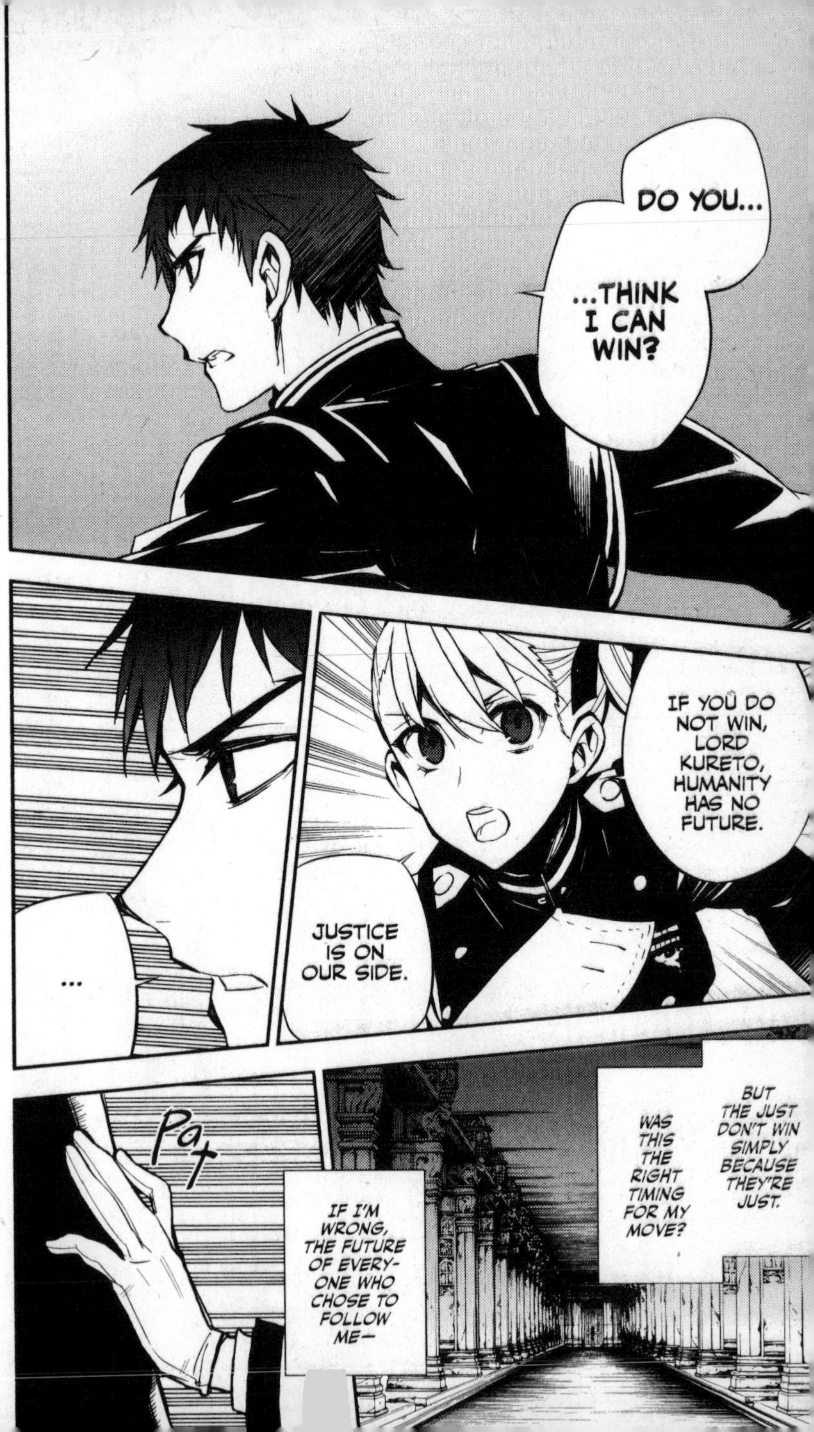
DO YOU...
...THINK I CAN WIN?
IF YOU DO NOT WIN, LORD KURETO, HUMANITY HAS NO FUTURE.
JUSTICE IS ON OUR SIDE.
...
BUT THE JUST DON'T WIN SIMPLY BECAUSE THEY'RE JUST.
WAS THIS THE RIGHT TIMING FOR MY MOVE?
IF I'M WRONG, THE FUTURE OF EVERY-ONE WHO CHOSE TO FOLLOW ME—
Pat

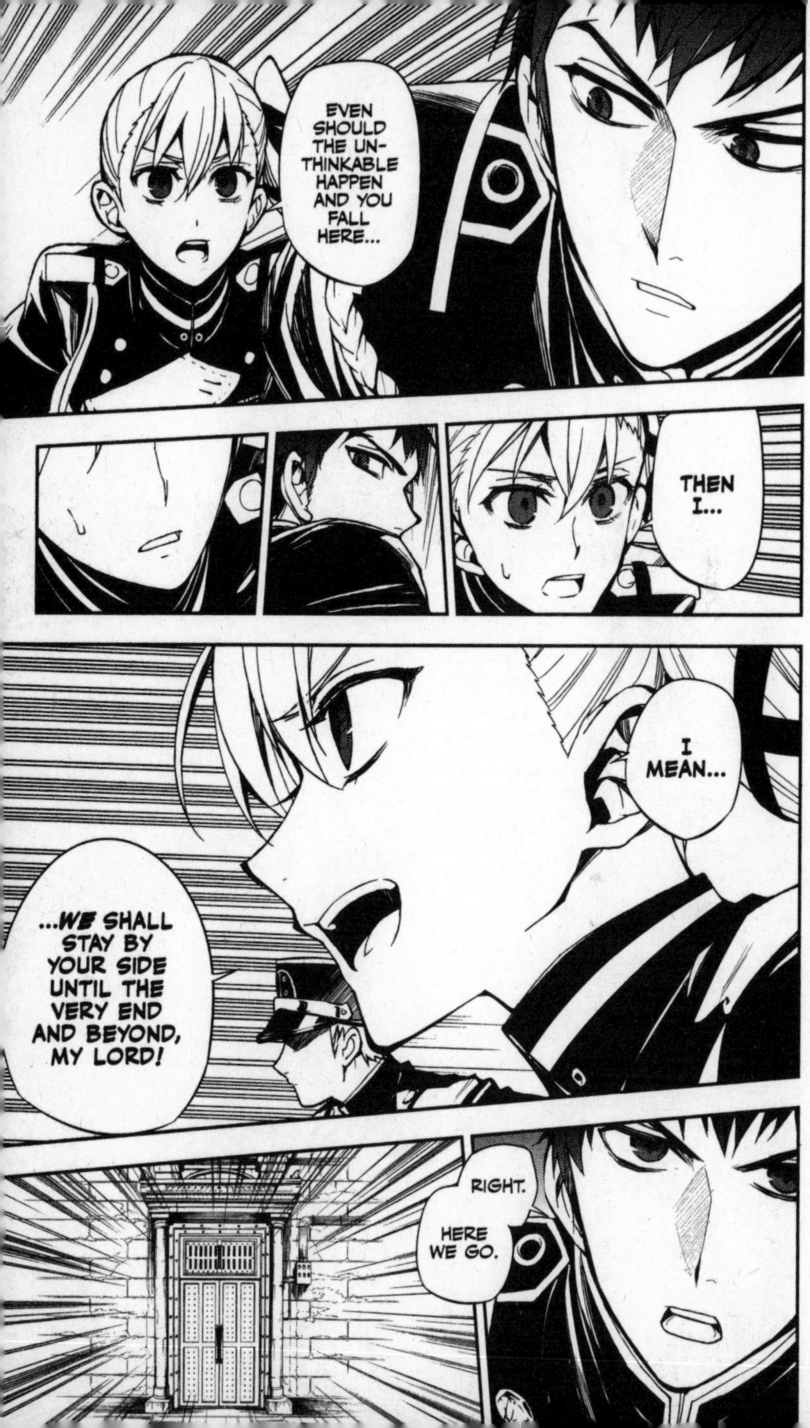
EVEN SHOULD THE UN-THINKABLE HAPPEN AND YOU FALL HERE...
THEN I...
I MEAN...
...*WE* SHALL STAY BY YOUR SIDE UNTIL THE VERY END AND BEYOND, MY LORD!
RIGHT.
HERE WE GO.

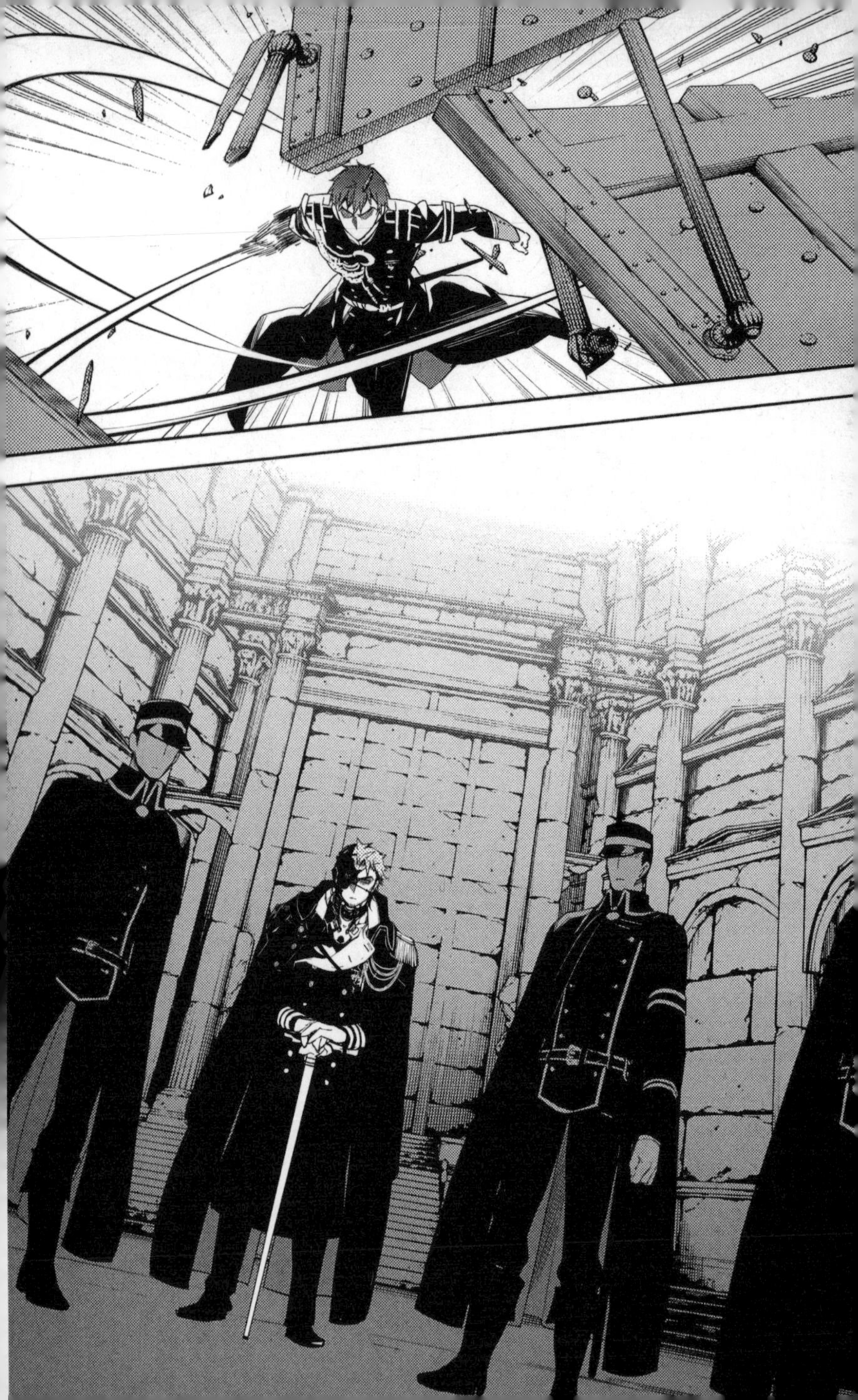

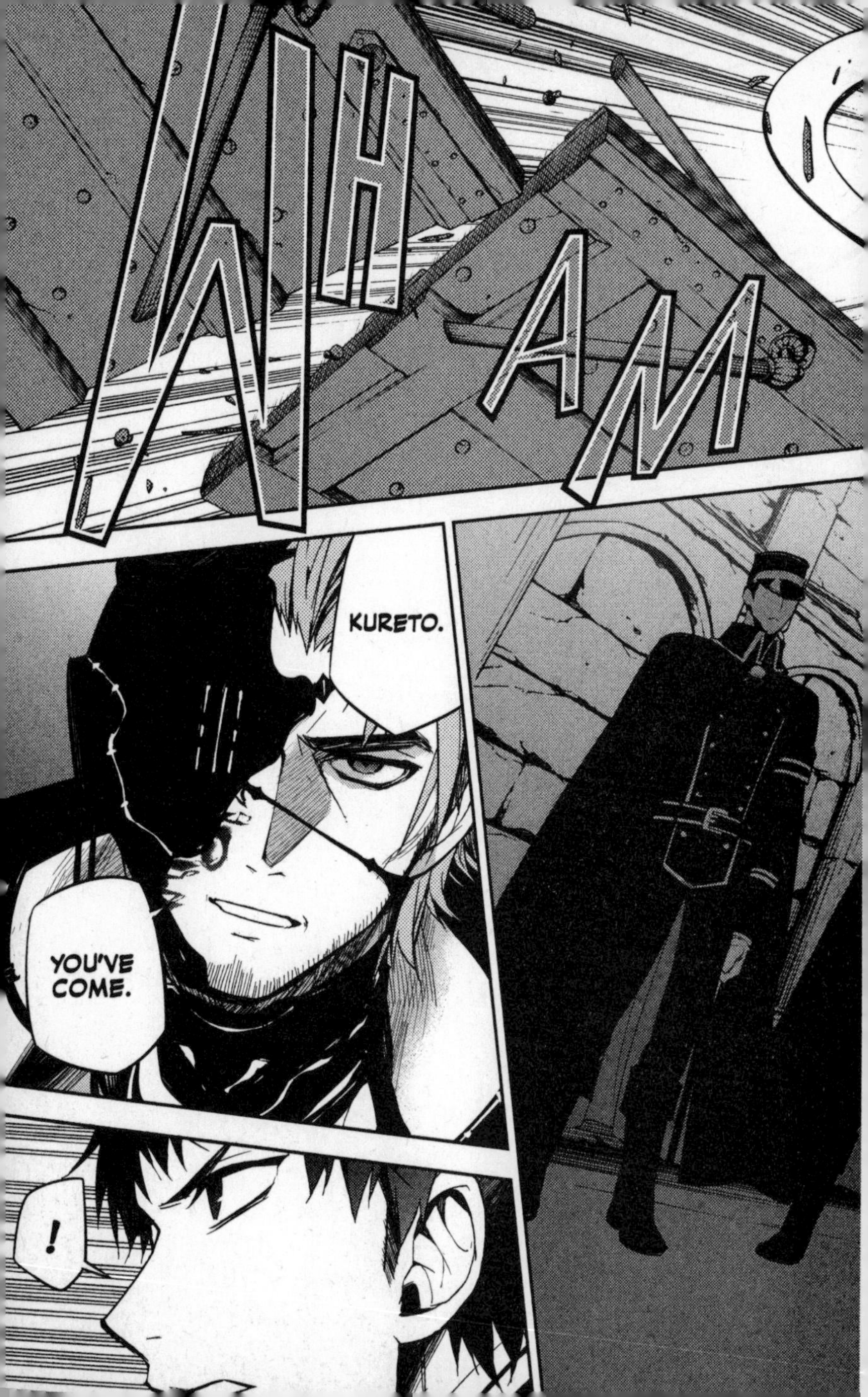
WHAM
KURETO.
YOU'VE COME.
!

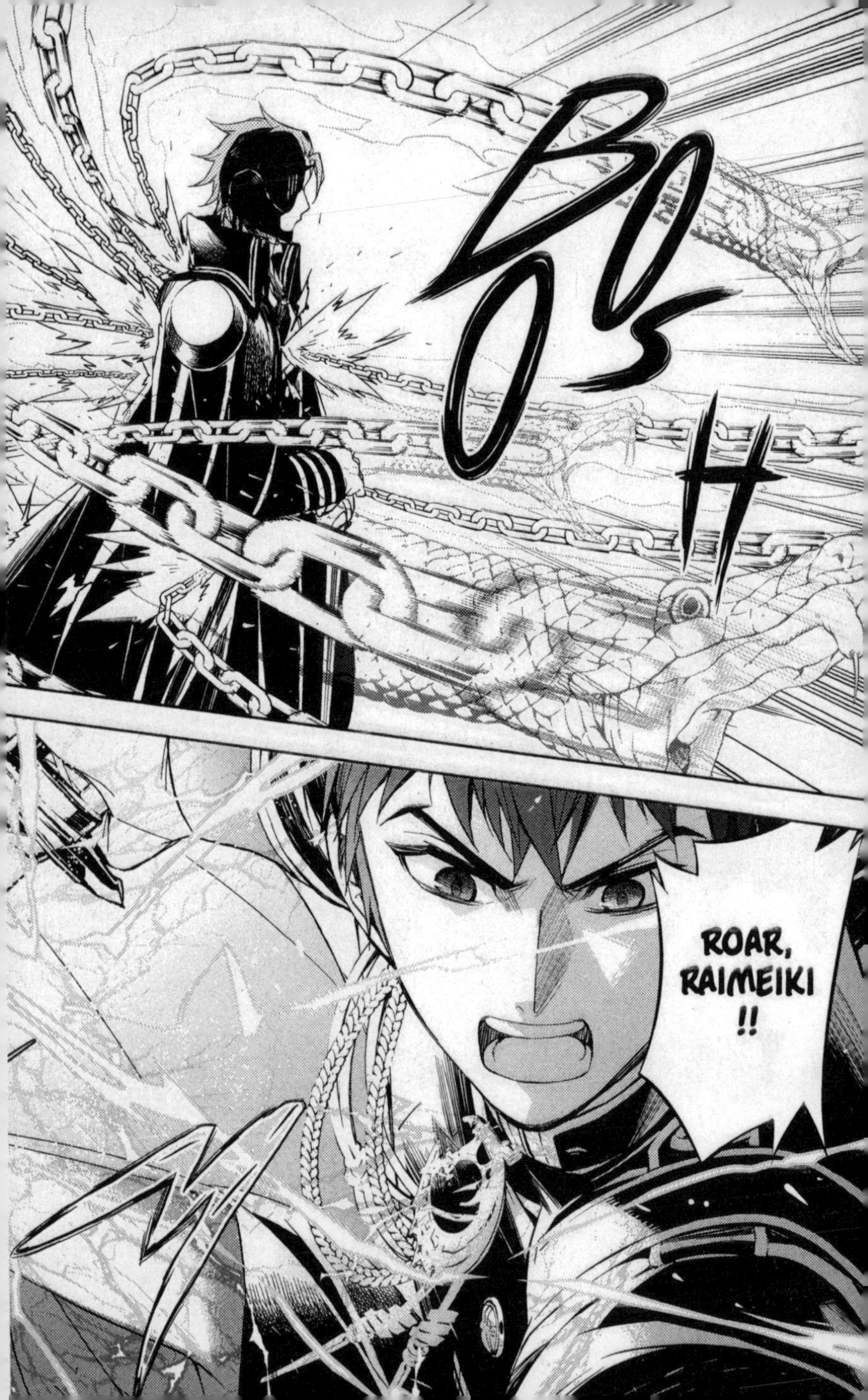
BOOSH
ROAR, RAIMEIKI !!

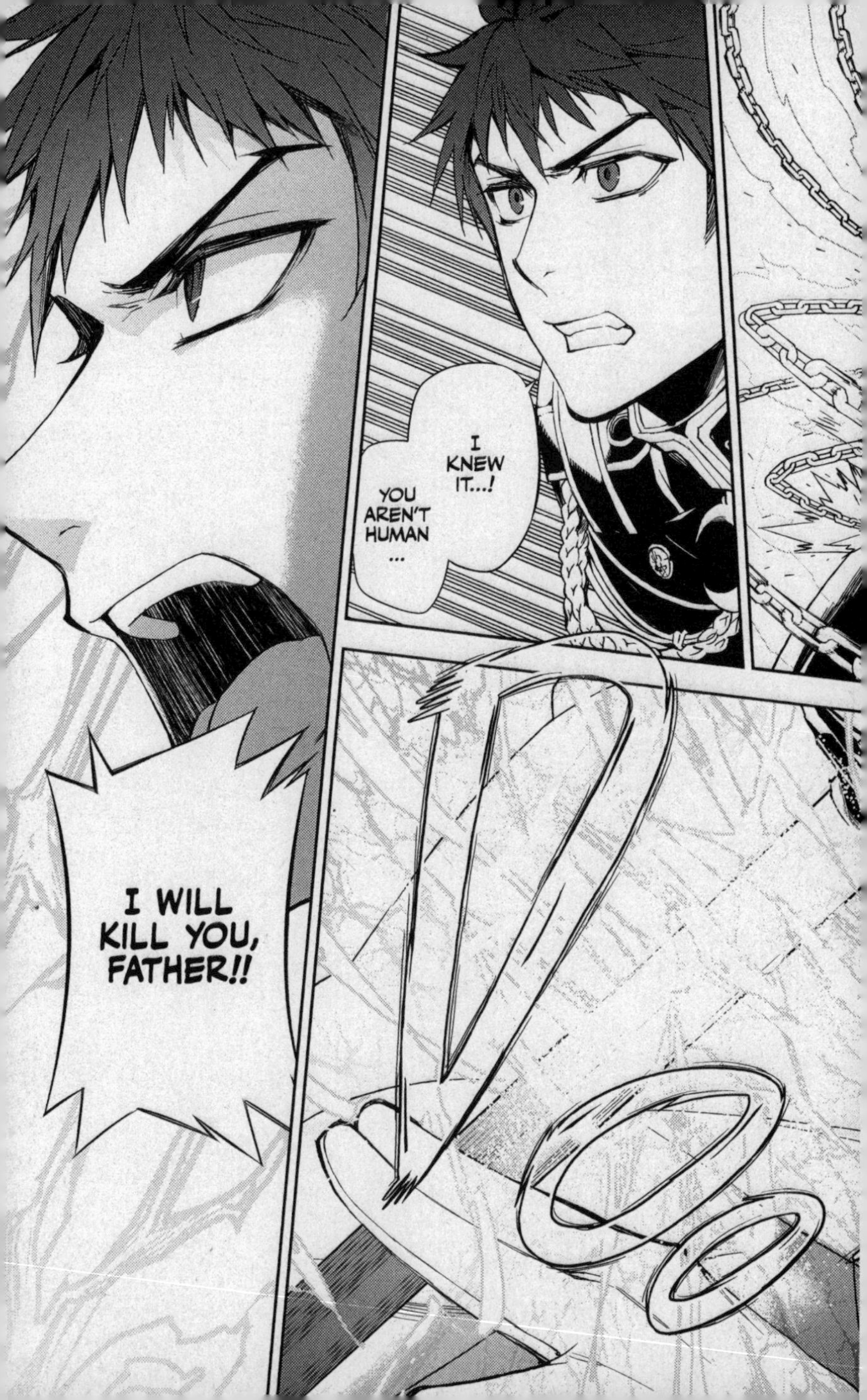
I KNEW IT...!
YOU AREN'T HUMAN...
I WILL KILL YOU, FATHER!!

Seraph of the End
—VAMPIRE REIGN—

Chapter 57
Defining a King

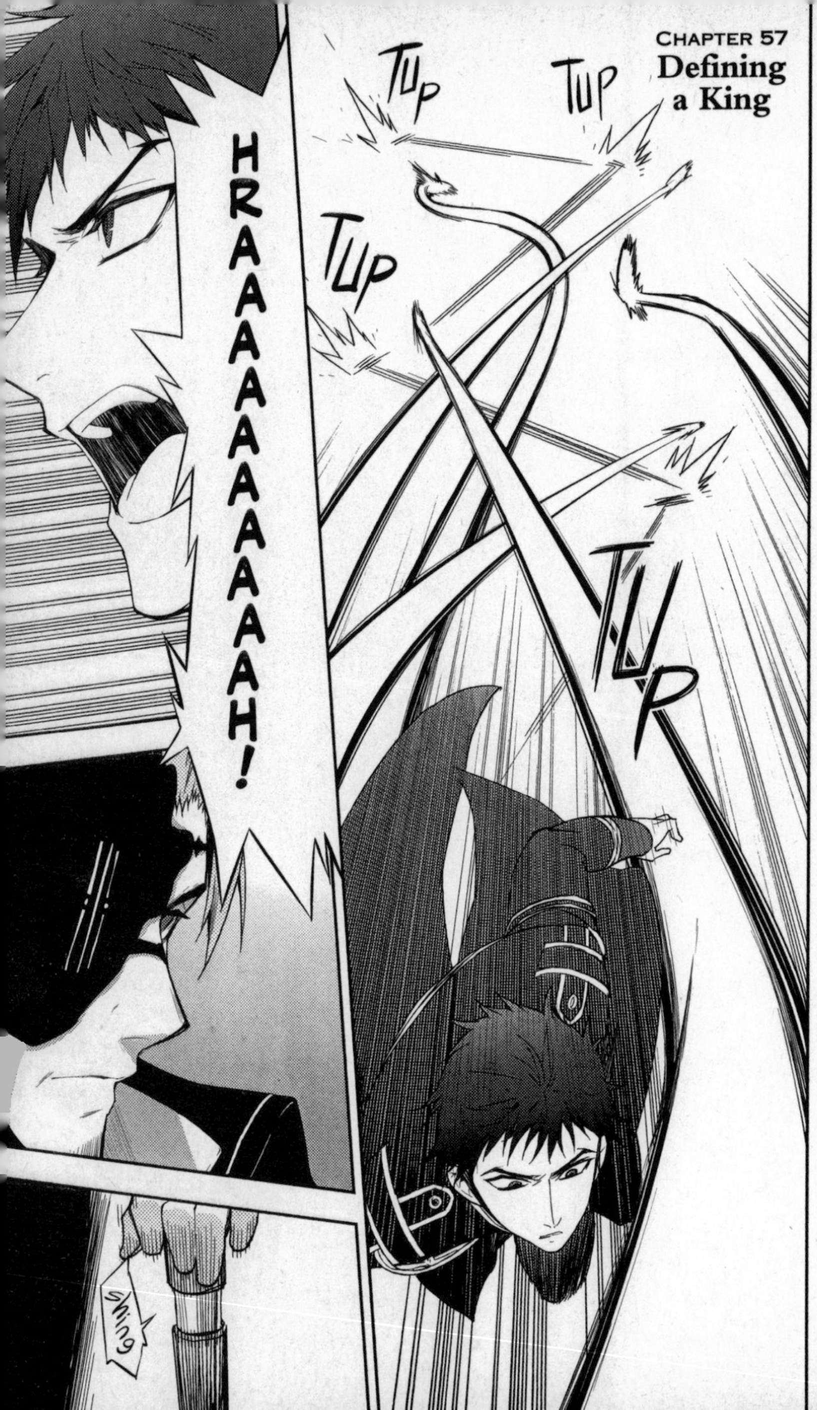
TUP
TUP
TUP
TUP
HRAAAAAAAAAAAAH!
shing

CHAPTER 57 Defining a King

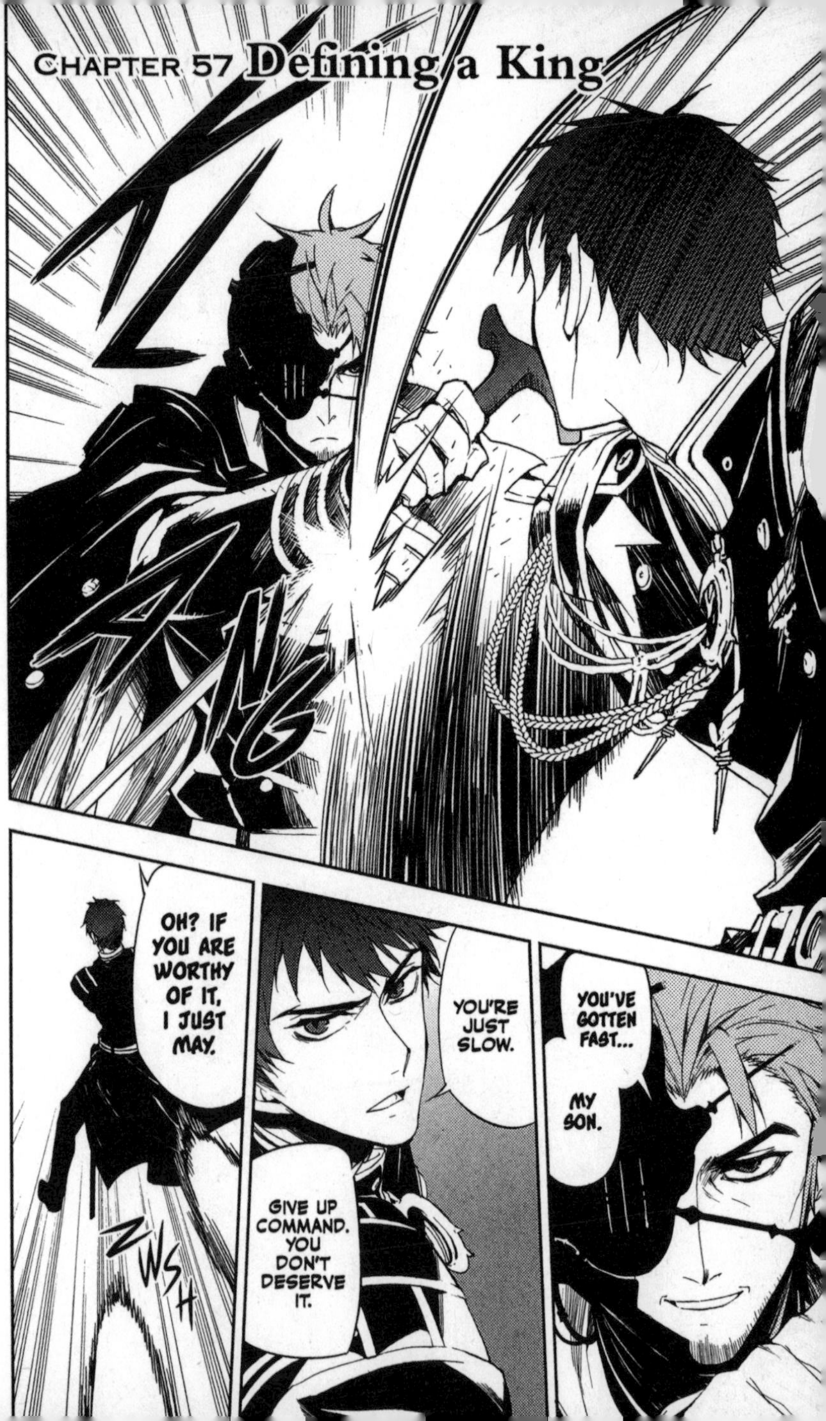
ZANG
YOU'VE GOTTEN FAST...
MY SON.
YOU'RE JUST SLOW.
GIVE UP COMMAND. YOU DON'T DESERVE IT.
OH? IF YOU ARE WORTHY OF IT, I JUST MAY.
ZWSH

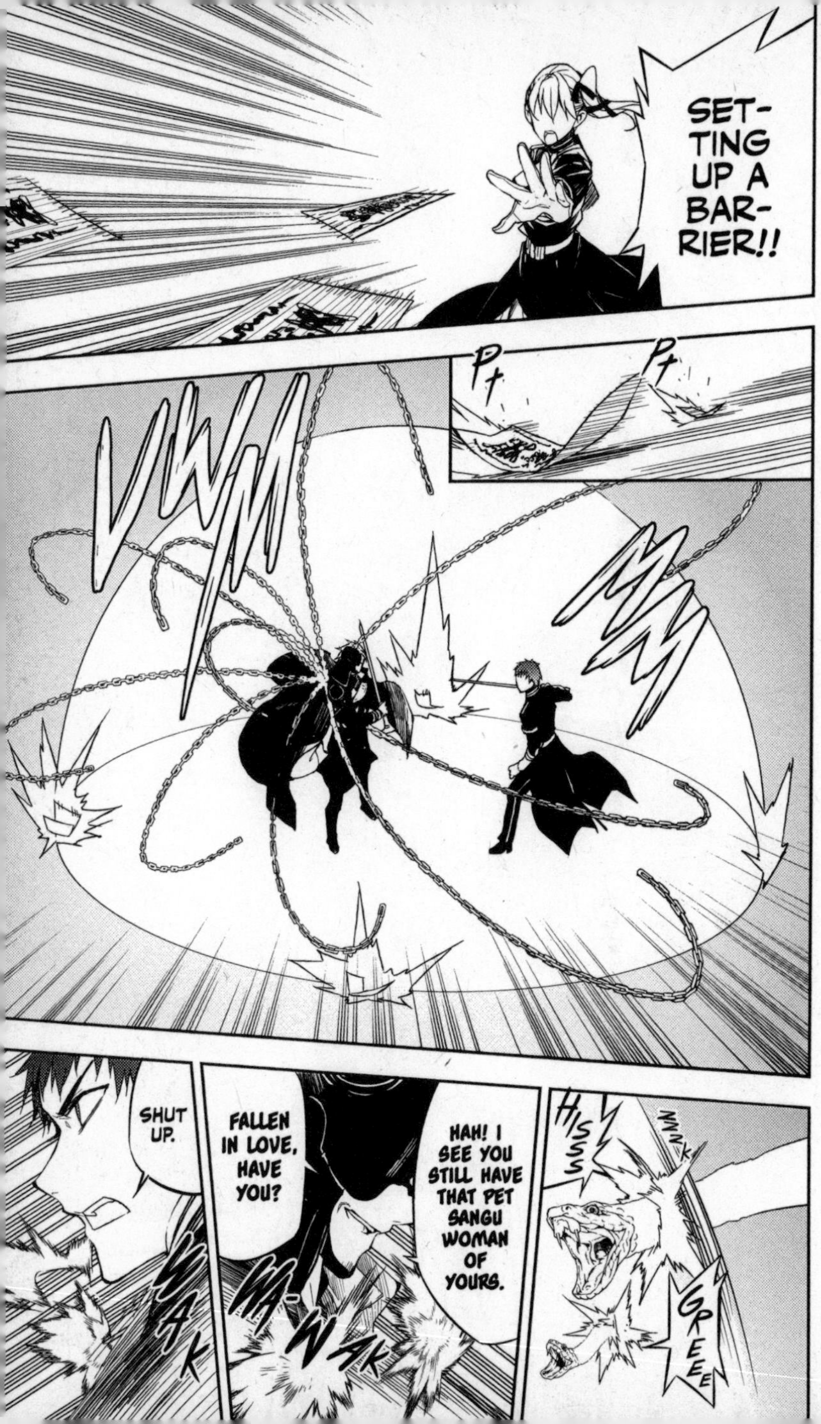
SET-TING UP A BAR-RIER!!
Pt
Pt
VWM
MMM
HISS
NNNK
GREEE
HAH! I SEE YOU STILL HAVE THAT PET SANGU WOMAN OF YOURS.
FALLEN IN LOVE, HAVE YOU?
WA-WAK
SHUT UP.
WAK

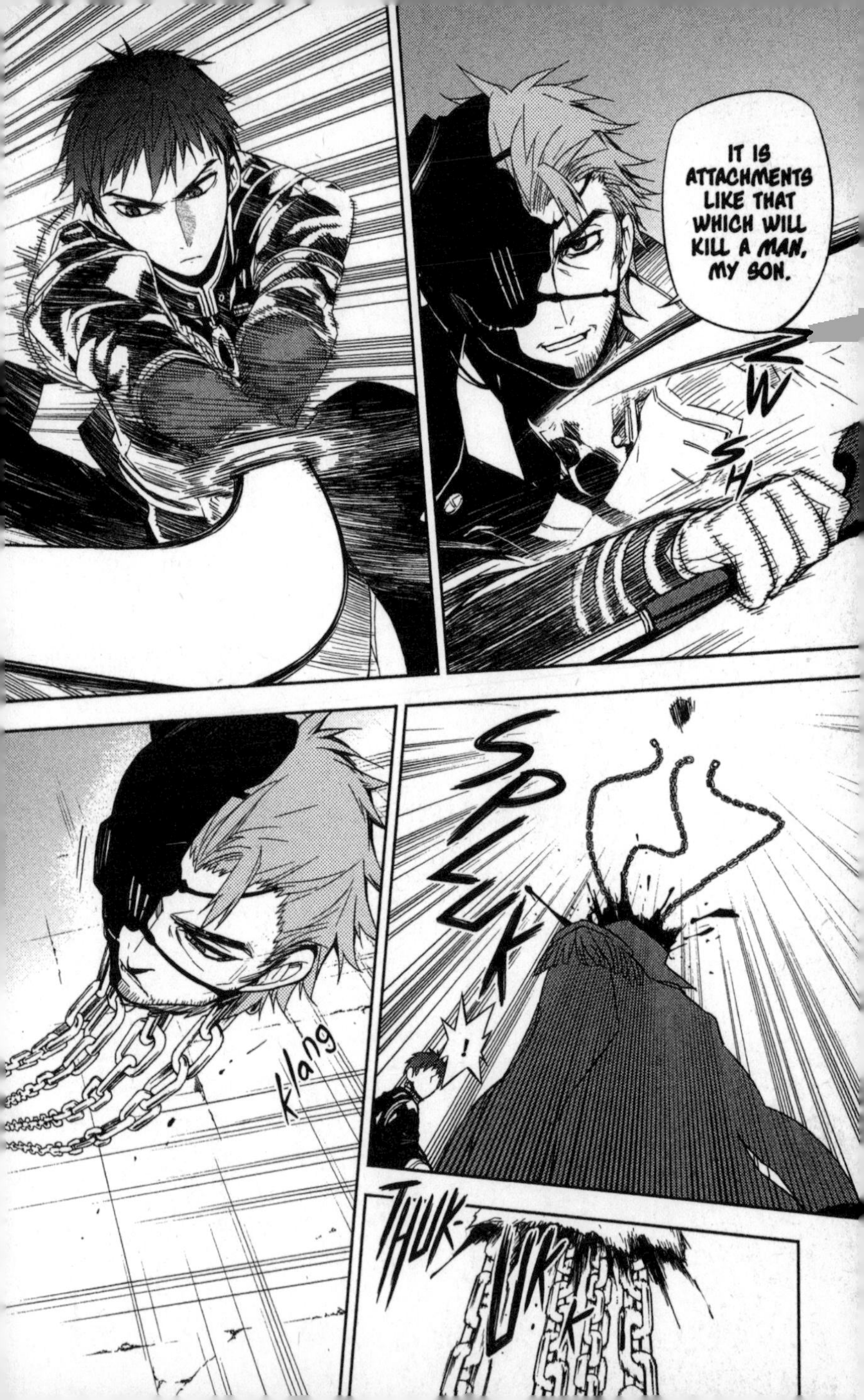
IT IS ATTACHMENTS LIKE THAT WHICH WILL KILL A MAN, MY SON.
ZWWSH
SPLUK
!
THUK-
klang

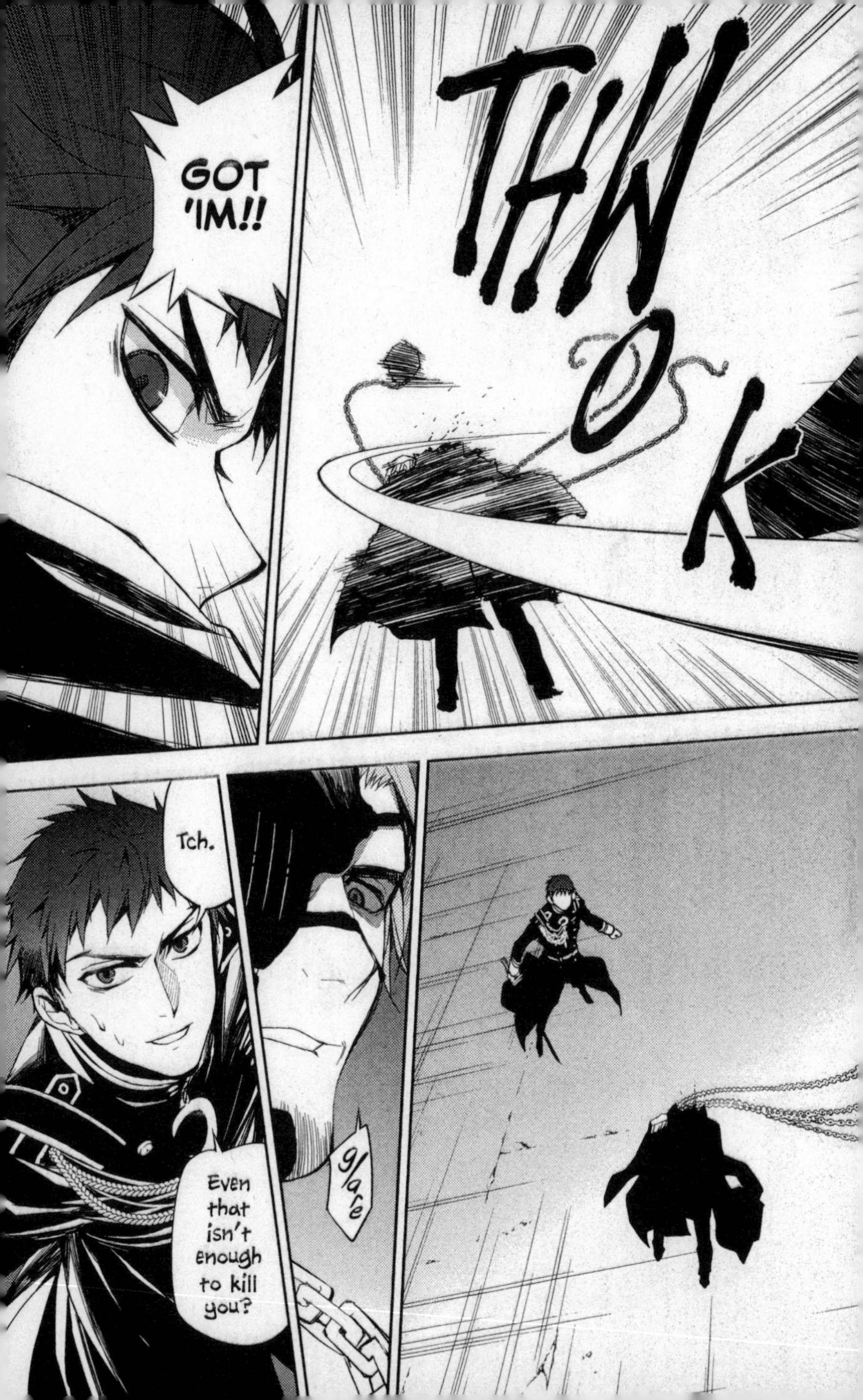
THWOK
GOT 'IM!!
Tch.
glare
Even that isn't enough to kill you?

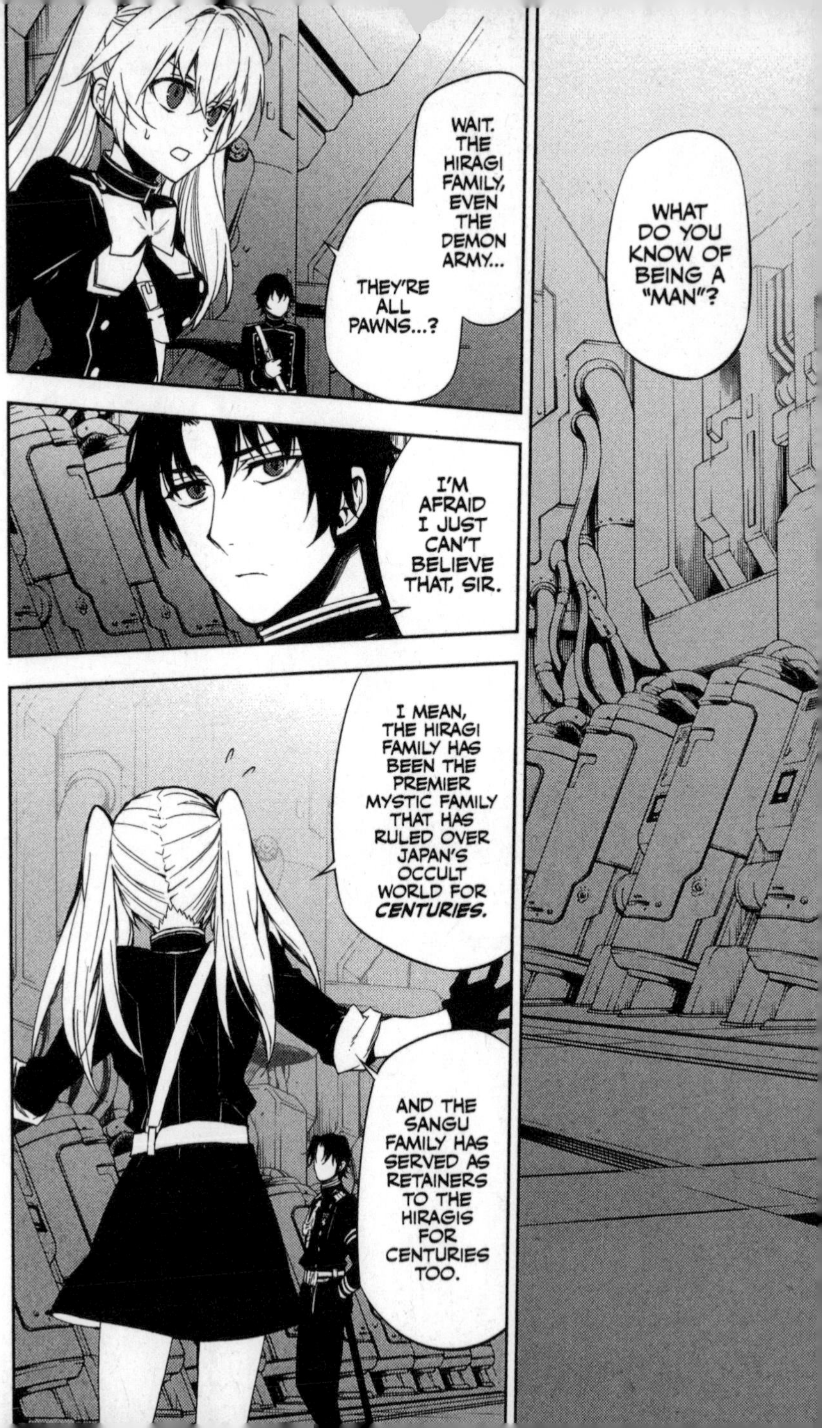
WHAT DO YOU KNOW OF BEING A "MAN"?
WAIT. THE HIRAGI FAMILY, EVEN THE DEMON ARMY...
THEY'RE ALL PAWNS...?
I'M AFRAID I JUST CAN'T BELIEVE THAT, SIR.
I MEAN, THE HIRAGI FAMILY HAS BEEN THE PREMIER MYSTIC FAMILY THAT HAS RULED OVER JAPAN'S OCCULT WORLD FOR CENTURIES.
AND THE SANGU FAMILY HAS SERVED AS RETAINERS TO THE HIRAGIS FOR CENTURIES TOO.

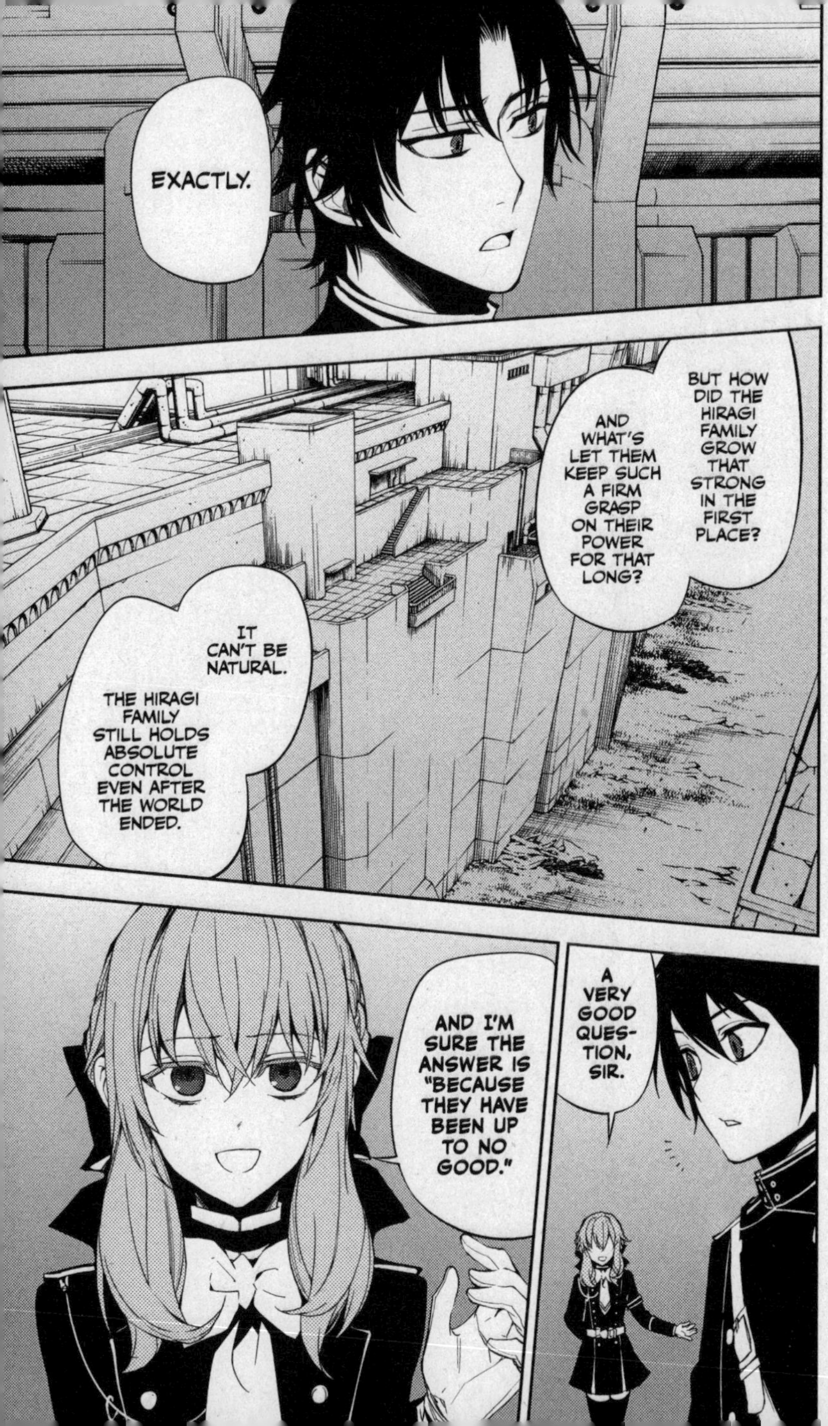
EXACTLY.
BUT HOW DID THE HIRAGI FAMILY GROW THAT STRONG IN THE FIRST PLACE?
AND WHAT'S LET THEM KEEP SUCH A FIRM GRASP ON THEIR POWER FOR THAT LONG?
IT CAN'T BE NATURAL.
THE HIRAGI FAMILY STILL HOLDS ABSOLUTE CONTROL EVEN AFTER THE WORLD ENDED.
A VERY GOOD QUES-TION, SIR.
AND I'M SURE THE ANSWER IS "BECAUSE THEY HAVE BEEN UP TO NO GOOD."

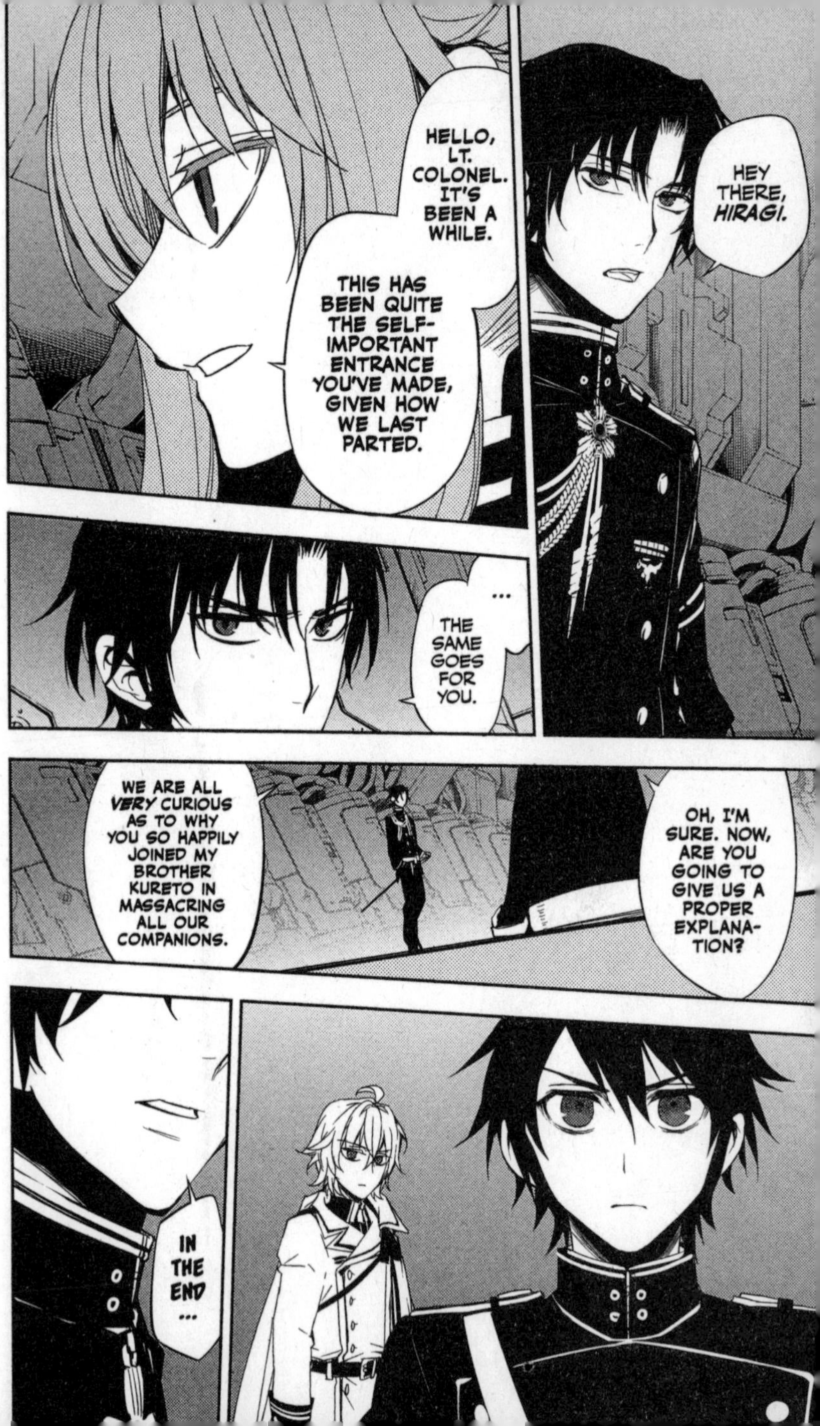
HEY THERE, *HIRAGI.*
HELLO, LT. COLONEL. IT'S BEEN A WHILE.
THIS HAS BEEN QUITE THE SELF-IMPORTANT ENTRANCE YOU'VE MADE, GIVEN HOW WE LAST PARTED.
... THE SAME GOES FOR YOU.
WE ARE ALL *VERY* CURIOUS AS TO WHY YOU SO HAPPILY JOINED MY BROTHER KURETO IN MASSACRING ALL OUR COMPANIONS.
OH, I'M SURE. NOW, ARE YOU GOING TO GIVE US A PROPER EXPLANATION?
IN THE END ...

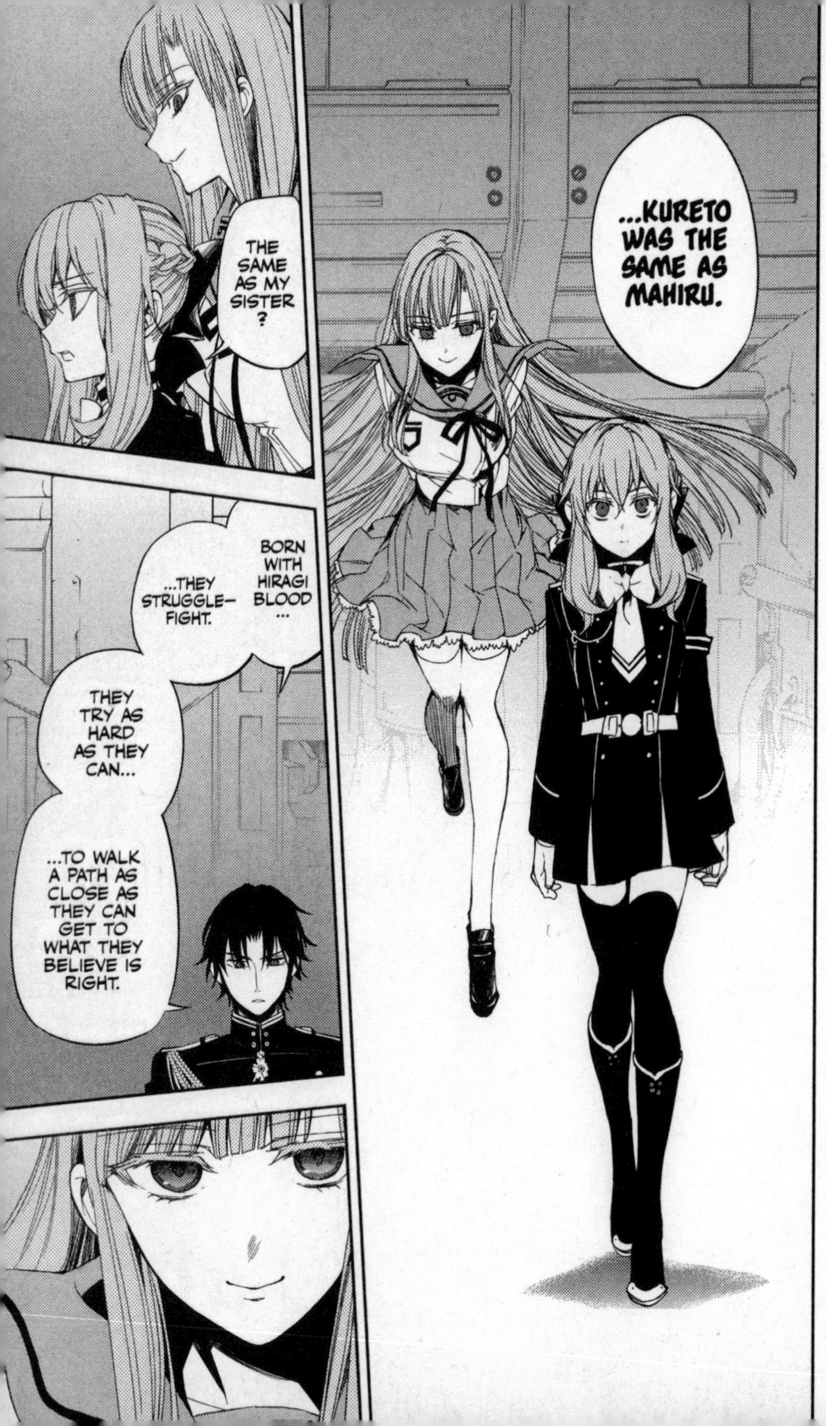
...KURETO WAS THE SAME AS MAHIRU.
THE SAME AS MY SISTER?
BORN WITH HIRAGI BLOOD...
...THEY STRUGGLE—FIGHT.
THEY TRY AS HARD AS THEY CAN...
...TO WALK A PATH AS CLOSE AS THEY CAN GET TO WHAT THEY BELIEVE IS RIGHT.

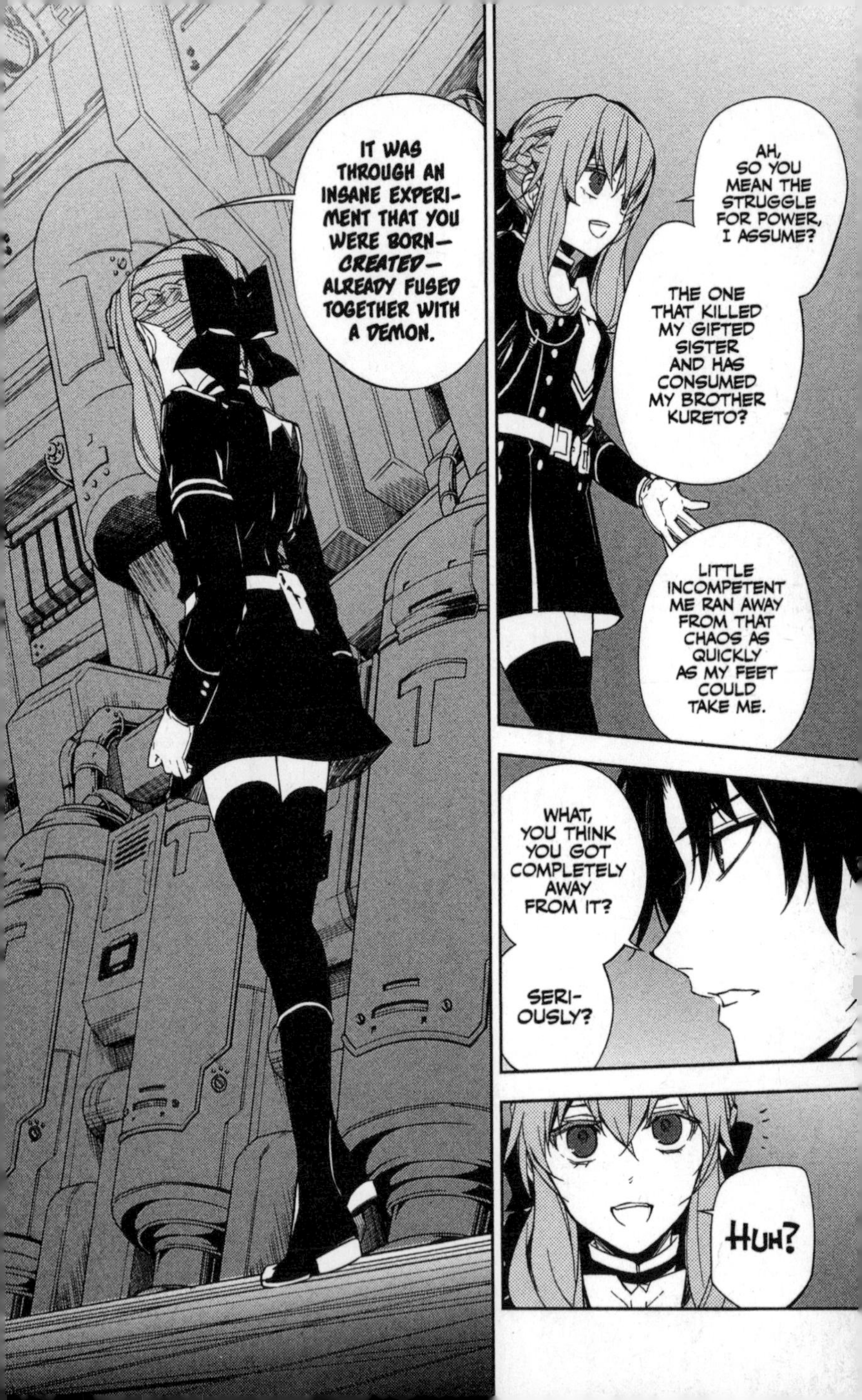
AH, SO YOU MEAN THE STRUGGLE FOR POWER, I ASSUME?
THE ONE THAT KILLED MY GIFTED SISTER AND HAS CONSUMED MY BROTHER KURETO?
LITTLE INCOMPETENT ME RAN AWAY FROM THAT CHAOS AS QUICKLY AS MY FEET COULD TAKE ME.
WHAT, YOU THINK YOU GOT COMPLETELY AWAY FROM IT?
SERI- OUSLY?
HUH?
IT WAS THROUGH AN INSANE EXPERI- MENT THAT YOU WERE BORN— CREATED— ALREADY FUSED TOGETHER WITH A DEMON.

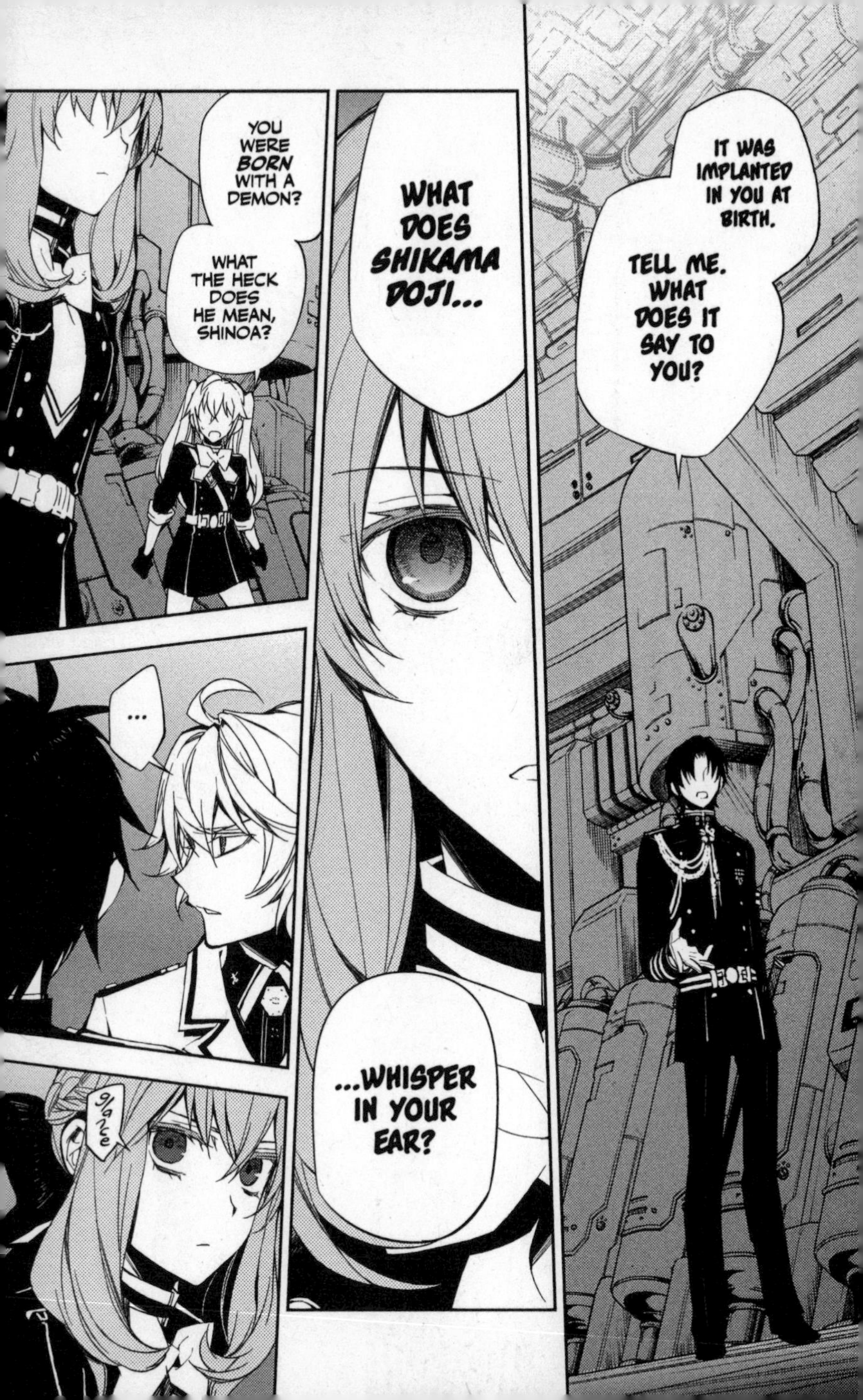
IT WAS IMPLANTED IN YOU AT BIRTH.
TELL ME. WHAT DOES IT SAY TO YOU?
WHAT DOES SHIKAMA DOJI...
...WHISPER IN YOUR EAR?
YOU WERE BORN WITH A DEMON?
WHAT THE HECK DOES HE MEAN, SHINOA?
...
glance

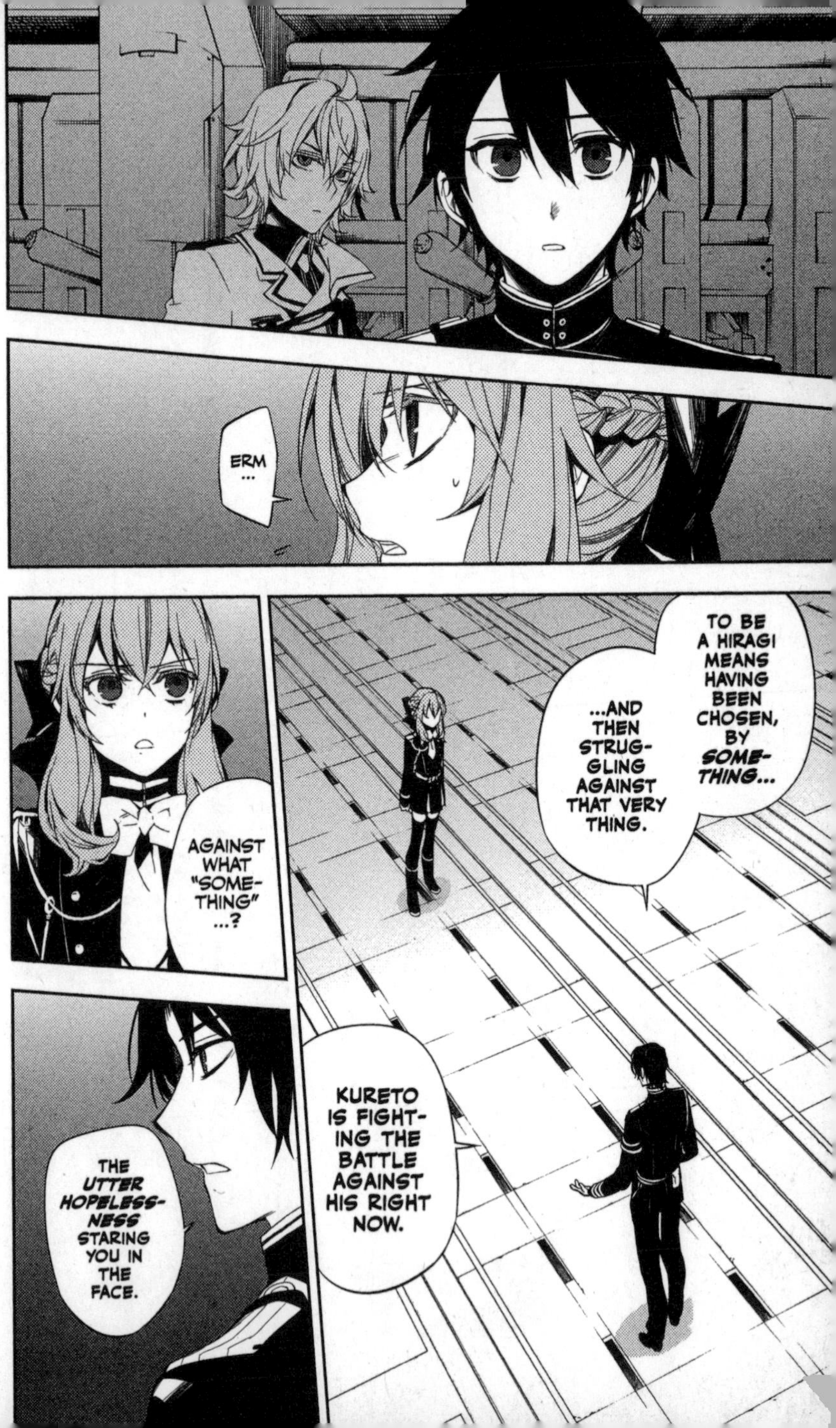
ERM ...
TO BE A HIRAGI MEANS HAVING BEEN CHOSEN, BY *SOME-THING*...
...AND THEN STRUG-GLING AGAINST THAT VERY THING.
KURETO IS FIGHT-ING THE BATTLE AGAINST HIS RIGHT NOW.
AGAINST WHAT "SOME-THING" ...?
THE *UTTER HOPELESS-NESS* STARING YOU IN THE FACE.

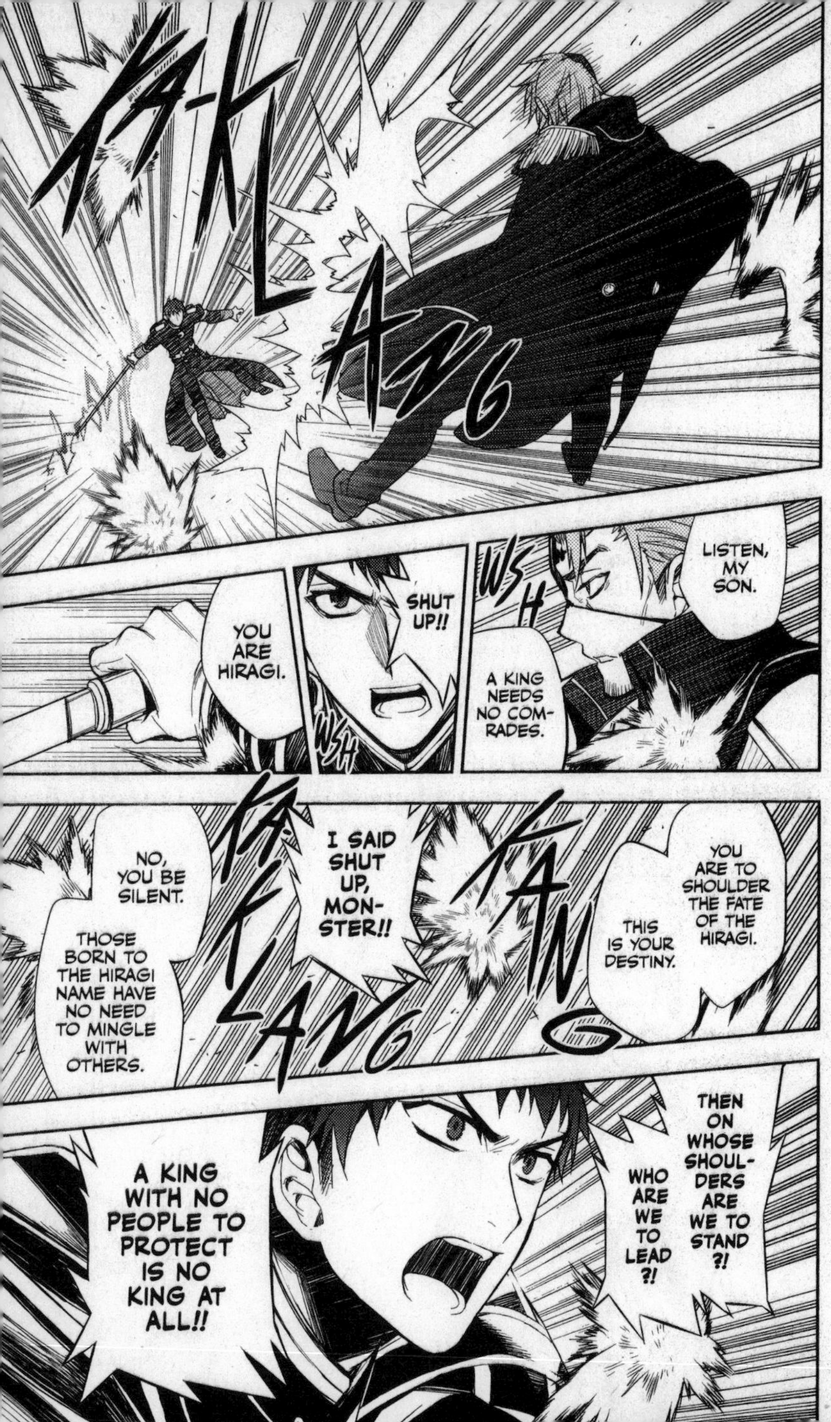
KA-KLANG
LISTEN, MY SON.
A KING NEEDS NO COM-RADES.
WSH
SHUT UP!!
WSH
YOU ARE HIRAGI.
YOU ARE TO SHOULDER THE FATE OF THE HIRAGI.
THIS IS YOUR DESTINY.
KANG
I SAID SHUT UP, MON-STER!!
KA-KLANG
NO, YOU BE SILENT.
THOSE BORN TO THE HIRAGI NAME HAVE NO NEED TO MINGLE WITH OTHERS.
THEN ON WHOSE SHOUL-DERS ARE WE TO STAND?!
WHO ARE WE TO LEAD?!
A KING WITH NO PEOPLE TO PROTECT IS NO KING AT ALL!!

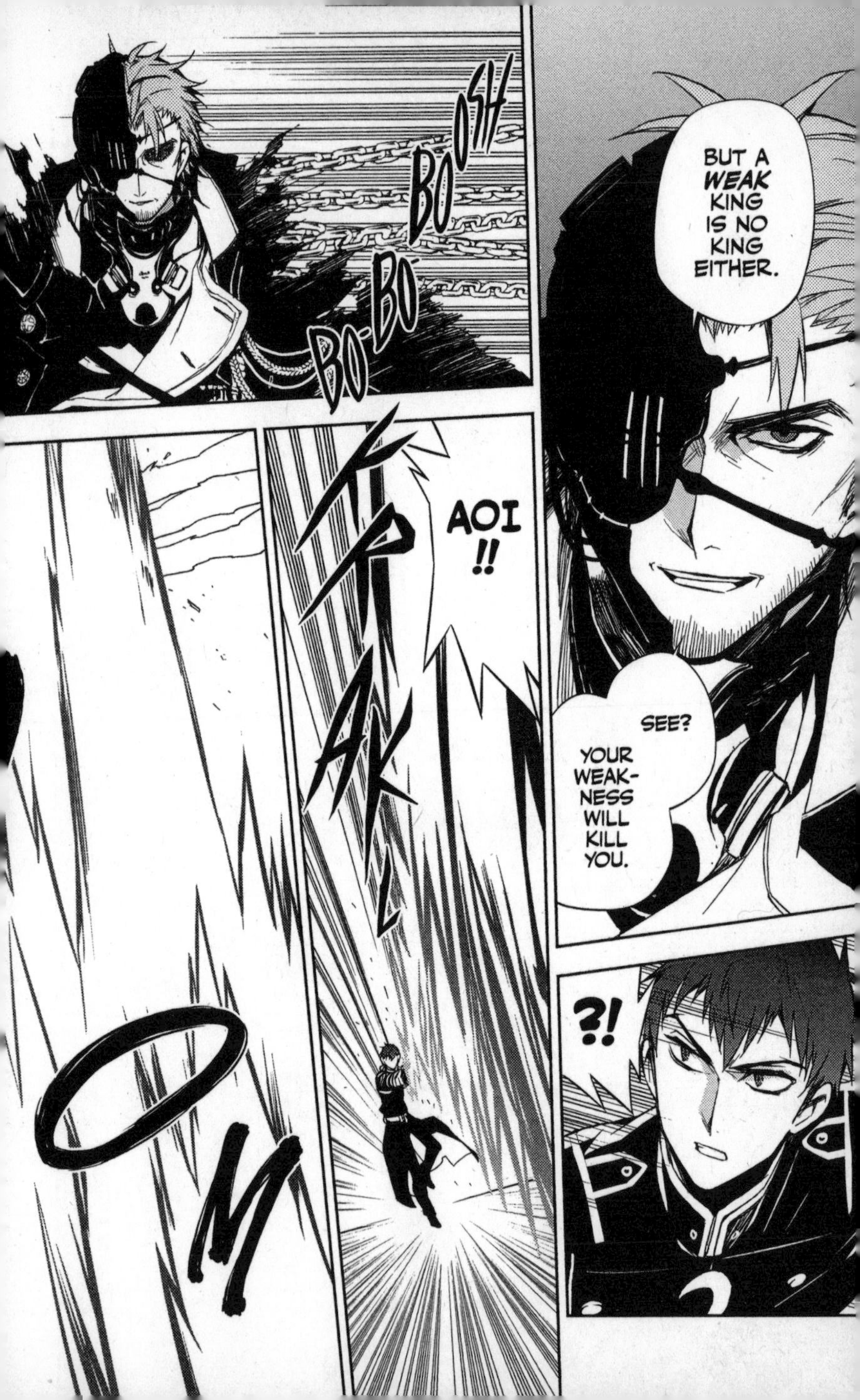
BUT A WEAK KING IS NO KING EITHER.
SEE? YOUR WEAK-NESS WILL KILL YOU.
BO-BO-BOOSH
?!
KRAKL
AOI!!
OM

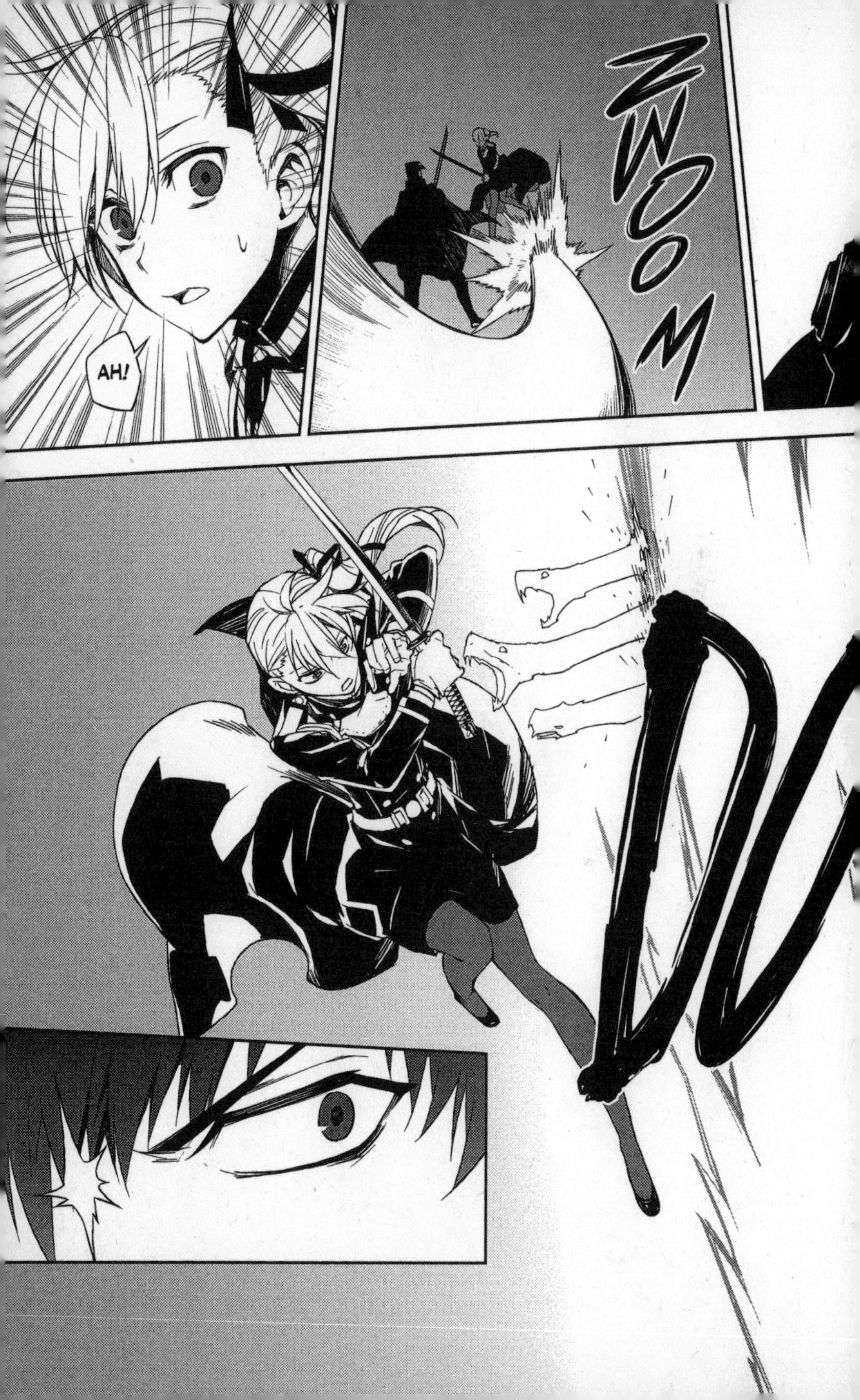
ZWOOM
AH!

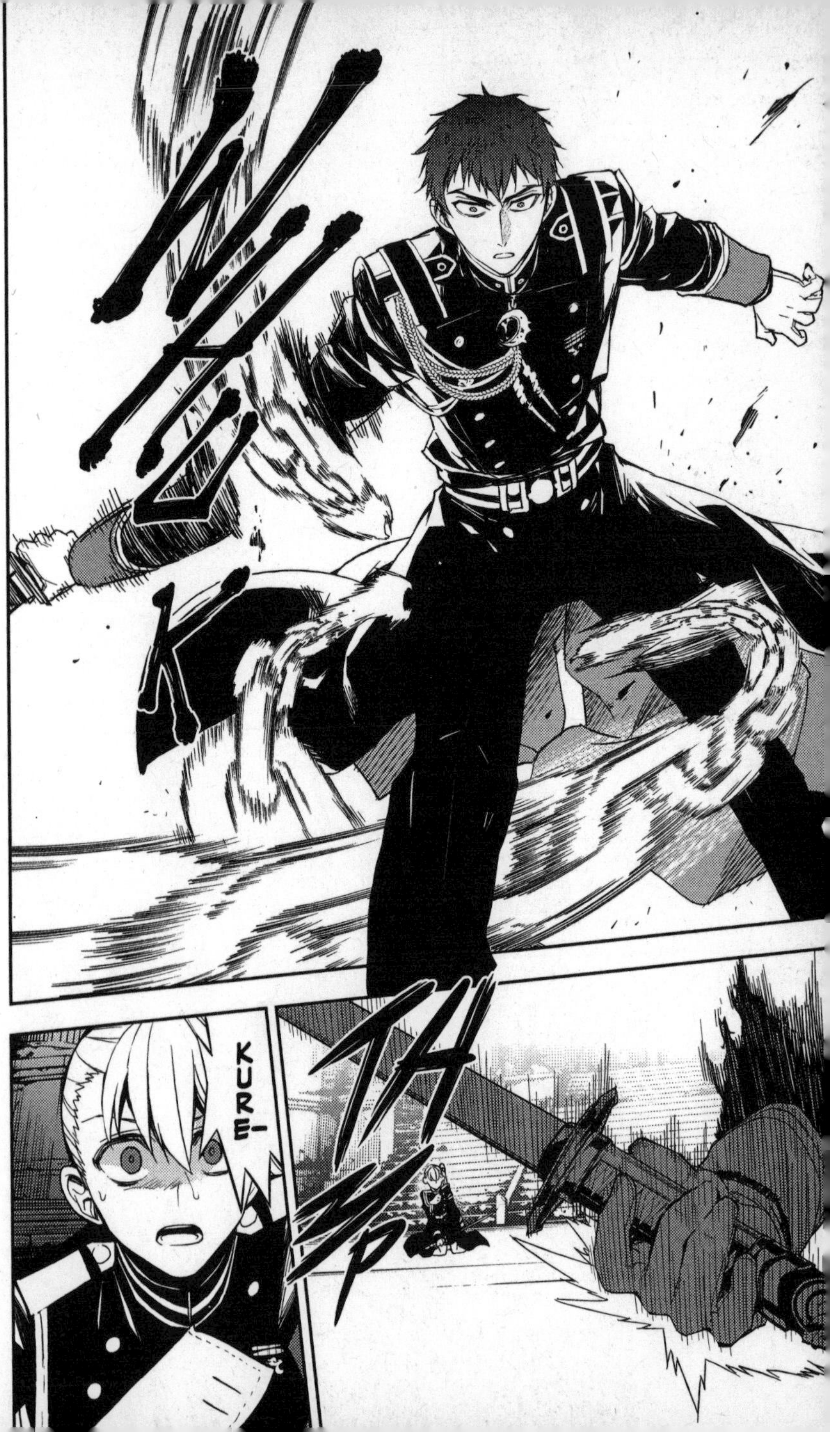
KURE–

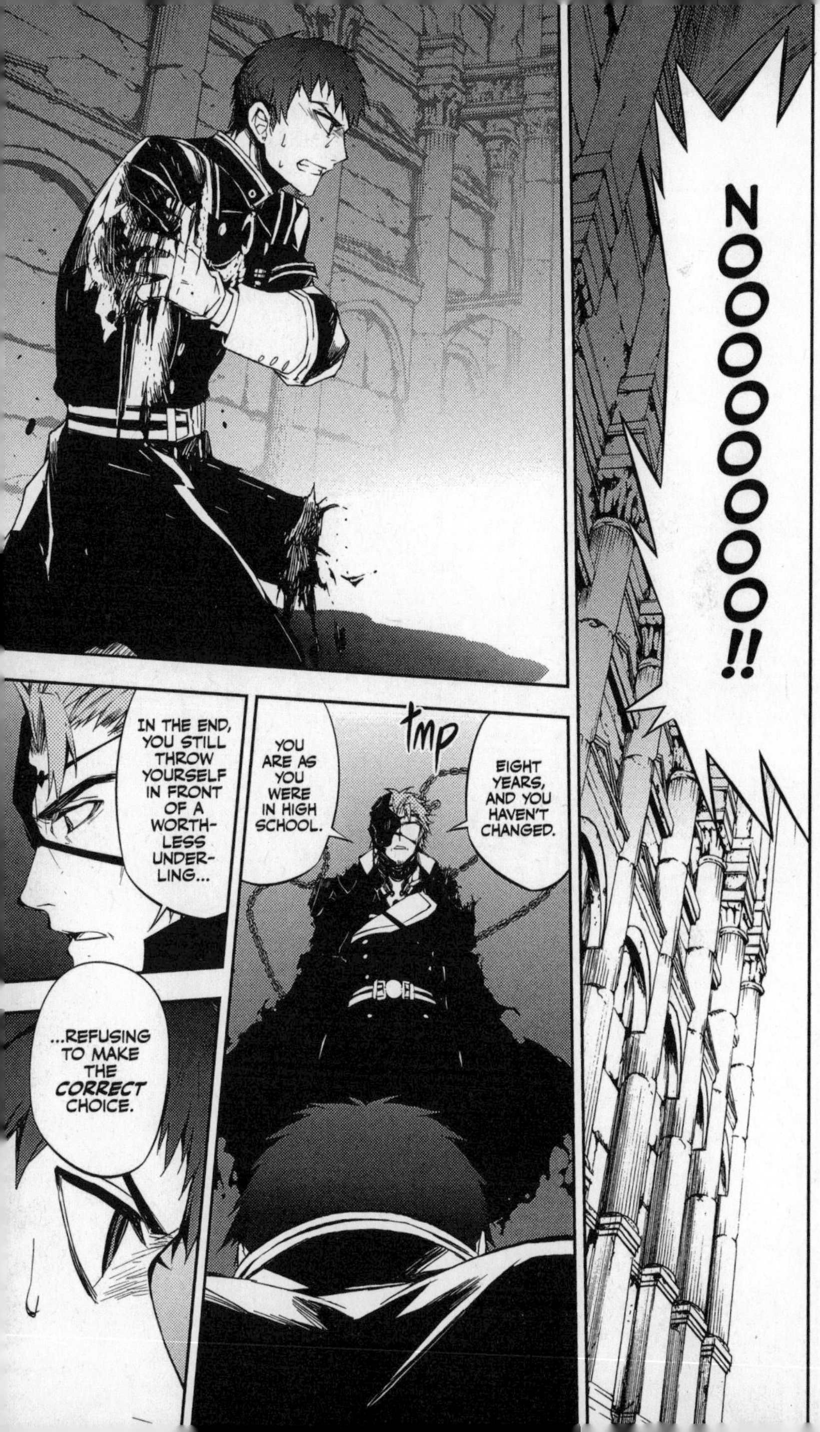
NOOOOOOOO!!
EIGHT YEARS, AND YOU HAVEN'T CHANGED.
tmp
YOU ARE AS YOU WERE IN HIGH SCHOOL.
IN THE END, YOU STILL THROW YOURSELF IN FRONT OF A WORTH-LESS UNDER-LING...
...REFUSING TO MAKE THE *CORRECT* CHOICE.

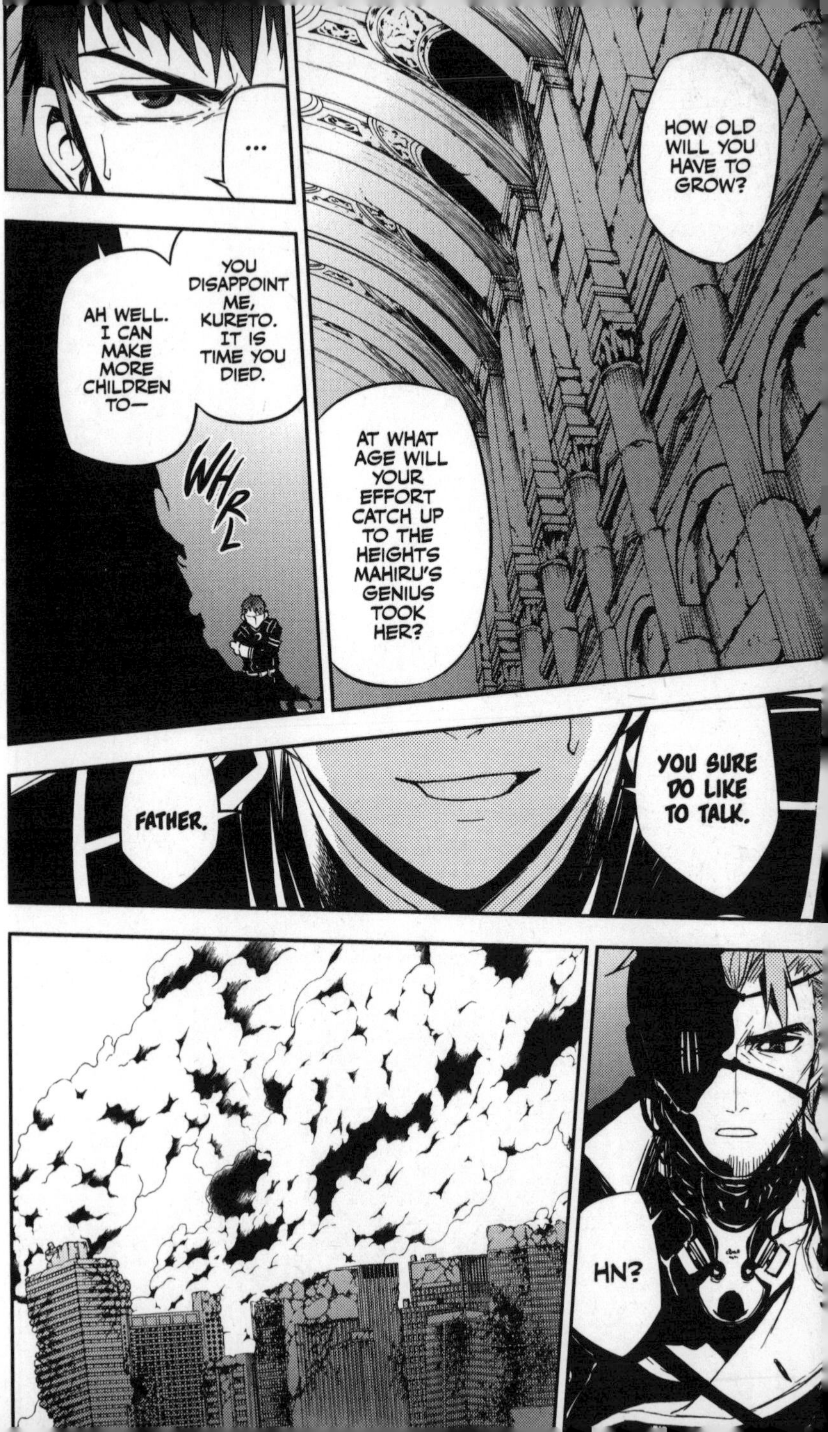
HOW OLD WILL YOU HAVE TO GROW?
AT WHAT AGE WILL YOUR EFFORT CATCH UP TO THE HEIGHTS MAHIRU'S GENIUS TOOK HER?
...
YOU DISAPPOINT ME, KURETO. IT IS TIME YOU DIED.
AH WELL. I CAN MAKE MORE CHILDREN TO—
WHRL
YOU SURE DO LIKE TO TALK.
FATHER.
HN?

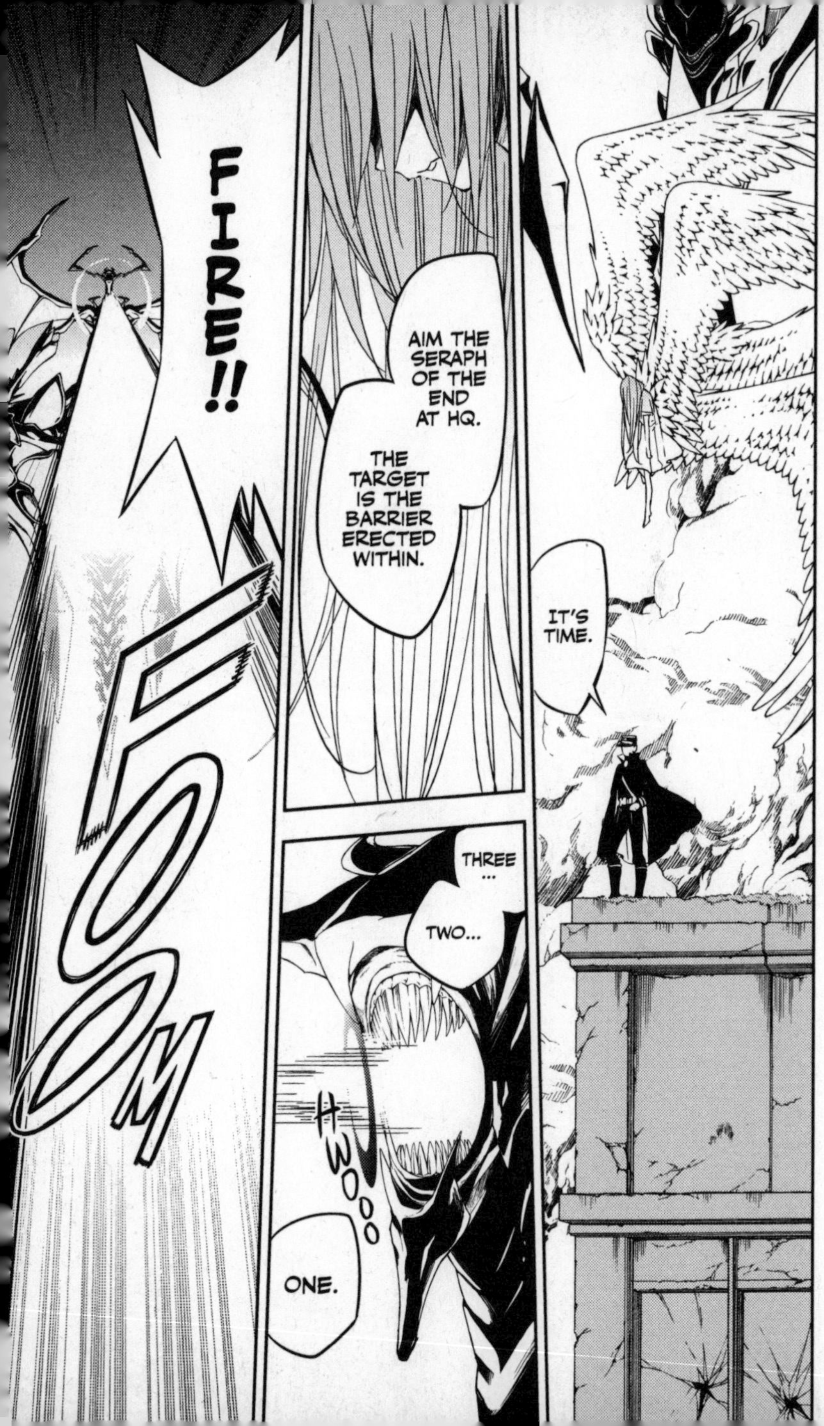
IT'S TIME.
AIM THE SERAPH OF THE END AT HQ.
THE TARGET IS THE BARRIER ERECTED WITHIN.
THREE...
TWO...
HWOOOO
ONE.
FIRE!!
FOOM

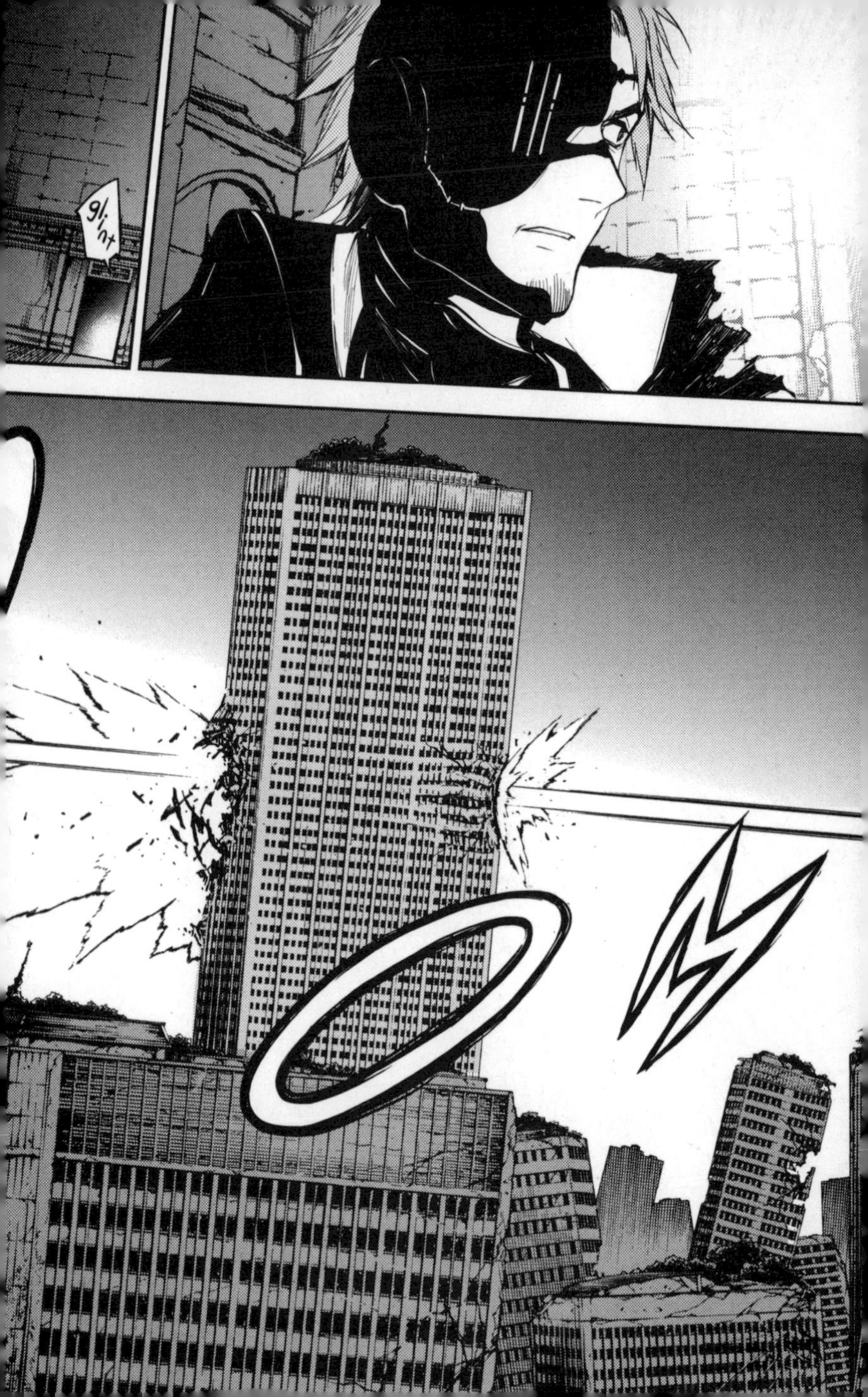
glint

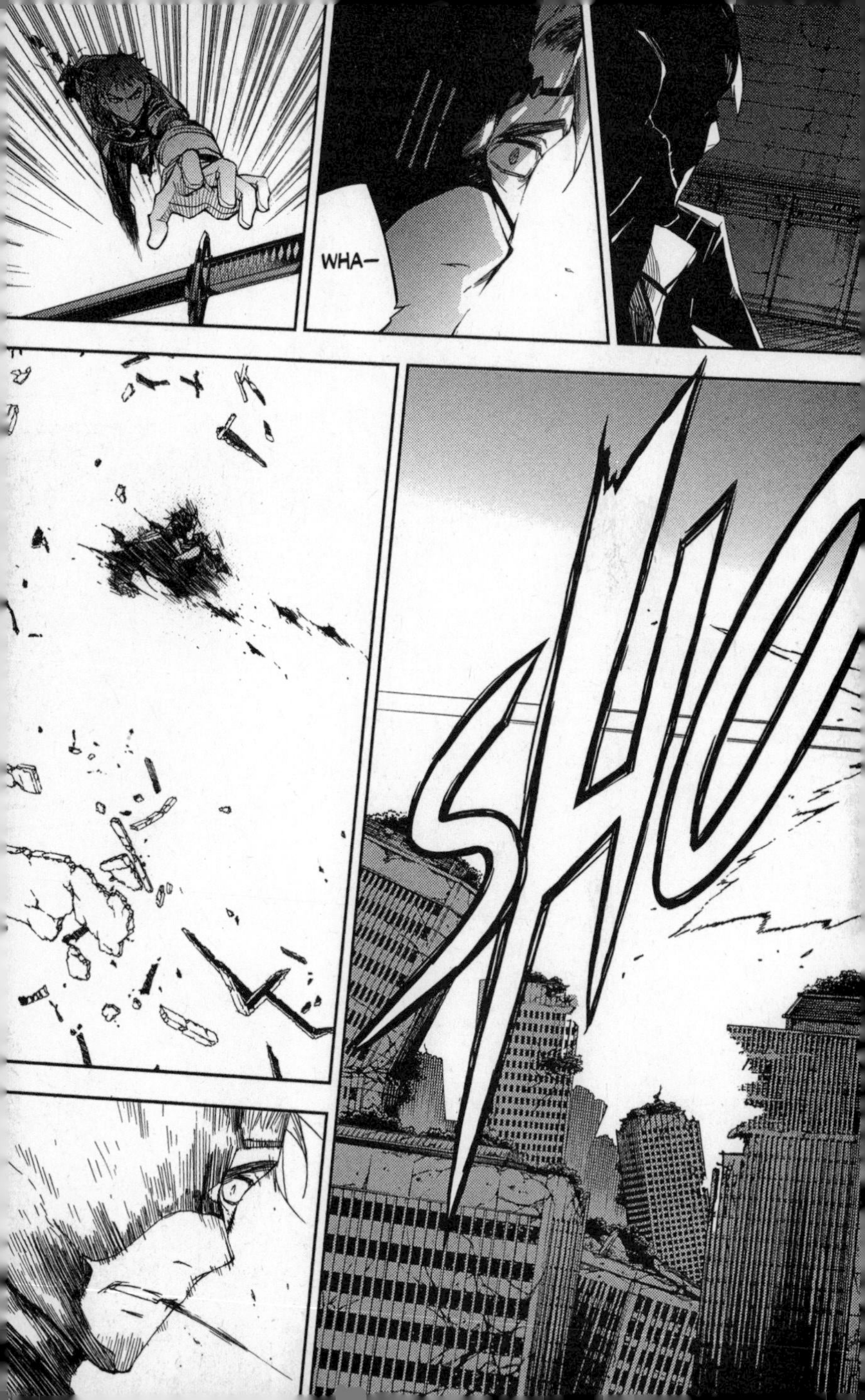
WHA–
SHO

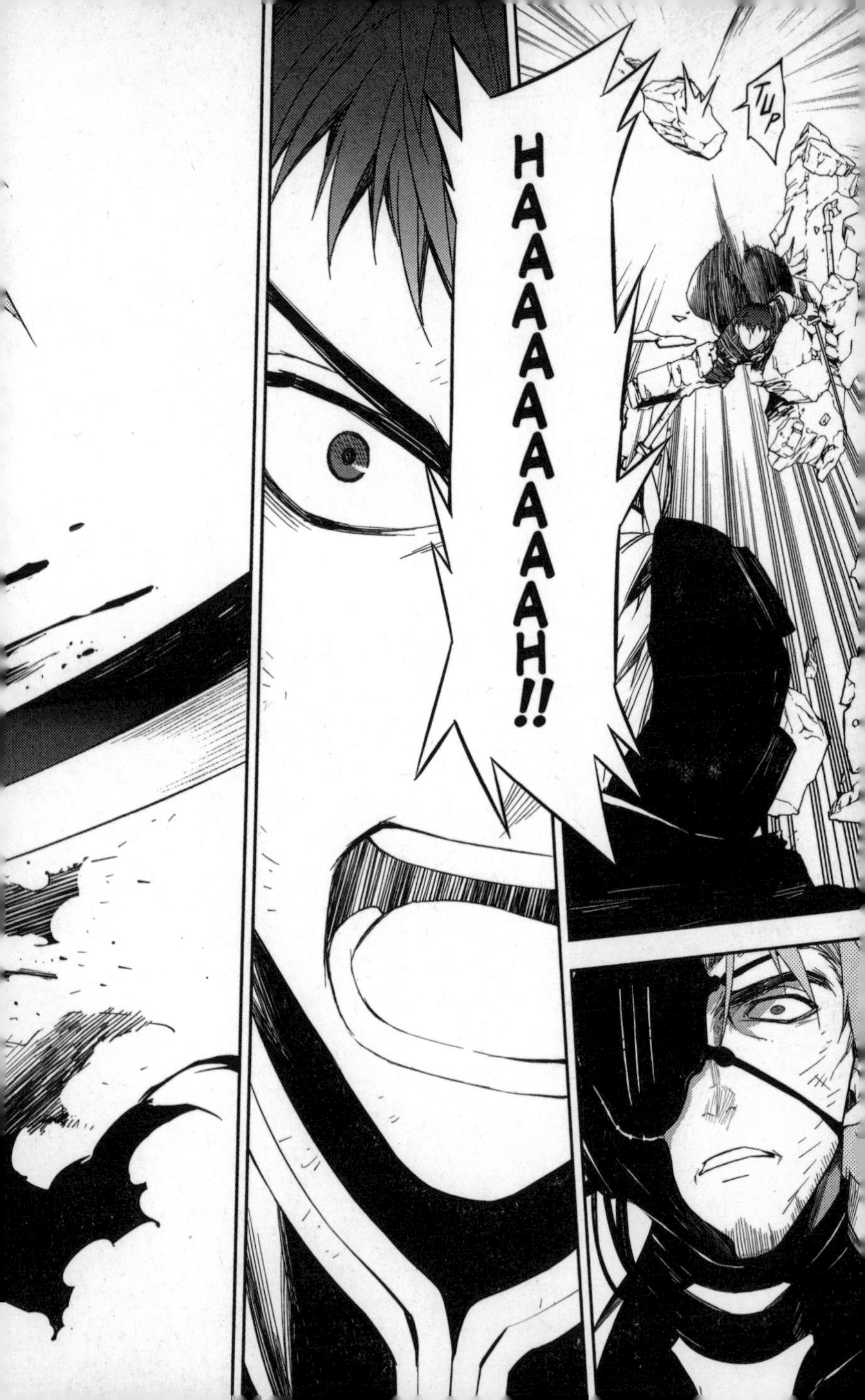
TUP
HAAAAAAAAAAH!!

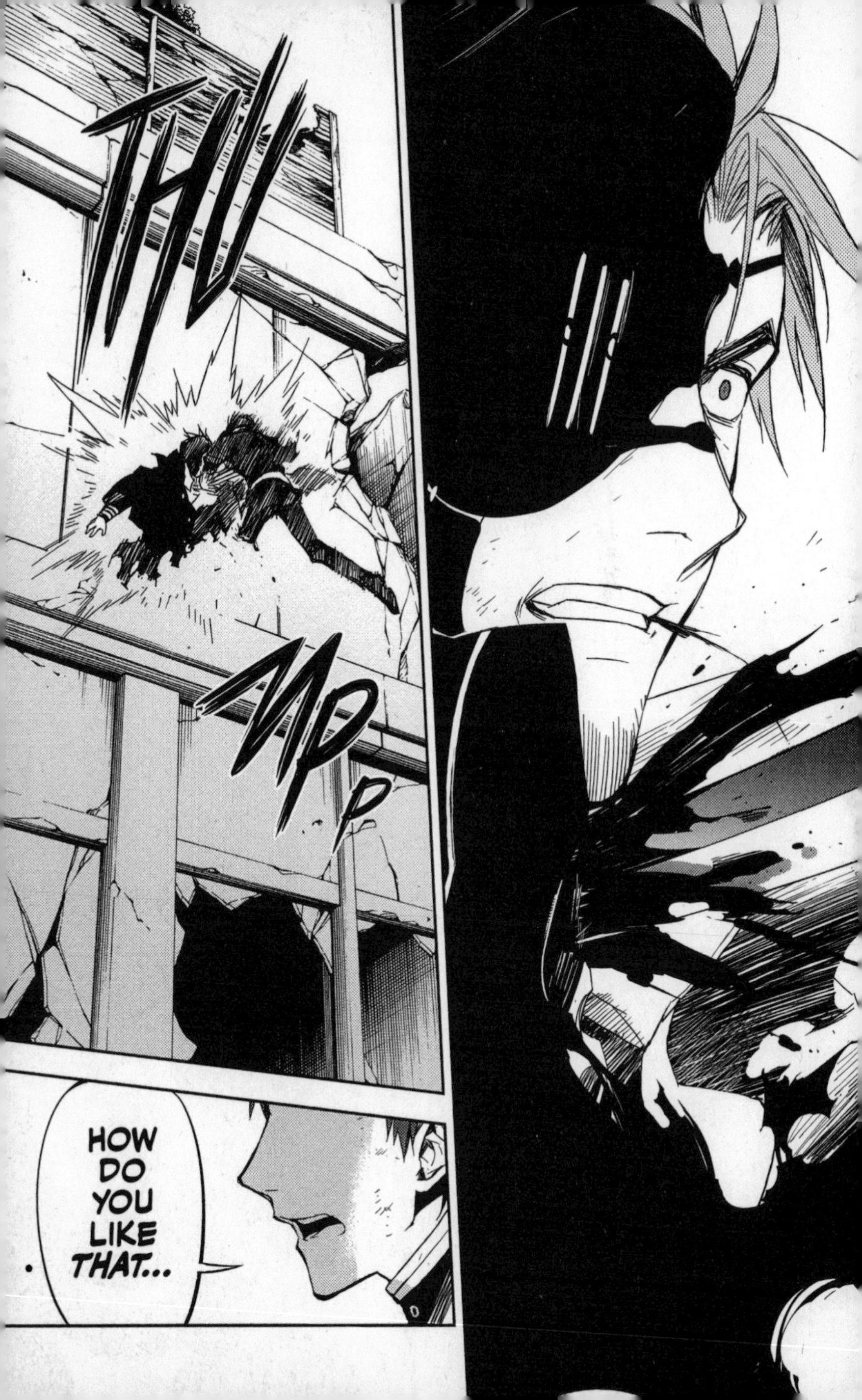
THUMPP
HOW DO YOU LIKE THAT...

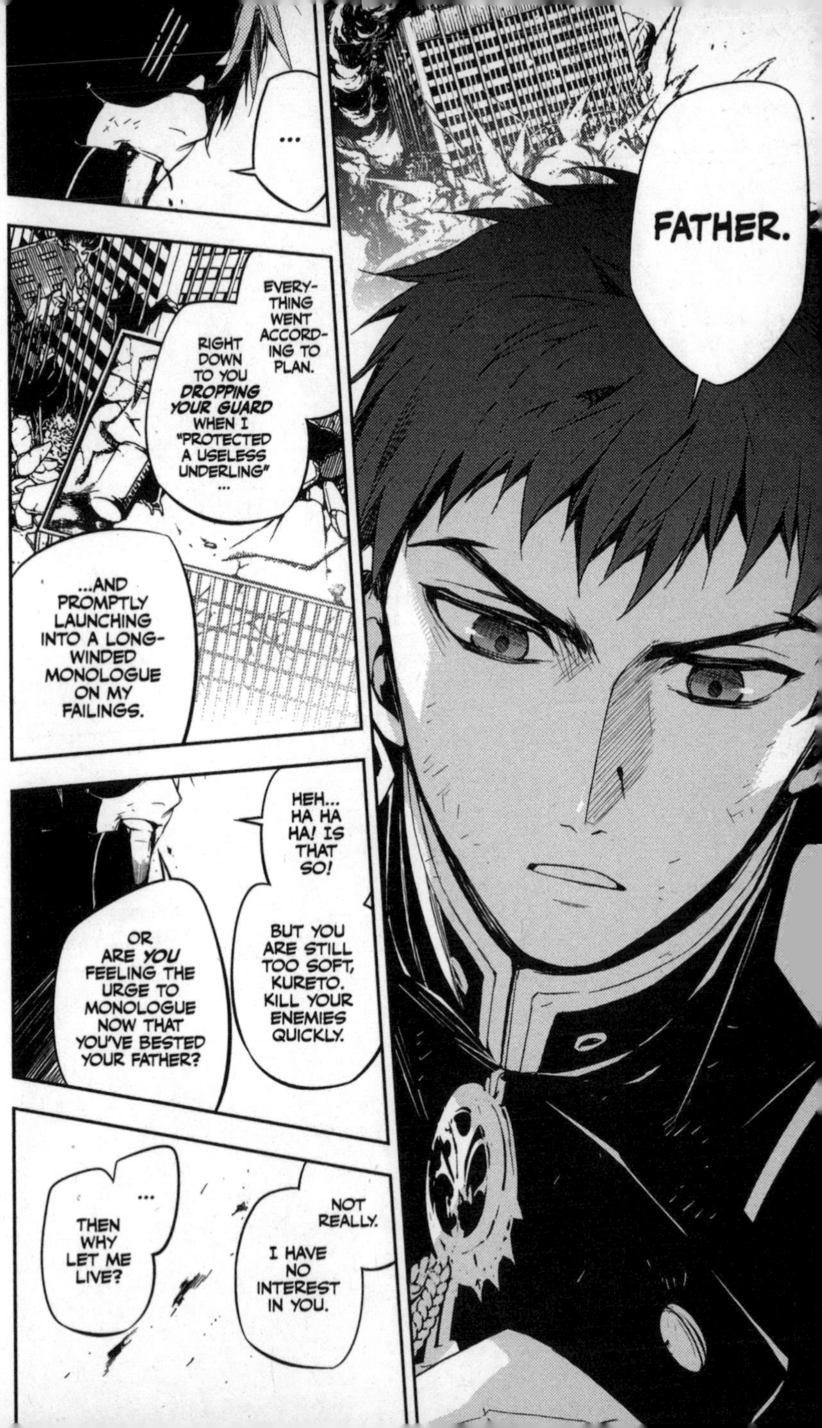
FATHER.
...
EVERY-THING WENT ACCORD-ING TO PLAN.
RIGHT DOWN TO YOU *DROPPING YOUR GUARD* WHEN I "PROTECTED A USELESS UNDERLING"...
...AND PROMPTLY LAUNCHING INTO A LONG-WINDED MONOLOGUE ON MY FAILINGS.
HEH... HA HA HA! IS THAT SO!
BUT YOU ARE STILL TOO SOFT, KURETO. KILL YOUR ENEMIES QUICKLY.
OR ARE *YOU* FEELING THE URGE TO MONOLOGUE NOW THAT YOU'VE BESTED YOUR FATHER?
NOT REALLY.
I HAVE NO INTEREST IN YOU.
...
THEN WHY LET ME LIVE?

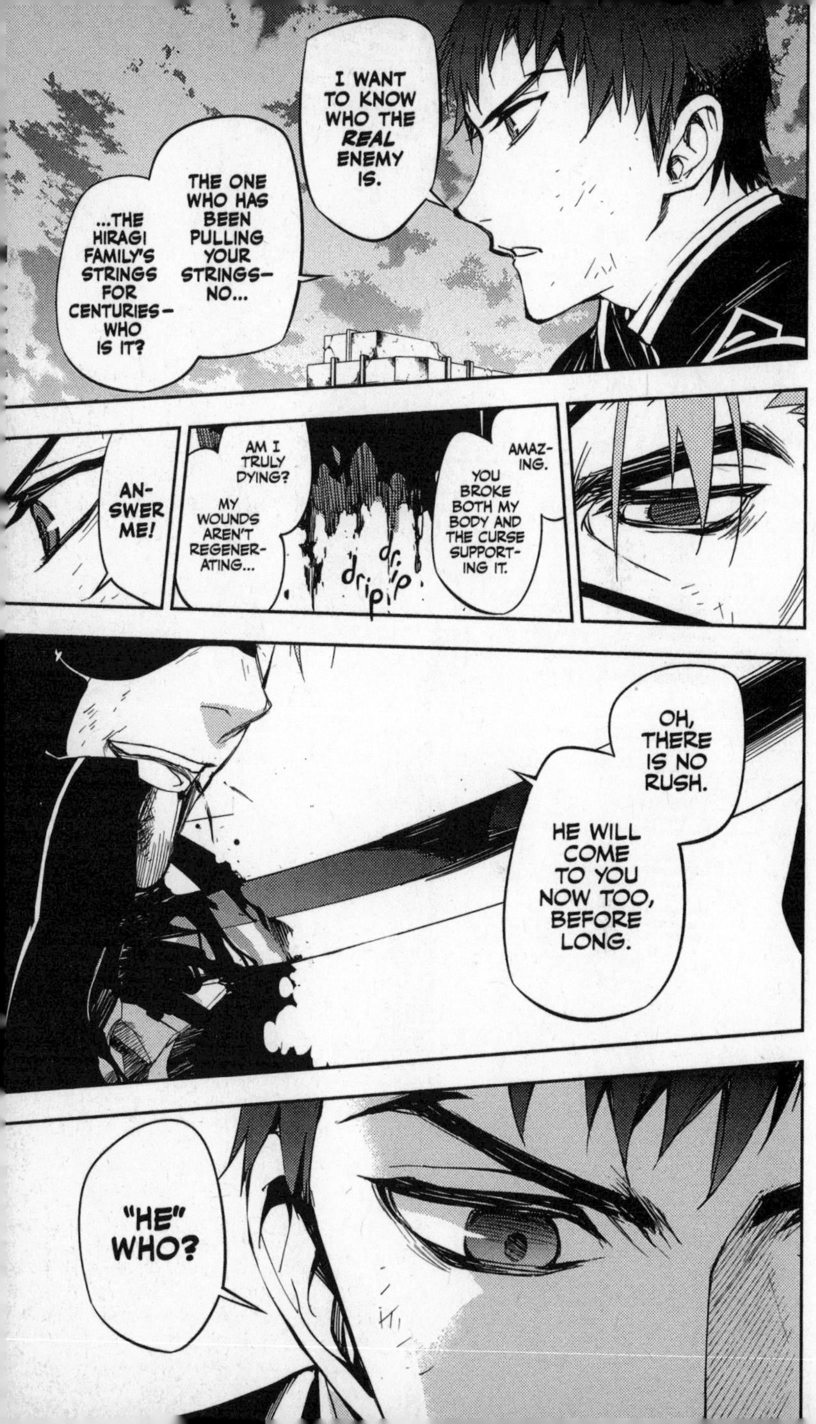
I WANT TO KNOW WHO THE REAL ENEMY IS.
THE ONE WHO HAS BEEN PULLING YOUR STRINGS—NO...
...THE HIRAGI FAMILY'S STRINGS FOR CENTURIES—WHO IS IT?
AMAZ-ING.
YOU BROKE BOTH MY BODY AND THE CURSE SUPPORT-ING IT.
drip
drip
AM I TRULY DYING?
MY WOUNDS AREN'T REGENER-ATING...
AN-SWER ME!
OH, THERE IS NO RUSH.
HE WILL COME TO YOU NOW TOO, BEFORE LONG.
"HE" WHO?

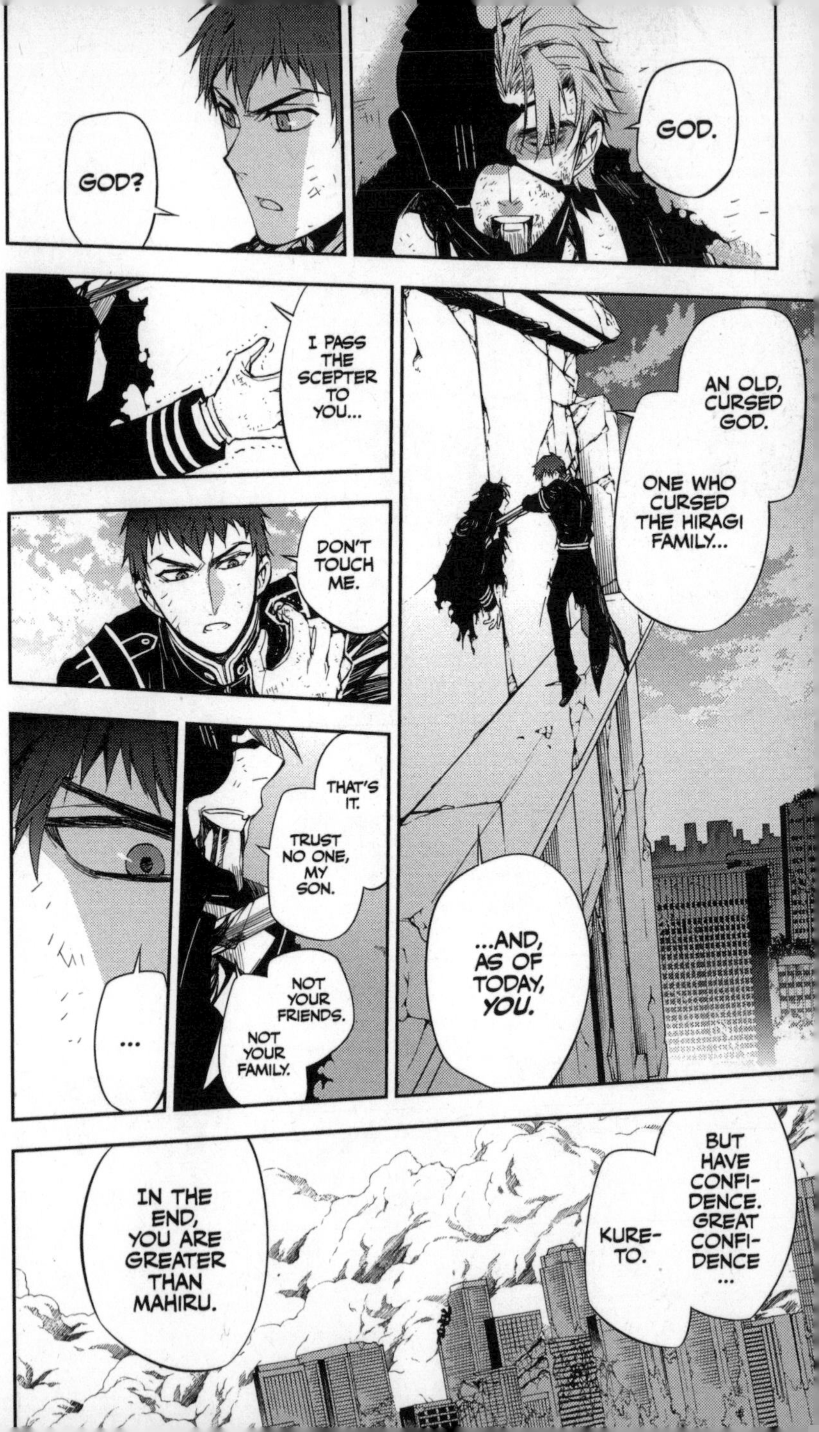
GOD.
GOD?
AN OLD, CURSED GOD.
ONE WHO CURSED THE HIRAGI FAMILY...
...AND, AS OF TODAY, *YOU.*
I PASS THE SCEPTER TO YOU...
DON'T TOUCH ME.
THAT'S IT.
TRUST NO ONE, MY SON.
NOT YOUR FRIENDS.
NOT YOUR FAMILY.
...
BUT HAVE CONFIDENCE. GREAT CONFIDENCE...
KURETO.
IN THE END, YOU ARE GREATER THAN MAHIRU.

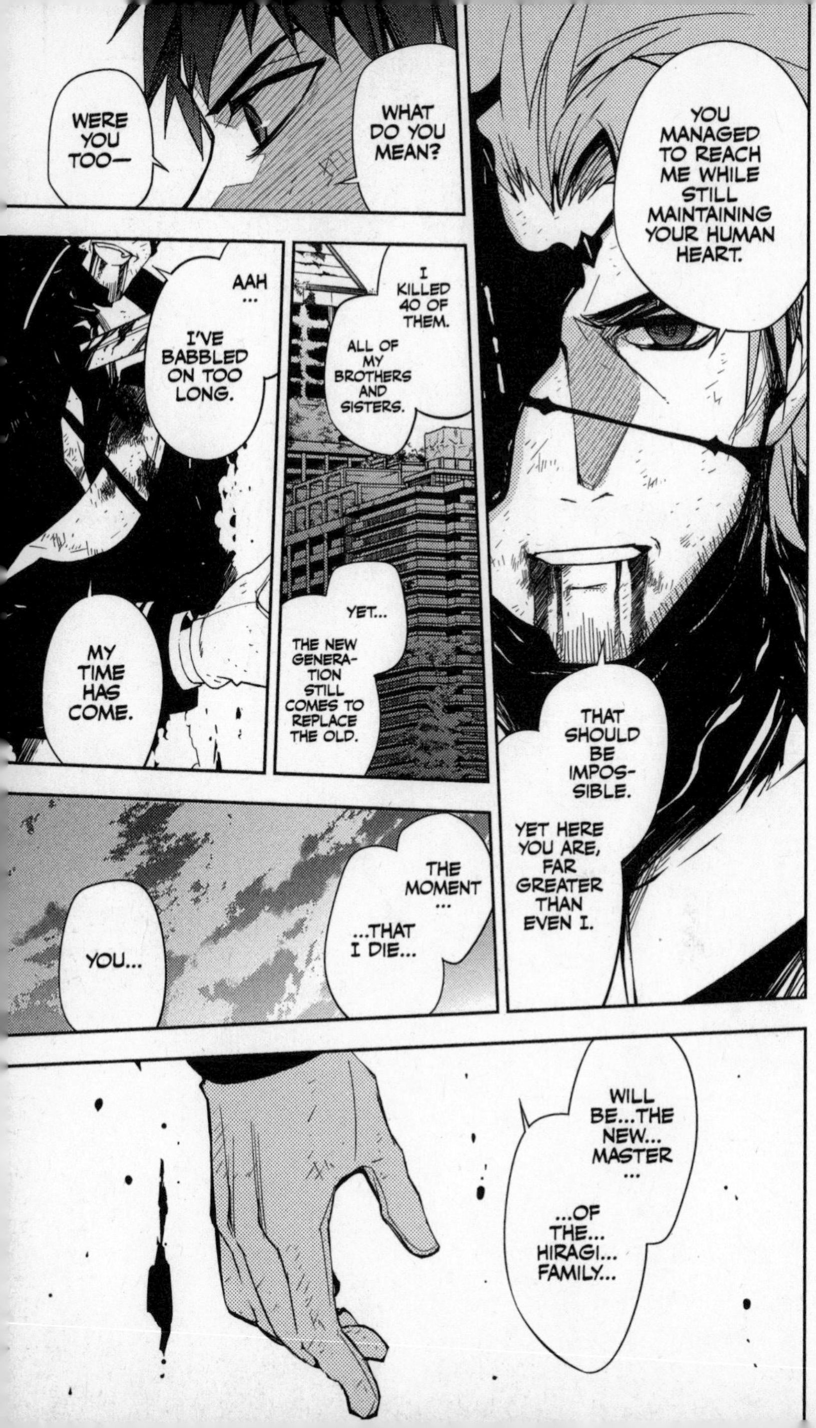
YOU MANAGED TO REACH ME WHILE STILL MAINTAINING YOUR HUMAN HEART.
THAT SHOULD BE IMPOS-SIBLE.
YET HERE YOU ARE, FAR GREATER THAN EVEN I.
WHAT DO YOU MEAN?
WERE YOU TOO—
I KILLED 40 OF THEM.
ALL OF MY BROTHERS AND SISTERS.
YET...
THE NEW GENERA-TION STILL COMES TO REPLACE THE OLD.
AAH ...
I'VE BABBLED ON TOO LONG.
MY TIME HAS COME.
THE MOMENT ...
...THAT I DIE...
YOU...
WILL BE...THE NEW... MASTER ...
...OF THE... HIRAGI... FAMILY...

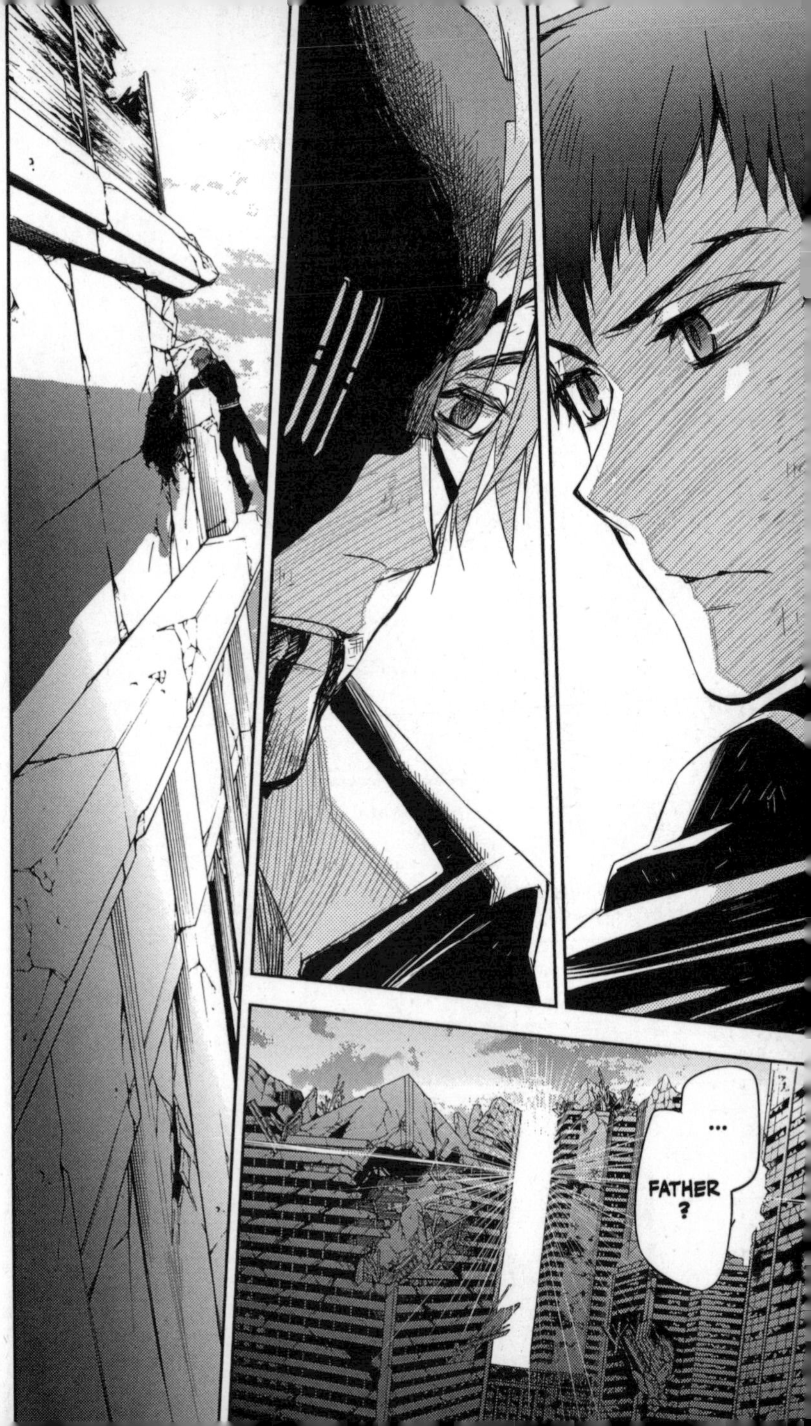
...
FATHER?

THAT WAS TOO EASY.

HE'S DEAD.

SO. WHAT COMES NEXT?

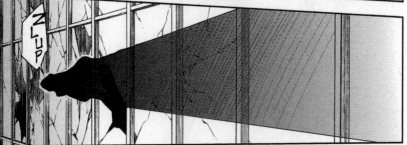

ZLUP

HELLO.

IT SEEMS ONE WHO COULD KILL TENRI HAS FINALLY APPEARED.

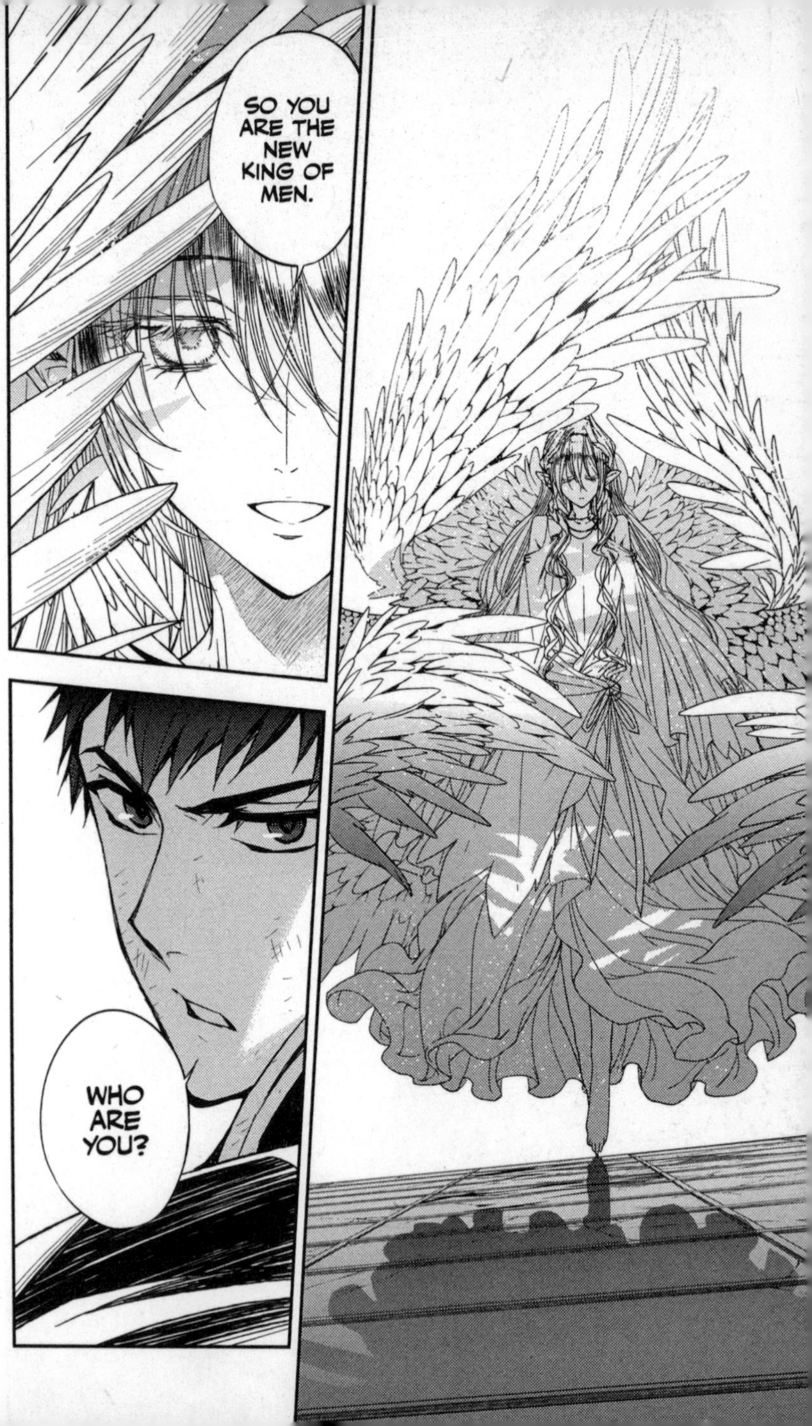
SO YOU ARE THE NEW KING OF MEN.
WHO ARE YOU?

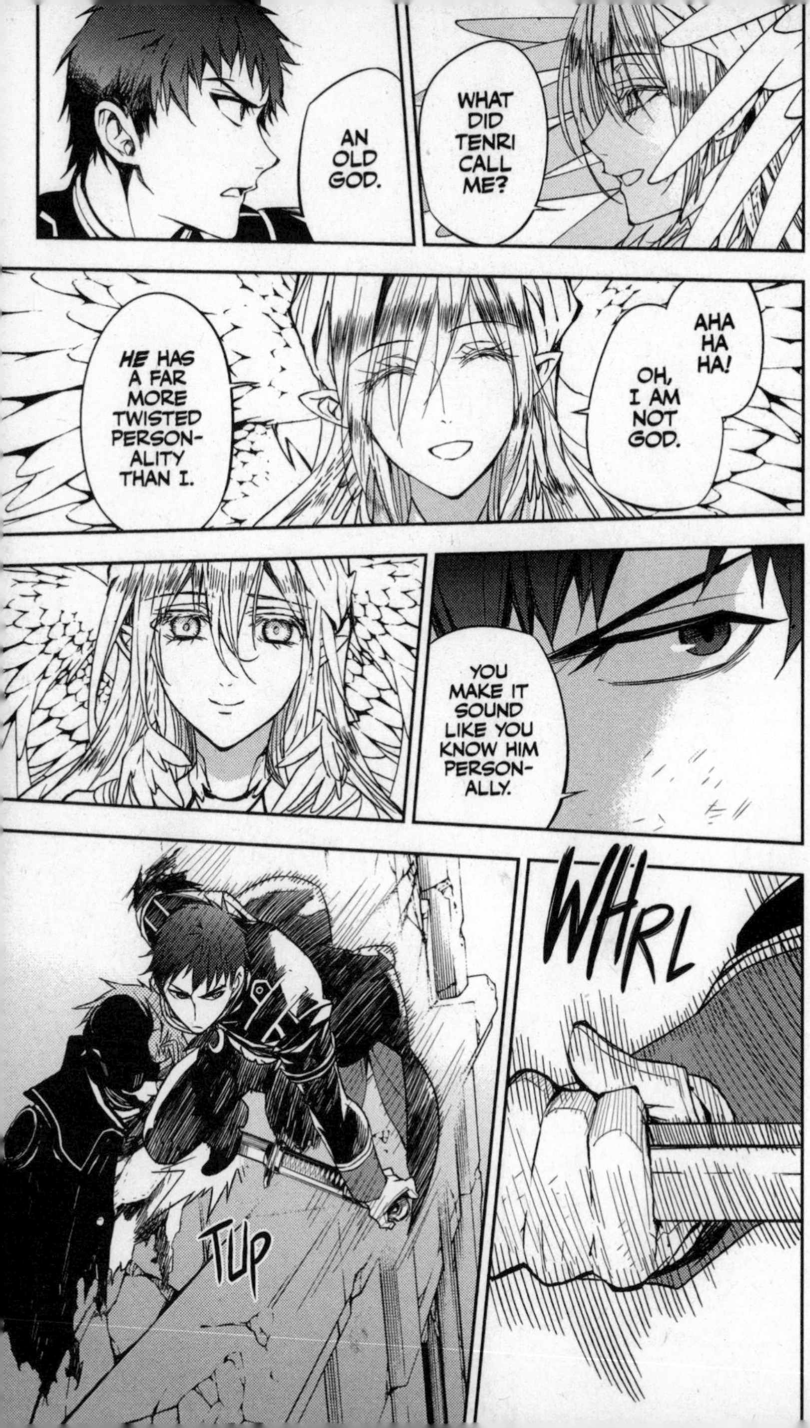
WHAT DID TENRI CALL ME?
AN OLD GOD.
AHA HA HA!
OH, I AM NOT GOD.
HE HAS A FAR MORE TWISTED PERSON-ALITY THAN I.
YOU MAKE IT SOUND LIKE YOU KNOW HIM PERSON-ALLY.
WHRL
TUP

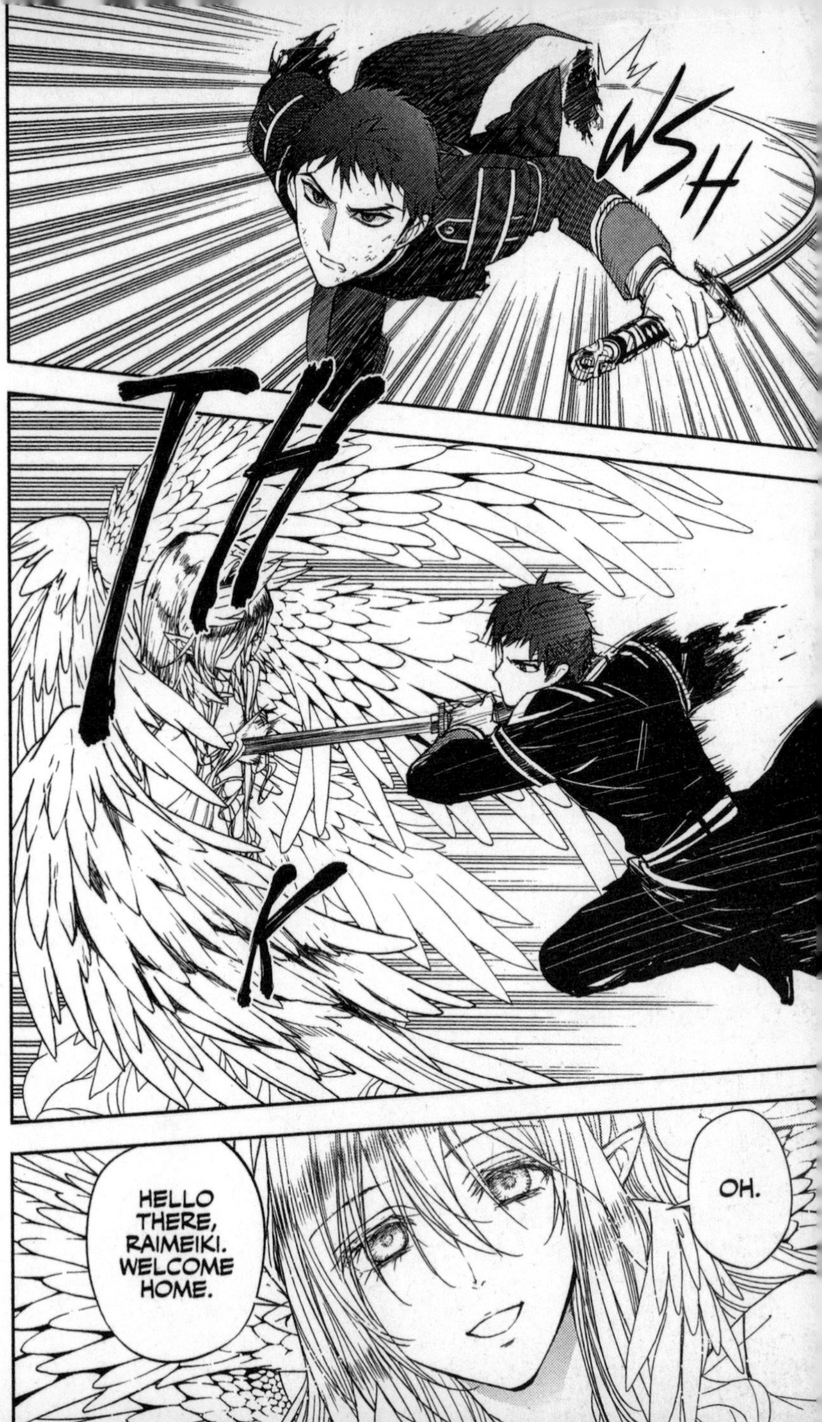
WSH
THK
OH.
HELLO THERE, RAIMEIKI. WELCOME HOME.

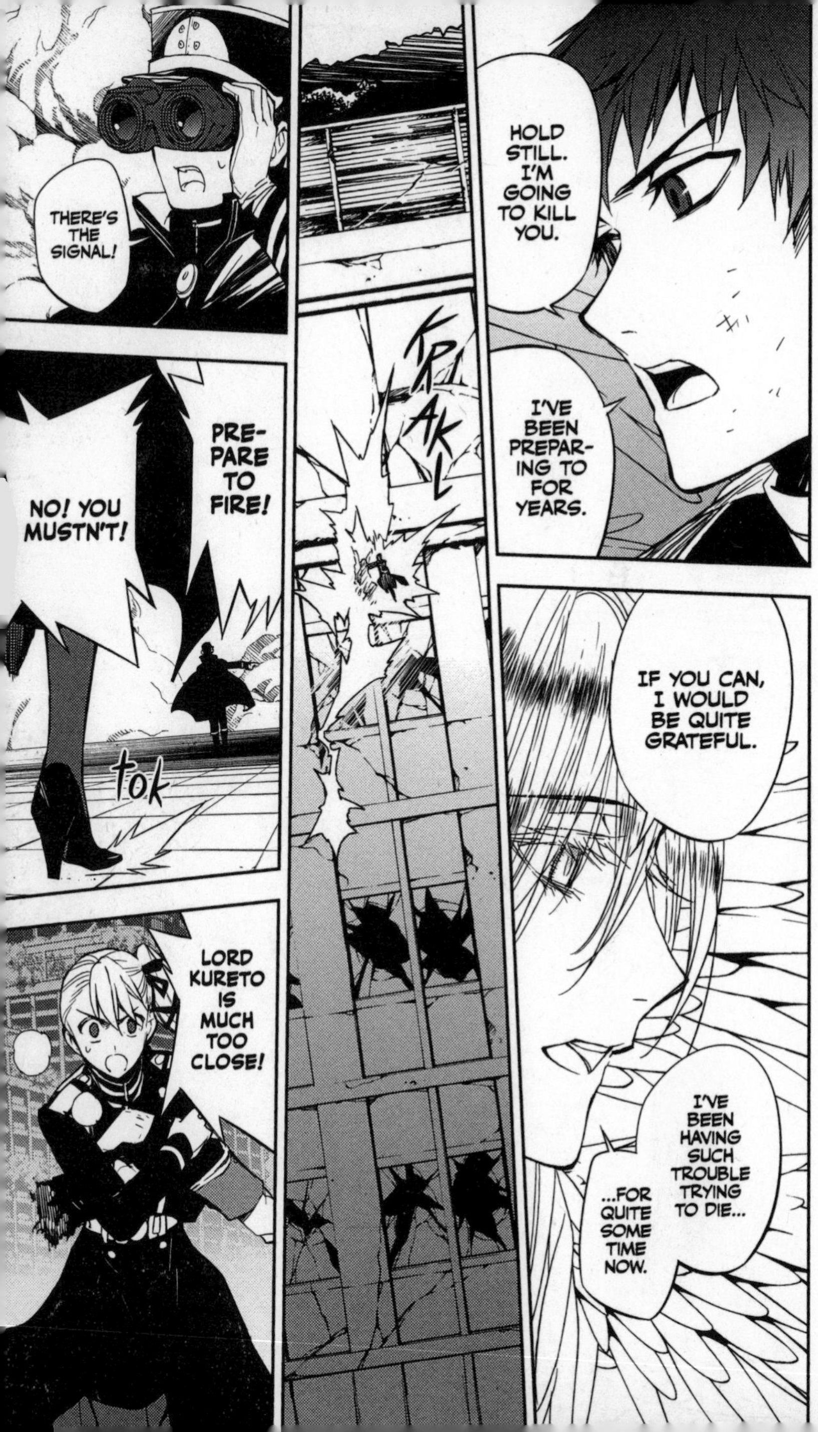
HOLD STILL. I'M GOING TO KILL YOU.
I'VE BEEN PREPAR-ING TO FOR YEARS.
IF YOU CAN, I WOULD BE QUITE GRATEFUL.
I'VE BEEN HAVING SUCH TROUBLE TRYING TO DIE...
...FOR QUITE SOME TIME NOW.
KRAKL
THERE'S THE SIGNAL!
PRE-PARE TO FIRE!
NO! YOU MUSTN'T!
tok
LORD KURETO IS MUCH TOO CLOSE!

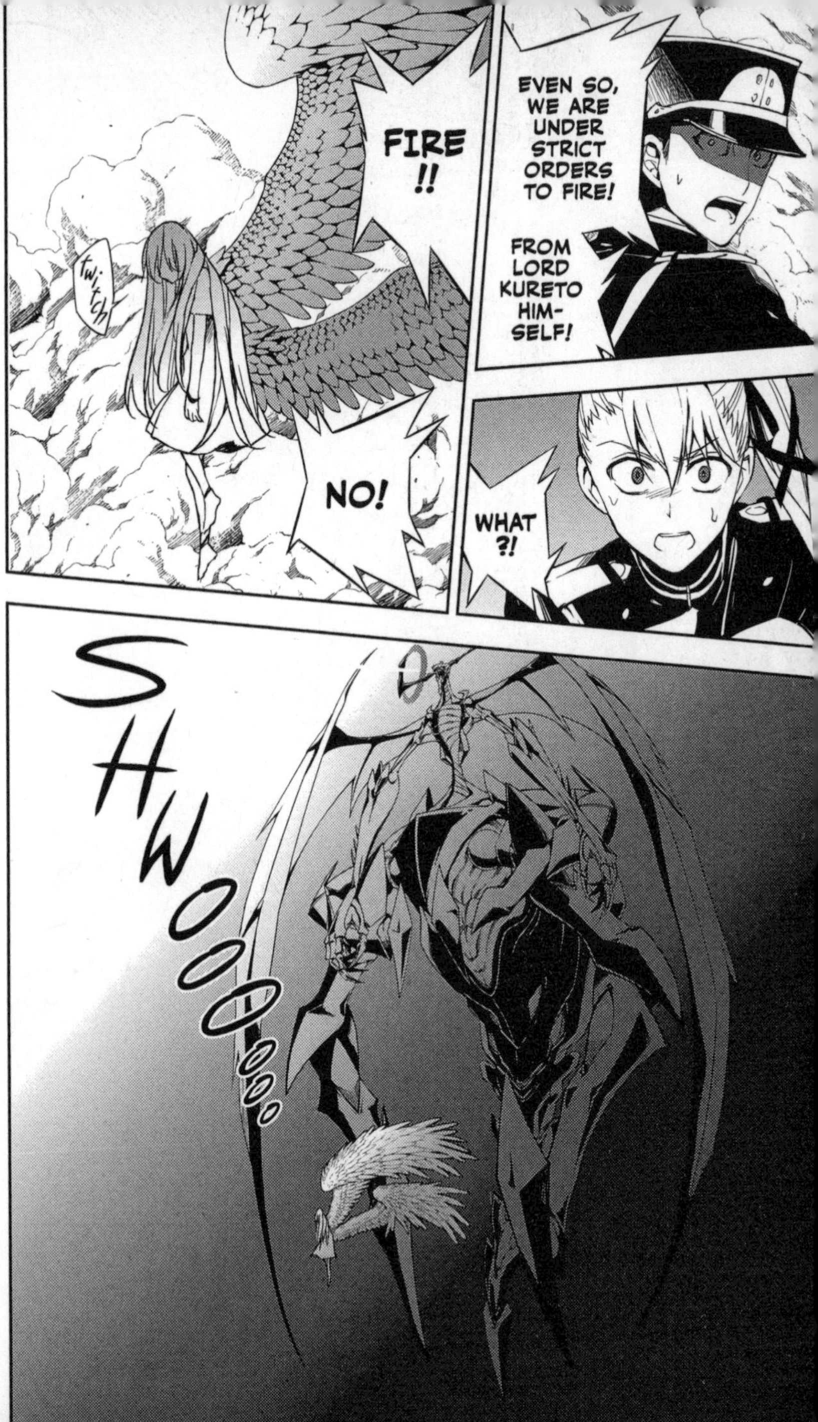
EVEN SO, WE ARE UNDER STRICT ORDERS TO FIRE!
FROM LORD KURETO HIMSELF!
WHAT ?!
FIRE !!
twitch
NO!
SHWOOOOooo

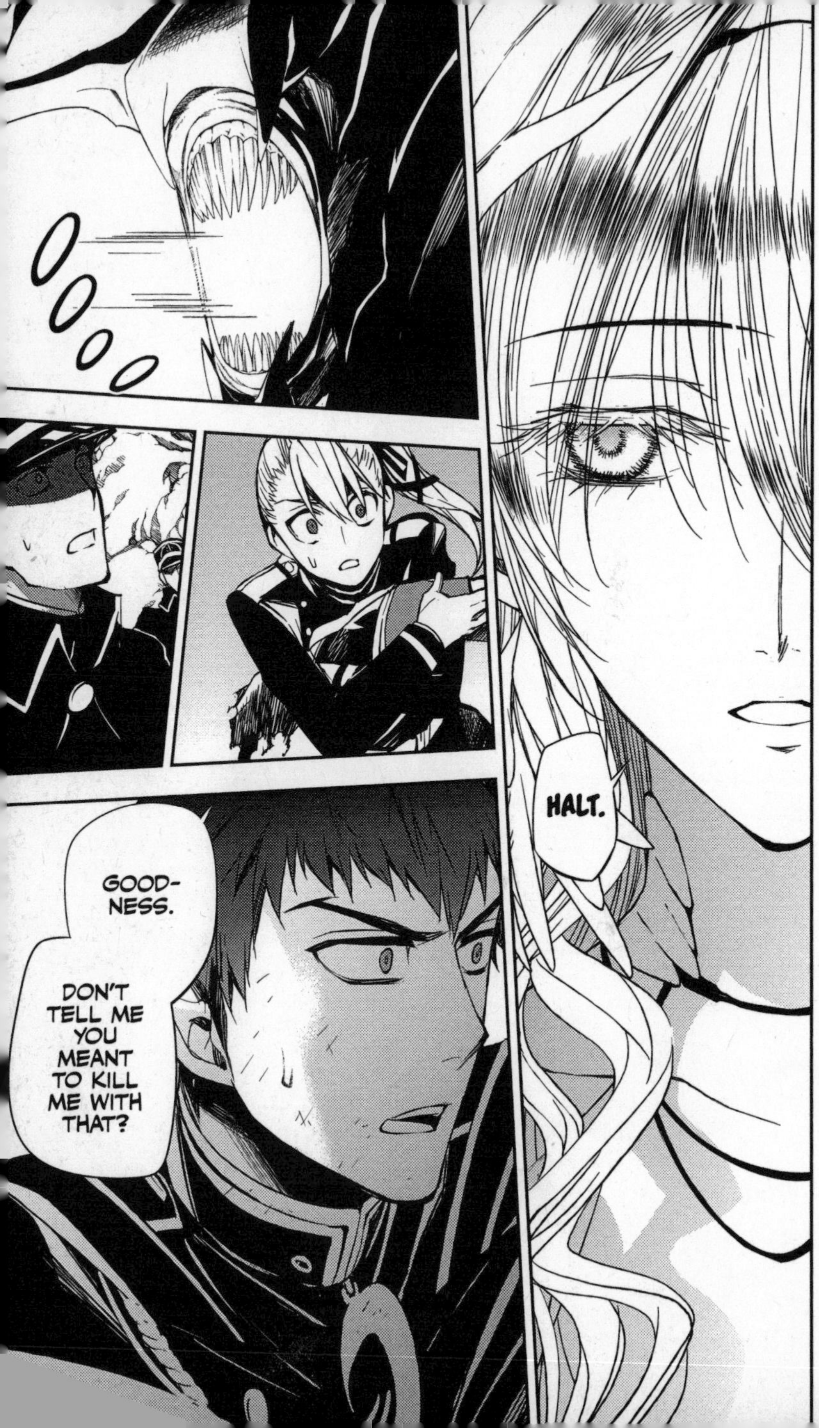
HALT.
GOOD-NESS.
DON'T TELL ME YOU MEANT TO KILL ME WITH THAT?

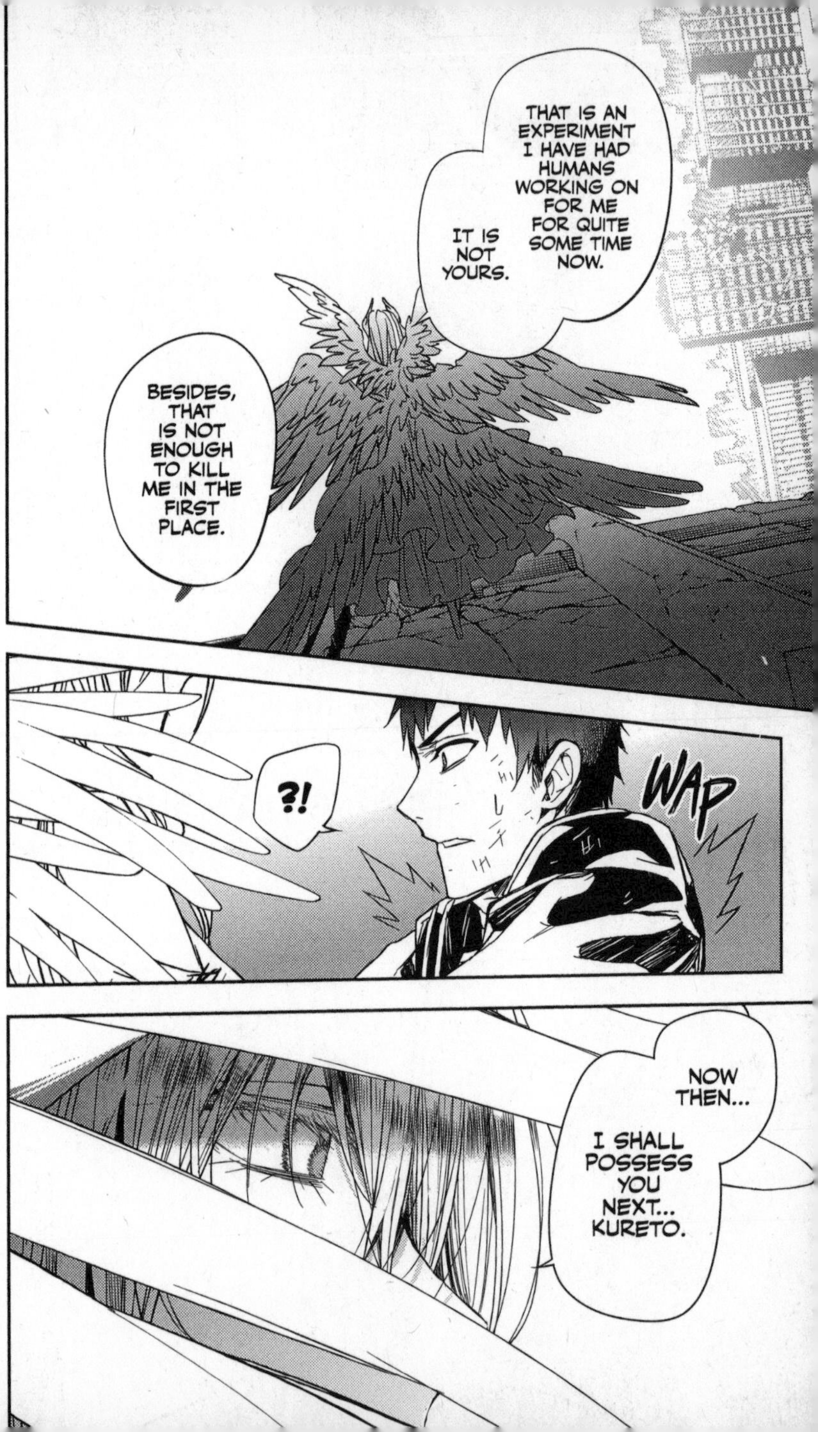
THAT IS AN EXPERIMENT I HAVE HAD HUMANS WORKING ON FOR ME FOR QUITE SOME TIME NOW.
IT IS NOT YOURS.
BESIDES, THAT IS NOT ENOUGH TO KILL ME IN THE FIRST PLACE.
WAP
?!
NOW THEN...
I SHALL POSSESS YOU NEXT... KURETO.

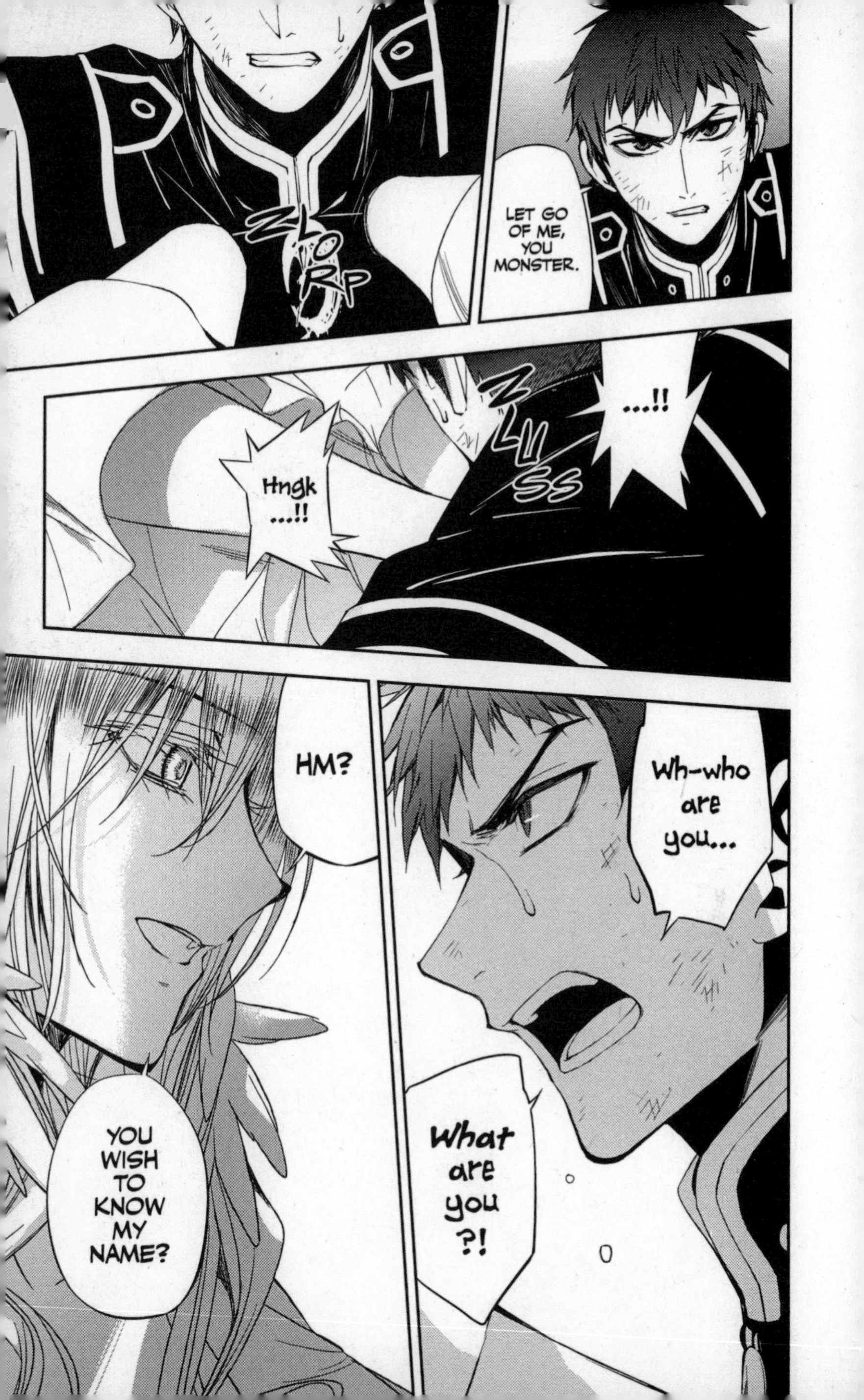
LET GO OF ME, YOU MONSTER.
ZLORP
...!!
ZLUSS
Hngk ...!!
Wh-who are you...
What are you ?!
HM?
YOU WISH TO KNOW MY NAME?

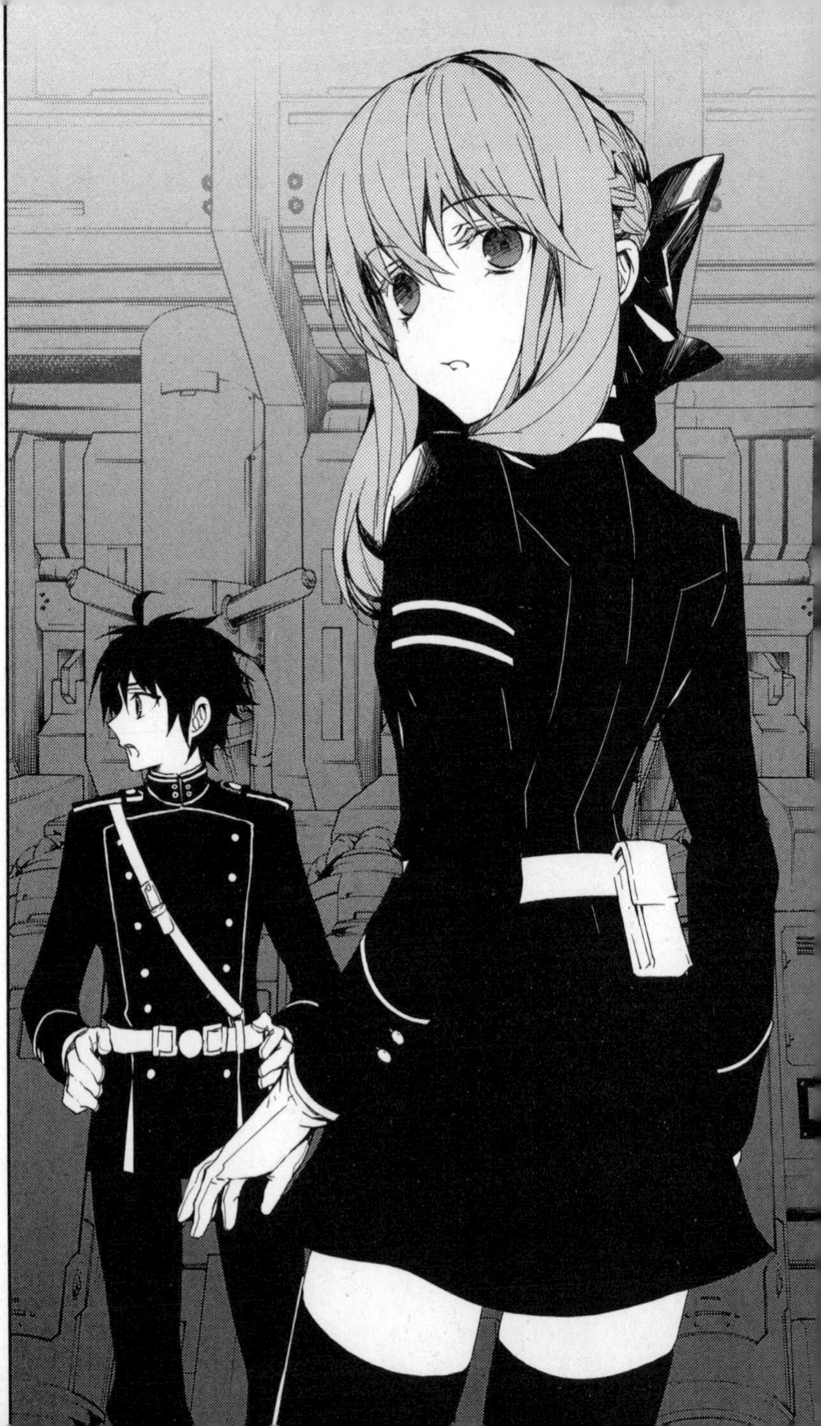

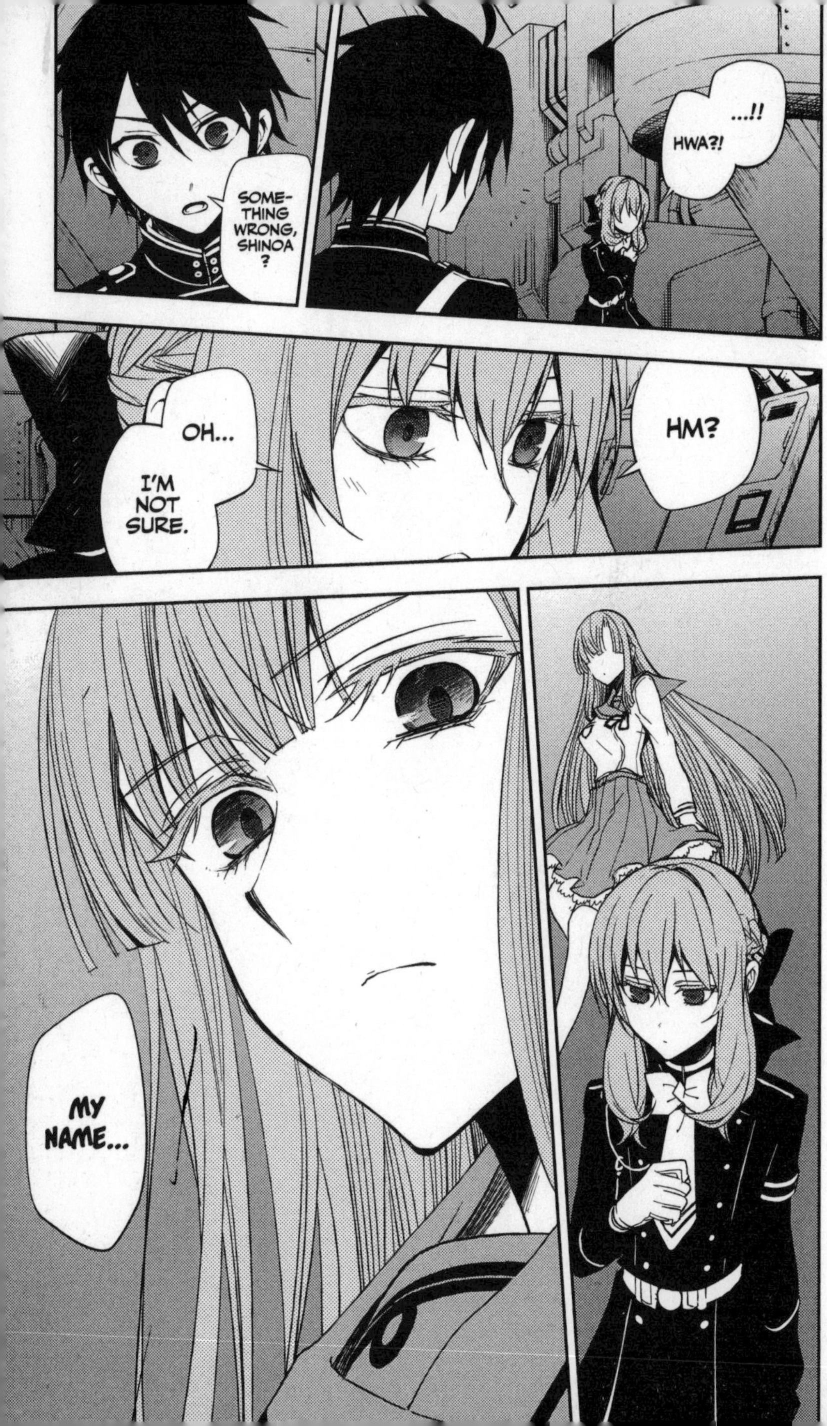
...!!
HWA?!
SOME-THING WRONG, SHINOA?
HM?
OH...
I'M NOT SURE.
MY NAME...

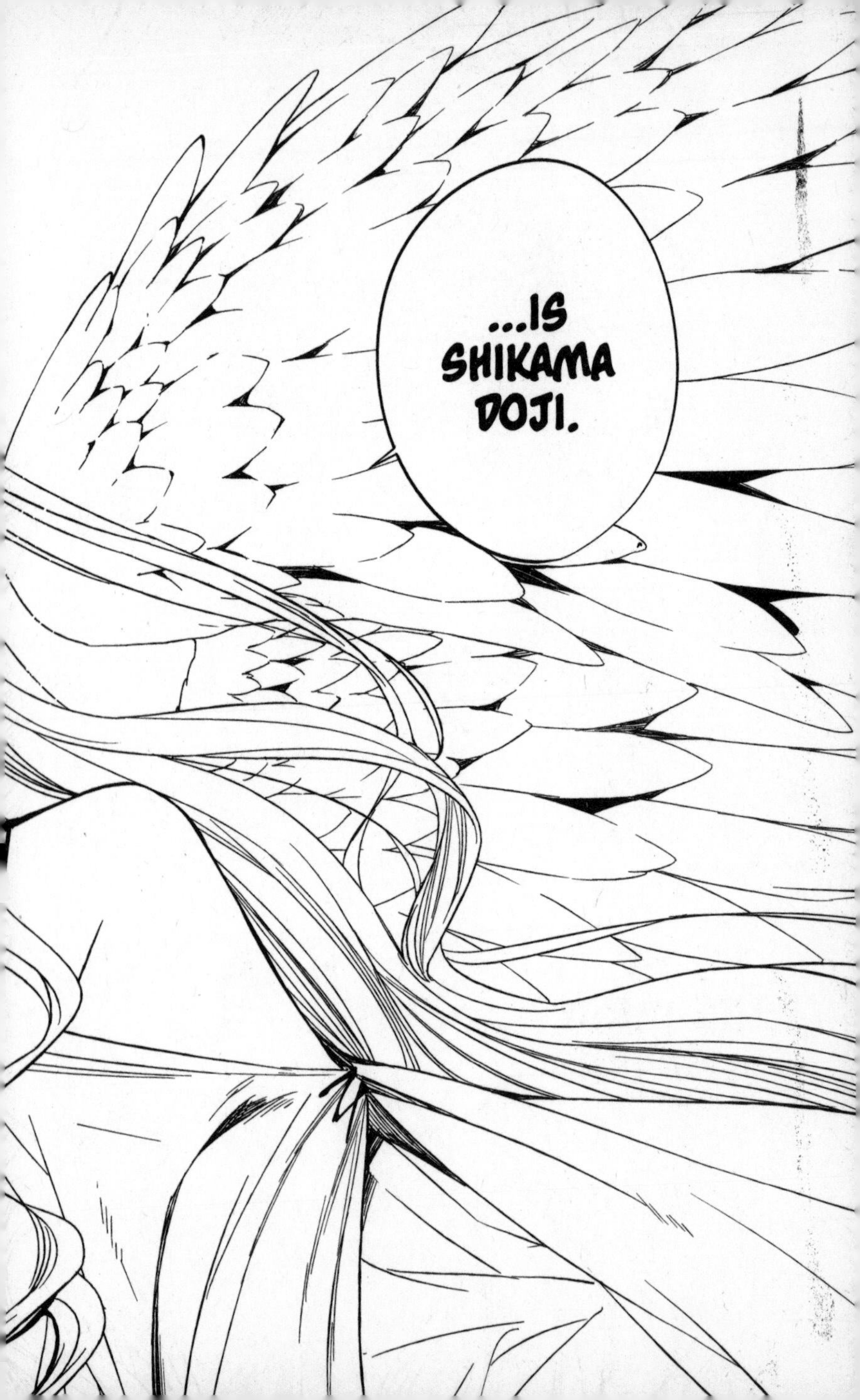
...IS SHIKAMA DOJI.

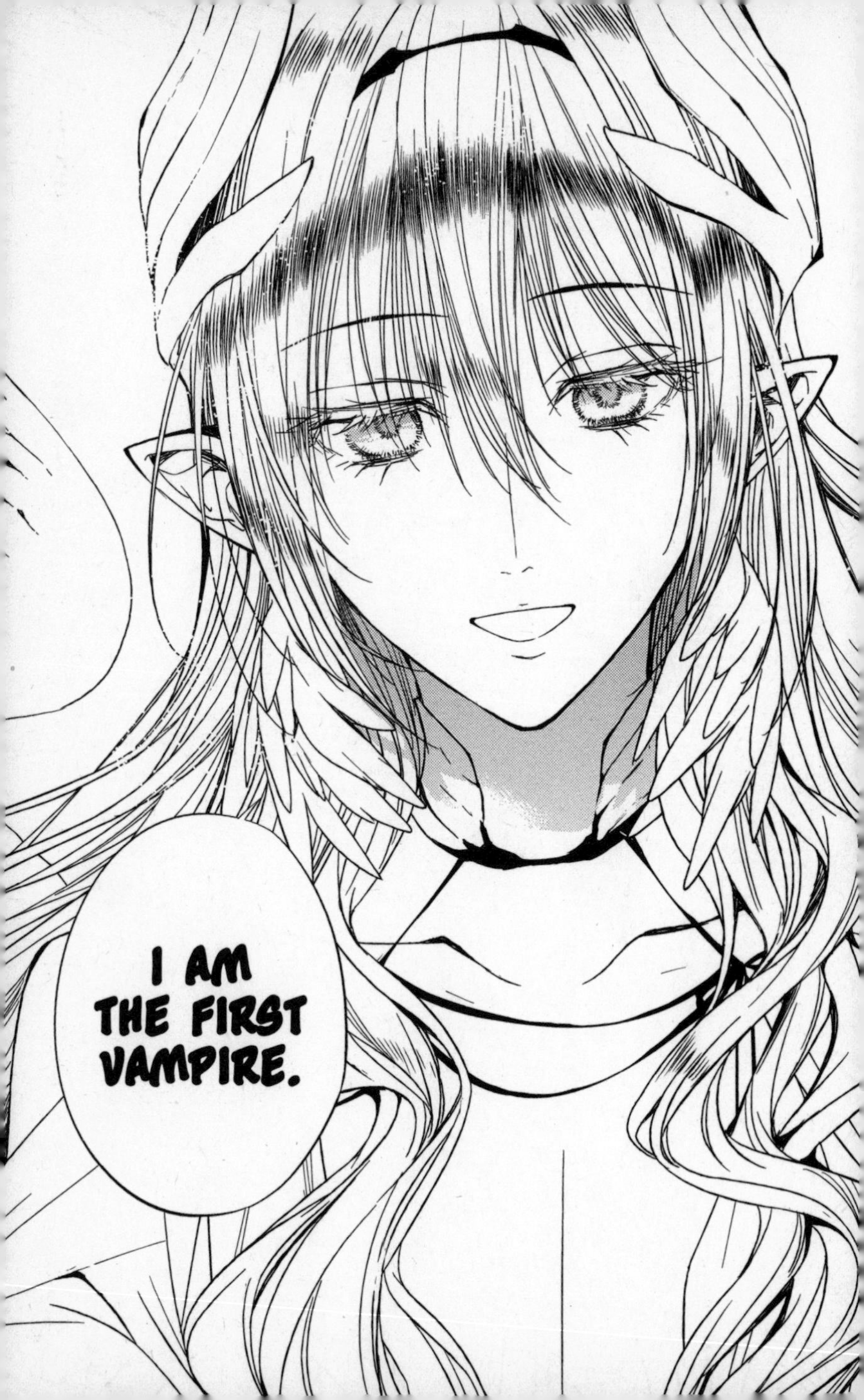
I AM THE FIRST VAMPIRE.

Seraph of the End
—VAMPIRE REIGN—

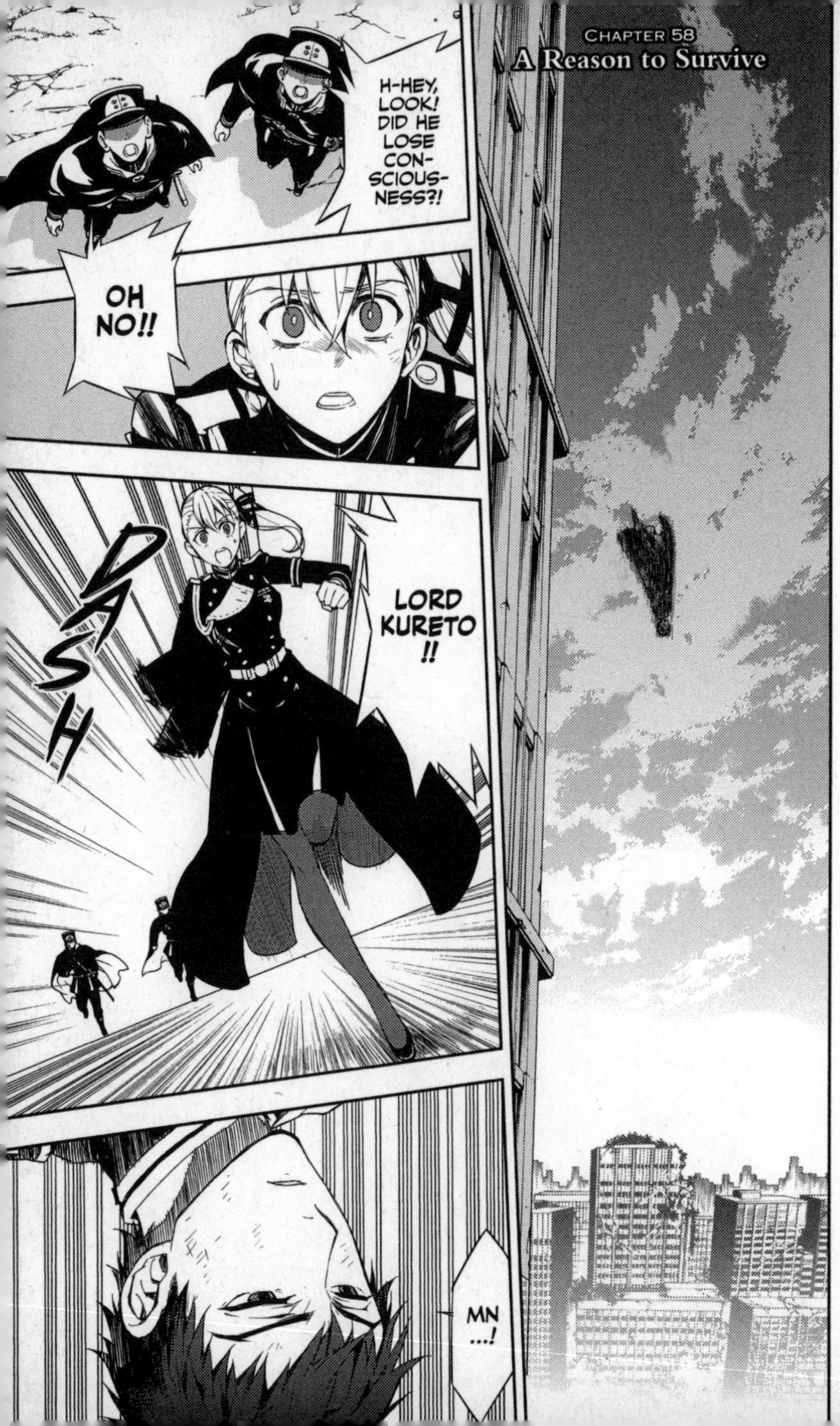
CHAPTER 58
A Reason to Survive
H-HEY, LOOK! DID HE LOSE CONSCIOUSNESS?!
OH NO!!
LORD KURETO!!
DASH
MN...!

Chapter 58
A Reason to Survive

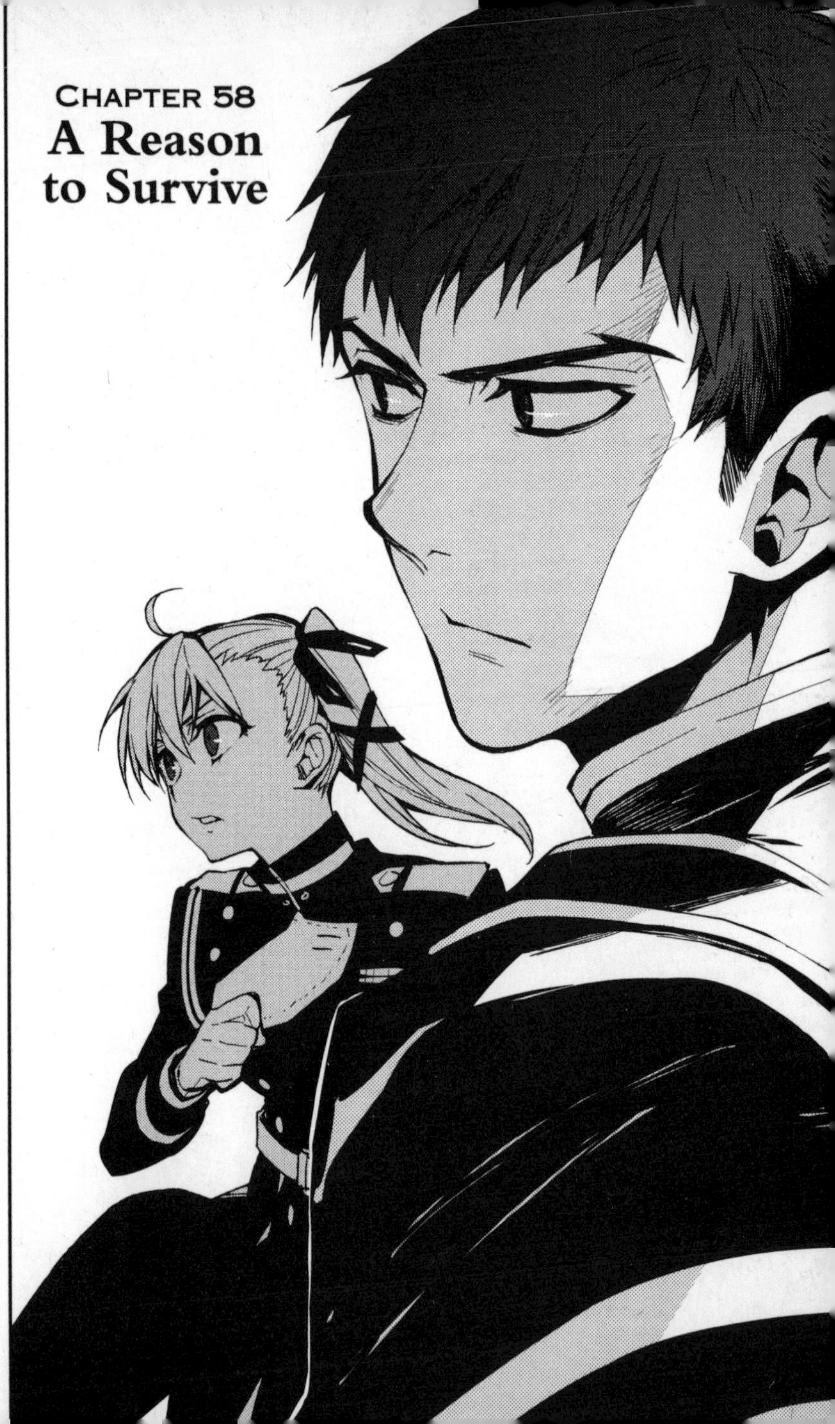

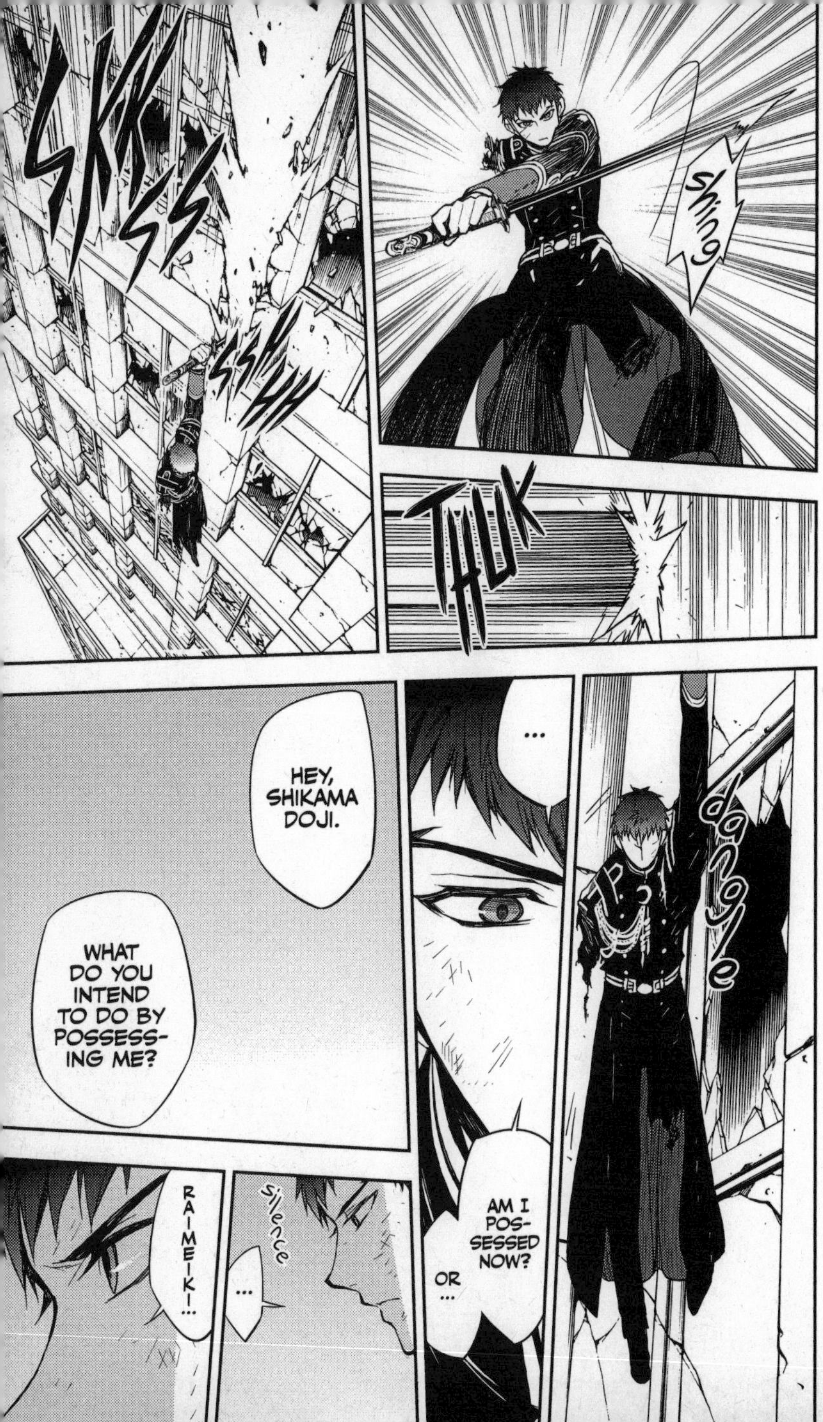
shiing
THUK
SKASSS
SSHHH
dangle
...
AM I POSSESSED NOW?
OR ...
HEY, SHIKAMA DOJI.
WHAT DO YOU INTEND TO DO BY POSSESSING ME?
silence
...
RAIMEIKI...

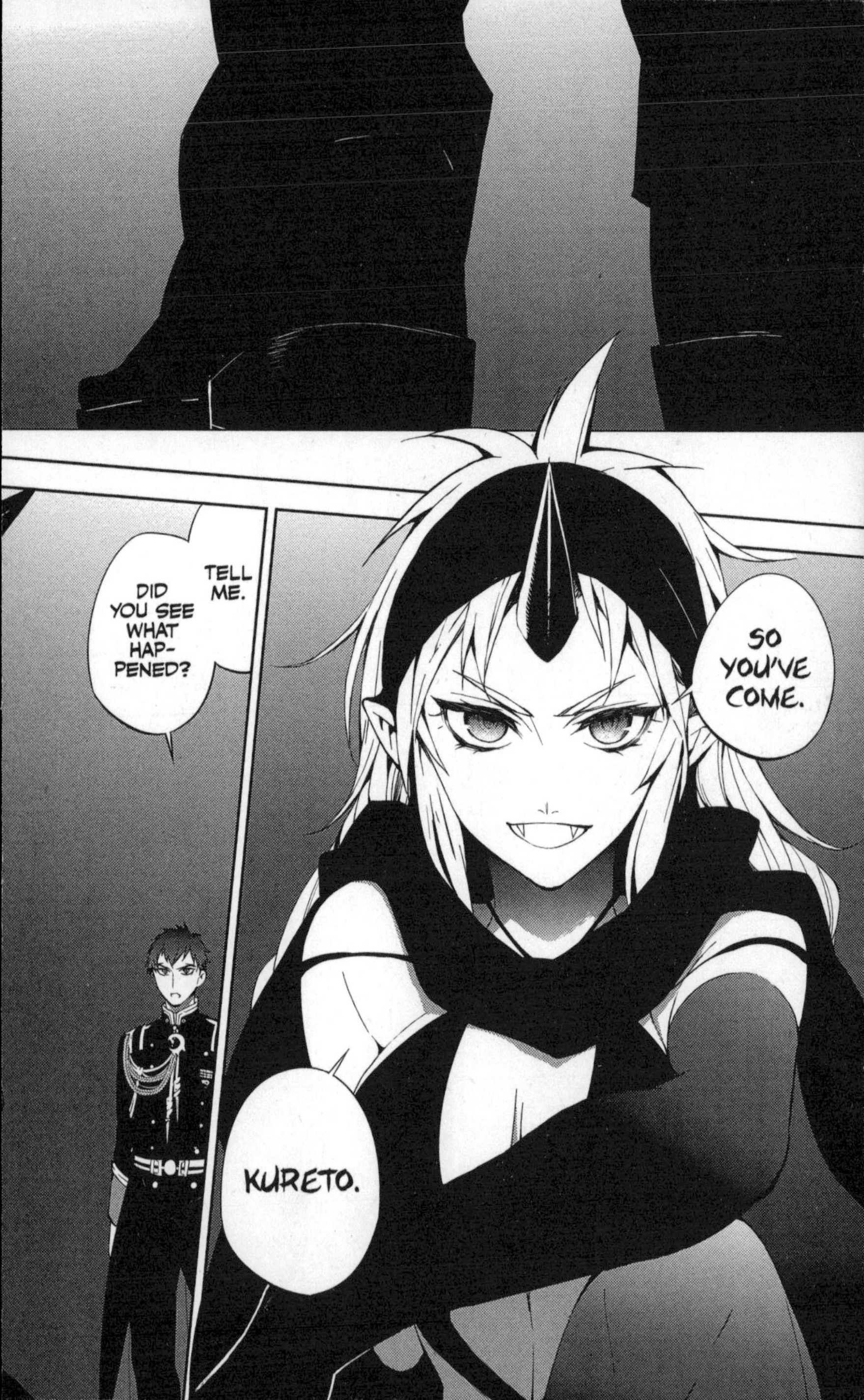
SO YOU'VE COME.
KURETO.
TELL ME.
DID YOU SEE WHAT HAPPENED?

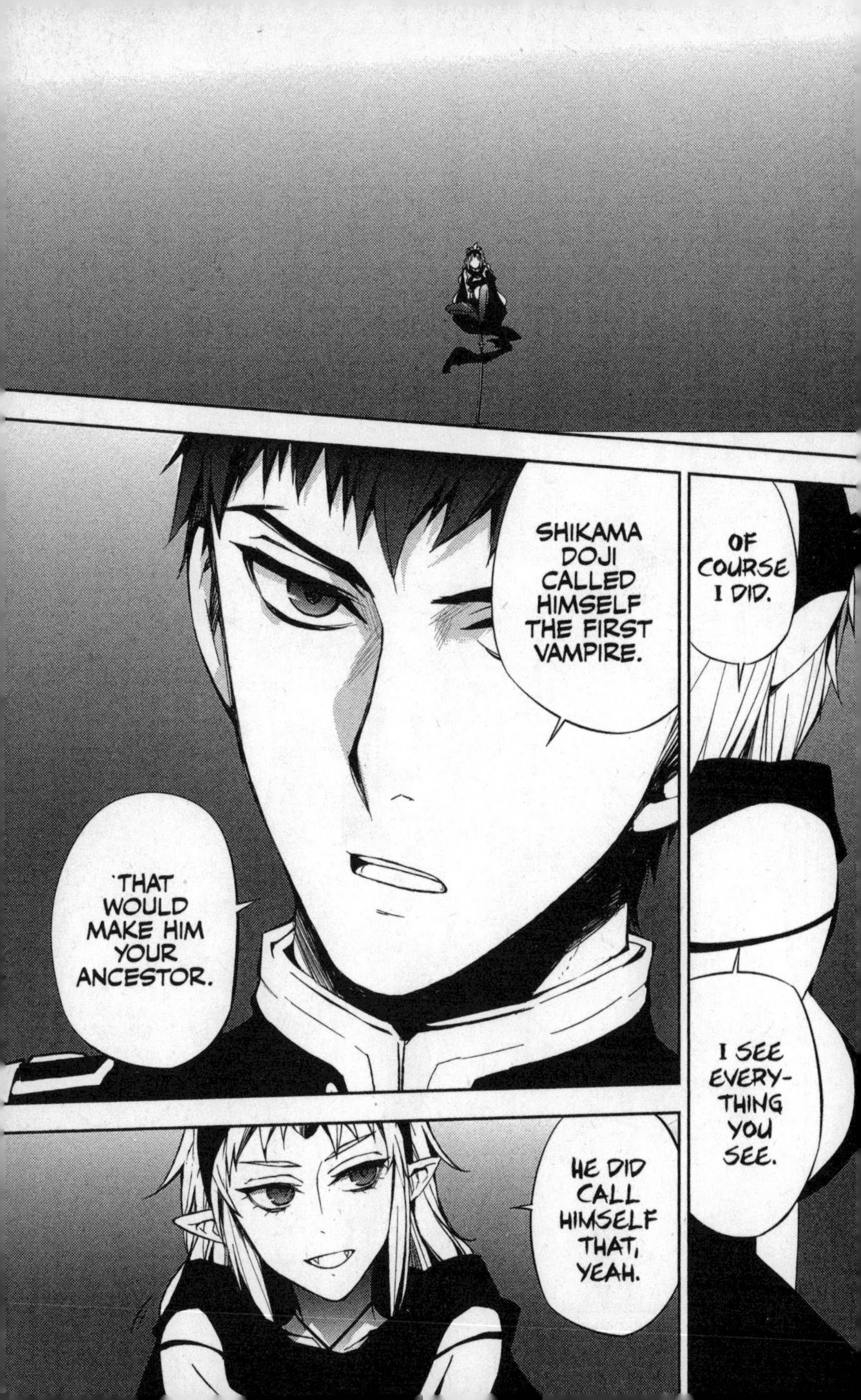
SHIKAMA DOJI CALLED HIMSELF THE FIRST VAMPIRE.
OF COURSE I DID.
THAT WOULD MAKE HIM YOUR ANCESTOR.
I SEE EVERY-THING YOU SEE.
HE DID CALL HIMSELF THAT, YEAH.

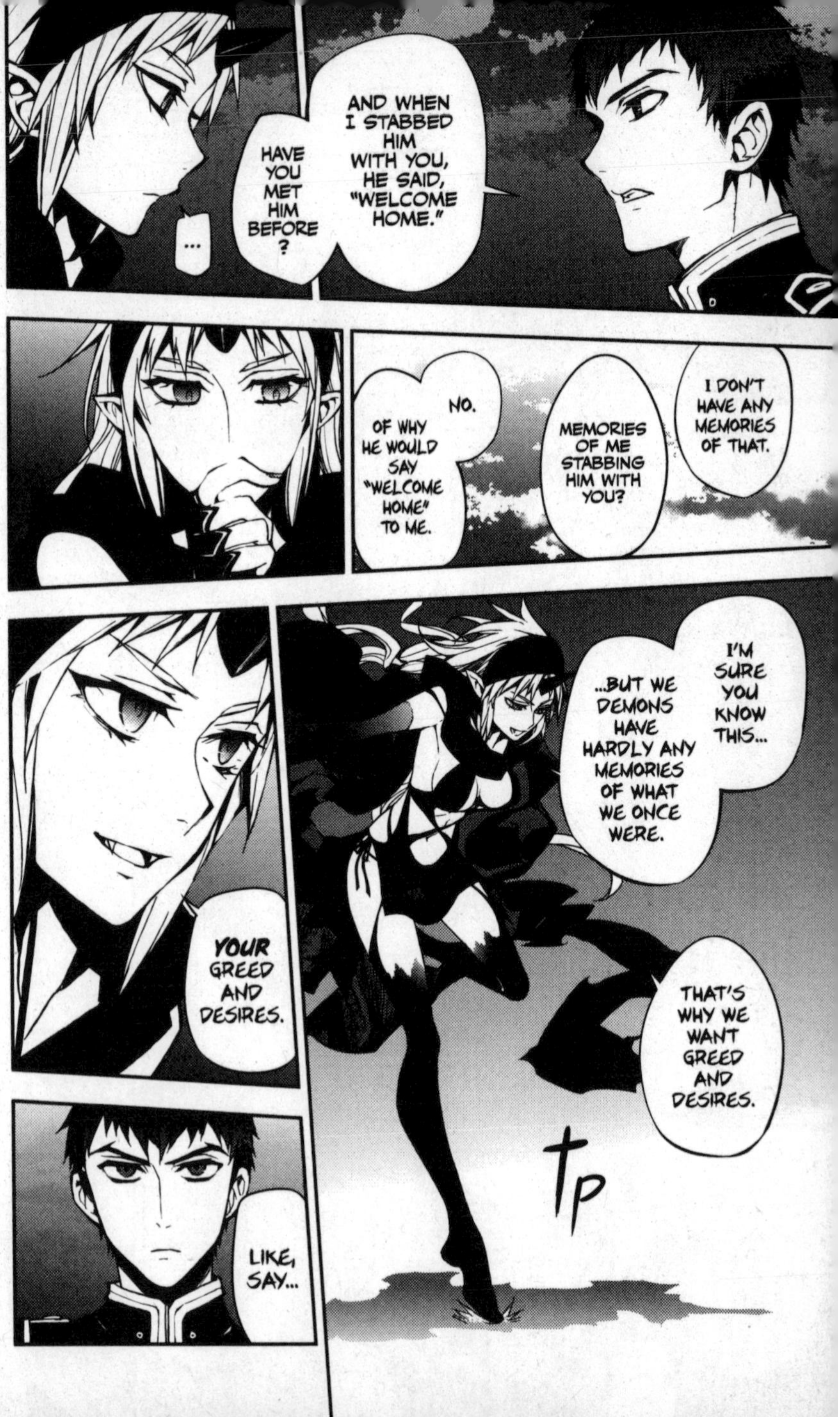
AND WHEN I STABBED HIM WITH YOU, HE SAID, "WELCOME HOME."
HAVE YOU MET HIM BEFORE?
...
I DON'T HAVE ANY MEMORIES OF THAT.
MEMORIES OF ME STABBING HIM WITH YOU?
NO.
OF WHY HE WOULD SAY "WELCOME HOME" TO ME.
I'M SURE YOU KNOW THIS...
...BUT WE DEMONS HAVE HARDLY ANY MEMORIES OF WHAT WE ONCE WERE.
THAT'S WHY WE WANT GREED AND DESIRES.
TP
YOUR GREED AND DESIRES.
LIKE, SAY...

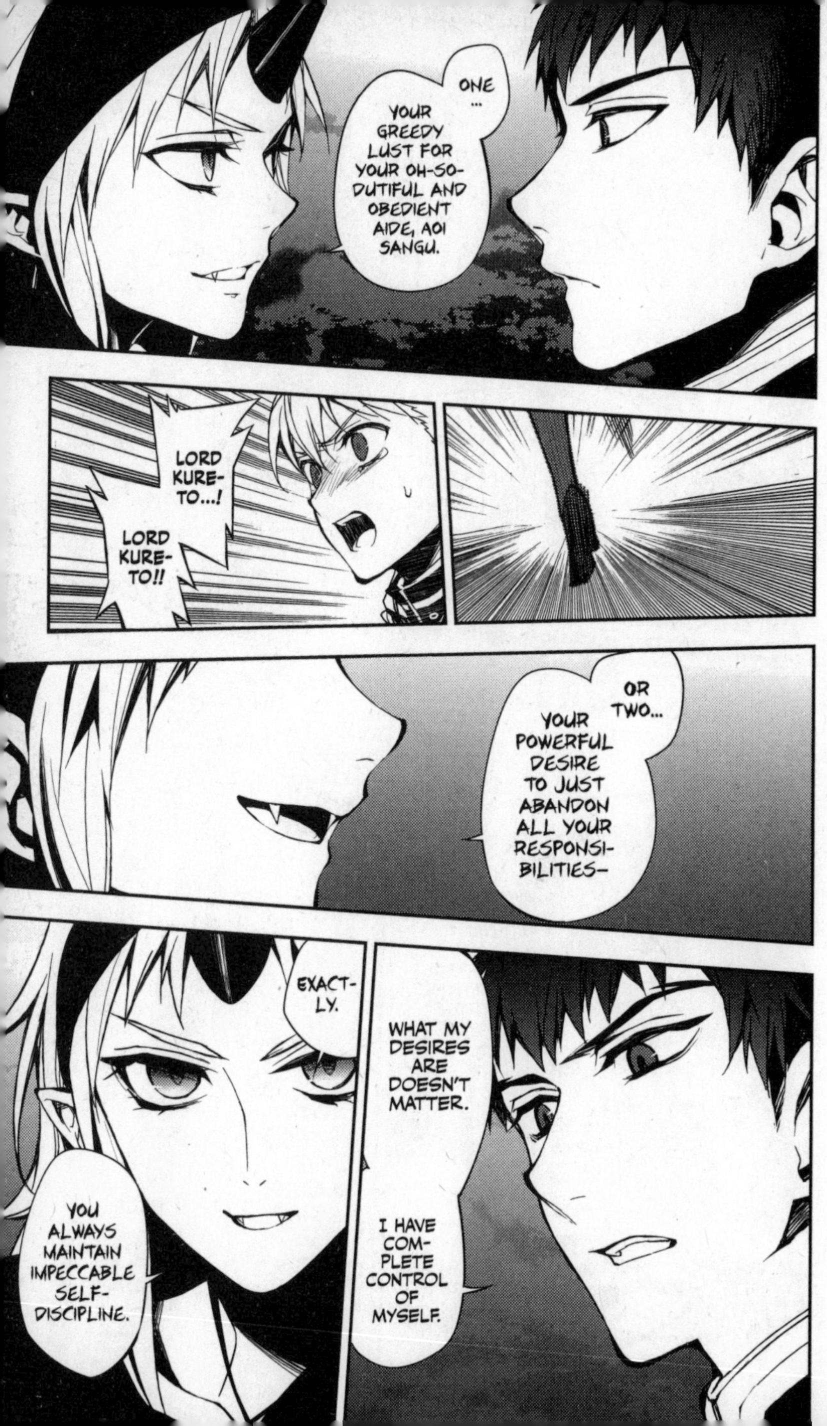
ONE... YOUR GREEDY LUST FOR YOUR OH-SO-DUTIFUL AND OBEDIENT AIDE, AOI SANGU.
LORD KURE-TO...!
LORD KURE-TO!!
OR TWO... YOUR POWERFUL DESIRE TO JUST ABANDON ALL YOUR RESPONSI-BILITIES—
WHAT MY DESIRES ARE DOESN'T MATTER.
I HAVE COM-PLETE CONTROL OF MYSELF.
EXACT-LY.
YOU ALWAYS MAINTAIN IMPECCABLE SELF-DISCIPLINE.

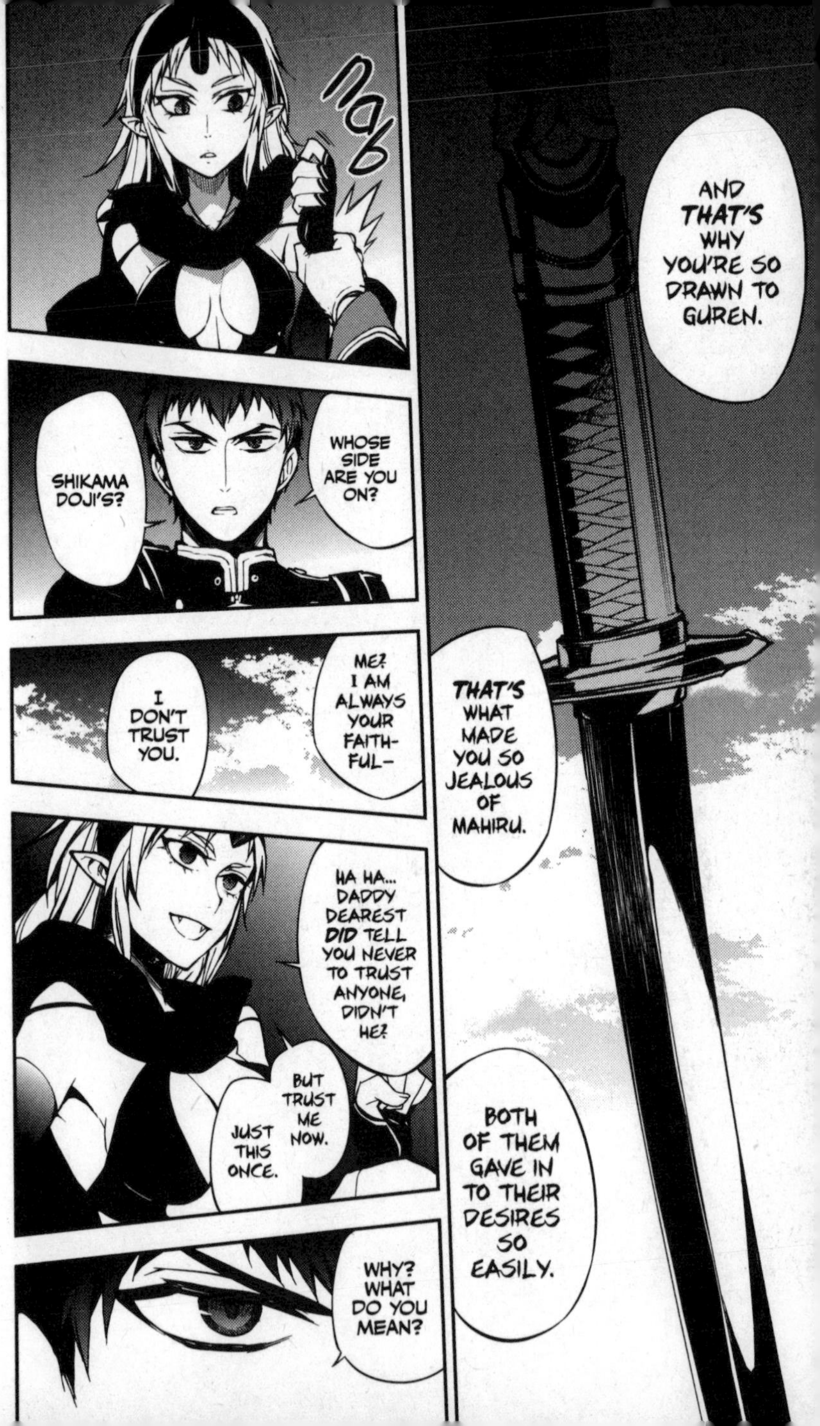
AND THAT'S WHY YOU'RE SO DRAWN TO GUREN.
THAT'S WHAT MADE YOU SO JEALOUS OF MAHIRU.
BOTH OF THEM GAVE IN TO THEIR DESIRES SO EASILY.
WHOSE SIDE ARE YOU ON?
SHIKAMA DOJI'S?
ME? I AM ALWAYS YOUR FAITH-FUL-
I DON'T TRUST YOU.
HA HA... DADDY DEAREST DID TELL YOU NEVER TO TRUST ANYONE, DIDN'T HE?
BUT TRUST ME NOW.
JUST THIS ONCE.
WHY? WHAT DO YOU MEAN?

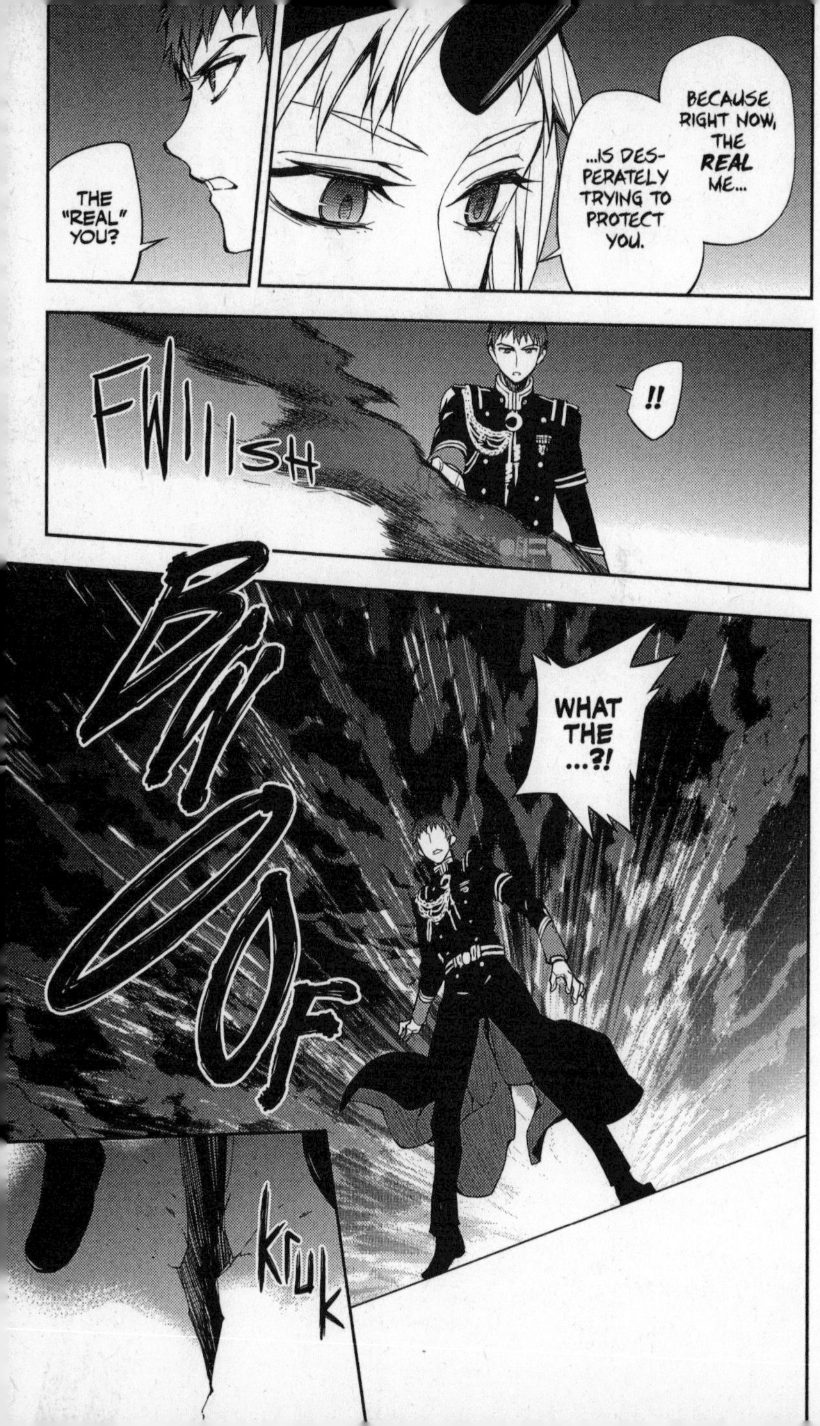
BECAUSE RIGHT NOW, THE REAL ME...
...IS DES-PERATELY TRYING TO PROTECT YOU.
THE "REAL" YOU?
FWIIISH
!!
WHAT THE ...?!
BWOOF
KRUK

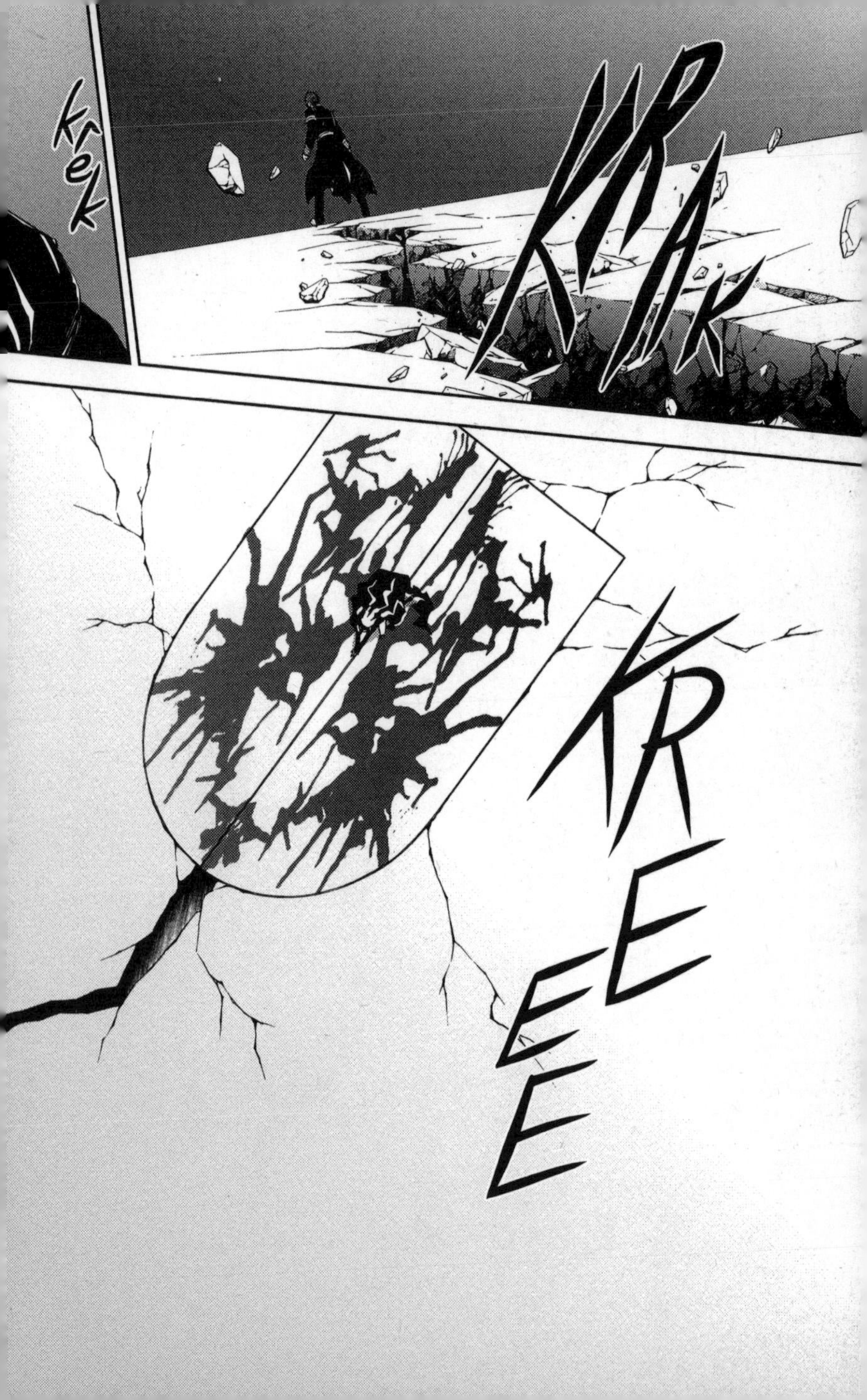
KRAK
krek
KREEEE

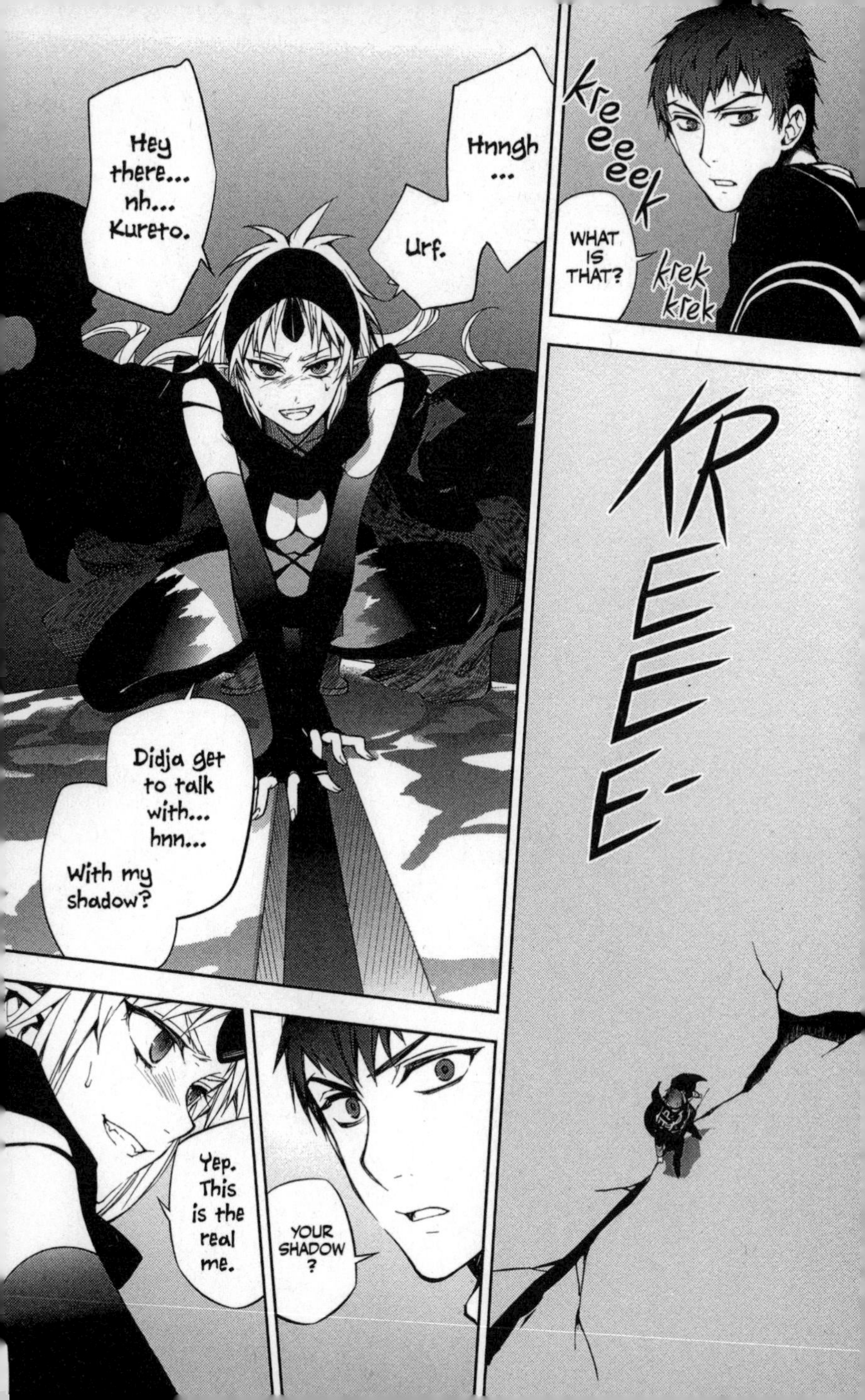
kreeeek
WHAT IS THAT?
krek krek
KREEEE-
Hnngh ...
Urf.
Hey there... nh... Kureto.
Didja get to talk with... hnn...
With my shadow?
YOUR SHADOW?
Yep. This is the real me.

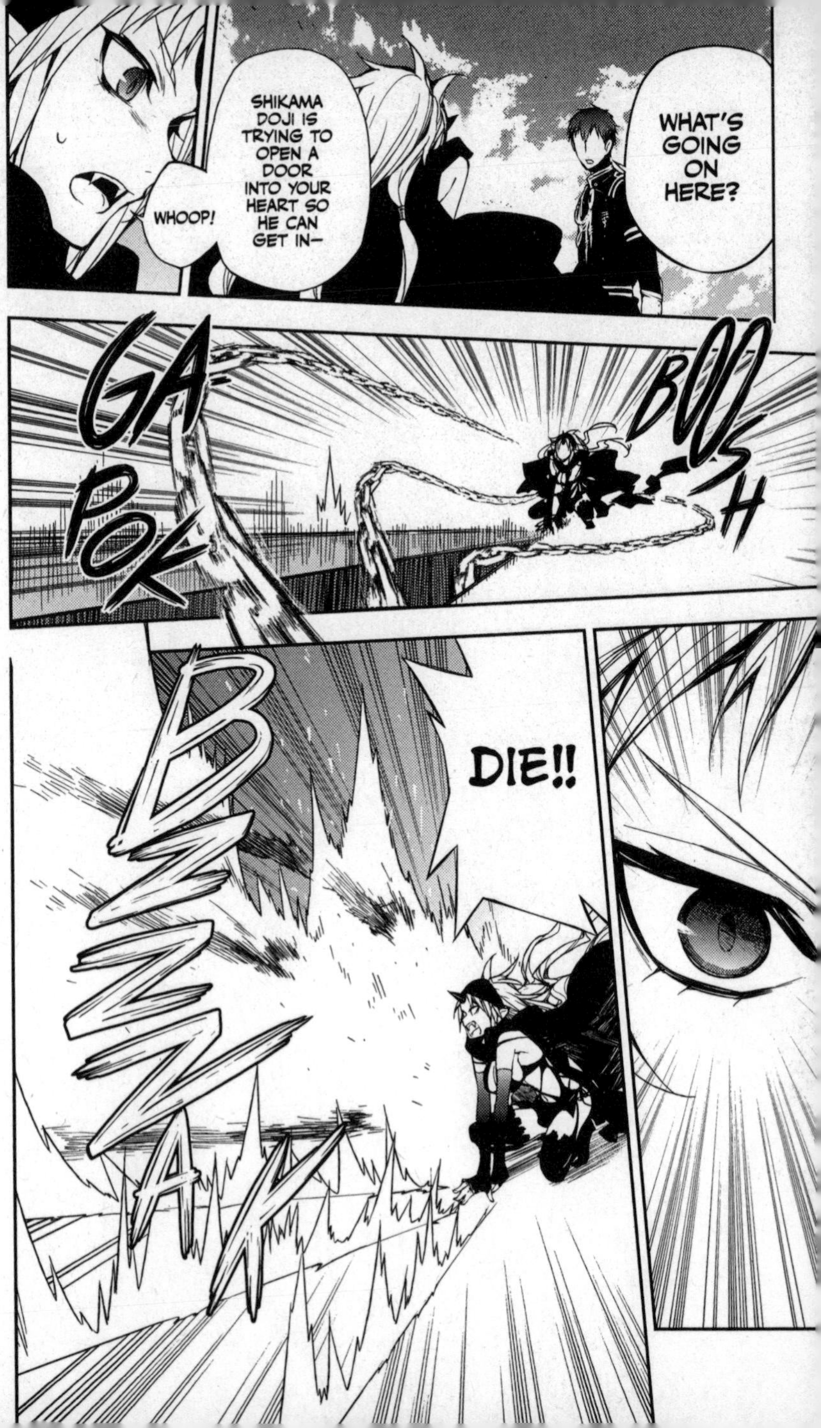
WHAT'S GOING ON HERE?
SHIKAMA DOJI IS TRYING TO OPEN A DOOR INTO YOUR HEART SO HE CAN GET IN—
WHOOP!
BOOOSH
GA-POK
DIE!!
BAMMMMAK

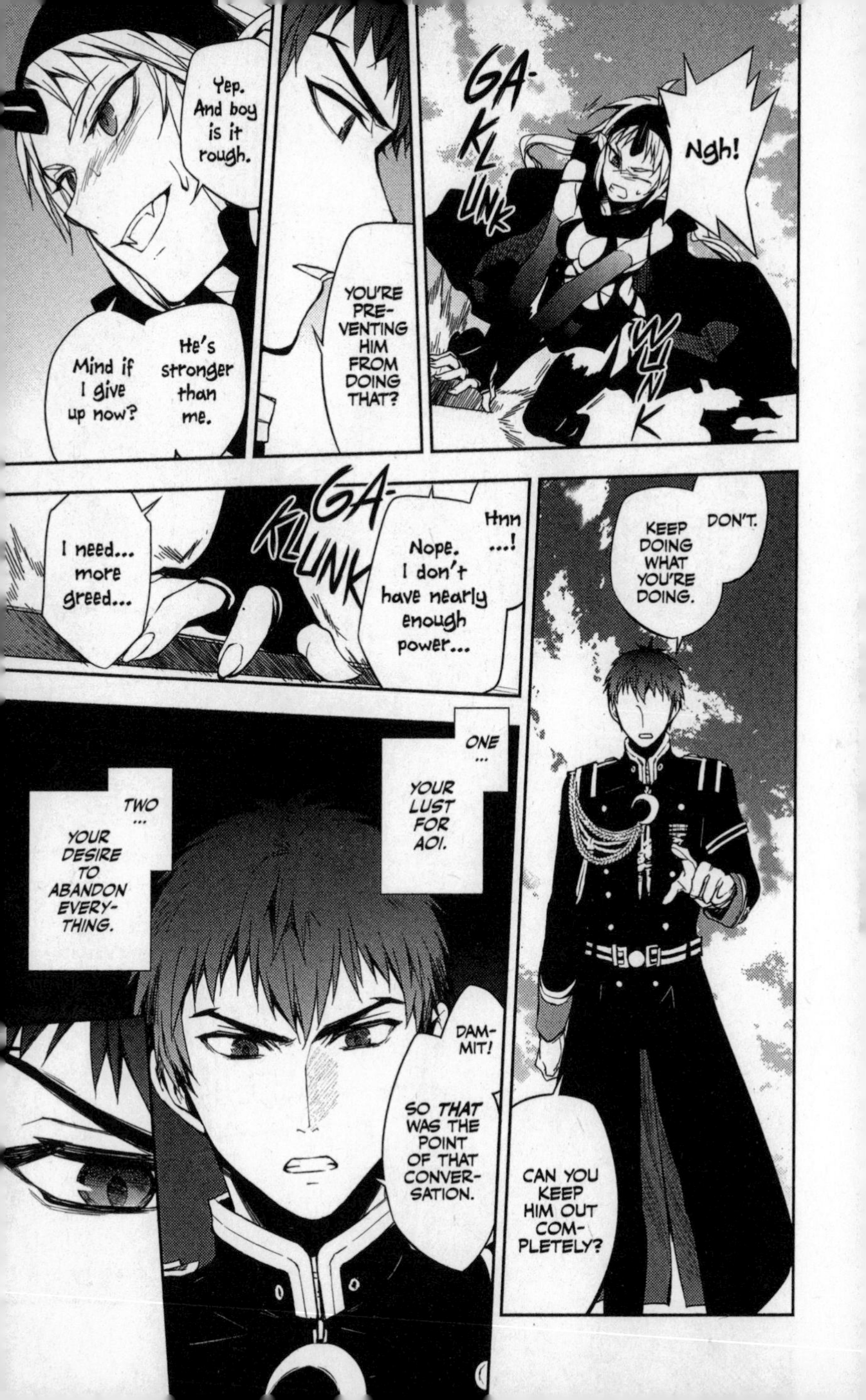
GA-KLUNK
Ngh!
WUNK
YOU'RE PREVENTING HIM FROM DOING THAT?
Yep. And boy is it rough.
He's stronger than me.
Mind if I give up now?
DON'T.
KEEP DOING WHAT YOU'RE DOING.
CAN YOU KEEP HIM OUT COMPLETELY?
Hnn...!
Nope. I don't have nearly enough power...
GA-KLUNK
I need... more greed...
ONE...
YOUR LUST FOR AOI.
TWO...
YOUR DESIRE TO ABANDON EVERYTHING.
DAMMIT!
SO THAT WAS THE POINT OF THAT CONVERSATION.

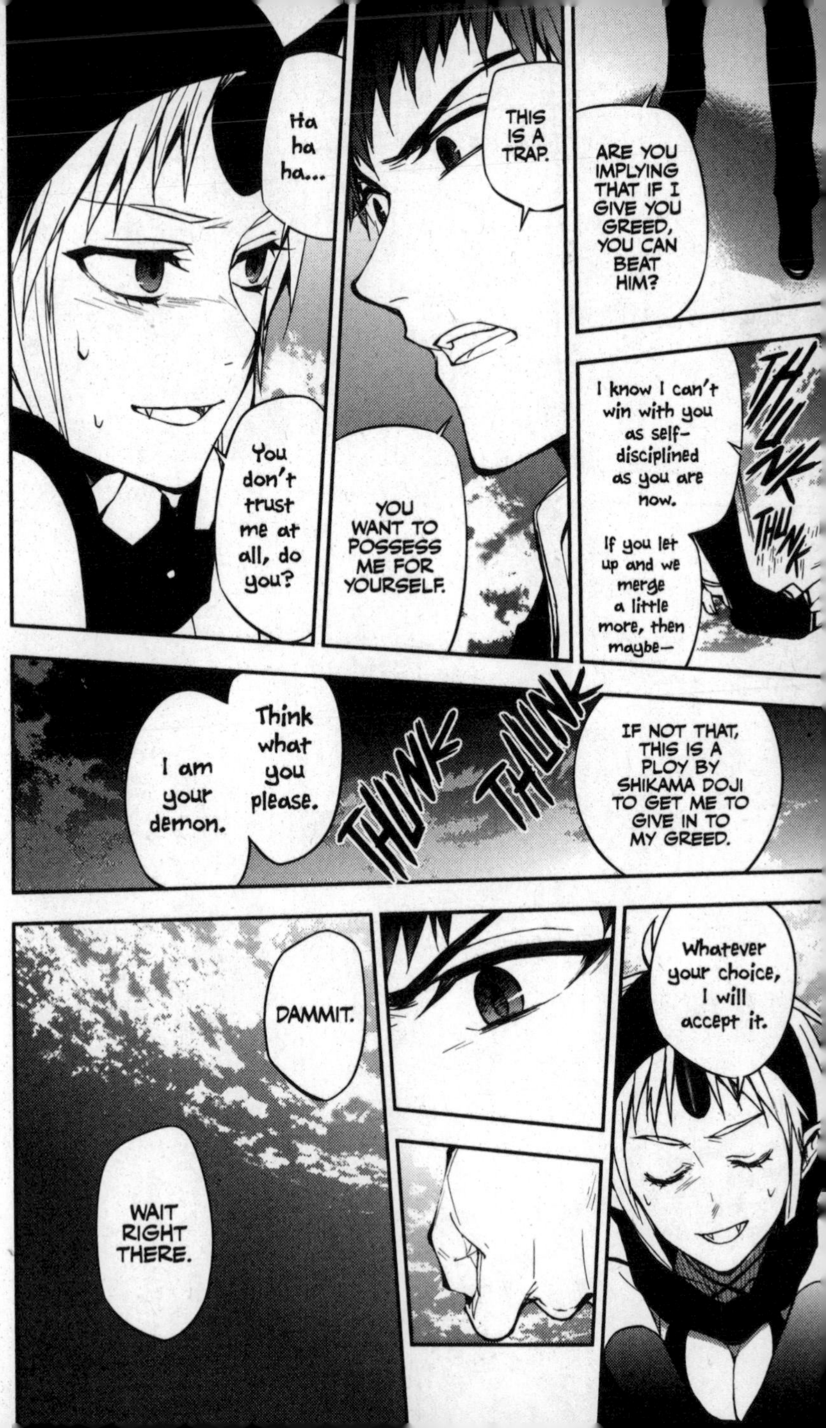
ARE YOU IMPLYING THAT IF I GIVE YOU GREED, YOU CAN BEAT HIM?
THUNK
THUNK
I know I can't win with you as self-disciplined as you are now.
If you let up and we merge a little more, then maybe—
THIS IS A TRAP.
YOU WANT TO POSSESS ME FOR YOURSELF.
Ha ha ha...
You don't trust me at all, do you?
IF NOT THAT, THIS IS A PLOY BY SHIKAMA DOJI TO GET ME TO GIVE IN TO MY GREED.
THUNK
THUNK
Think what you please.
I am your demon.
Whatever your choice, I will accept it.
DAMMIT.
WAIT RIGHT THERE.

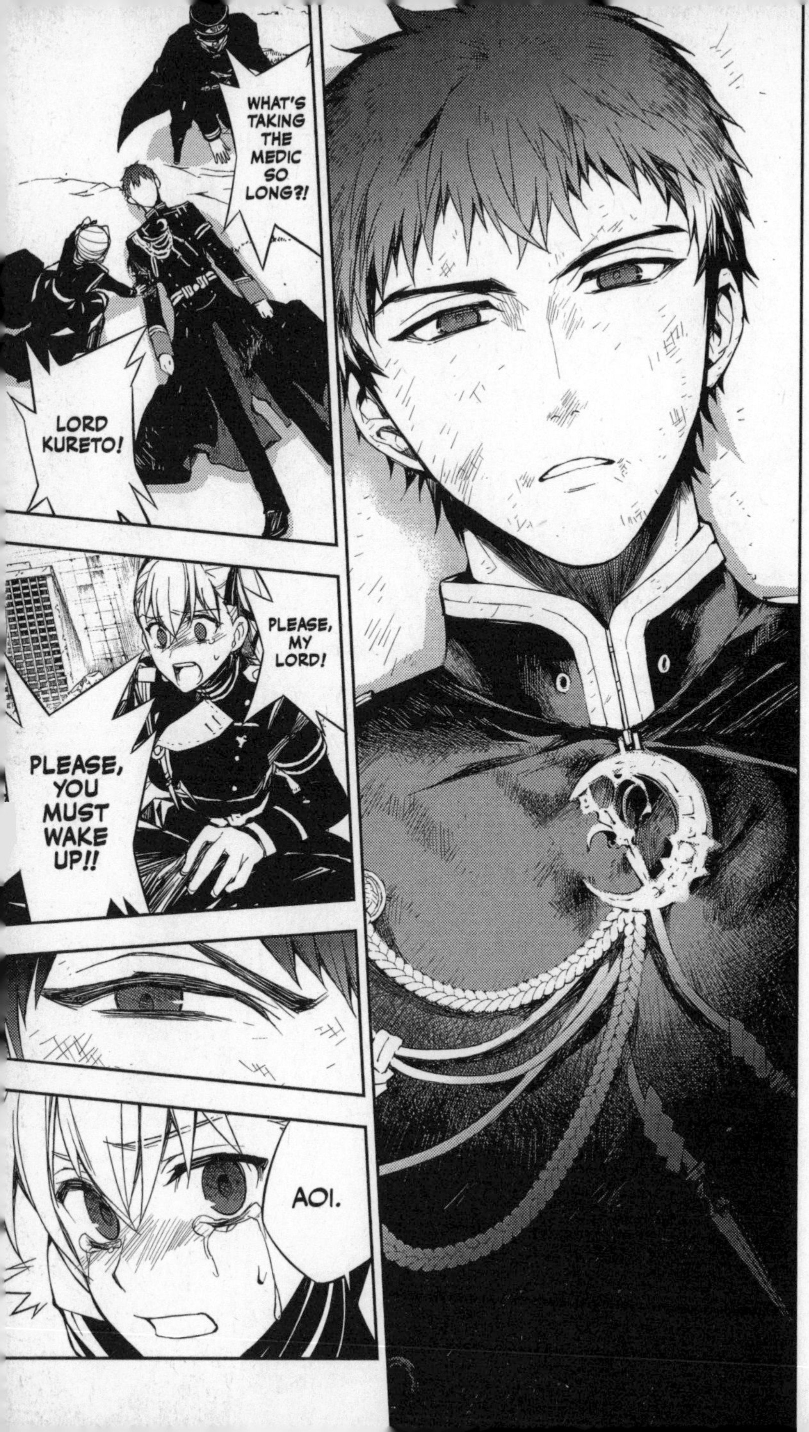
WHAT'S TAKING THE MEDIC SO LONG?!
LORD KURETO!
PLEASE, MY LORD!
PLEASE, YOU MUST WAKE UP!!
AOI.

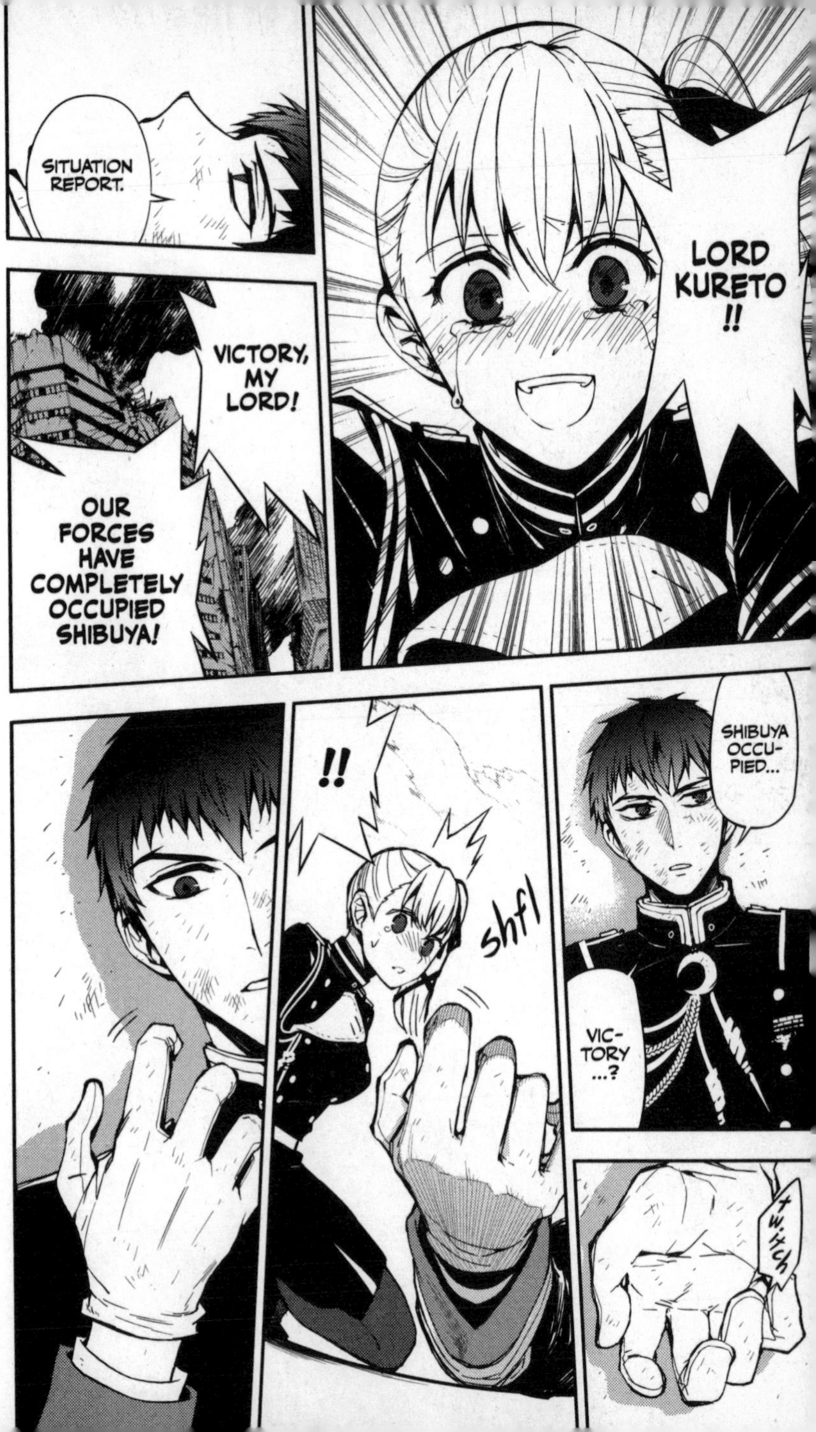
LORD KURETO !!
SITUATION REPORT.
VICTORY, MY LORD!
OUR FORCES HAVE COMPLETELY OCCUPIED SHIBUYA!
SHIBUYA OCCU-PIED...
VIC-TORY ...?
twitch
!!
shfl

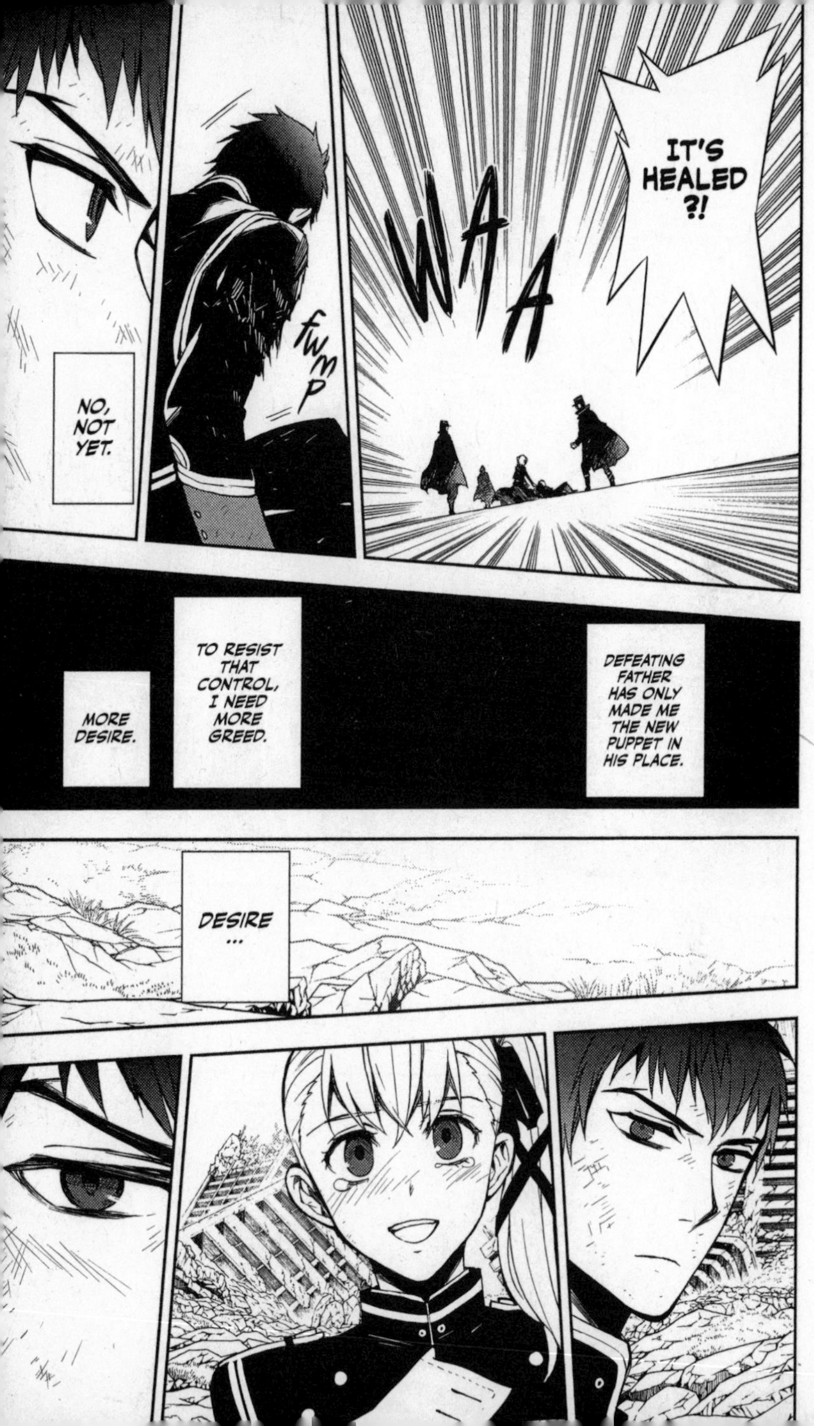
IT'S HEALED ?!
WAA
FWMP
NO, NOT YET.
DEFEATING FATHER HAS ONLY MADE ME THE NEW PUPPET IN HIS PLACE.
TO RESIST THAT CONTROL, I NEED MORE GREED.
MORE DESIRE.
DESIRE ...

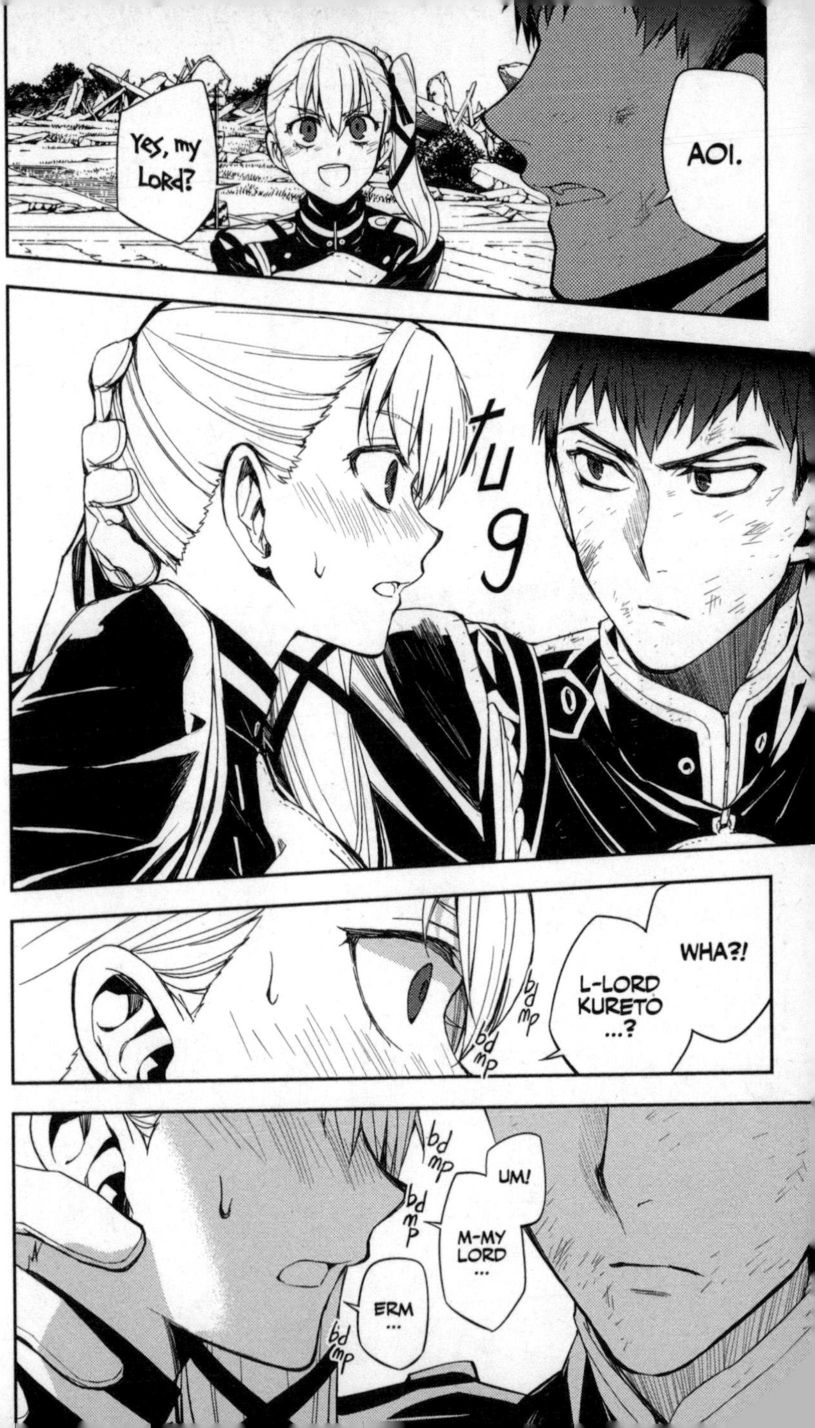
AOI.
Yes, my Lord?
tug
WHA?!
L-LORD KURETO ...?
bdmp
bdmp
bdmp
UM!
bdmp
M-MY LORD ...
ERM ...
bdmp

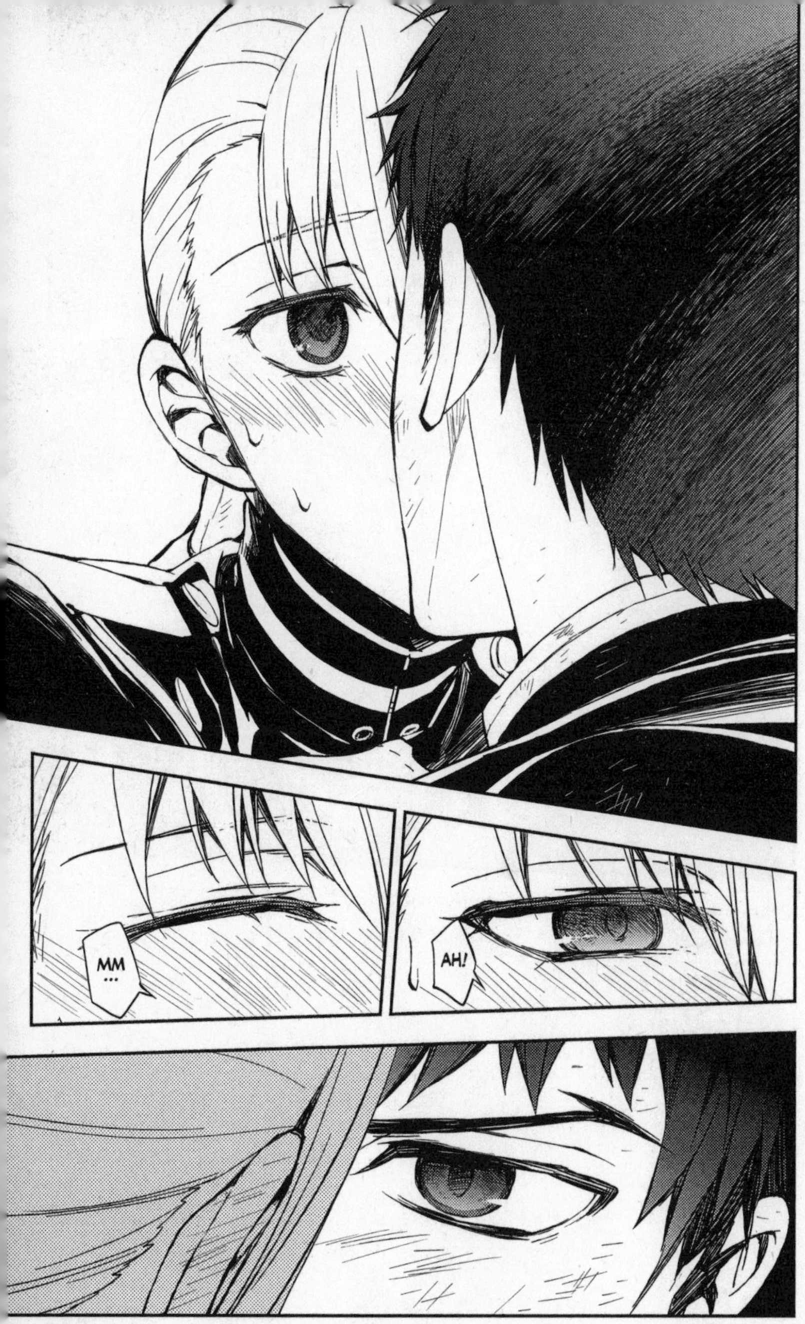
AH!
MM
...

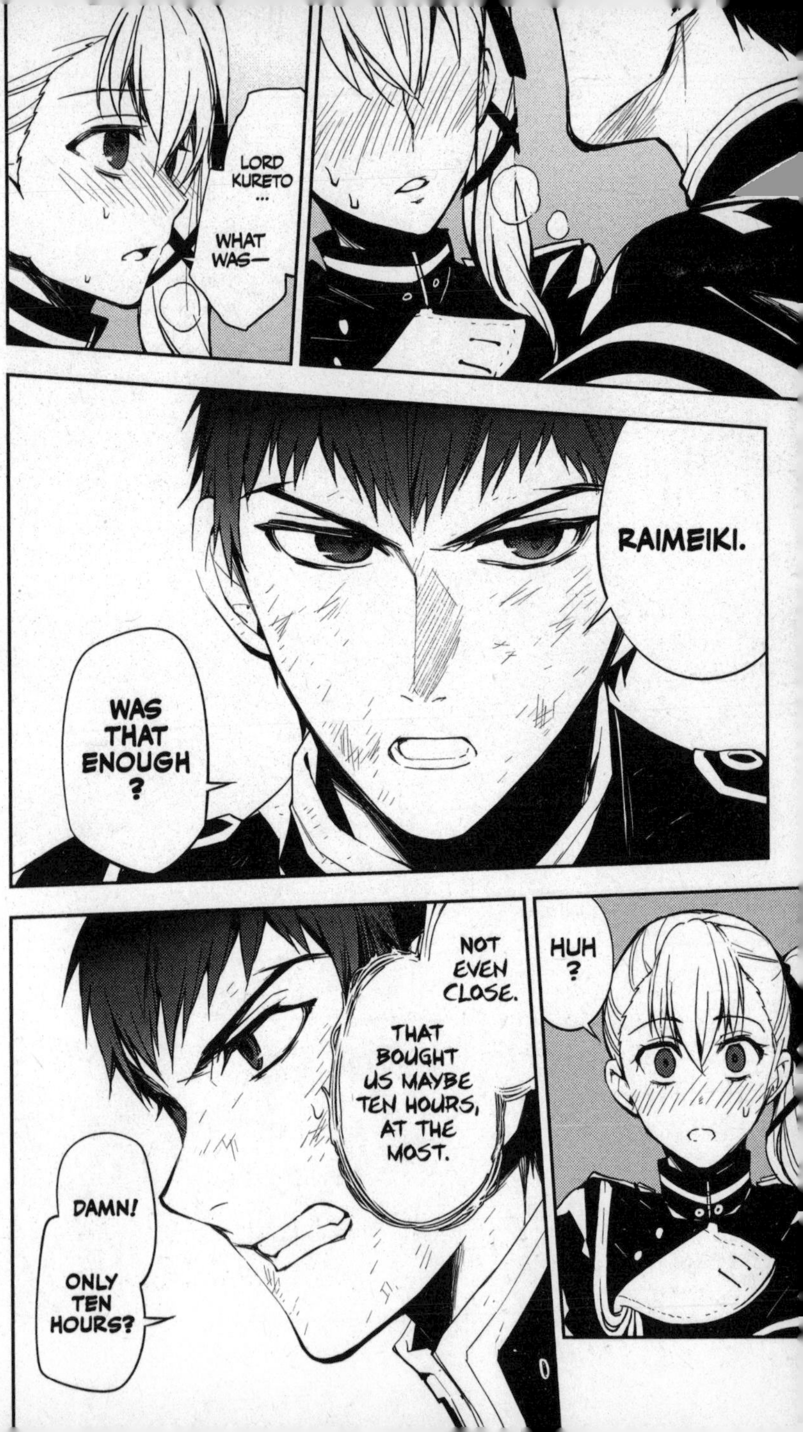
LORD KURETO...
WHAT WAS—
RAIMEIKI.
WAS THAT ENOUGH?
HUH?
NOT EVEN CLOSE.
THAT BOUGHT US MAYBE TEN HOURS, AT THE MOST.
DAMN!
ONLY TEN HOURS?

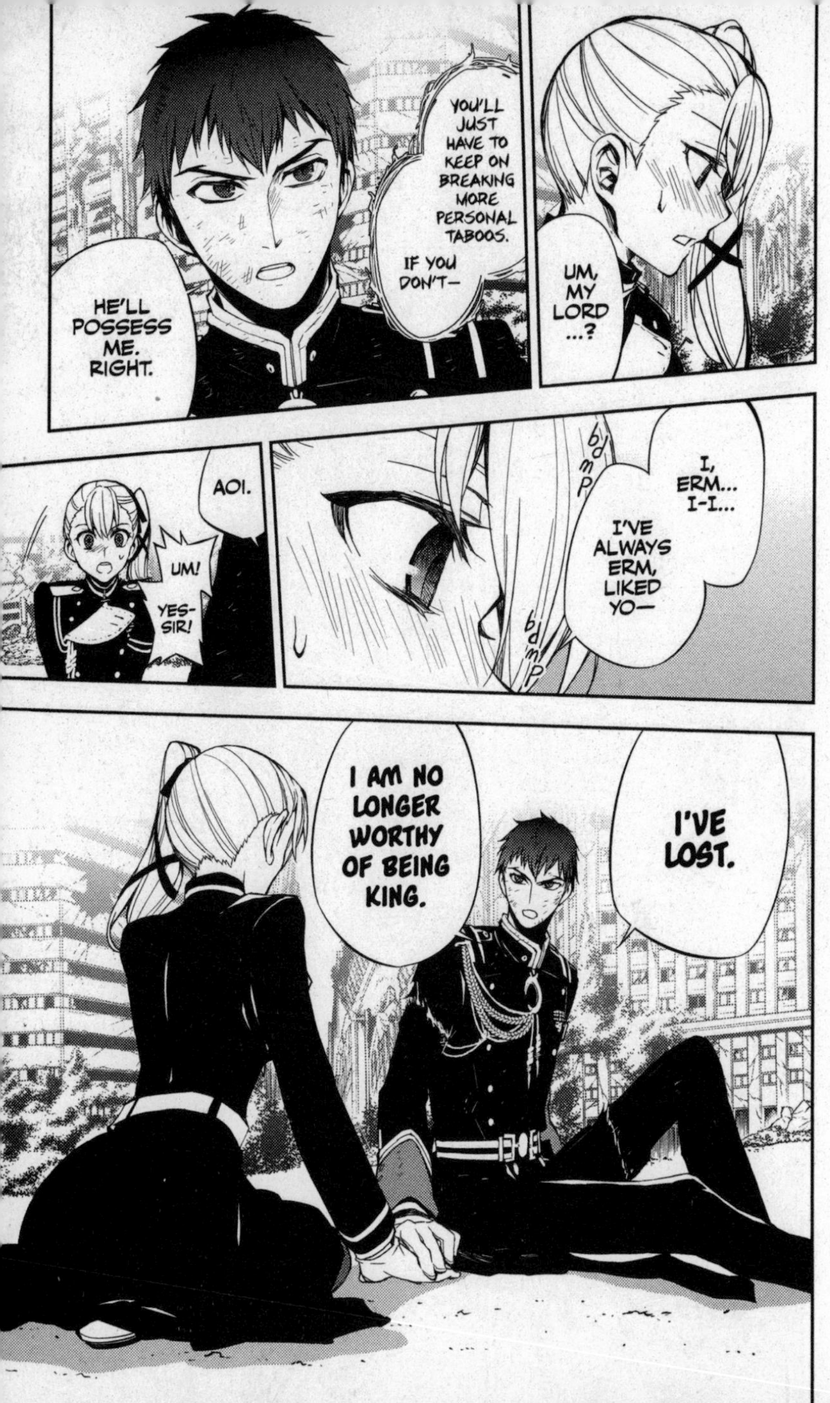
UM, MY LORD ...?
YOU'LL JUST HAVE TO KEEP ON BREAKING MORE PERSONAL TABOOS.
IF YOU DON'T—
HE'LL POSSESS ME. RIGHT.
bdmp
I, ERM... I-I...
I'VE ALWAYS ERM, LIKED YO—
bdmp
AOI.
UM!
YES-SIR!
I'VE LOST.
I AM NO LONGER WORTHY OF BEING KING.

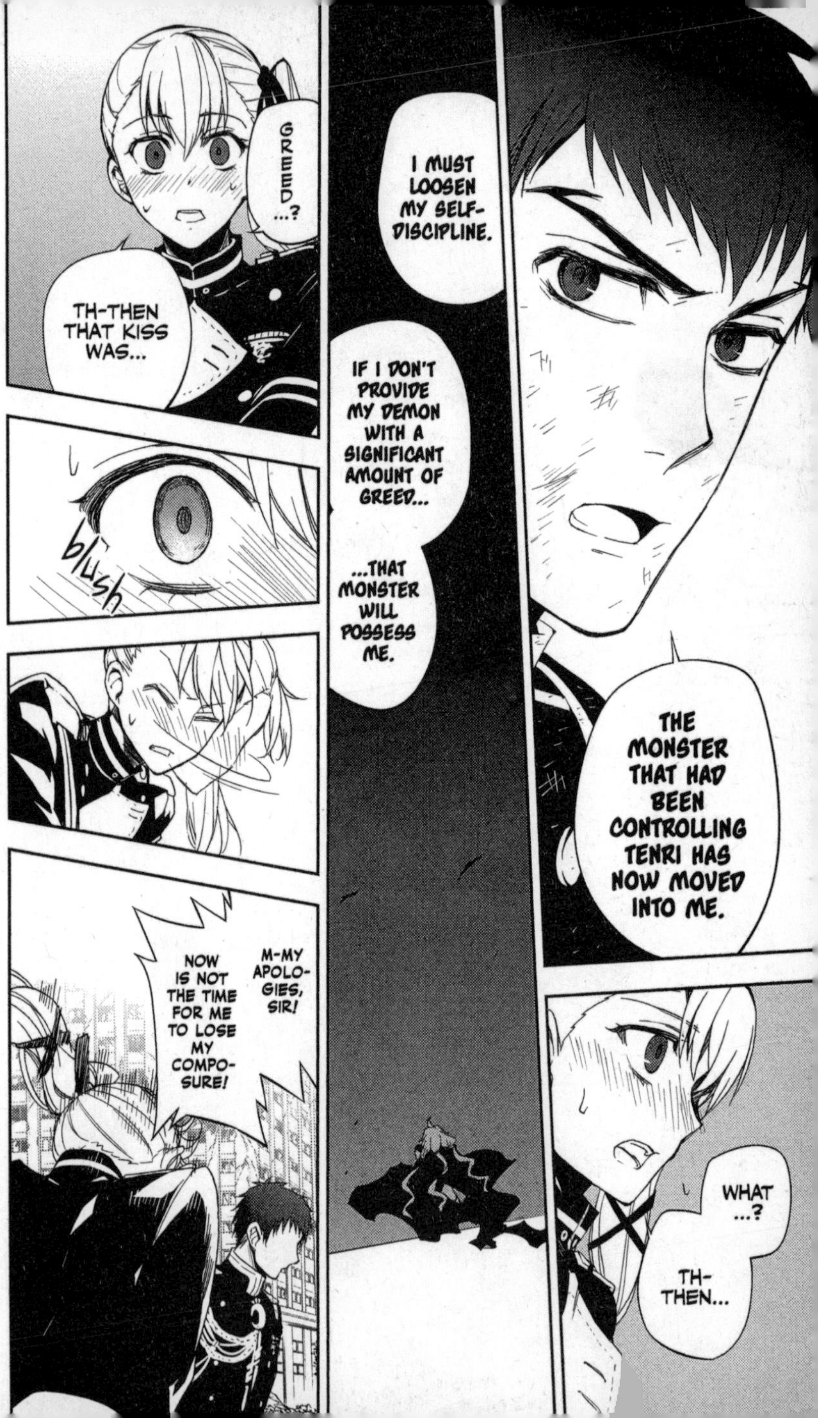
THE MONSTER THAT HAD BEEN CONTROLLING TENRI HAS NOW MOVED INTO ME.
I MUST LOOSEN MY SELF-DISCIPLINE.
IF I DON'T PROVIDE MY DEMON WITH A SIGNIFICANT AMOUNT OF GREED...
...THAT MONSTER WILL POSSESS ME.
WHAT ...?
TH- THEN...
GREED ...?
TH-THEN THAT KISS WAS...
blush
M-MY APOLO-GIES, SIR!
NOW IS NOT THE TIME FOR ME TO LOSE MY COMPO-SURE!

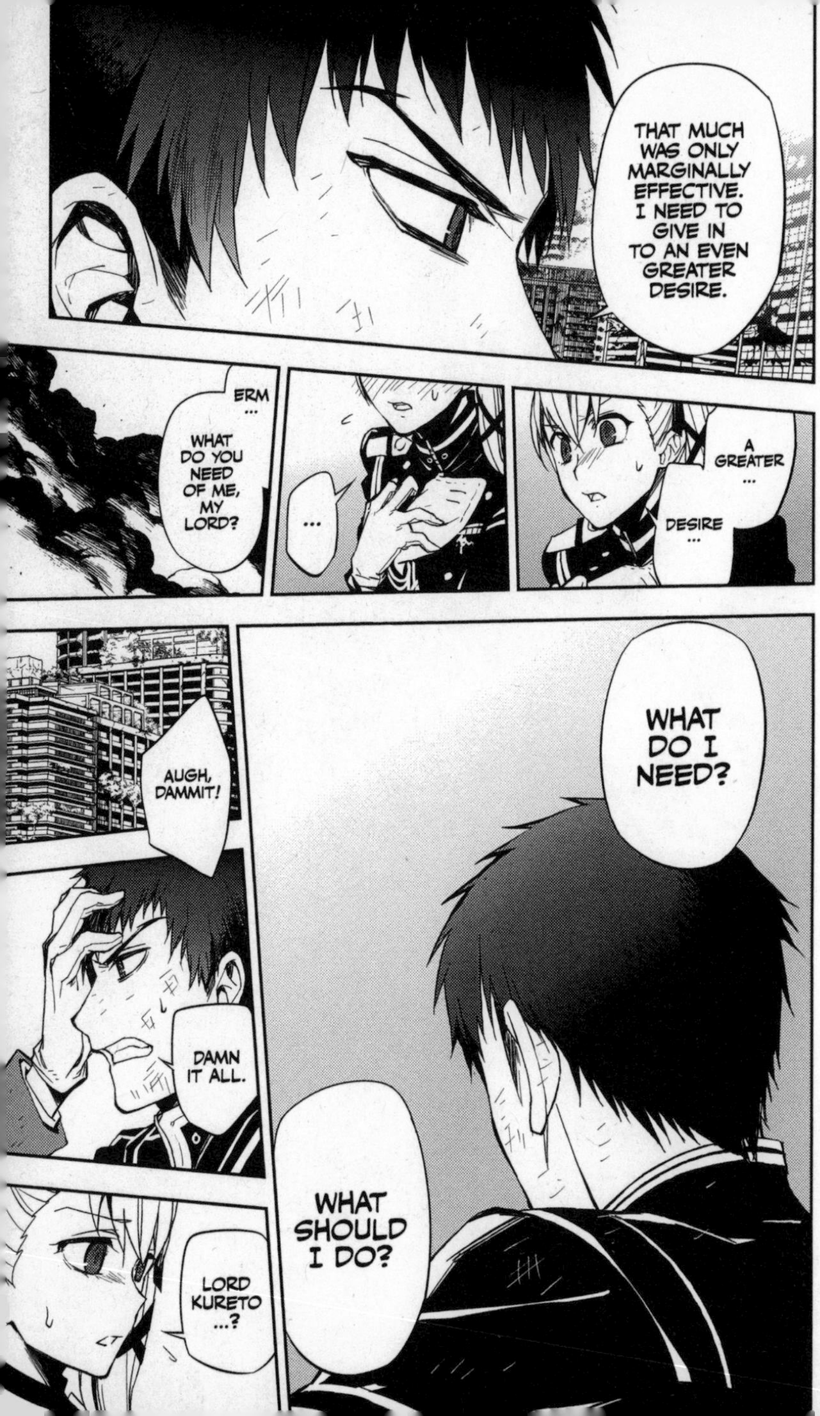
THAT MUCH WAS ONLY MARGINALLY EFFECTIVE. I NEED TO GIVE IN TO AN EVEN GREATER DESIRE.
A GREATER ...
DESIRE ...
...
ERM ...
WHAT DO YOU NEED OF ME, MY LORD?
WHAT DO I NEED?
WHAT SHOULD I DO?
AUGH, DAMMIT!
DAMN IT ALL.
LORD KURETO ...?

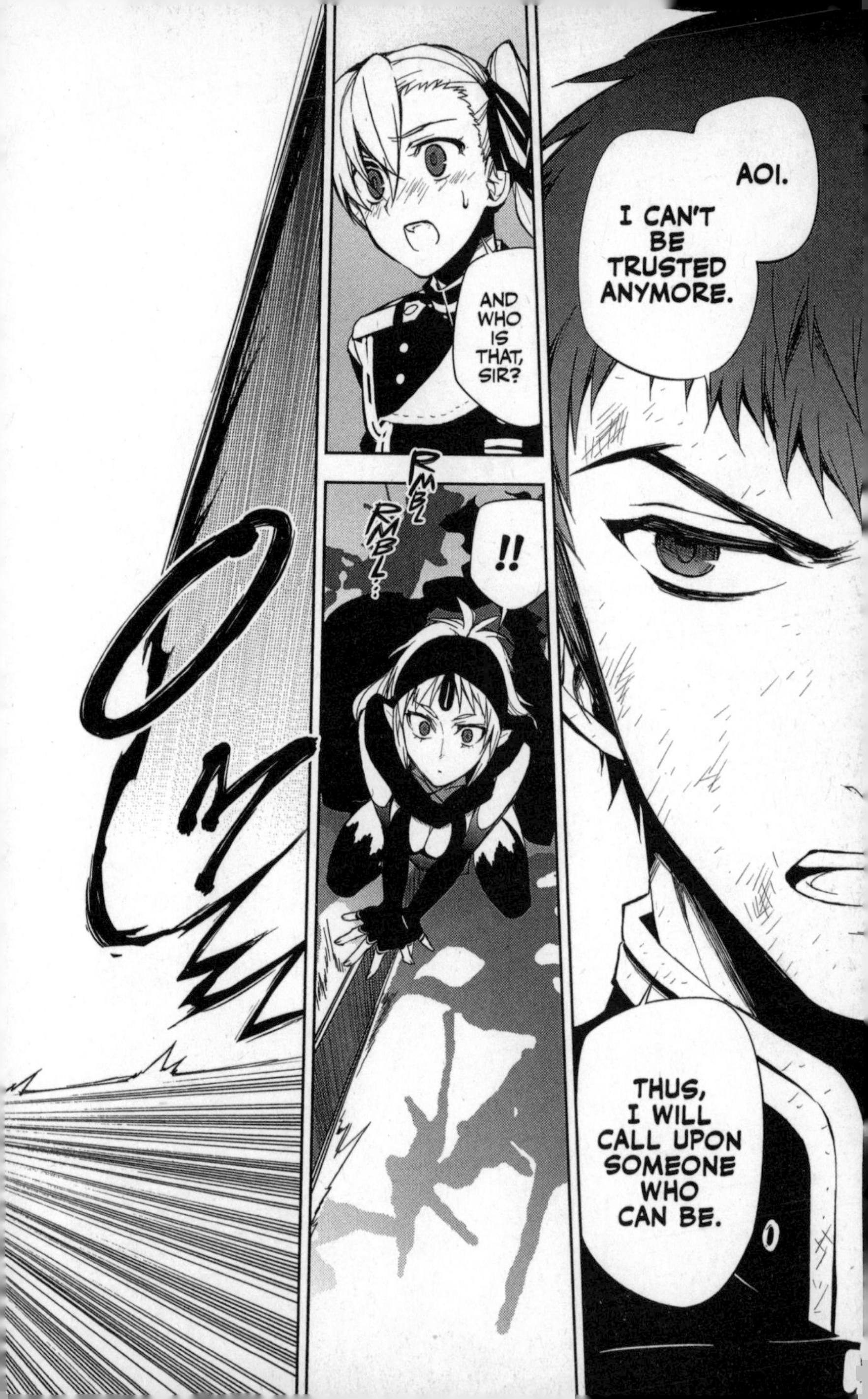
AOI.
I CAN'T BE TRUSTED ANYMORE.
THUS, I WILL CALL UPON SOMEONE WHO CAN BE.
AND WHO IS THAT, SIR?
RMBL RMBL...
!!
OMM

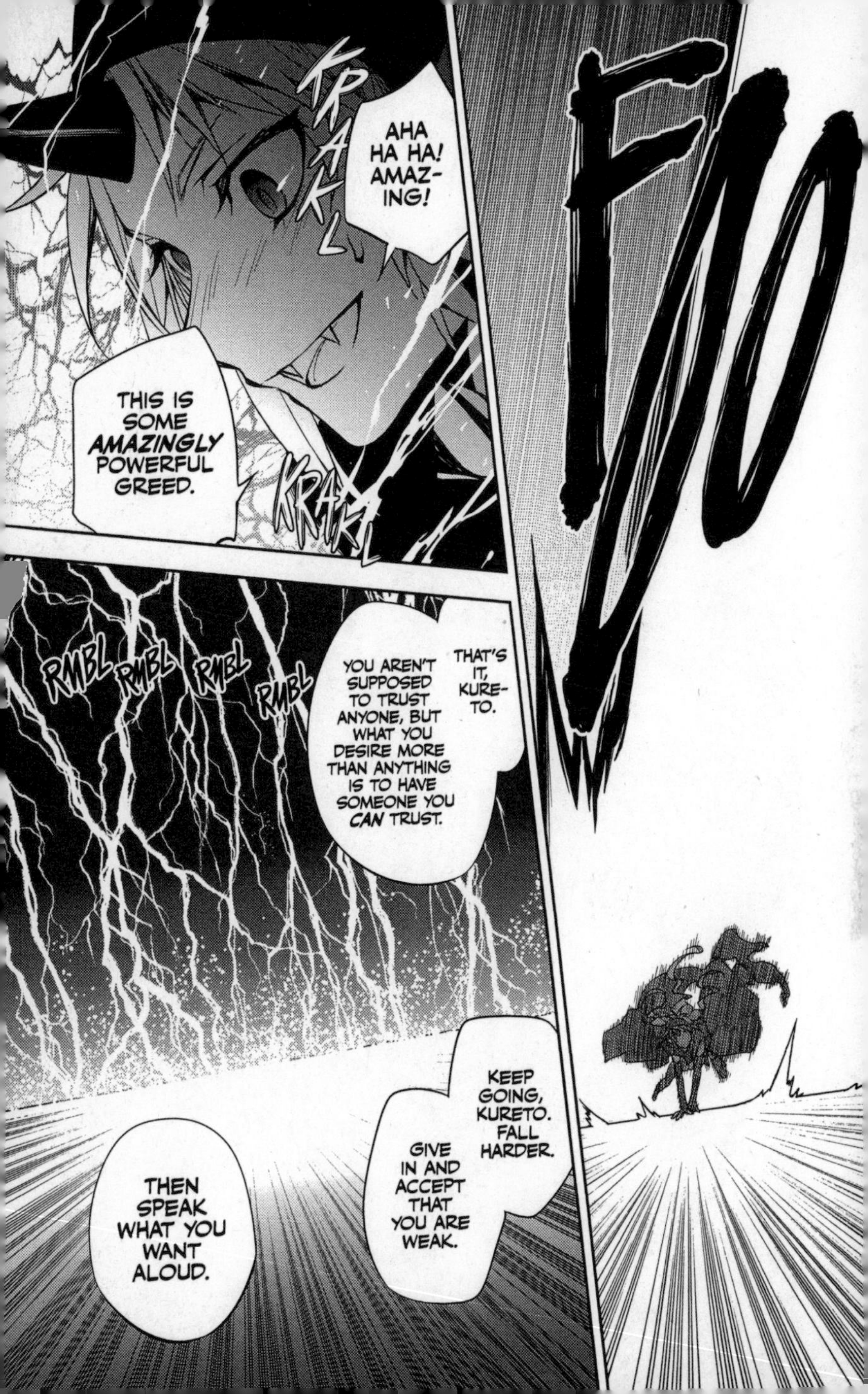
FOO
AHA HA HA! AMAZING!
KRAKL
THIS IS SOME AMAZINGLY POWERFUL GREED.
KRAKL
RMBL RMBL RMBL RMBL
THAT'S IT, KURETO.
YOU AREN'T SUPPOSED TO TRUST ANYONE, BUT WHAT YOU DESIRE MORE THAN ANYTHING IS TO HAVE SOMEONE YOU CAN TRUST.
KEEP GOING, KURETO. FALL HARDER.
GIVE IN AND ACCEPT THAT YOU ARE WEAK.
THEN SPEAK WHAT YOU WANT ALOUD.

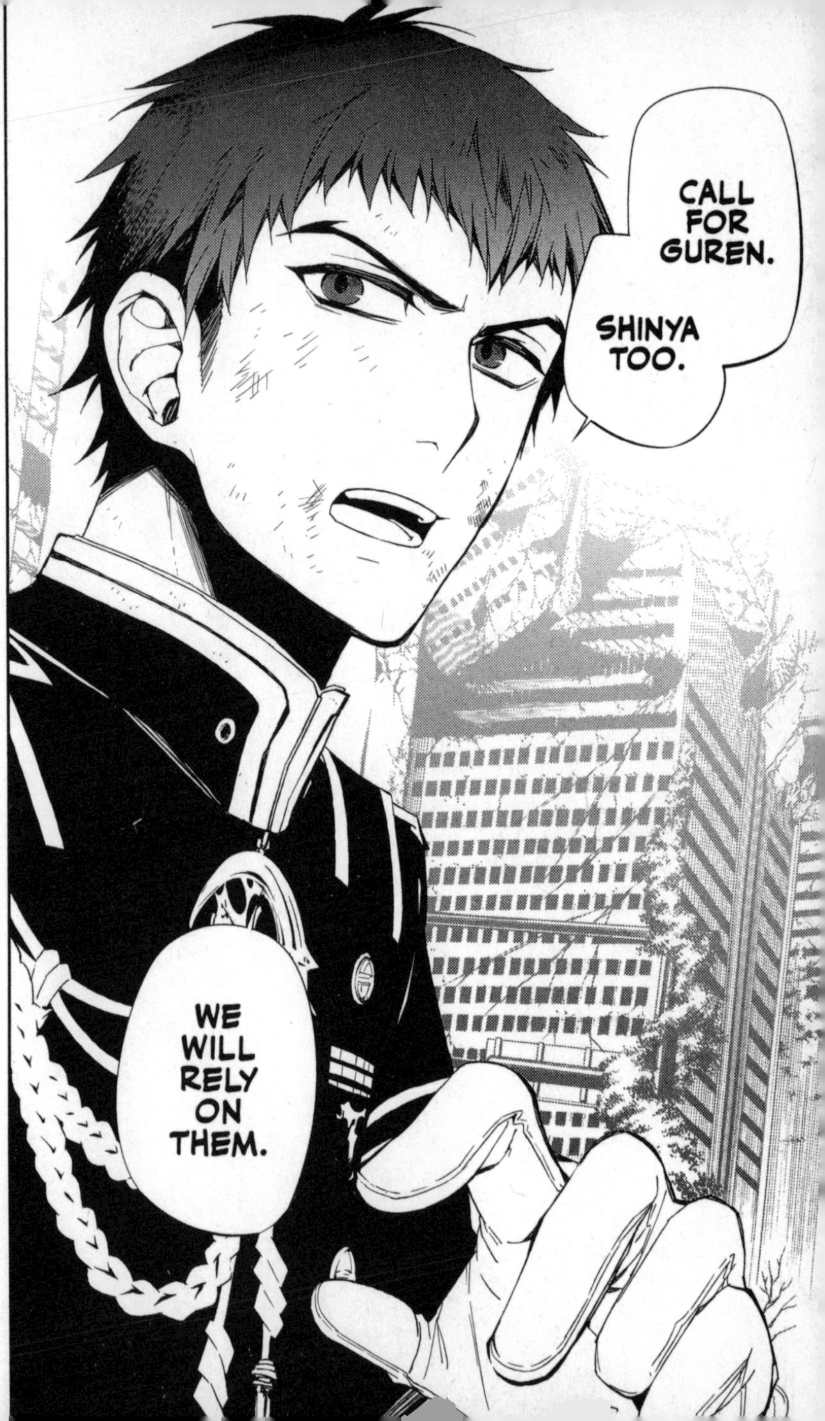
CALL FOR GUREN.
SHINYA TOO.
WE WILL RELY ON THEM.

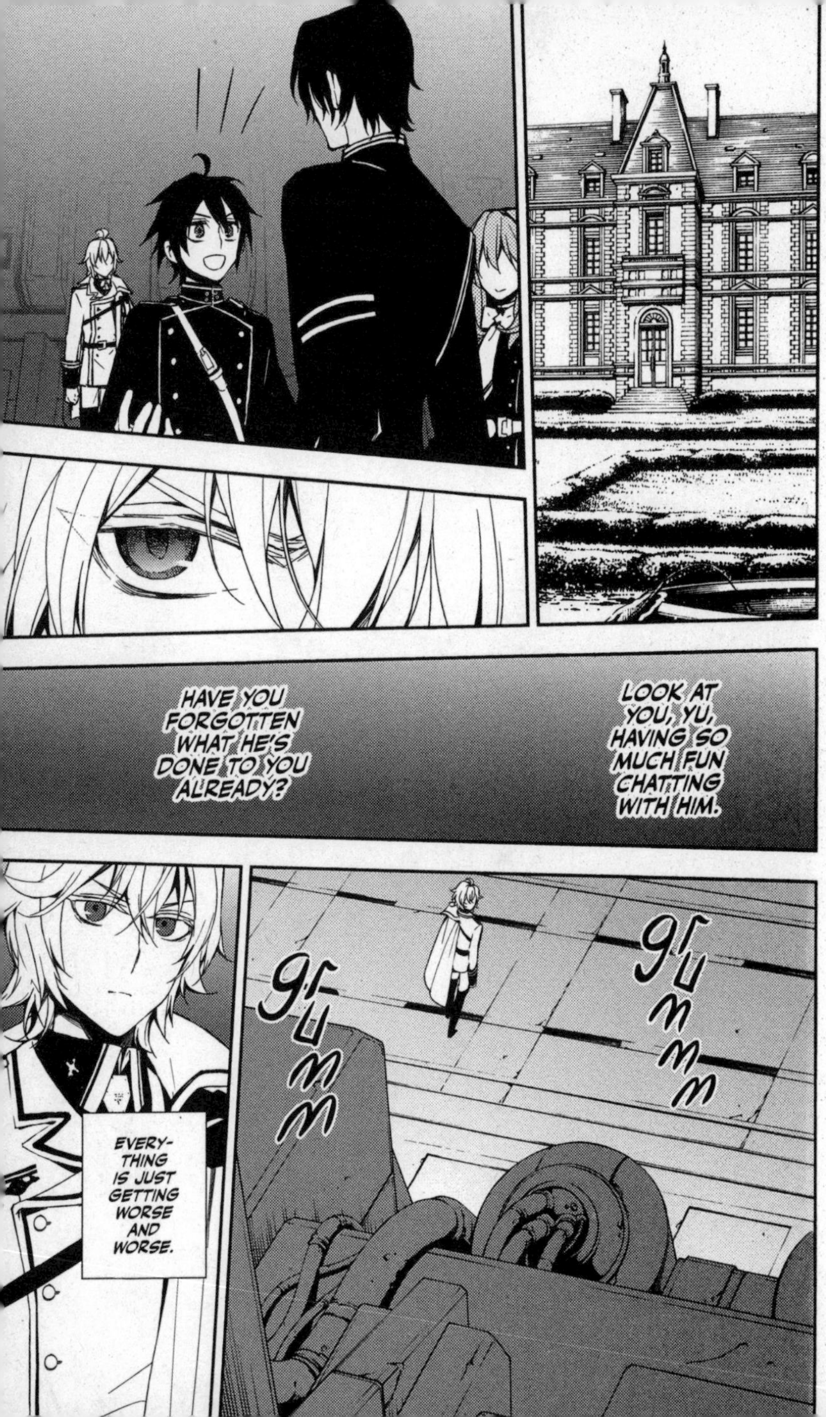
LOOK AT YOU, YU, HAVING SO MUCH FUN CHATTING WITH HIM.
HAVE YOU FORGOTTEN WHAT HE'S DONE TO YOU ALREADY?
EVERY-THING IS JUST GETTING WORSE AND WORSE.

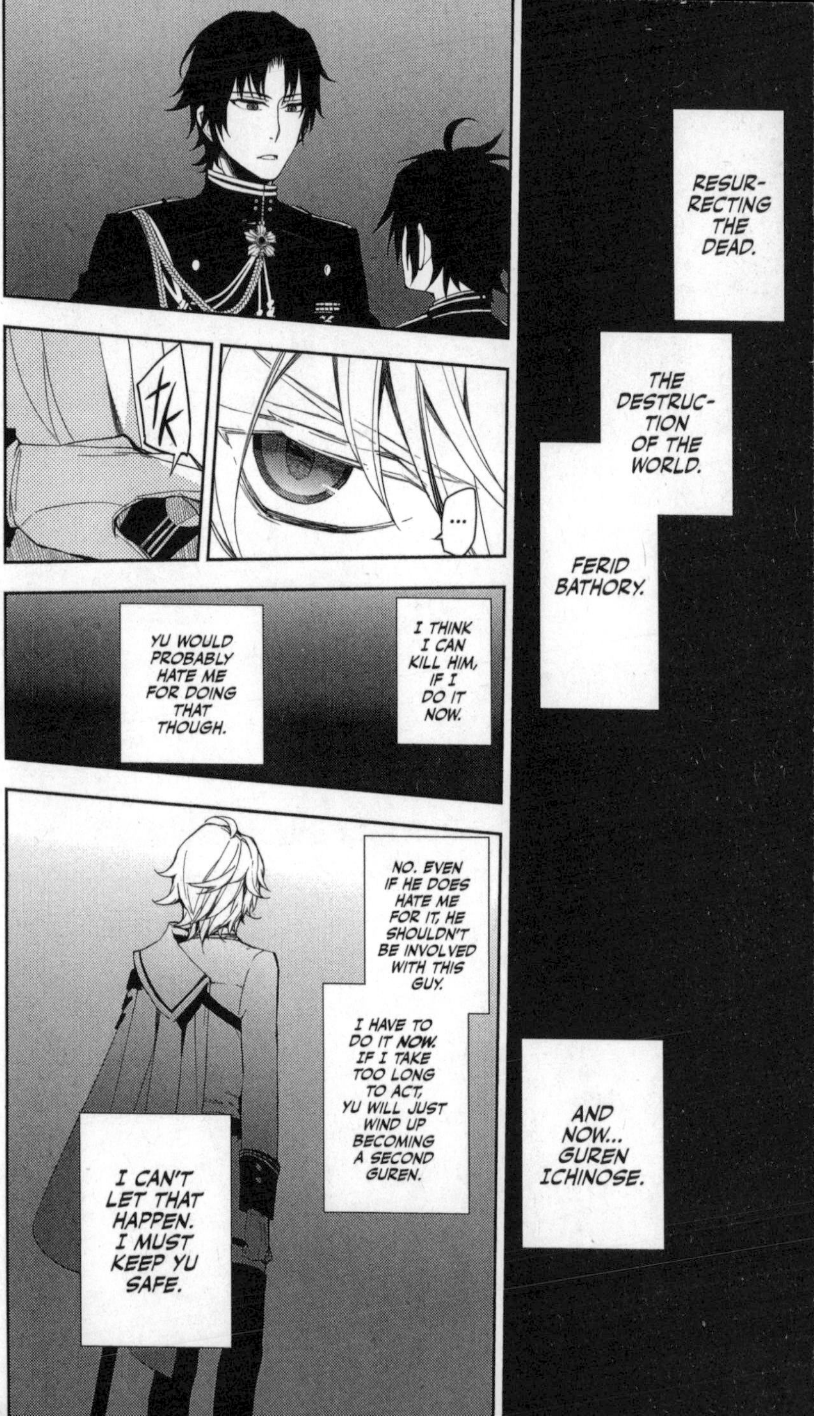
RESUR-RECTING THE DEAD.
THE DESTRUC-TION OF THE WORLD.
FERID BATHORY.
AND NOW... GUREN ICHINOSE.
...
TK
I THINK I CAN KILL HIM, IF I DO IT NOW.
YU WOULD PROBABLY HATE ME FOR DOING THAT THOUGH.
NO. EVEN IF HE DOES HATE ME FOR IT, HE SHOULDN'T BE INVOLVED WITH THIS GUY.
I HAVE TO DO IT NOW. IF I TAKE TOO LONG TO ACT, YU WILL JUST WIND UP BECOMING A SECOND GUREN.
I CAN'T LET THAT HAPPEN. I MUST KEEP YU SAFE.

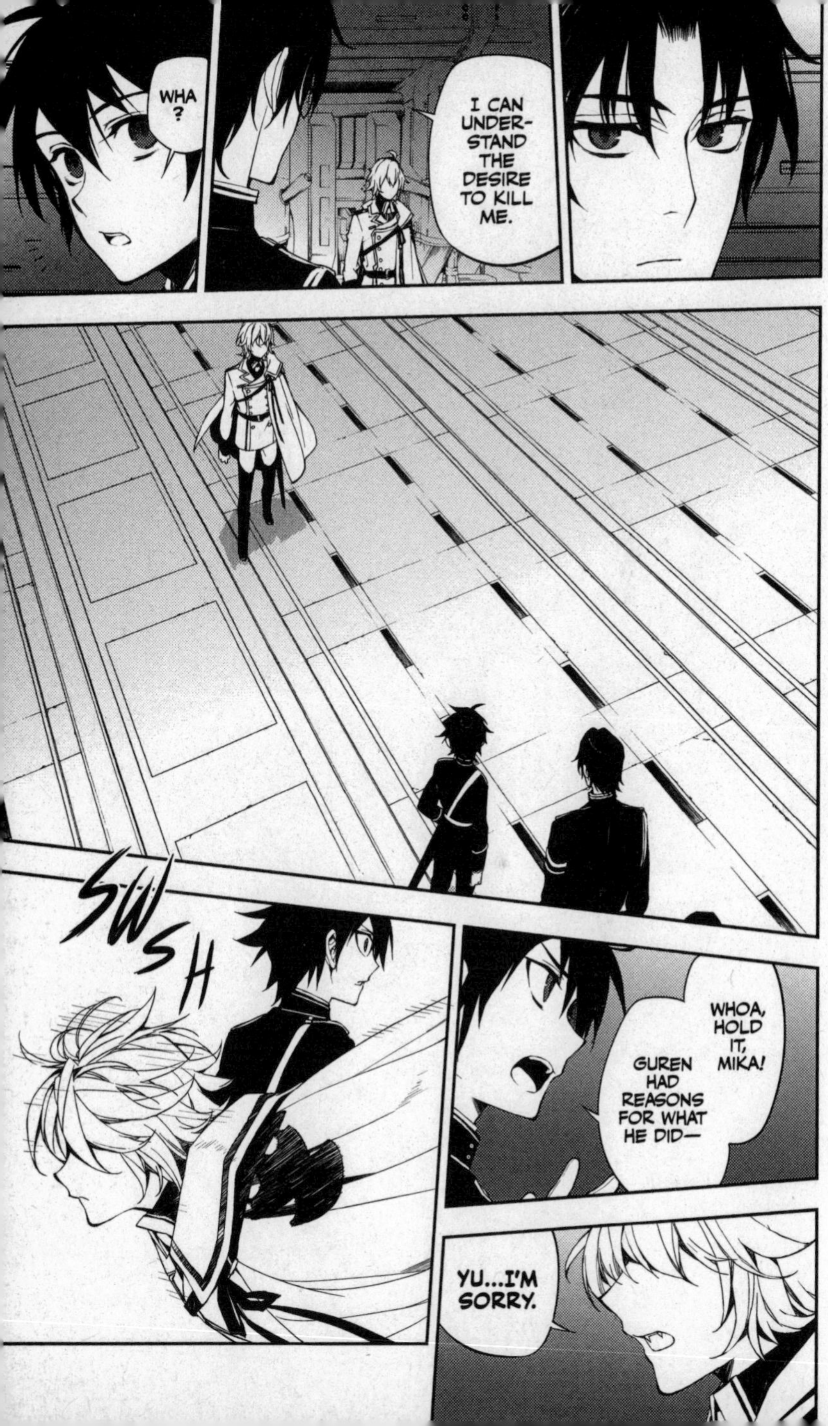
I CAN UNDER-STAND THE DESIRE TO KILL ME.
WHA?
WHOA, HOLD IT, MIKA!
GUREN HAD REASONS FOR WHAT HE DID—
YU...I'M SORRY.
SWSH

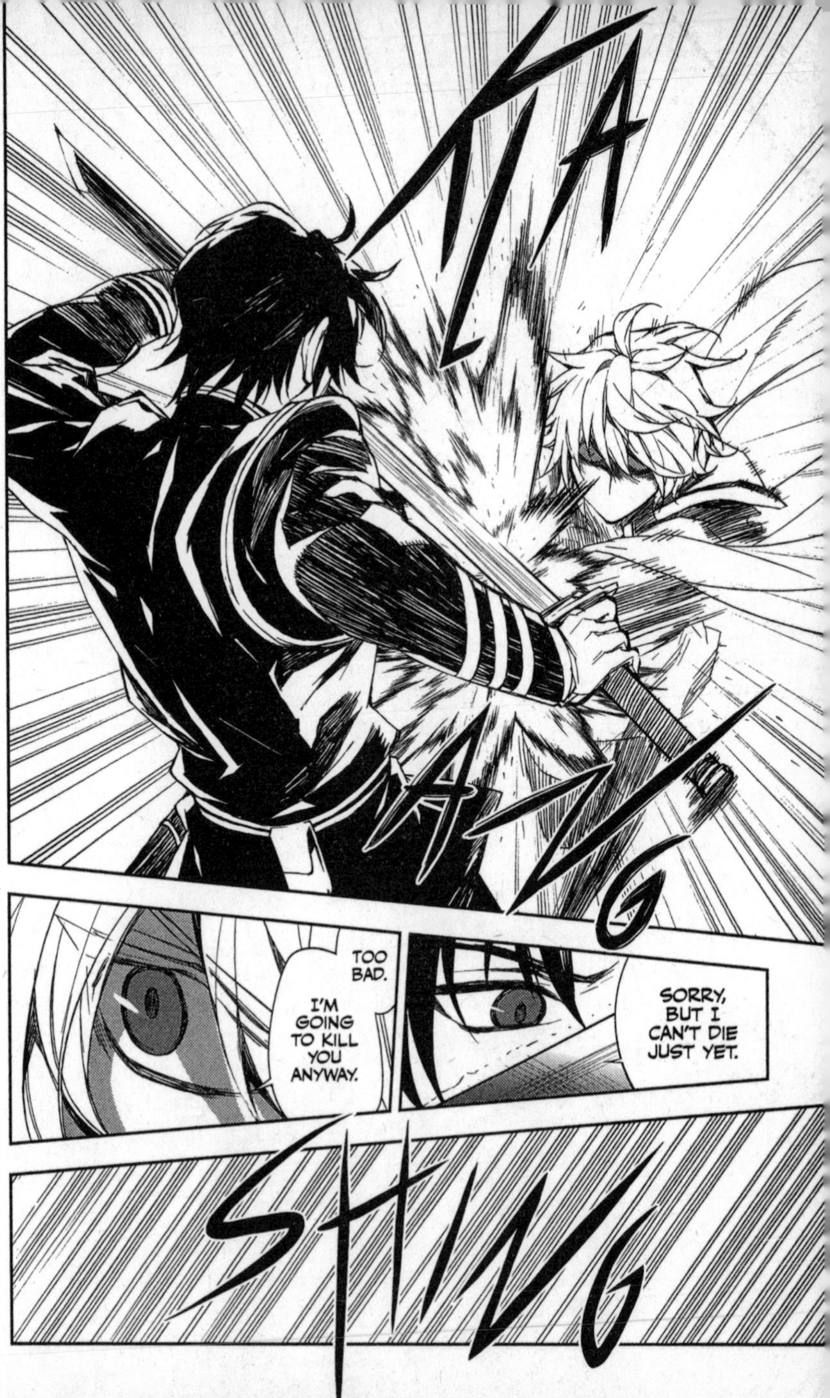
SORRY, BUT I CAN'T DIE JUST YET.
TOO BAD.
I'M GOING TO KILL YOU ANYWAY.
SHING

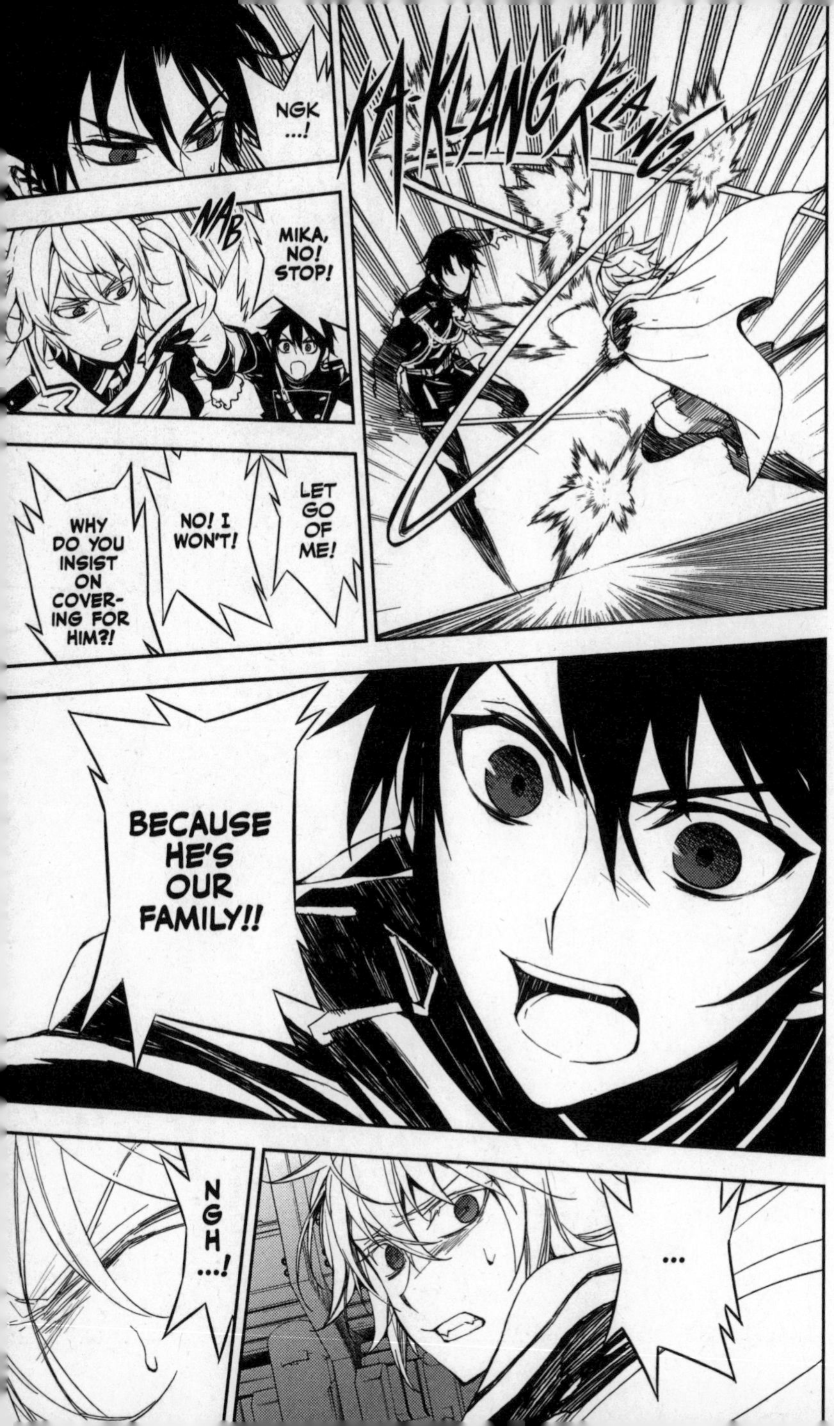
KA-KLANG KLANG
NGK ...!
NAB
MIKA, NO! STOP!
LET GO OF ME!
NO! I WON'T!
WHY DO YOU INSIST ON COVERING FOR HIM?!
BECAUSE HE'S OUR FAMILY!!
...
NGH ...!

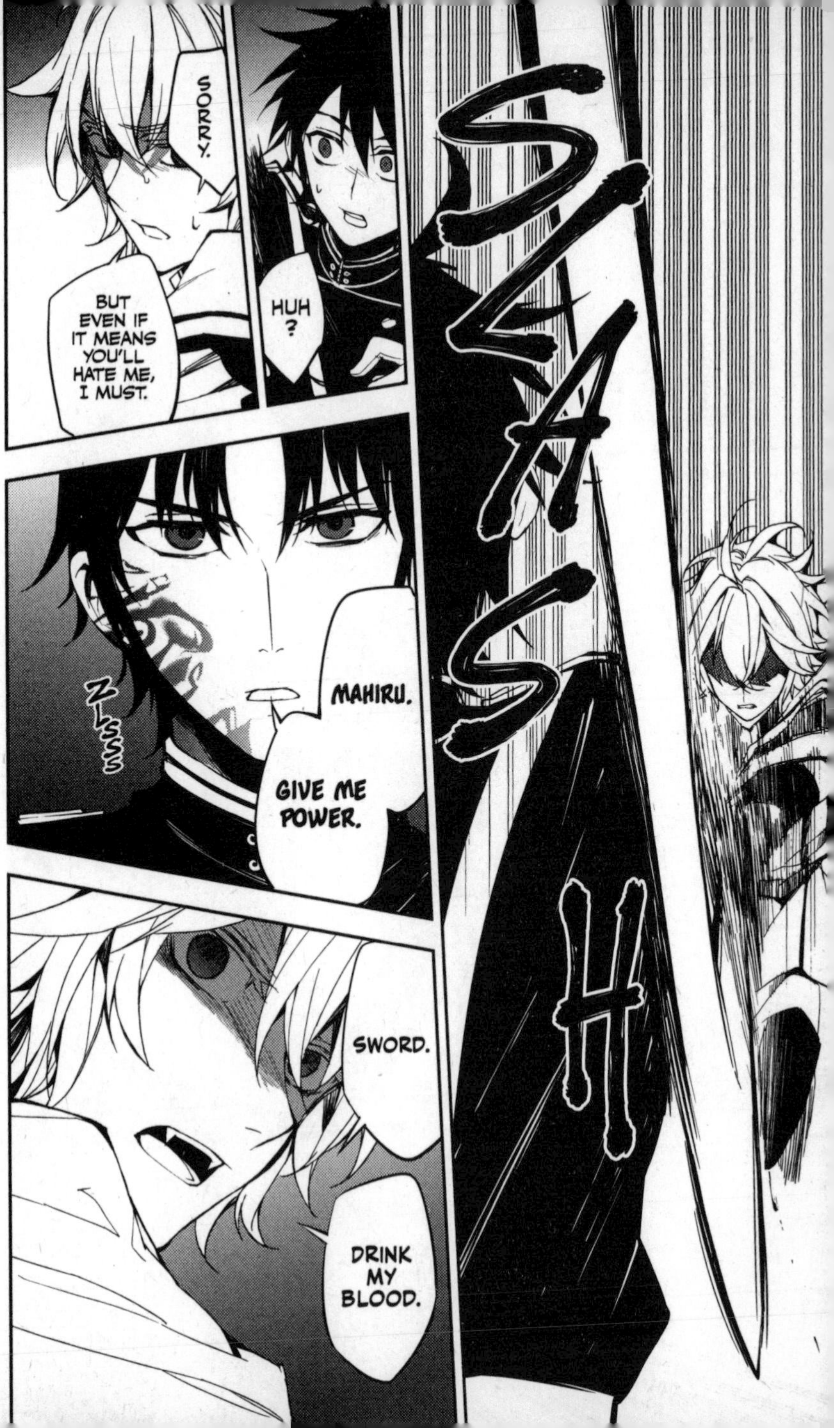
SHASSH
HUH?
SORRY.
BUT EVEN IF IT MEANS YOU'LL HATE ME, I MUST.
MAHIRU.
GIVE ME POWER.
ZLSSS
SWORD.
DRINK MY BLOOD.

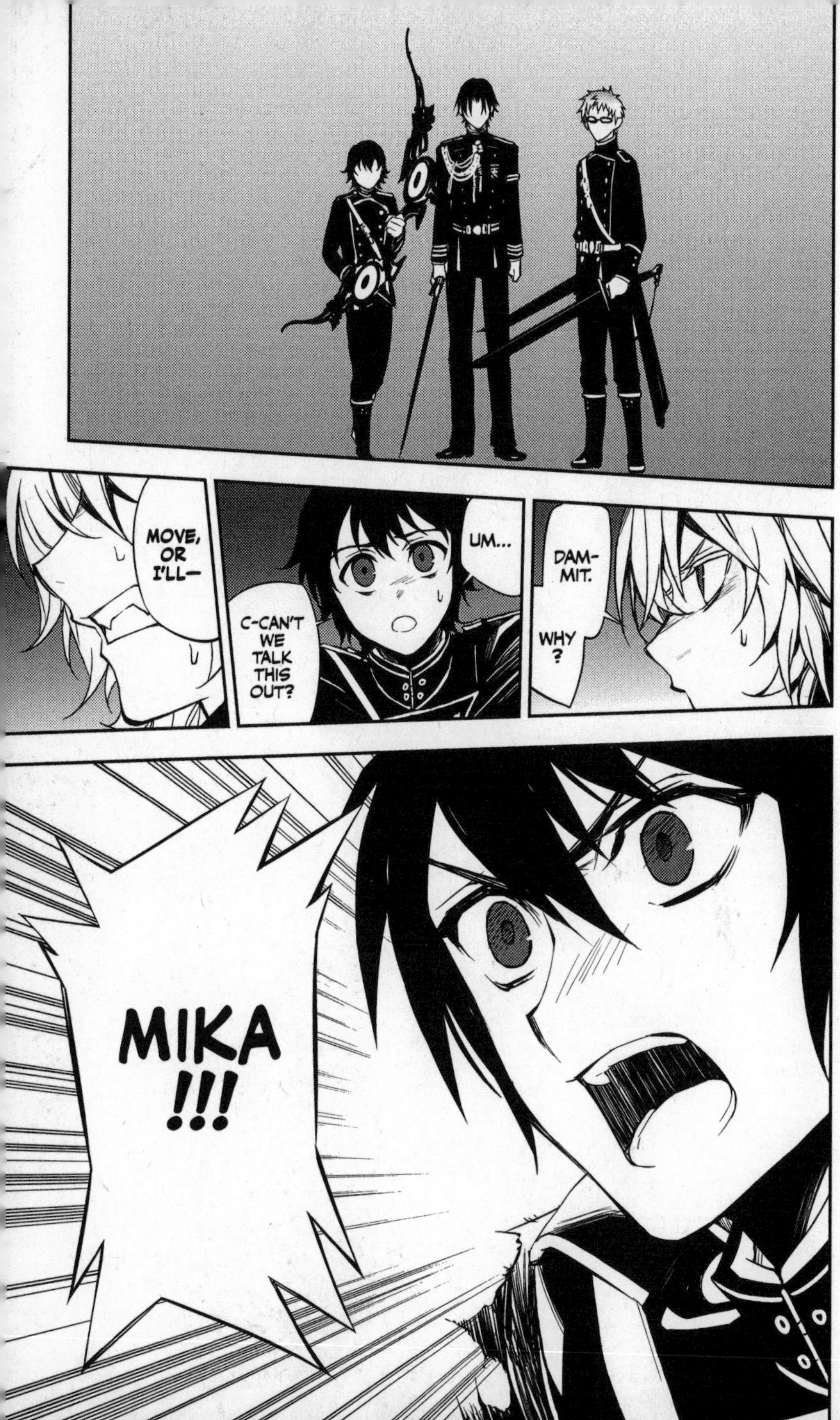
DAM-MIT.
WHY?
UM...
C-CAN'T WE TALK THIS OUT?
MOVE, OR I'LL—
MIKA!!!

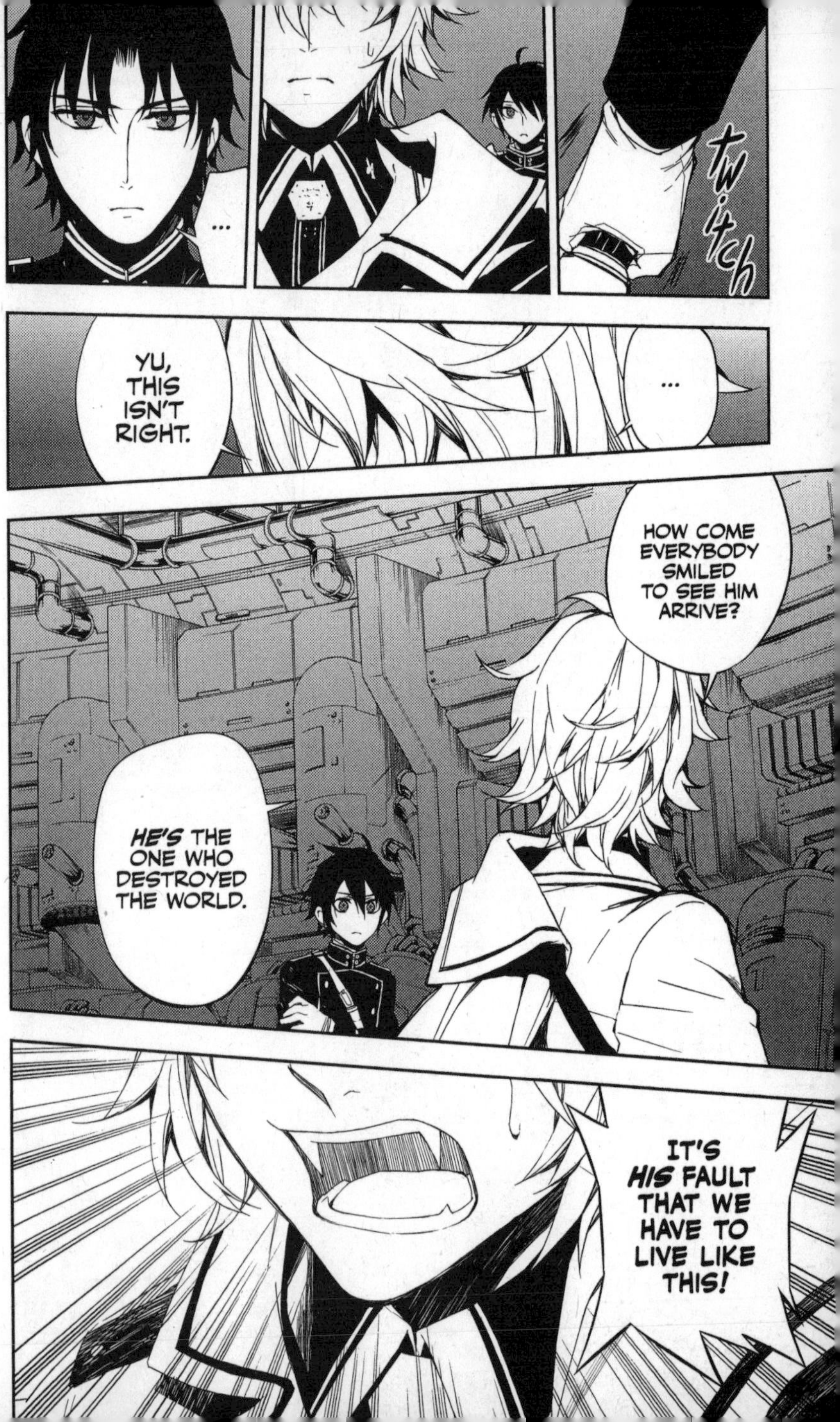

twitch
...
...
YU, THIS ISN'T RIGHT.
HOW COME EVERYBODY SMILED TO SEE HIM ARRIVE?
HE'S THE ONE WHO DESTROYED THE WORLD.
IT'S *HIS* FAULT THAT WE HAVE TO LIVE LIKE THIS!

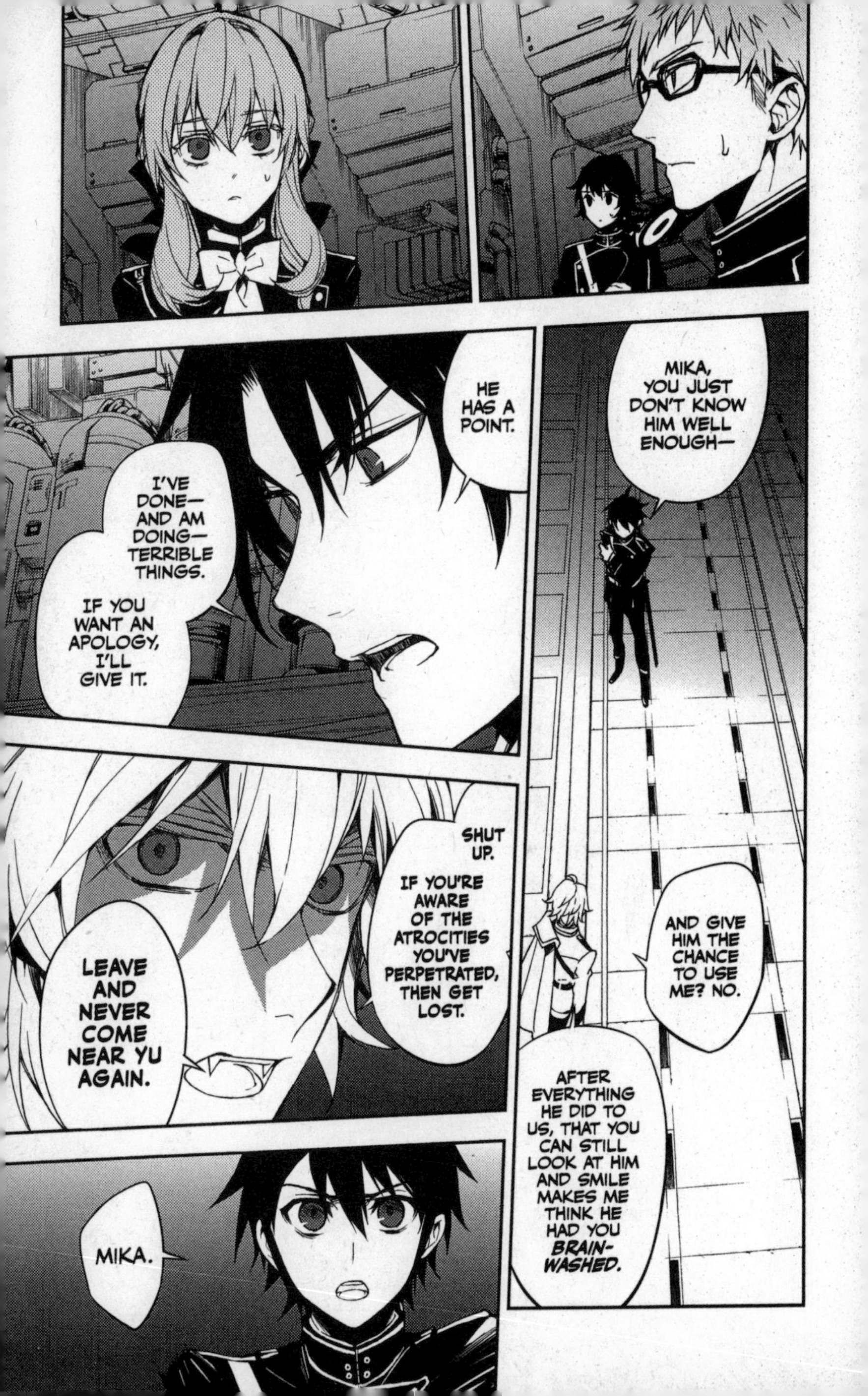
MIKA, YOU JUST DON'T KNOW HIM WELL ENOUGH—
AND GIVE HIM THE CHANCE TO USE ME? NO.
AFTER EVERYTHING HE DID TO US, THAT YOU CAN STILL LOOK AT HIM AND SMILE MAKES ME THINK HE HAD YOU *BRAIN-WASHED*.
HE HAS A POINT.
I'VE DONE—AND AM DOING—TERRIBLE THINGS.
IF YOU WANT AN APOLOGY, I'LL GIVE IT.
SHUT UP.
IF YOU'RE AWARE OF THE ATROCITIES YOU'VE PERPETRATED, THEN GET LOST.
LEAVE AND NEVER COME NEAR YU AGAIN.
MIKA.

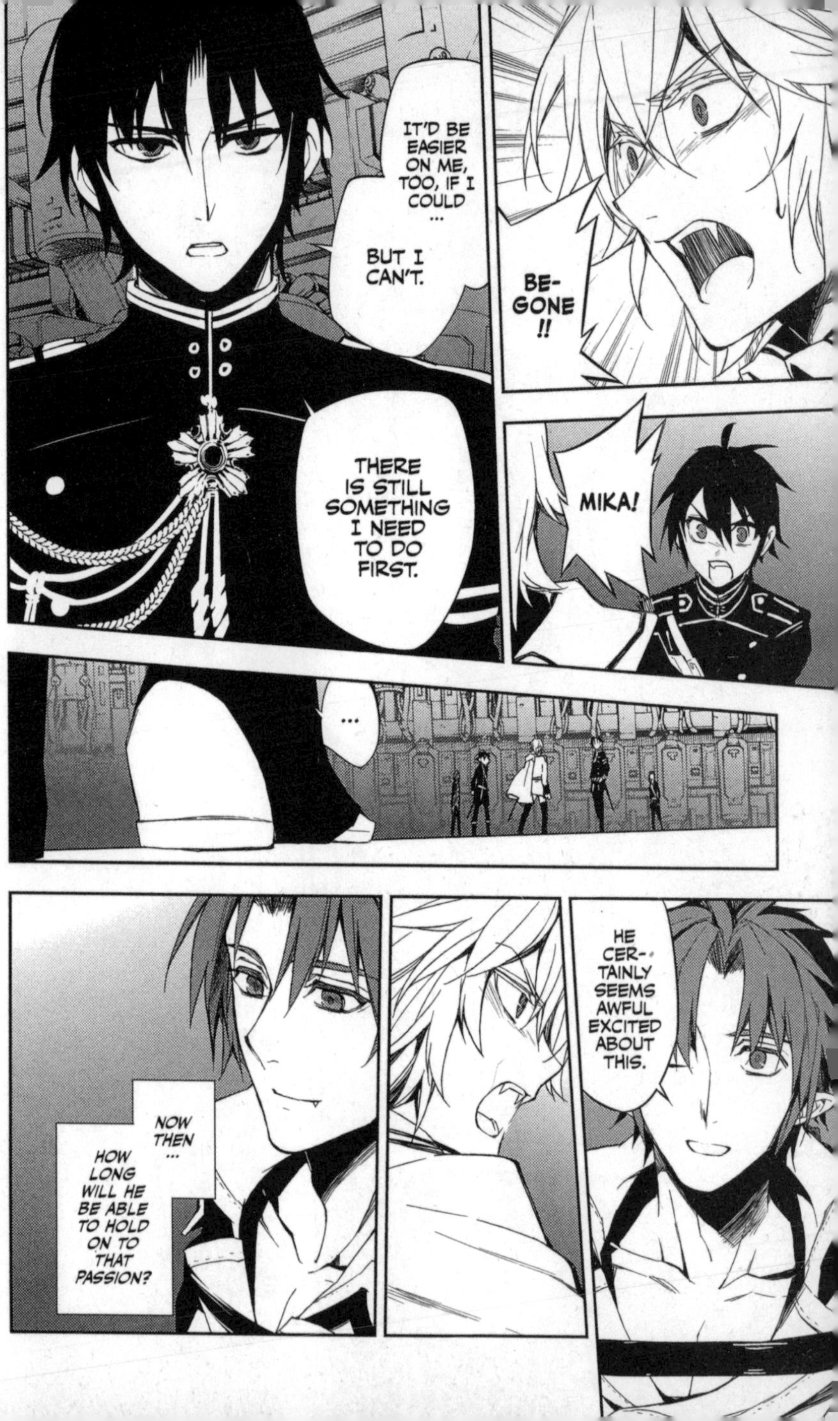
BE-GONE!!
MIKA!
IT'D BE EASIER ON ME, TOO, IF I COULD ...
BUT I CAN'T.
THERE IS STILL SOMETHING I NEED TO DO FIRST.
...
HE CER-TAINLY SEEMS AWFUL EXCITED ABOUT THIS.
NOW THEN ...
HOW LONG WILL HE BE ABLE TO HOLD ON TO THAT PASSION?

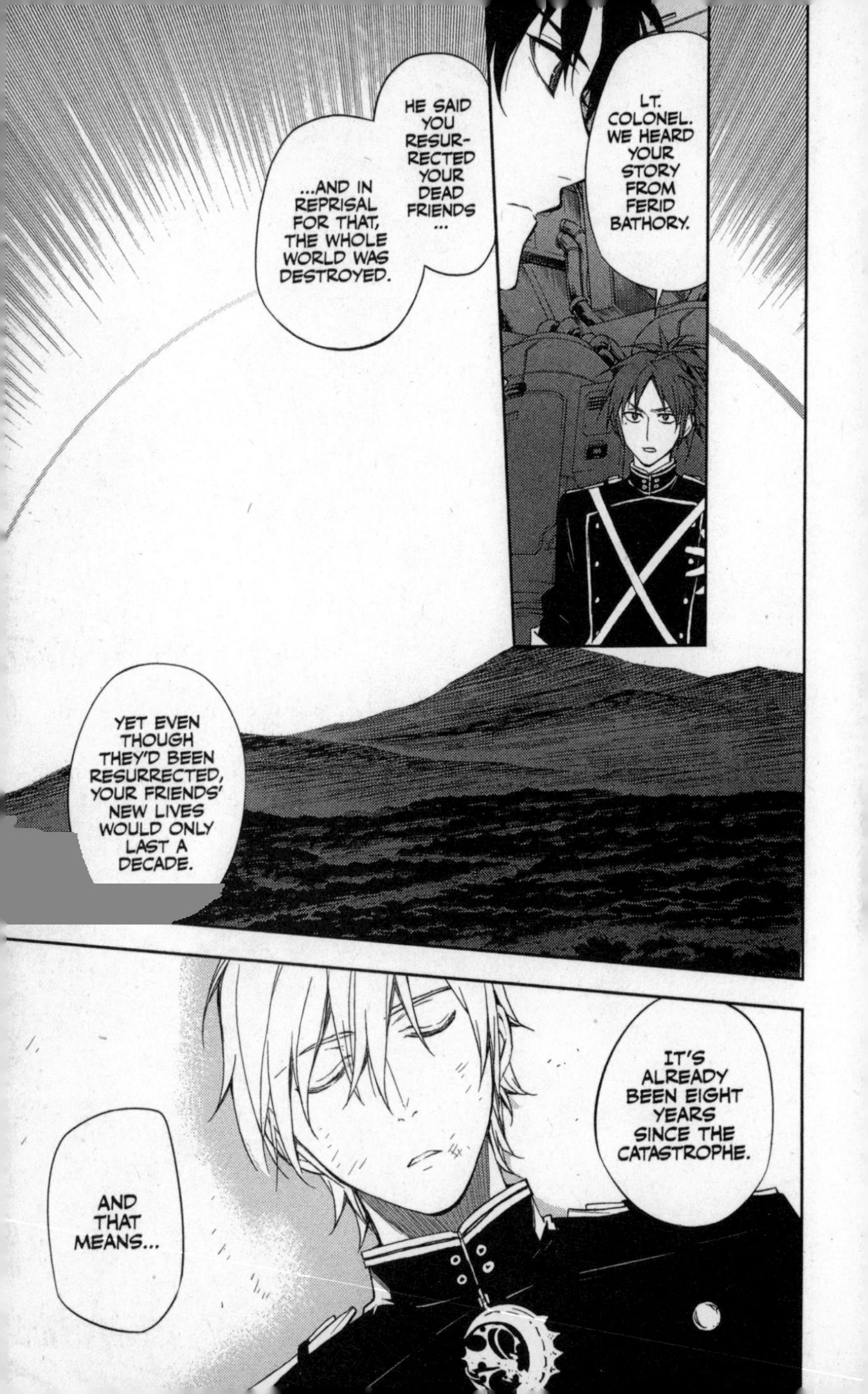
LT. COLONEL. WE HEARD YOUR STORY FROM FERID BATHORY.
HE SAID YOU RESUR-RECTED YOUR DEAD FRIENDS ...
...AND IN REPRISAL FOR THAT, THE WHOLE WORLD WAS DESTROYED.
YET EVEN THOUGH THEY'D BEEN RESURRECTED, YOUR FRIENDS' NEW LIVES WOULD ONLY LAST A DECADE.
IT'S ALREADY BEEN EIGHT YEARS SINCE THE CATASTROPHE.
AND THAT MEANS...

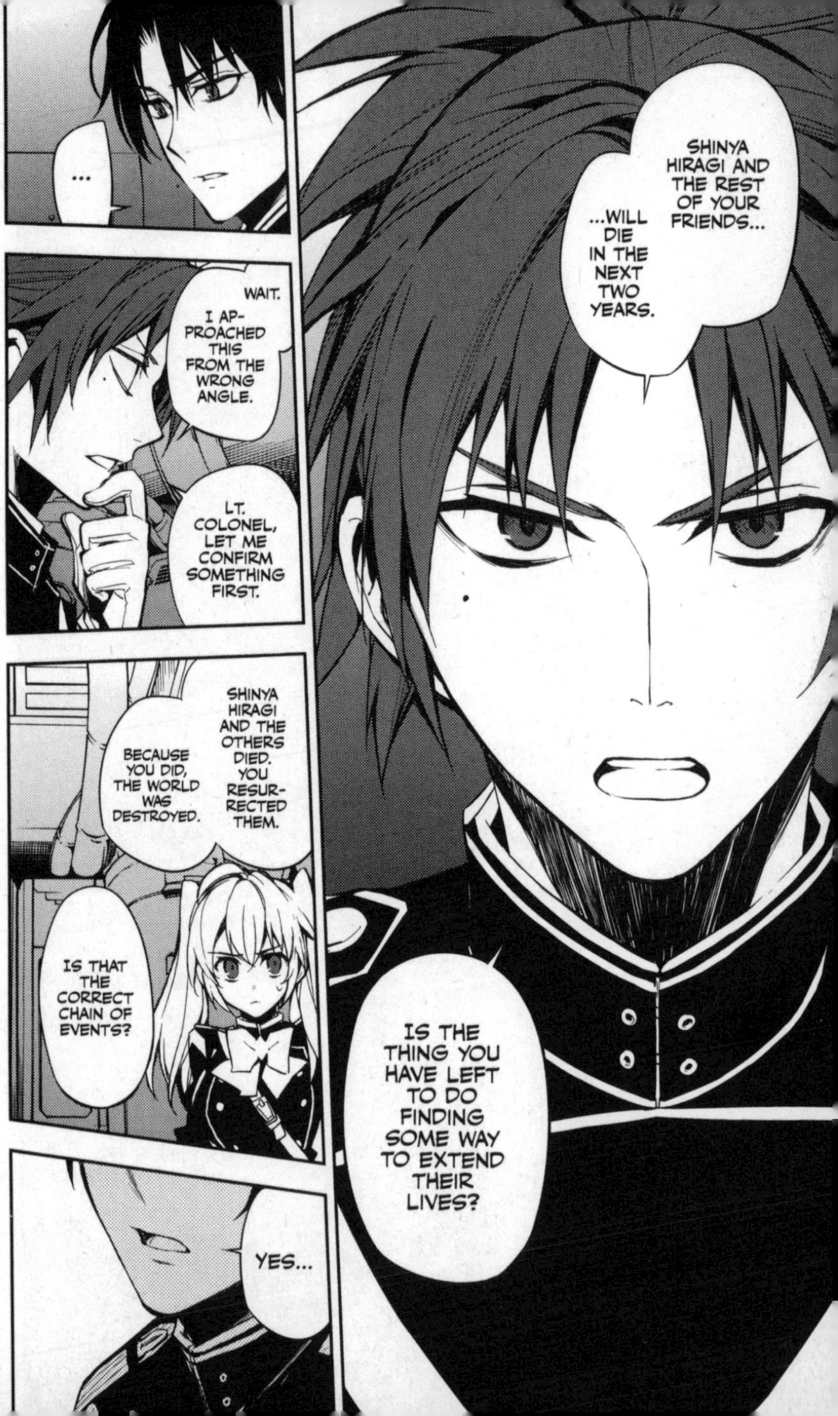
SHINYA HIRAGI AND THE REST OF YOUR FRIENDS...
...WILL DIE IN THE NEXT TWO YEARS.
IS THE THING YOU HAVE LEFT TO DO FINDING SOME WAY TO EXTEND THEIR LIVES?
...
WAIT. I APPROACHED THIS FROM THE WRONG ANGLE.
LT. COLONEL, LET ME CONFIRM SOMETHING FIRST.
SHINYA HIRAGI AND THE OTHERS DIED. YOU RESURRECTED THEM.
BECAUSE YOU DID, THE WORLD WAS DESTROYED.
IS THAT THE CORRECT CHAIN OF EVENTS?
YES...

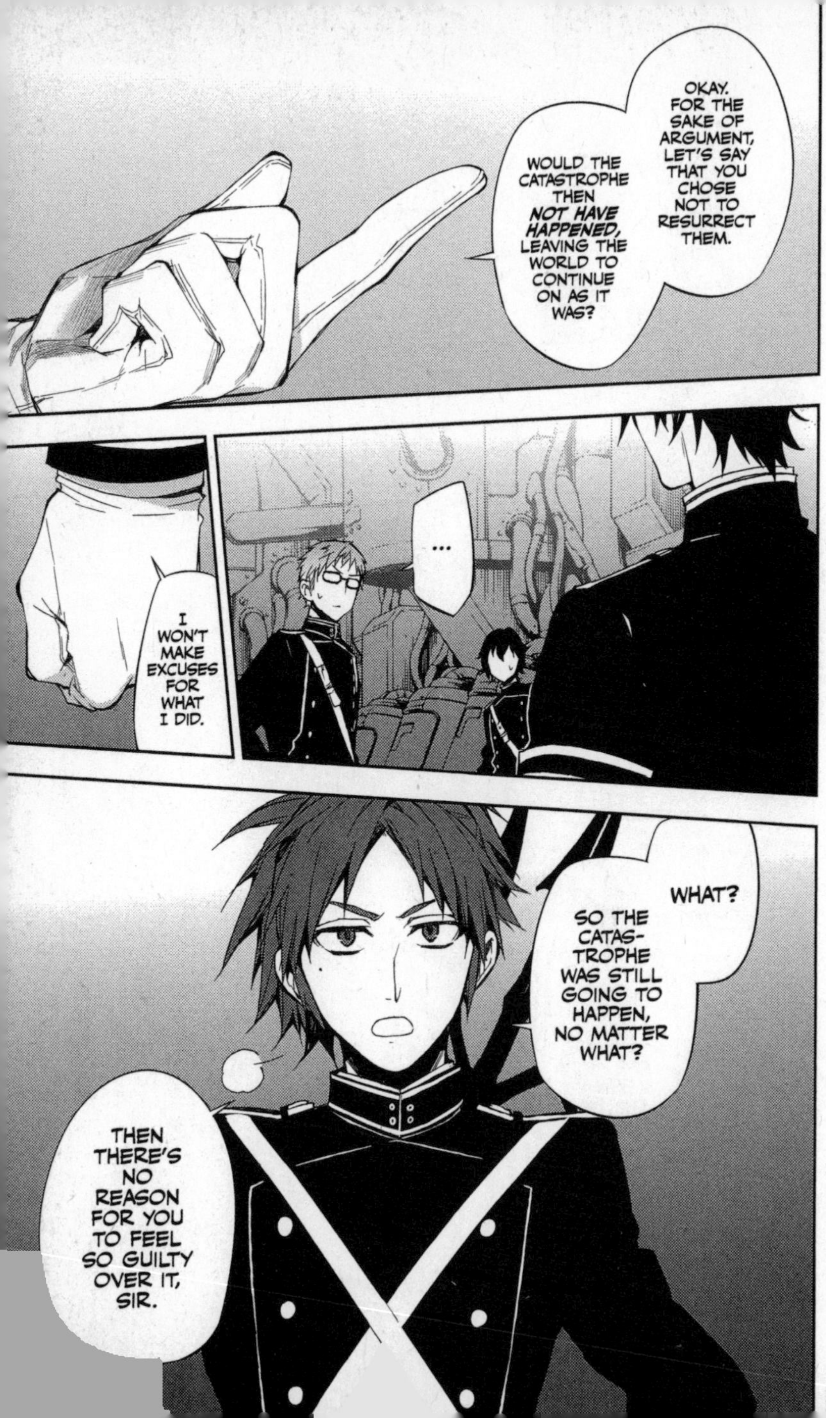
OKAY. FOR THE SAKE OF ARGUMENT, LET'S SAY THAT YOU CHOSE NOT TO RESURRECT THEM.
WOULD THE CATASTROPHE THEN NOT HAVE HAPPENED, LEAVING THE WORLD TO CONTINUE ON AS IT WAS?
...
I WON'T MAKE EXCUSES FOR WHAT I DID.
WHAT?
SO THE CATAS-TROPHE WAS STILL GOING TO HAPPEN, NO MATTER WHAT?
THEN THERE'S NO REASON FOR YOU TO FEEL SO GUILTY OVER IT, SIR.

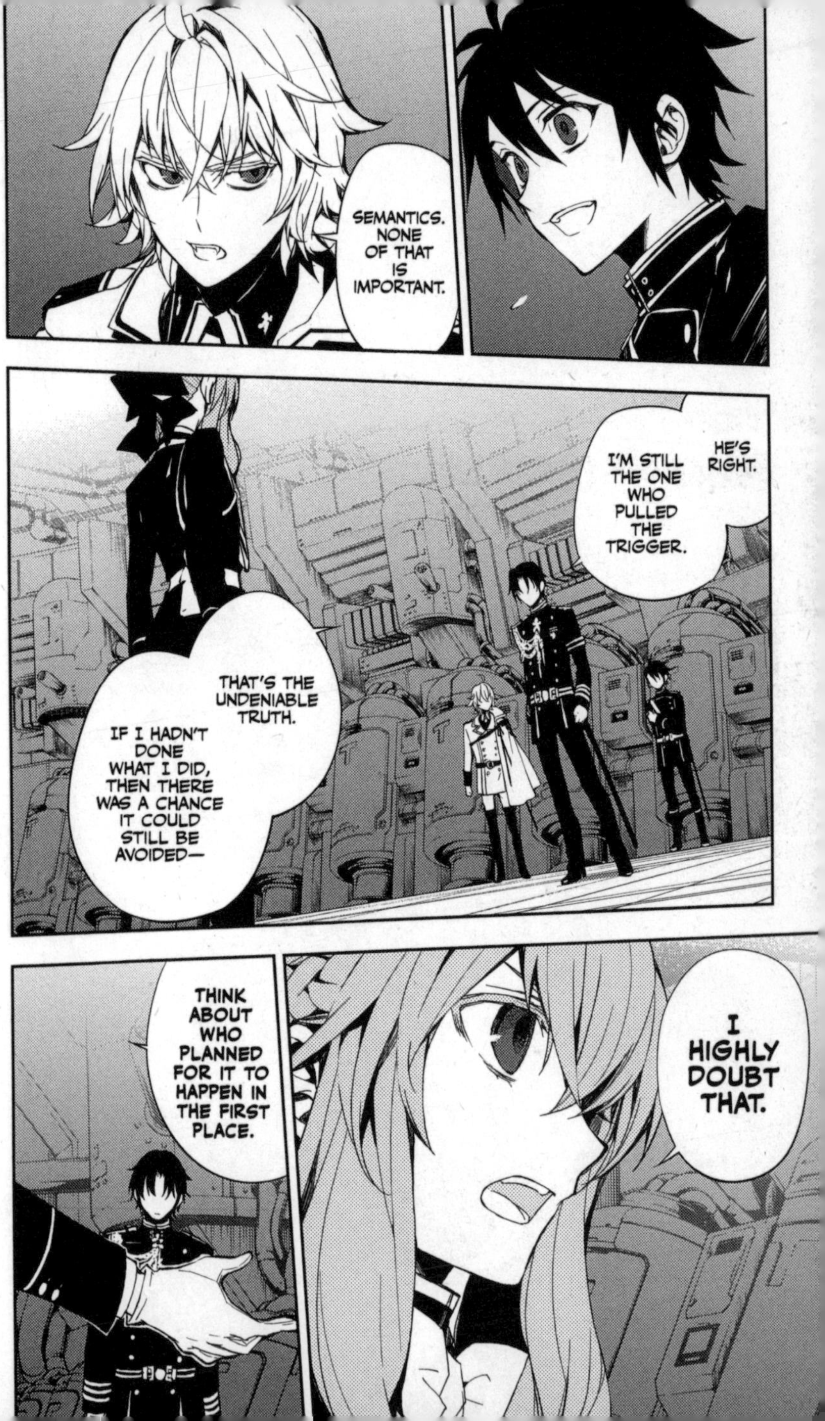
SEMANTICS. NONE OF THAT IS IMPORTANT.
HE'S RIGHT.
I'M STILL THE ONE WHO PULLED THE TRIGGER.
THAT'S THE UNDENIABLE TRUTH.
IF I HADN'T DONE WHAT I DID, THEN THERE WAS A CHANCE IT COULD STILL BE AVOIDED—
I HIGHLY DOUBT THAT.
THINK ABOUT WHO PLANNED FOR IT TO HAPPEN IN THE FIRST PLACE.

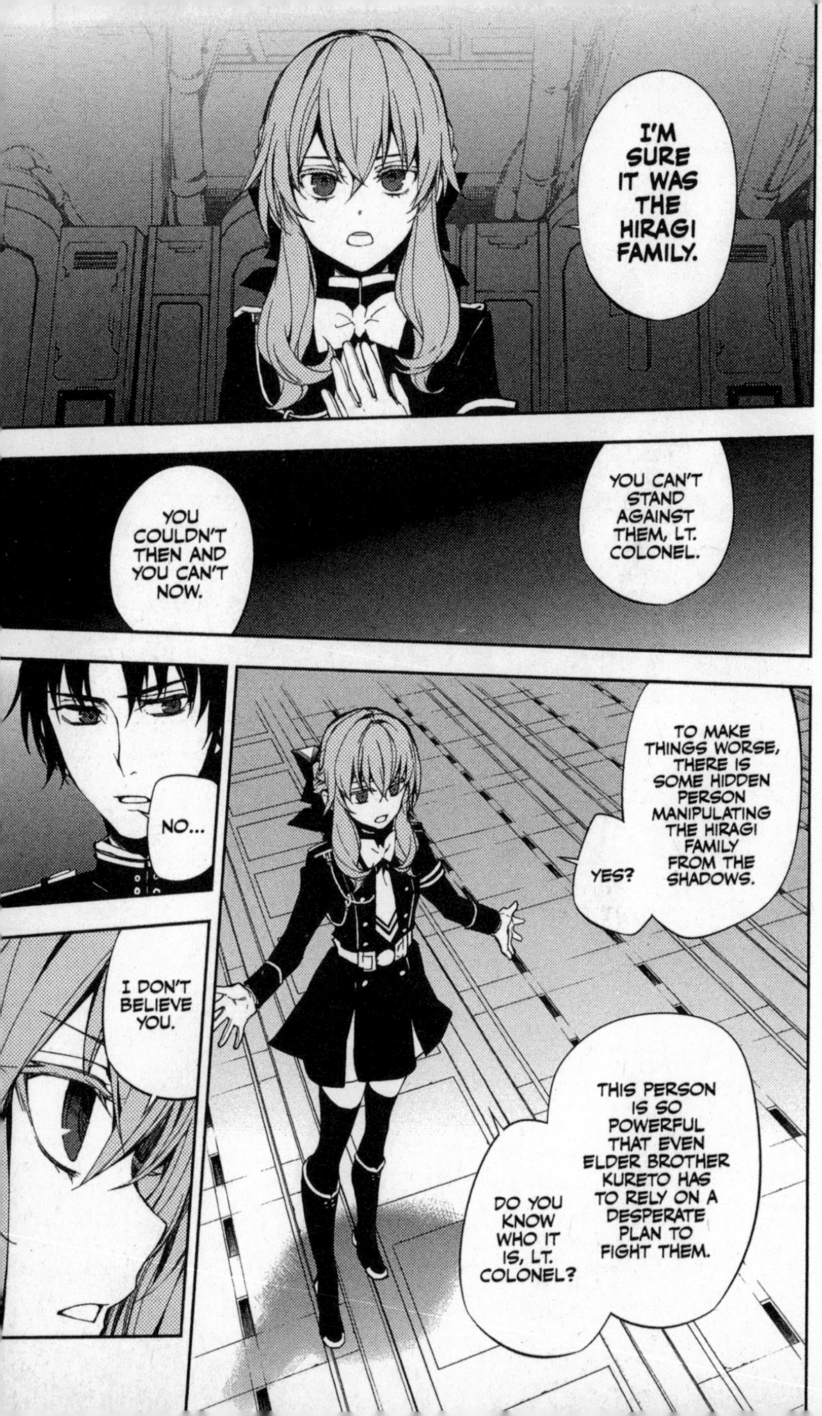

I'M SURE IT WAS THE HIRAGI FAMILY.
YOU CAN'T STAND AGAINST THEM, LT. COLONEL.
YOU COULDN'T THEN AND YOU CAN'T NOW.
TO MAKE THINGS WORSE, THERE IS SOME HIDDEN PERSON MANIPULATING THE HIRAGI FAMILY FROM THE SHADOWS.
YES?
THIS PERSON IS SO POWERFUL THAT EVEN ELDER BROTHER KURETO HAS TO RELY ON A DESPERATE PLAN TO FIGHT THEM.
DO YOU KNOW WHO IT IS, LT. COLONEL?
NO...
I DON'T BELIEVE YOU.

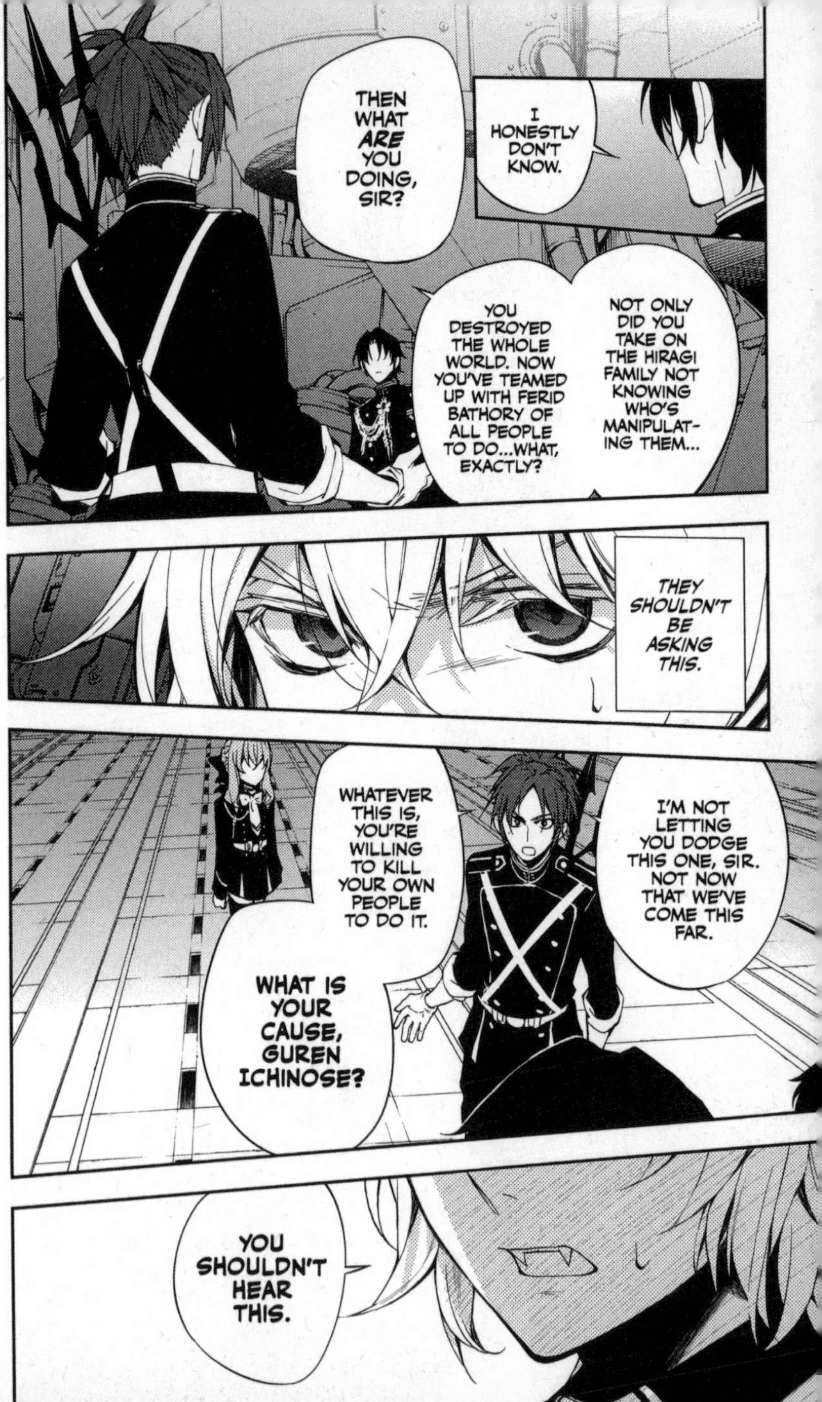
I HONESTLY DON'T KNOW.
THEN WHAT *ARE* YOU DOING, SIR?
NOT ONLY DID YOU TAKE ON THE HIRAGI FAMILY NOT KNOWING WHO'S MANIPULATING THEM...
YOU DESTROYED THE WHOLE WORLD. NOW YOU'VE TEAMED UP WITH FERID BATHORY OF ALL PEOPLE TO DO...WHAT, EXACTLY?
THEY SHOULDN'T BE ASKING THIS.
I'M NOT LETTING YOU DODGE THIS ONE, SIR. NOT NOW THAT WE'VE COME THIS FAR.
WHATEVER THIS IS, YOU'RE WILLING TO KILL YOUR OWN PEOPLE TO DO IT.
WHAT IS YOUR CAUSE, GUREN ICHINOSE?
YOU SHOULDN'T HEAR THIS.

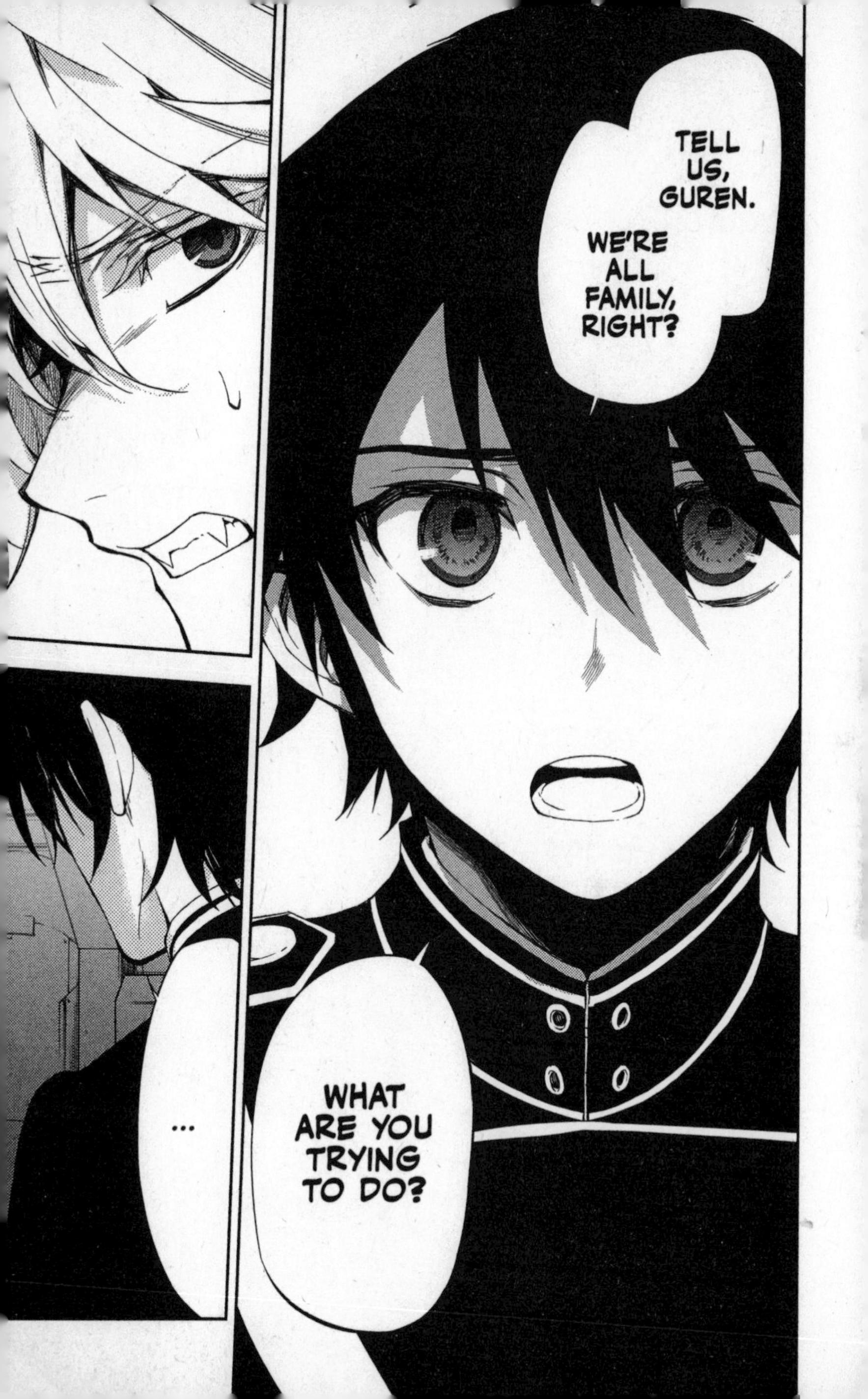
TELL US, GUREN.
WE'RE ALL FAMILY, RIGHT?
WHAT ARE YOU TRYING TO DO?
...

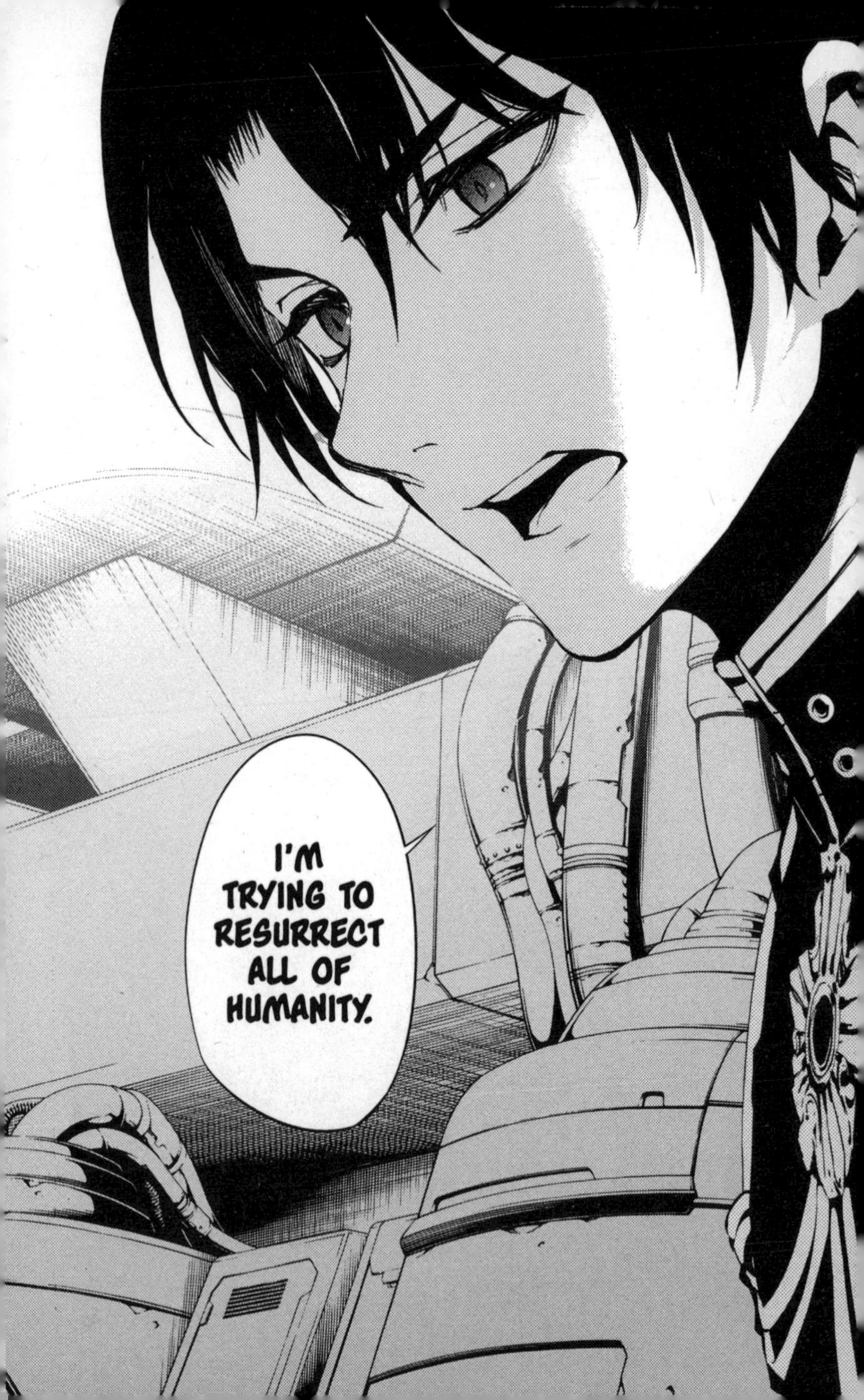
I'M TRYING TO RESURRECT ALL OF HUMANITY.

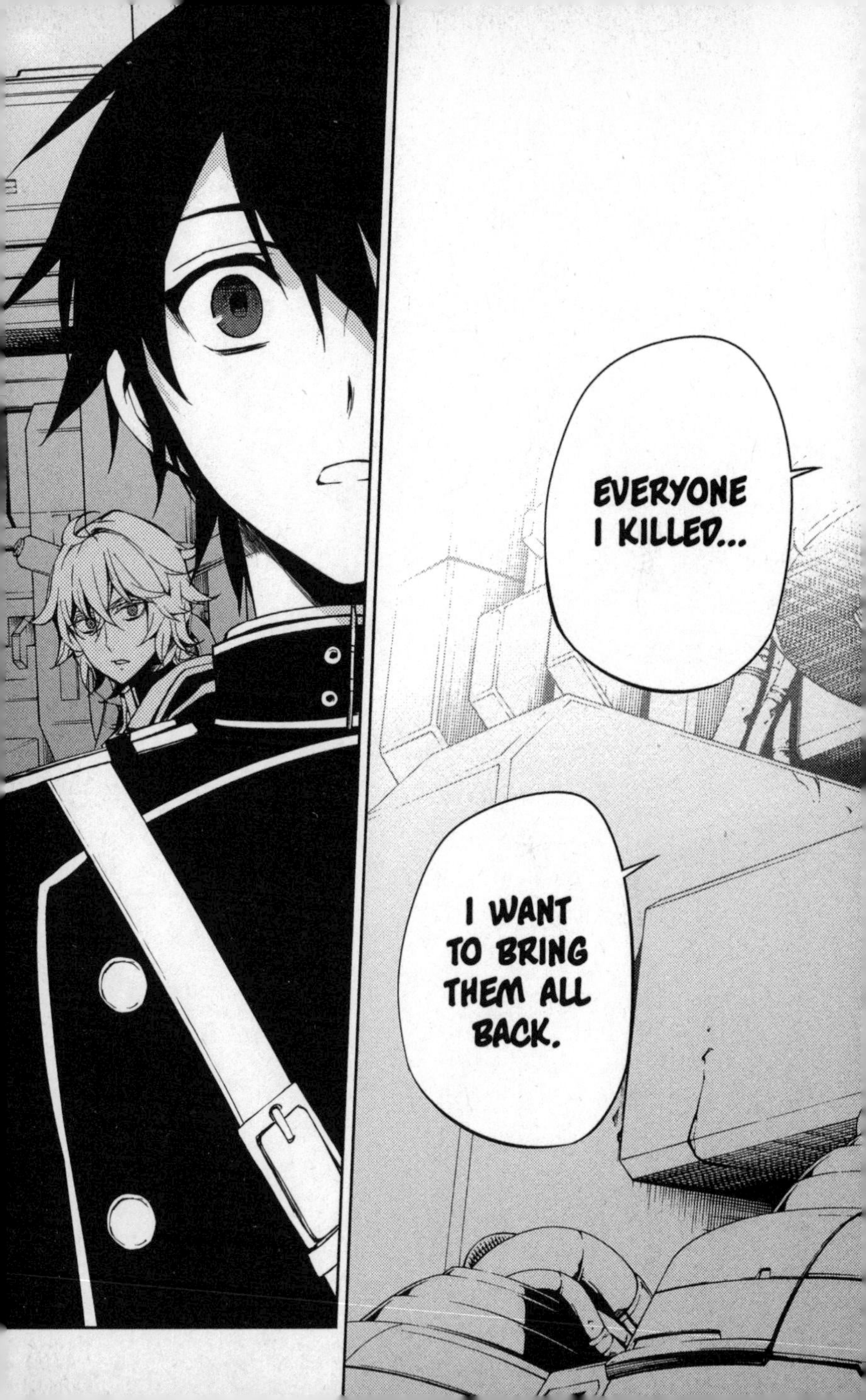
EVERYONE I KILLED...
I WANT TO BRING THEM ALL BACK.

Seraph of the End
VAMPIRE REIGN

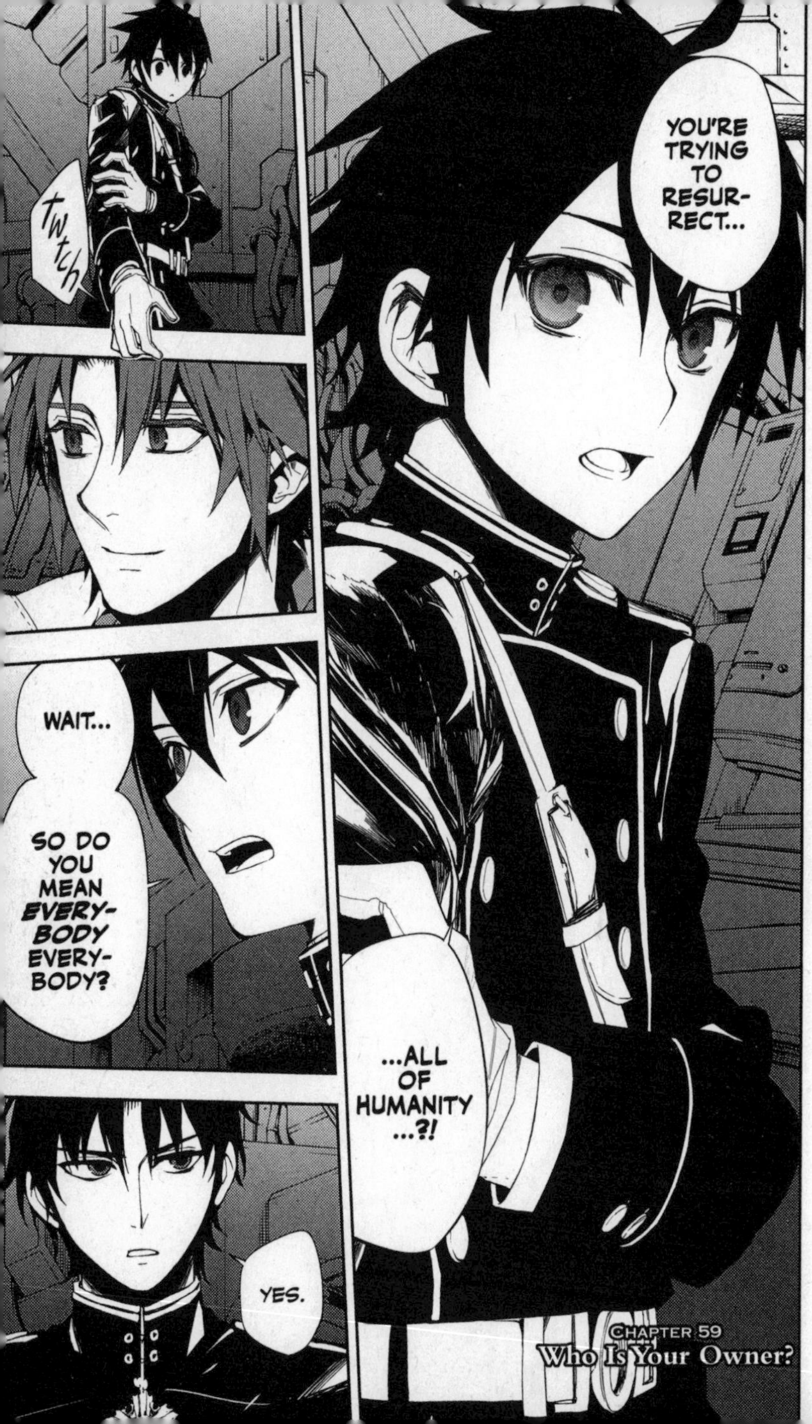
YOU'RE TRYING TO RESUR-RECT...
twitch
WAIT...
SO DO YOU MEAN *EVERY-BODY* EVERY-BODY?
...ALL OF HUMANITY ...?!
YES.
CHAPTER 59
Who Is Your Owner?

Chapter 59 Who Is Your Owner?

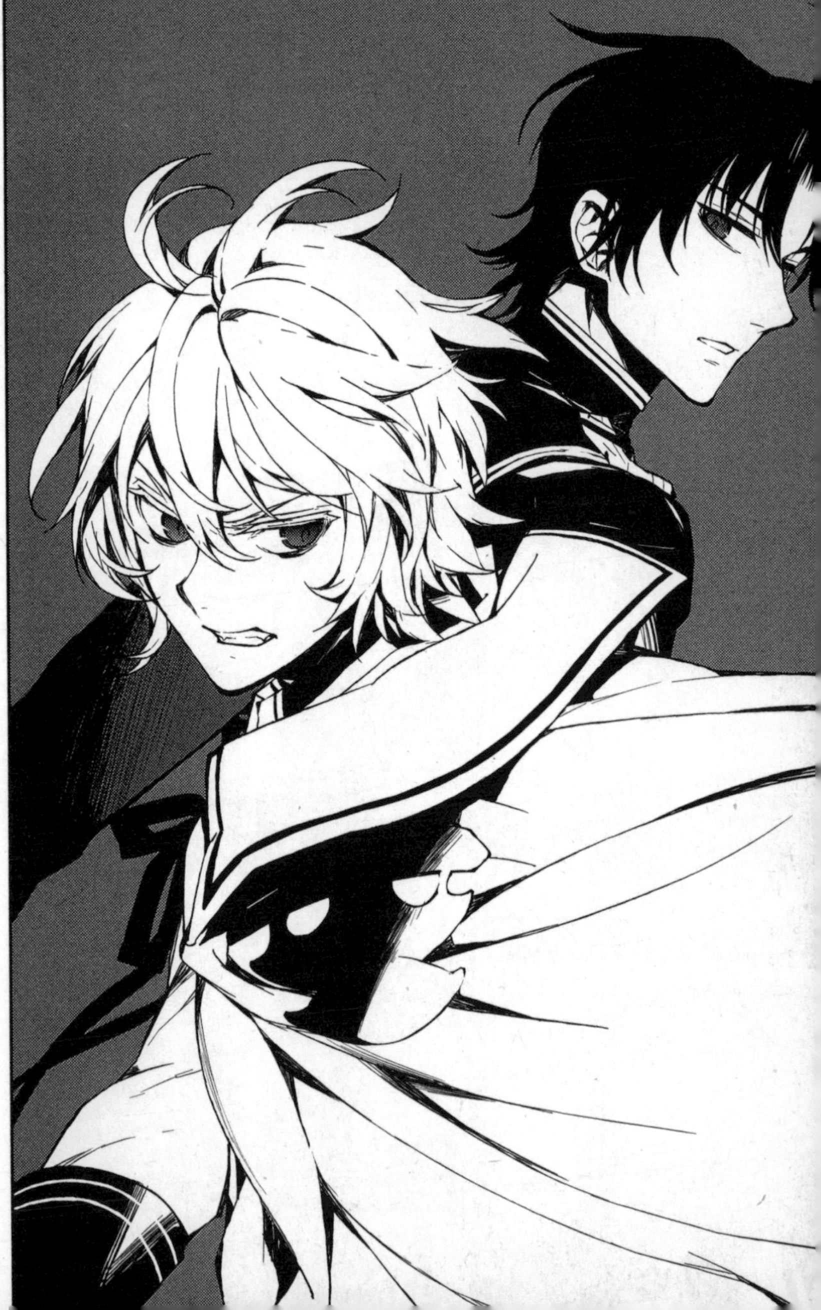

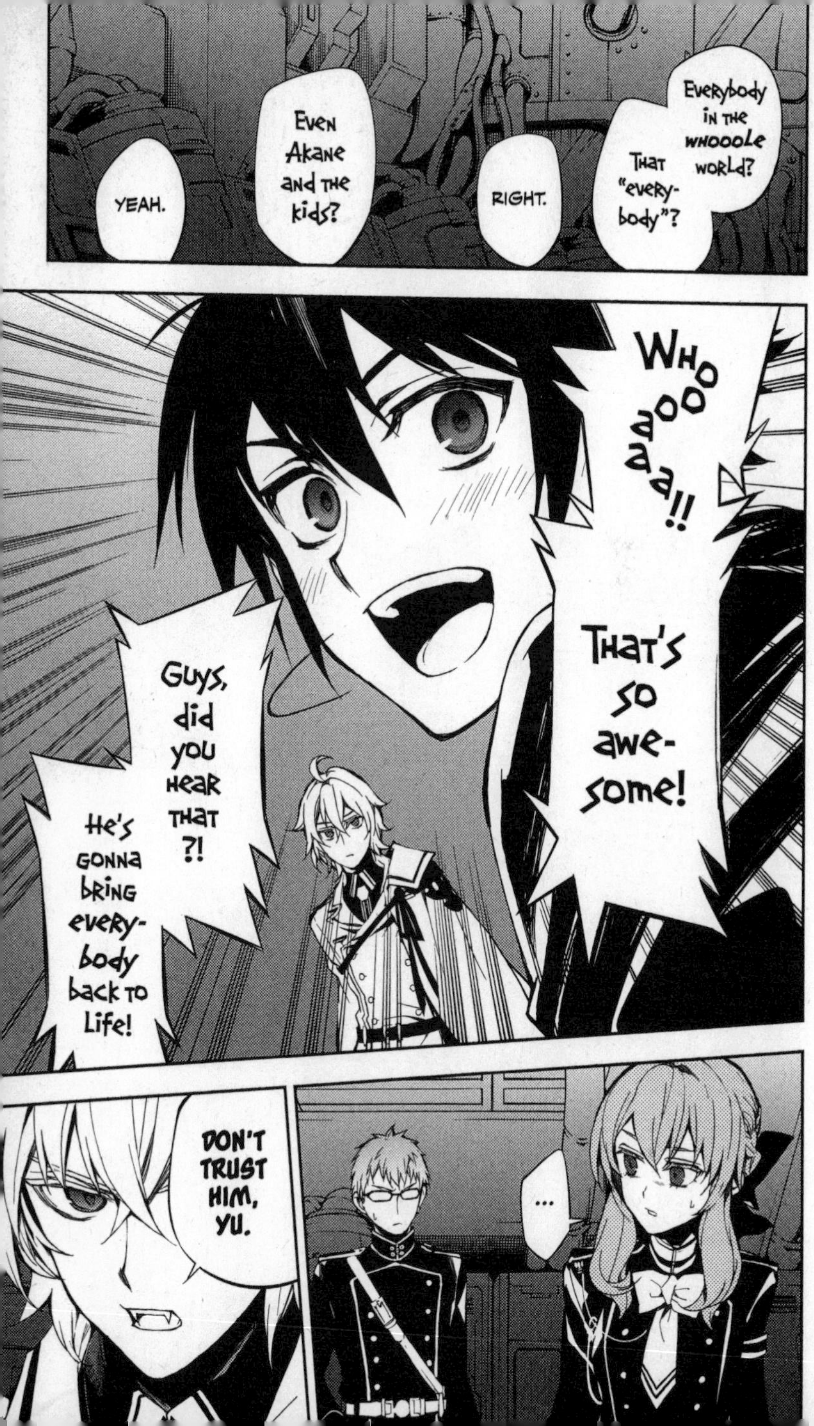
Everybody in the whoooole world?
That "everybody"?
Right.
Even Akane and the kids?
Yeah.
Whoooaaaa!!
That's so awesome!
Guys, did you hear that?!
He's gonna bring everybody back to life!
...
Don't trust him, Yu.

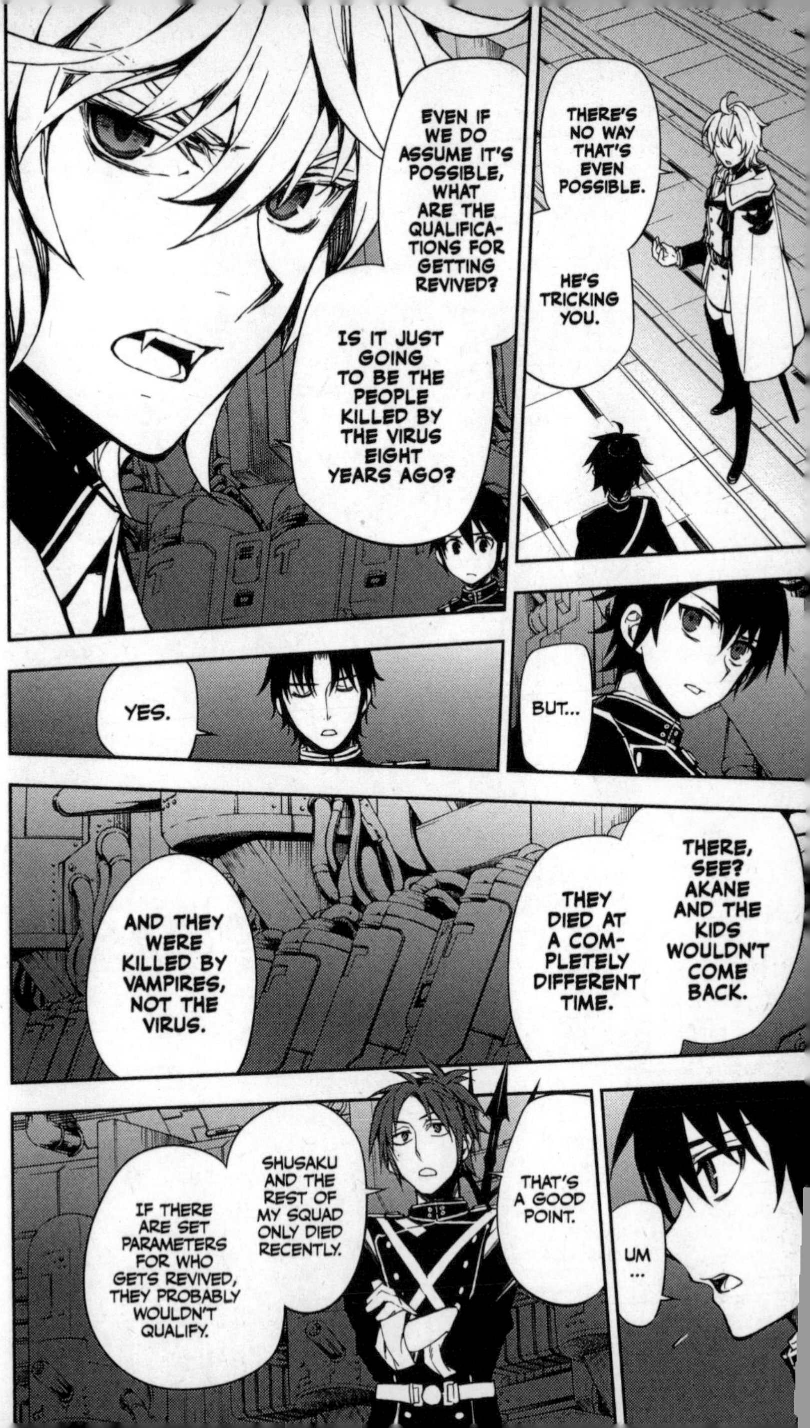
THERE'S NO WAY THAT'S EVEN POSSIBLE.
HE'S TRICKING YOU.
EVEN IF WE DO ASSUME IT'S POSSIBLE, WHAT ARE THE QUALIFICATIONS FOR GETTING REVIVED?
IS IT JUST GOING TO BE THE PEOPLE KILLED BY THE VIRUS EIGHT YEARS AGO?
BUT...
YES.
THERE, SEE? AKANE AND THE KIDS WOULDN'T COME BACK.
THEY DIED AT A COMPLETELY DIFFERENT TIME.
AND THEY WERE KILLED BY VAMPIRES, NOT THE VIRUS.
UM ...
THAT'S A GOOD POINT.
SHUSAKU AND THE REST OF MY SQUAD ONLY DIED RECENTLY.
IF THERE ARE SET PARAMETERS FOR WHO GETS REVIVED, THEY PROBABLY WOULDN'T QUALIFY.

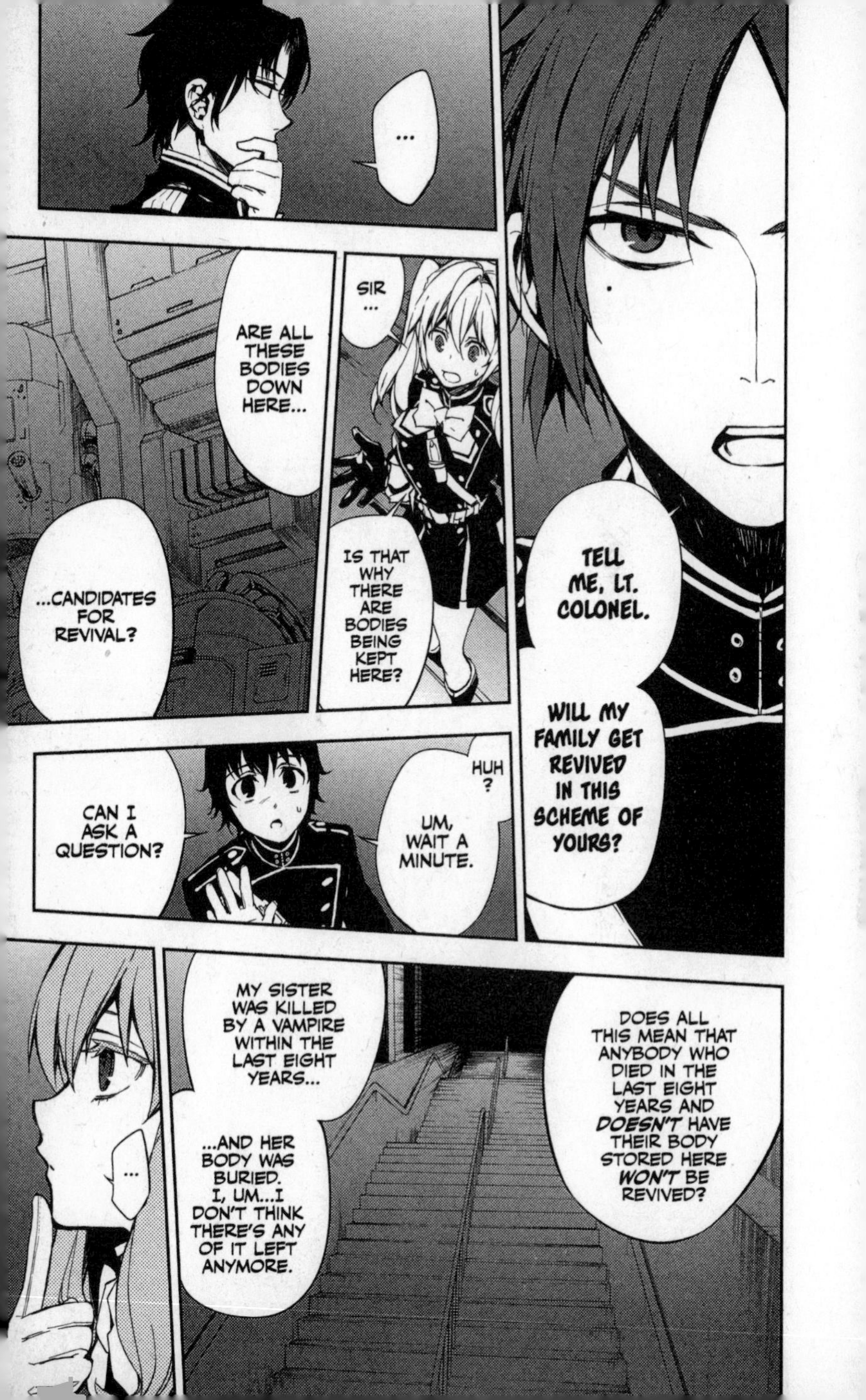
TELL ME, LT. COLONEL.
WILL MY FAMILY GET REVIVED IN THIS SCHEME OF YOURS?
...
SIR...
ARE ALL THESE BODIES DOWN HERE...
IS THAT WHY THERE ARE BODIES BEING KEPT HERE?
...CANDIDATES FOR REVIVAL?
HUH?
UM, WAIT A MINUTE.
CAN I ASK A QUESTION?
DOES ALL THIS MEAN THAT ANYBODY WHO DIED IN THE LAST EIGHT YEARS AND *DOESN'T* HAVE THEIR BODY STORED HERE *WON'T* BE REVIVED?
MY SISTER WAS KILLED BY A VAMPIRE WITHIN THE LAST EIGHT YEARS...
...AND HER BODY WAS BURIED. I, UM...I DON'T THINK THERE'S ANY OF IT LEFT ANYMORE.
...

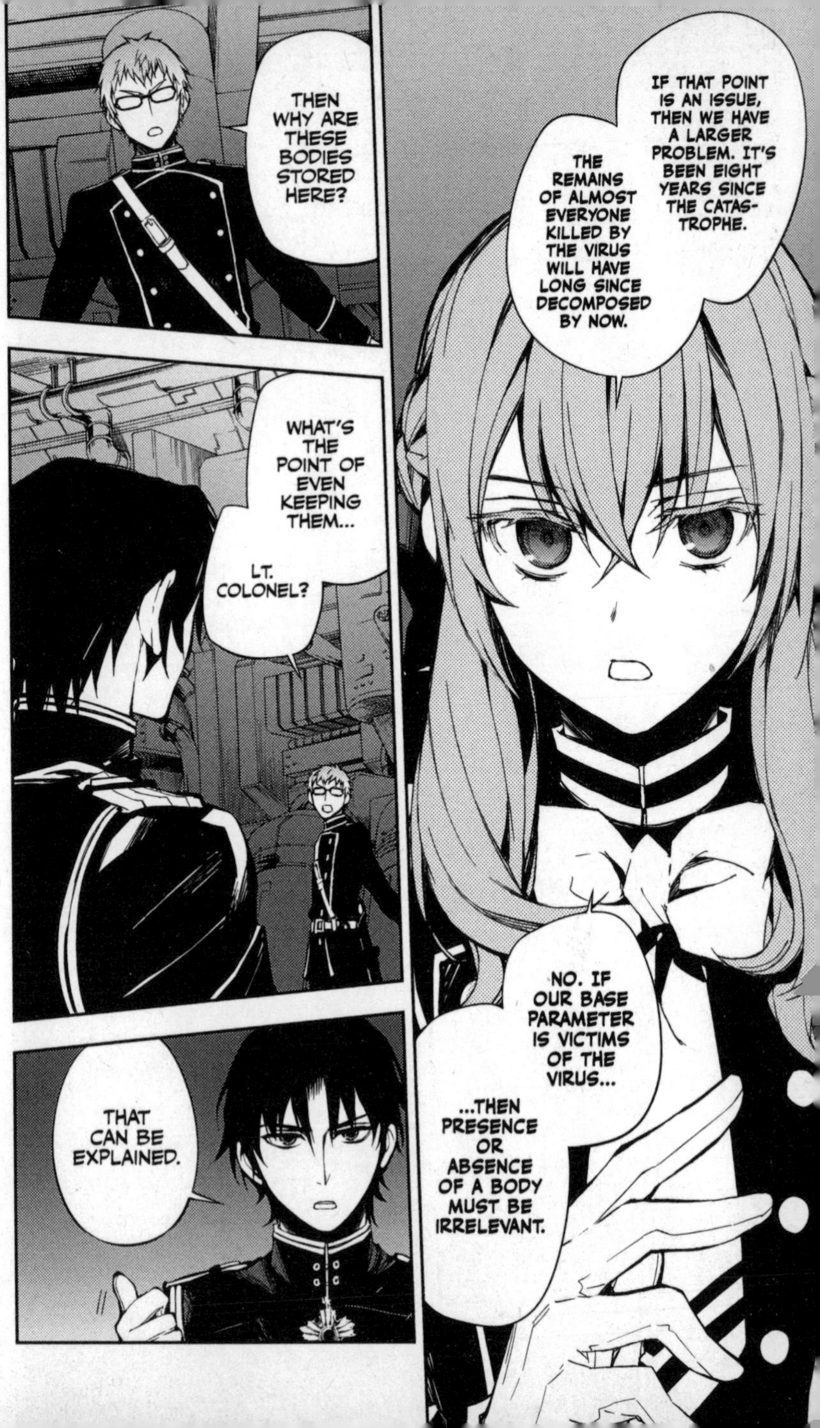
IF THAT POINT IS AN ISSUE, THEN WE HAVE A LARGER PROBLEM. IT'S BEEN EIGHT YEARS SINCE THE CATASTROPHE.
THE REMAINS OF ALMOST EVERYONE KILLED BY THE VIRUS WILL HAVE LONG SINCE DECOMPOSED BY NOW.
NO. IF OUR BASE PARAMETER IS VICTIMS OF THE VIRUS...
...THEN PRESENCE OR ABSENCE OF A BODY MUST BE IRRELEVANT.
THEN WHY ARE THESE BODIES STORED HERE?
WHAT'S THE POINT OF EVEN KEEPING THEM...
LT. COLONEL?
THAT CAN BE EXPLAINED.

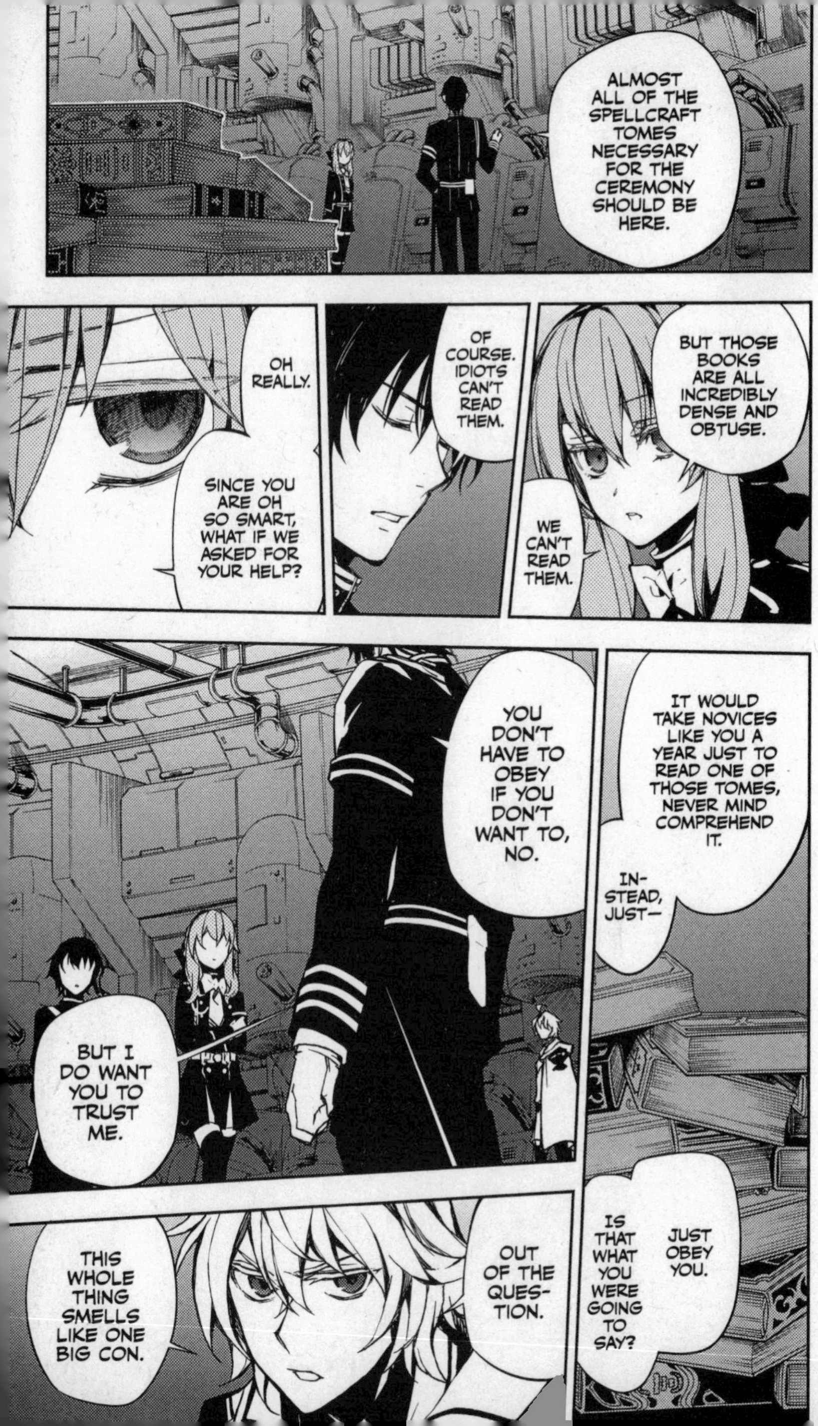
ALMOST ALL OF THE SPELLCRAFT TOMES NECESSARY FOR THE CEREMONY SHOULD BE HERE.
BUT THOSE BOOKS ARE ALL INCREDIBLY DENSE AND OBTUSE.
WE CAN'T READ THEM.
OF COURSE. IDIOTS CAN'T READ THEM.
OH REALLY.
SINCE YOU ARE OH SO SMART, WHAT IF WE ASKED FOR YOUR HELP?
IT WOULD TAKE NOVICES LIKE YOU A YEAR JUST TO READ ONE OF THOSE TOMES, NEVER MIND COMPREHEND IT.
IN-STEAD, JUST—
YOU DON'T HAVE TO OBEY IF YOU DON'T WANT TO, NO.
BUT I DO WANT YOU TO TRUST ME.
JUST OBEY YOU.
IS THAT WHAT YOU WERE GOING TO SAY?
OUT OF THE QUES-TION.
THIS WHOLE THING SMELLS LIKE ONE BIG CON.

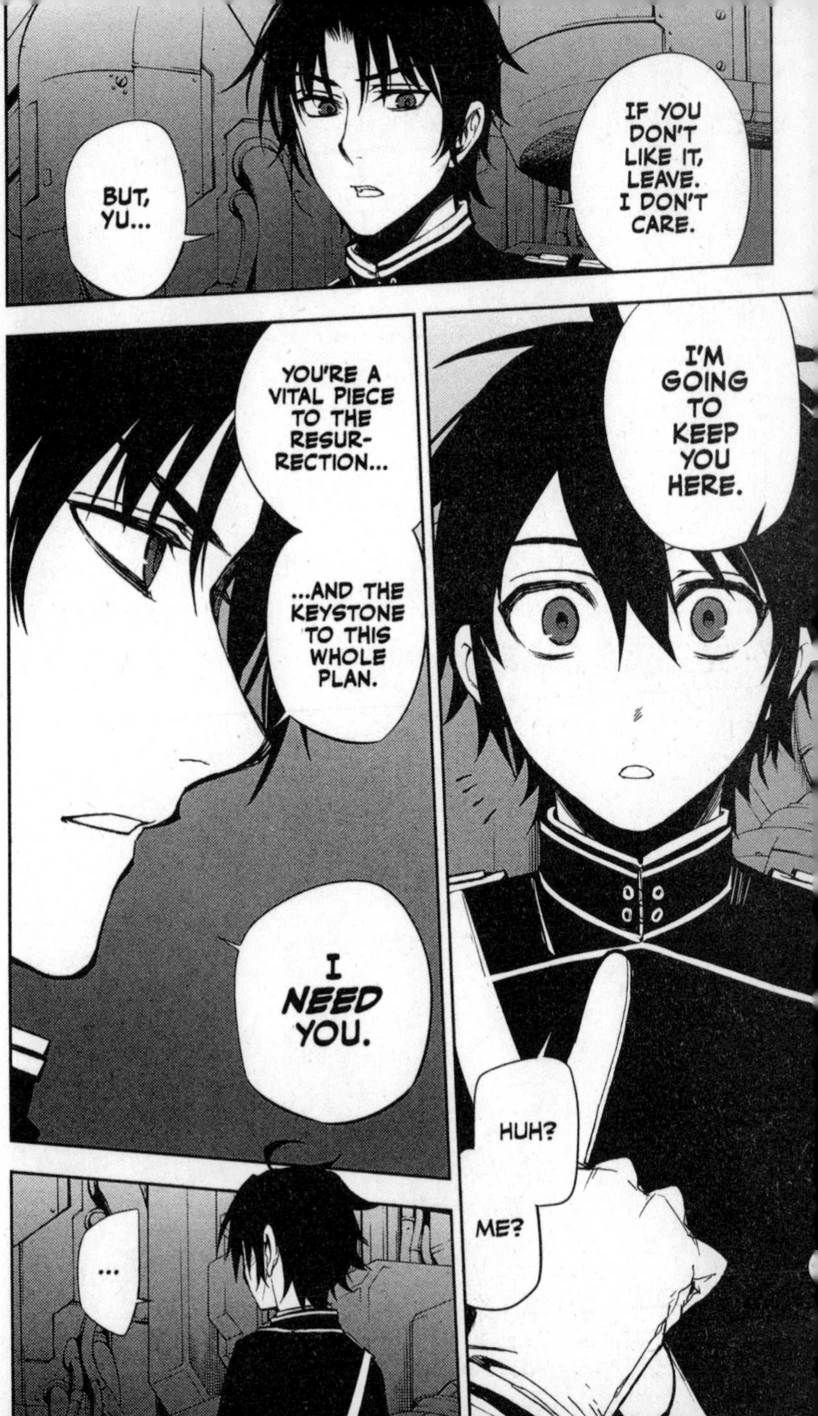
IF YOU DON'T LIKE IT, LEAVE. I DON'T CARE.
BUT, YU...
I'M GOING TO KEEP YOU HERE.
HUH?
ME?
YOU'RE A VITAL PIECE TO THE RESURRECTION...
...AND THE KEYSTONE TO THIS WHOLE PLAN.
I *NEED* YOU.
...

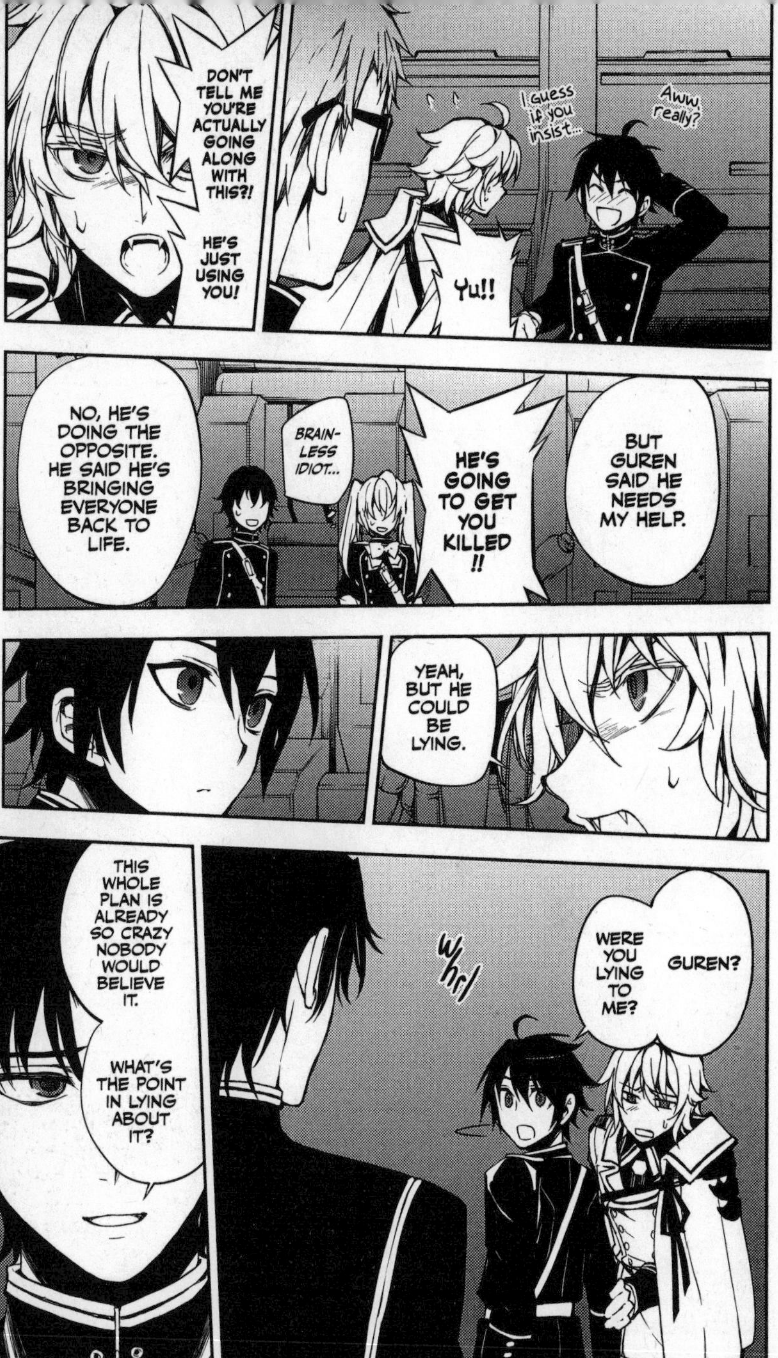

Aww, really?
I guess if you insist...
Yu!!
DON'T TELL ME YOU'RE ACTUALLY GOING ALONG WITH THIS?!
HE'S JUST USING YOU!
BUT GUREN SAID HE NEEDS MY HELP.
HE'S GOING TO GET YOU KILLED!!
BRAIN-LESS IDIOT...
NO, HE'S DOING THE OPPOSITE. HE SAID HE'S BRINGING EVERYONE BACK TO LIFE.
YEAH, BUT HE COULD BE LYING.
GUREN?
WERE YOU LYING TO ME?
whrl
THIS WHOLE PLAN IS ALREADY SO CRAZY NOBODY WOULD BELIEVE IT.
WHAT'S THE POINT IN LYING ABOUT IT?

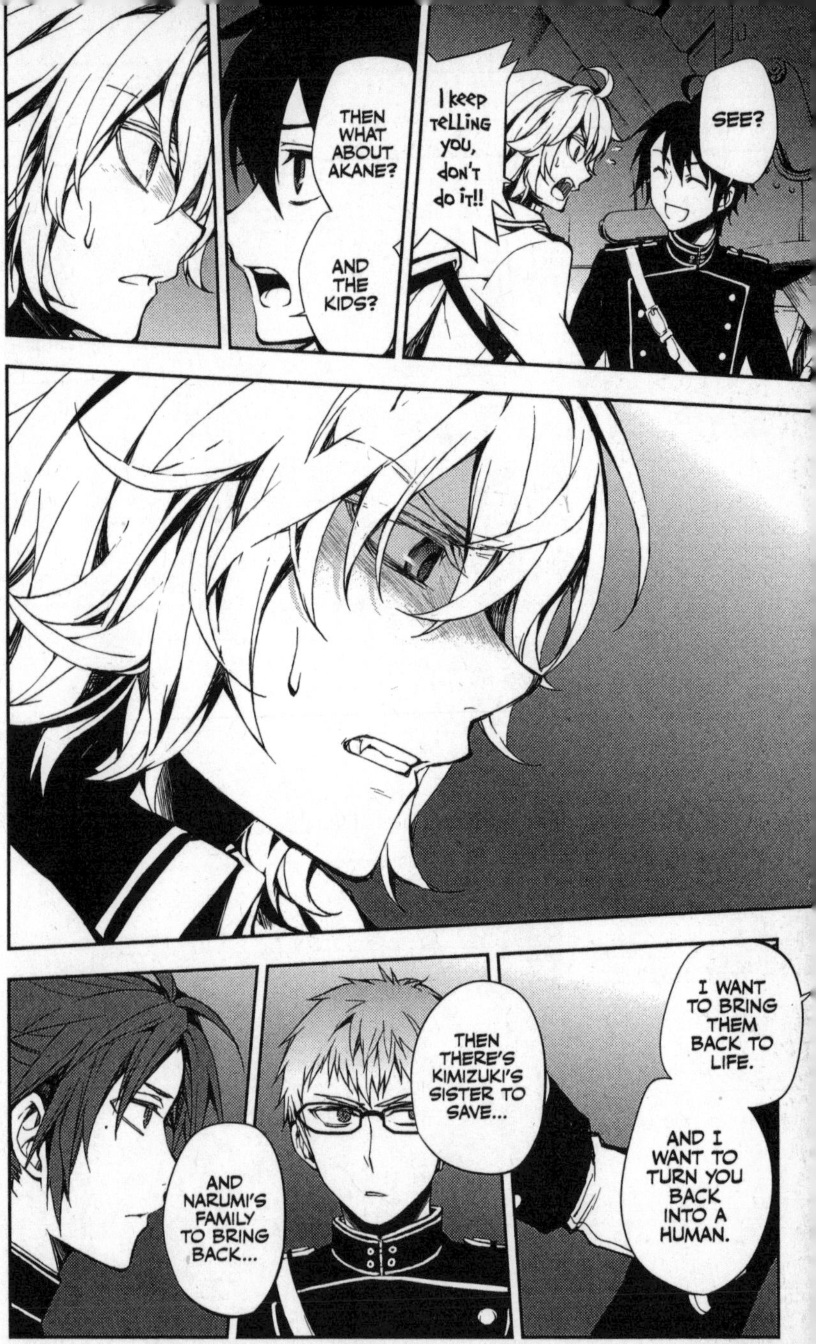
SEE?
I keep telling you, don't do it!!
THEN WHAT ABOUT AKANE?
AND THE KIDS?
I WANT TO BRING THEM BACK TO LIFE.
AND I WANT TO TURN YOU BACK INTO A HUMAN.
THEN THERE'S KIMIZUKI'S SISTER TO SAVE...
AND NARUMI'S FAMILY TO BRING BACK...

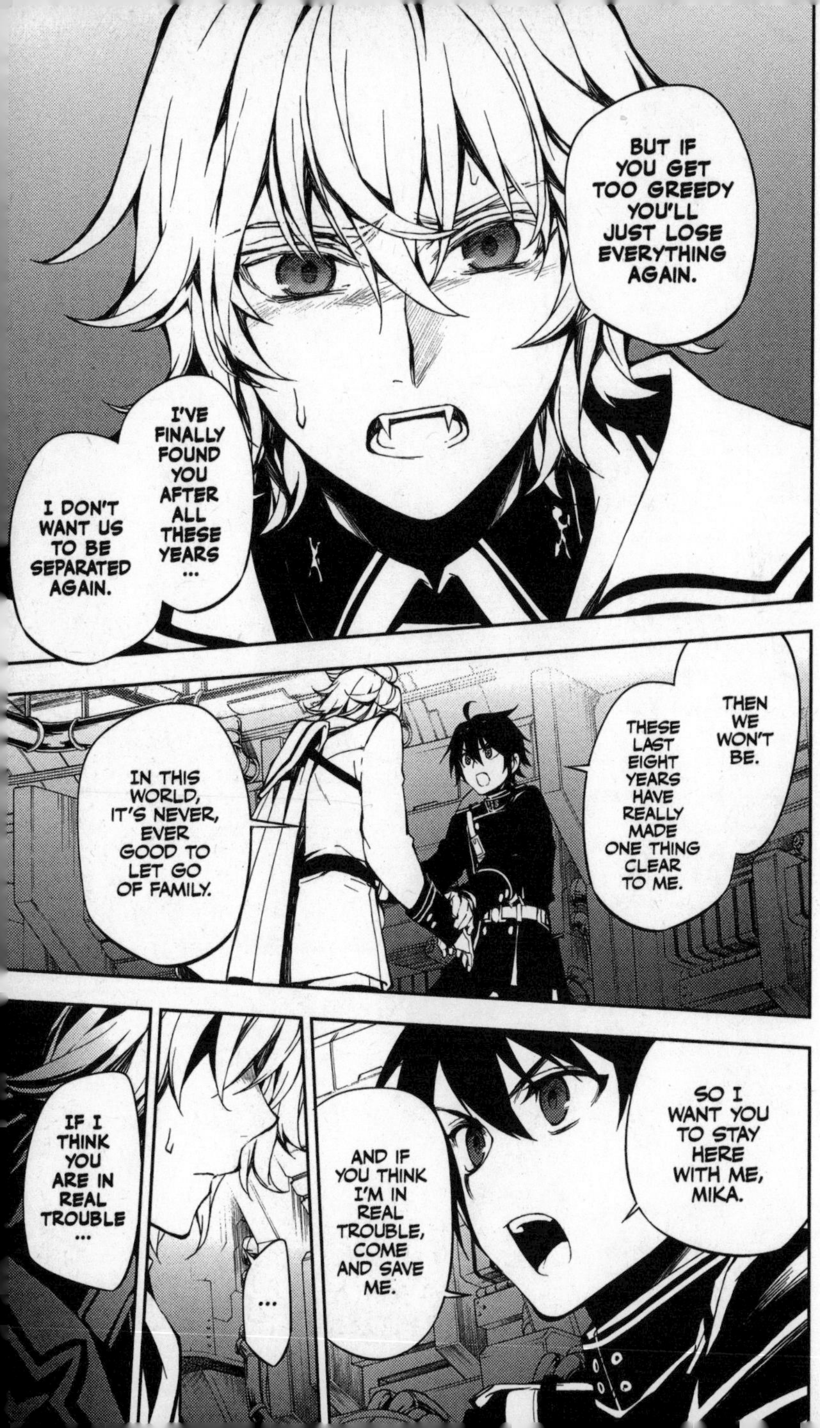
BUT IF YOU GET TOO GREEDY YOU'LL JUST LOSE EVERYTHING AGAIN.
I'VE FINALLY FOUND YOU AFTER ALL THESE YEARS...
I DON'T WANT US TO BE SEPARATED AGAIN.
THEN WE WON'T BE.
THESE LAST EIGHT YEARS HAVE REALLY MADE ONE THING CLEAR TO ME.
IN THIS WORLD, IT'S NEVER, EVER GOOD TO LET GO OF FAMILY.
SO I WANT YOU TO STAY HERE WITH ME, MIKA.
AND IF YOU THINK I'M IN REAL TROUBLE, COME AND SAVE ME.
...
IF I THINK YOU ARE IN REAL TROUBLE...

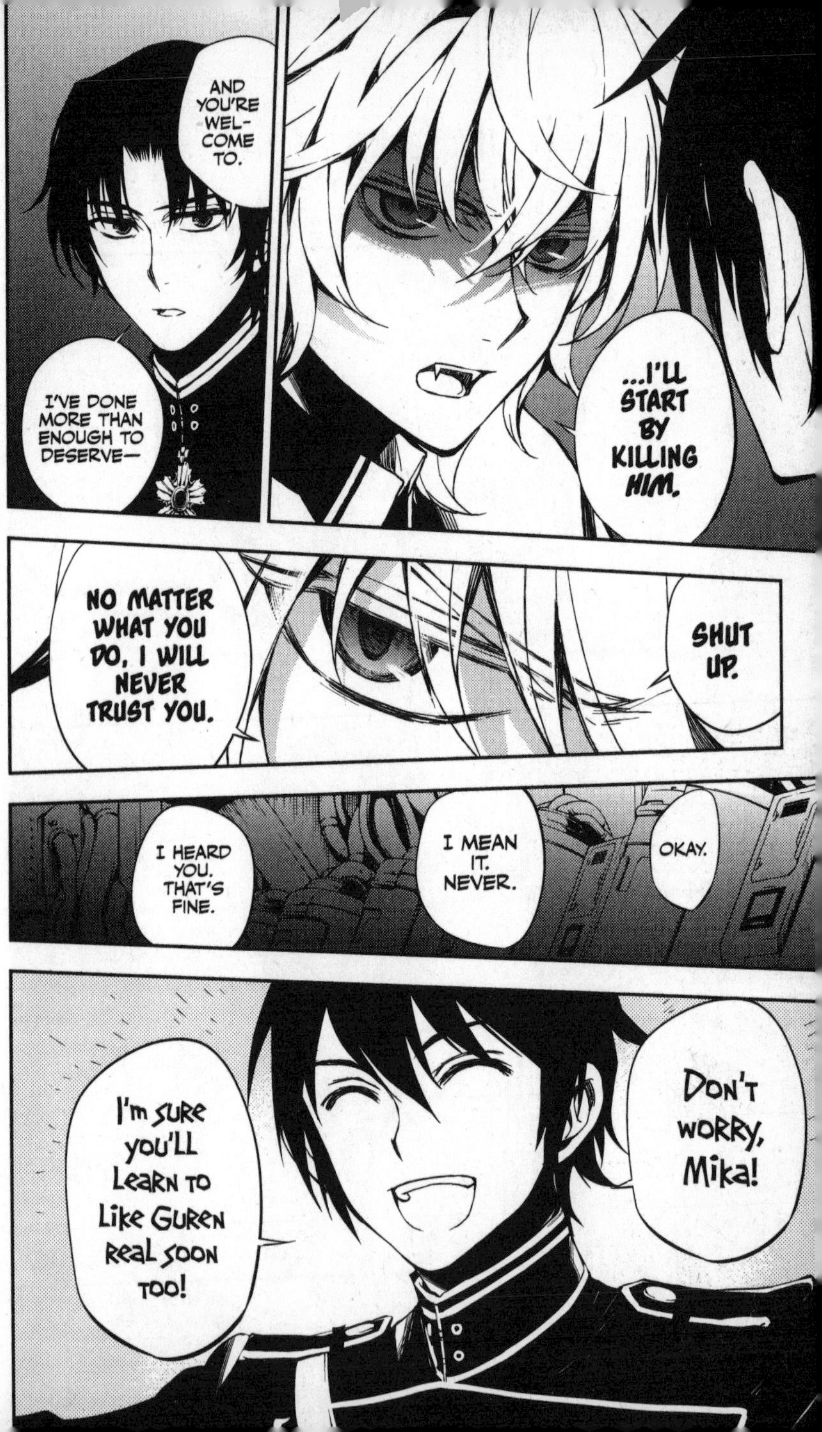
...I'LL START BY KILLING HIM.
AND YOU'RE WEL-COME TO.
I'VE DONE MORE THAN ENOUGH TO DESERVE—
SHUT UP.
NO MATTER WHAT YOU DO, I WILL NEVER TRUST YOU.
OKAY.
I MEAN IT. NEVER.
I HEARD YOU. THAT'S FINE.
Don't worry, Mika!
I'm sure you'll learn to like Guren real soon too!

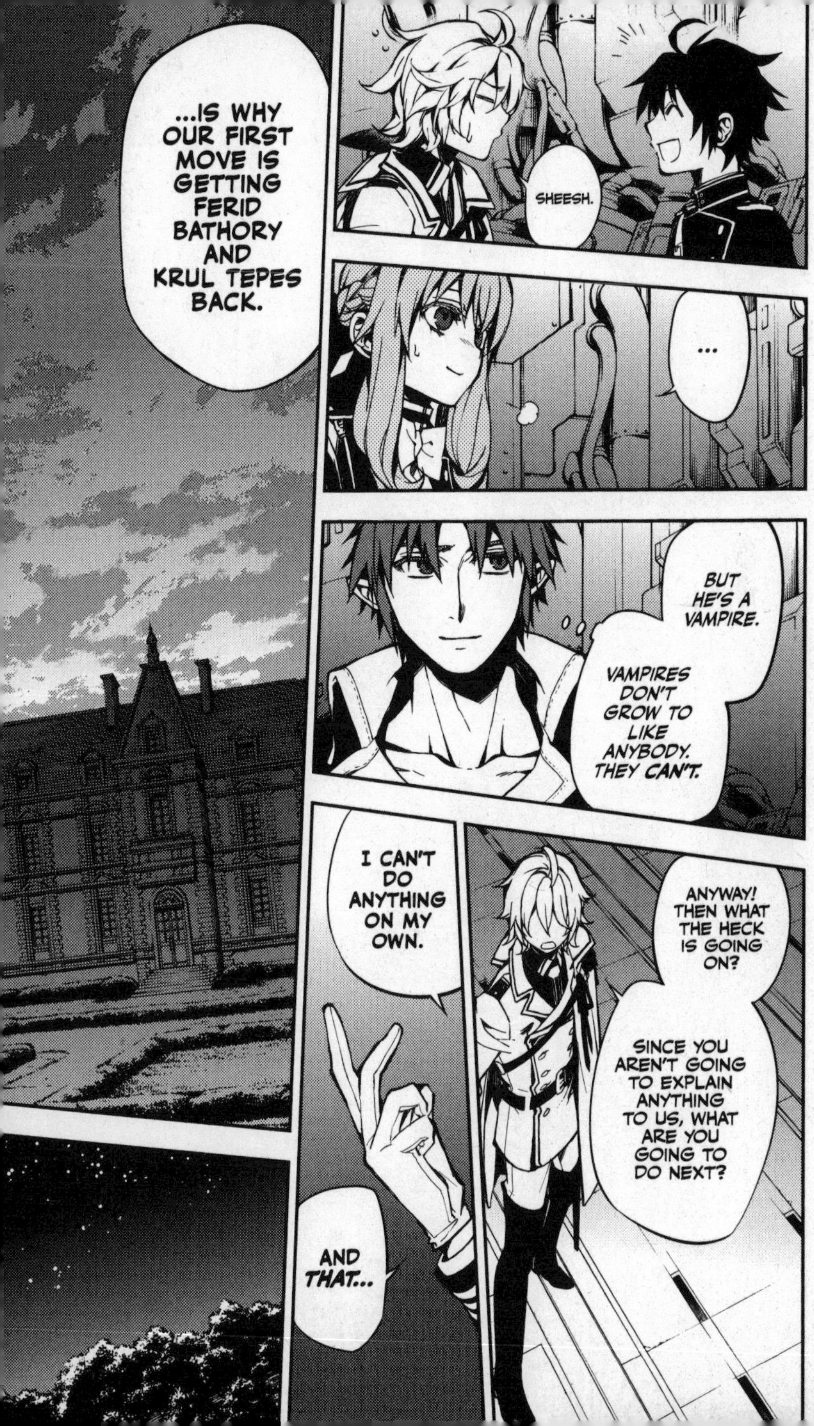
SHEESH.
...
BUT HE'S A VAMPIRE.
VAMPIRES DON'T GROW TO LIKE ANYBODY. THEY *CAN'T.*
...IS WHY OUR FIRST MOVE IS GETTING FERID BATHORY AND KRUL TEPES BACK.
ANYWAY! THEN WHAT THE HECK IS GOING ON?
SINCE YOU AREN'T GOING TO EXPLAIN ANYTHING TO US, WHAT ARE YOU GOING TO DO NEXT?
I CAN'T DO ANYTHING ON MY OWN.
AND *THAT...*

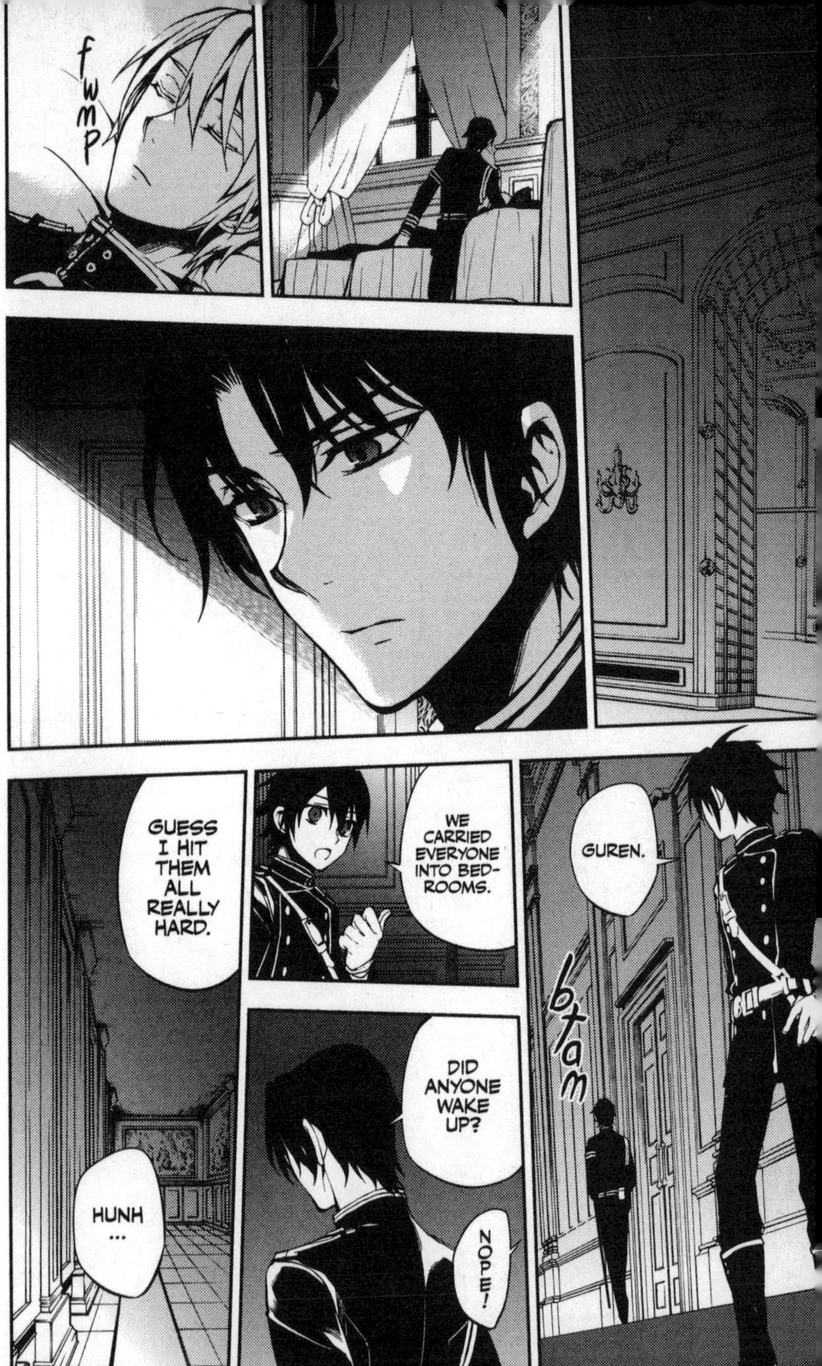
fwmp
GUREN.
btam
WE CARRIED EVERYONE INTO BED-ROOMS.
DID ANYONE WAKE UP?
NOPE!
GUESS I HIT THEM ALL REALLY HARD.
HUNH ...

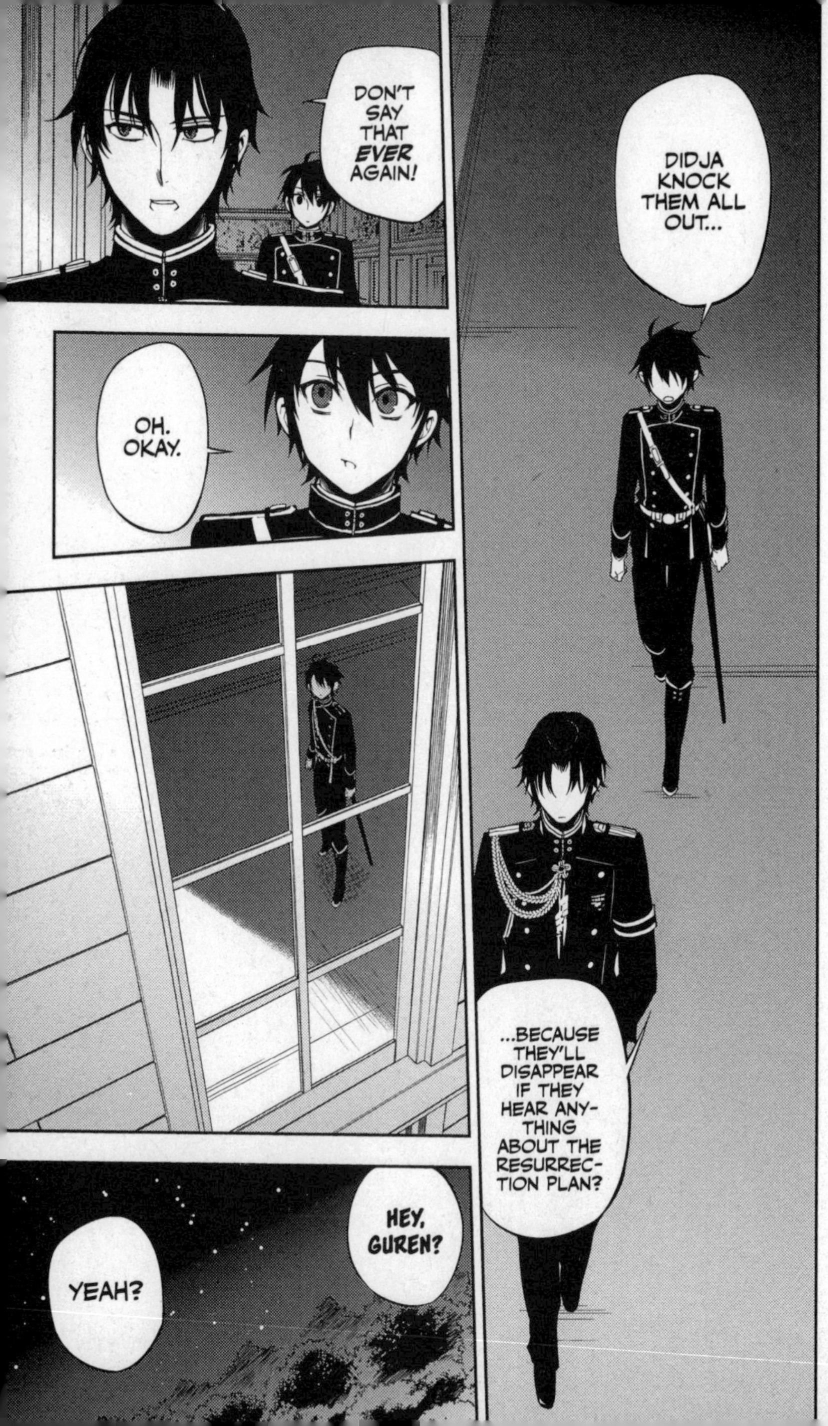
DIDJA KNOCK THEM ALL OUT...
...BECAUSE THEY'LL DISAPPEAR IF THEY HEAR ANYTHING ABOUT THE RESURRECTION PLAN?
DON'T SAY THAT *EVER* AGAIN!
OH. OKAY.
HEY, GUREN?
YEAH?

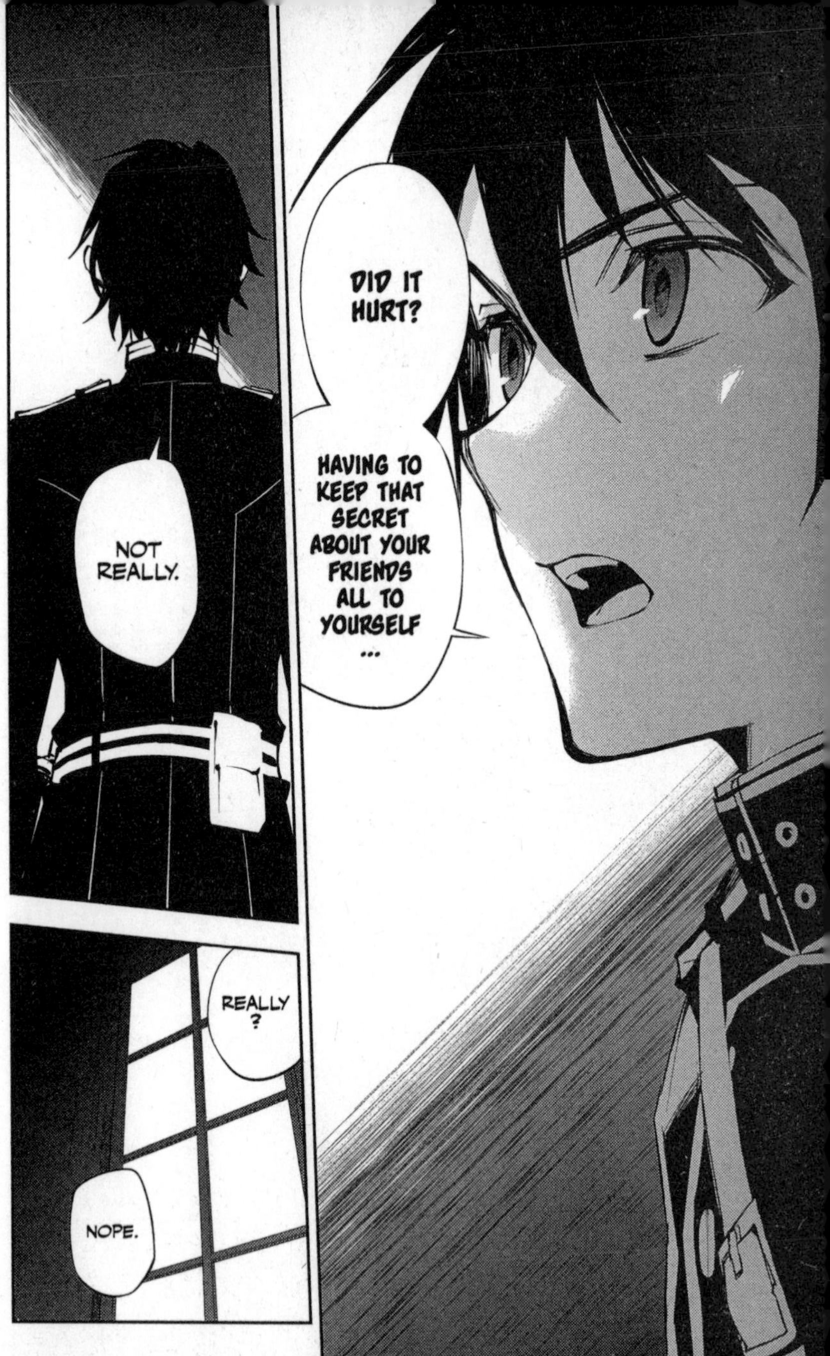
DID IT HURT?
HAVING TO KEEP THAT SECRET ABOUT YOUR FRIENDS ALL TO YOURSELF ...
NOT REALLY.
REALLY ?
NOPE.

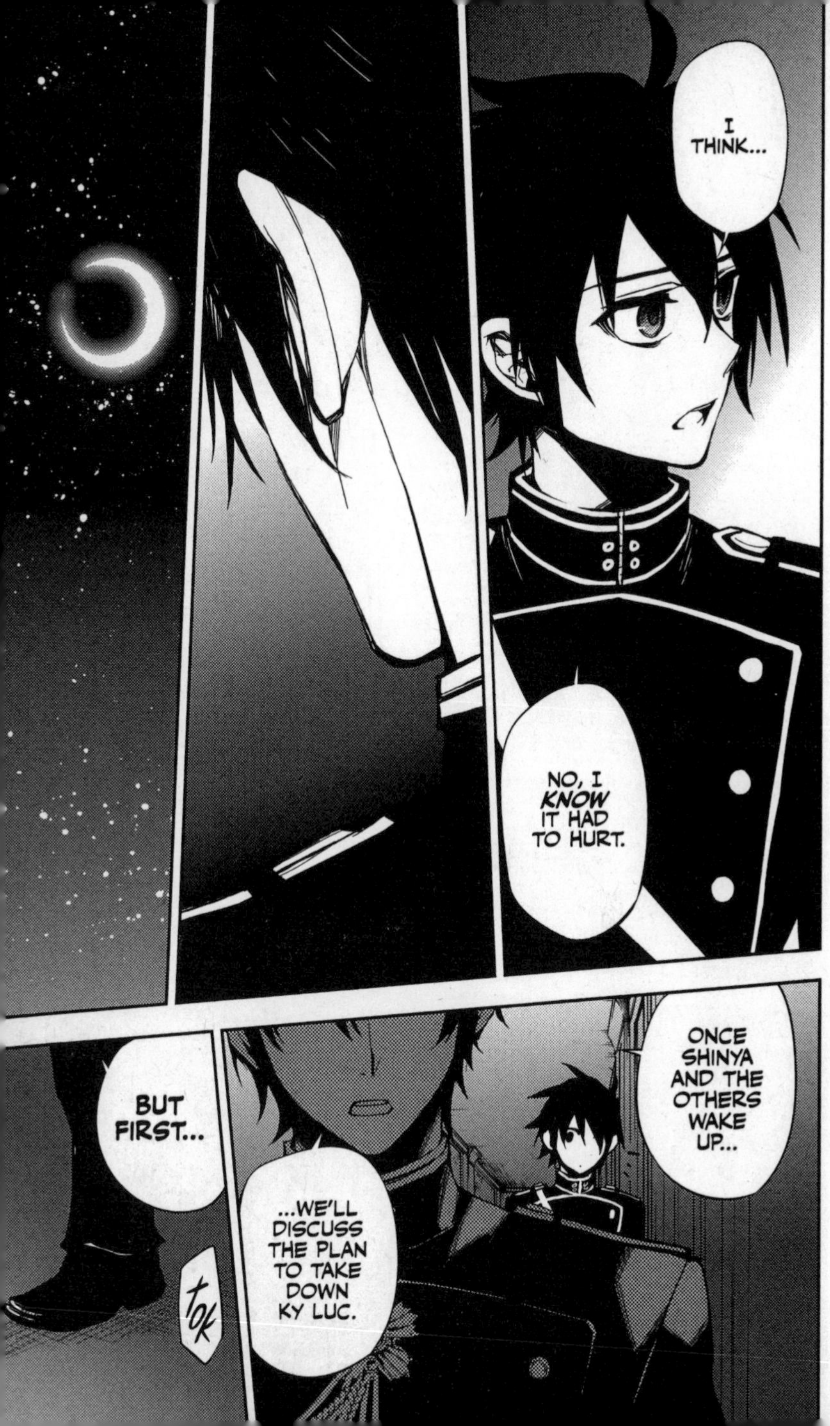
I THINK...
NO, I *KNOW* IT HAD TO HURT.
ONCE SHINYA AND THE OTHERS WAKE UP...
...WE'LL DISCUSS THE PLAN TO TAKE DOWN KY LUC.
BUT FIRST...
tok

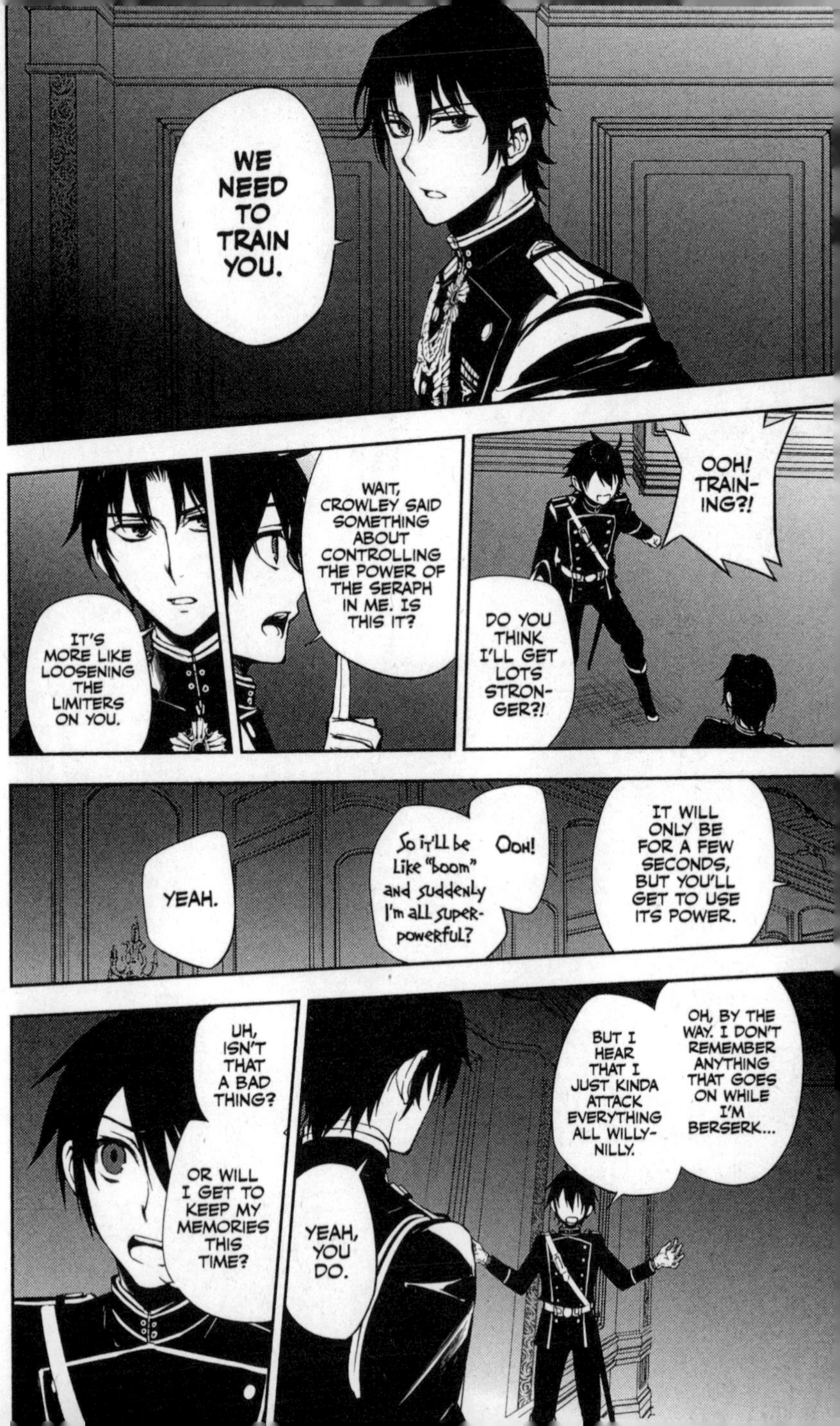
WE NEED TO TRAIN YOU.
OOH! TRAINING?!
DO YOU THINK I'LL GET LOTS STRONGER?!
WAIT, CROWLEY SAID SOMETHING ABOUT CONTROLLING THE POWER OF THE SERAPH IN ME. IS THIS IT?
IT'S MORE LIKE LOOSENING THE LIMITERS ON YOU.
IT WILL ONLY BE FOR A FEW SECONDS, BUT YOU'LL GET TO USE ITS POWER.
Ooh!
So it'll be like "boom" and suddenly I'm all super-powerful?
YEAH.
OH, BY THE WAY. I DON'T REMEMBER ANYTHING THAT GOES ON WHILE I'M BERSERK...
BUT I HEAR THAT I JUST KINDA ATTACK EVERYTHING ALL WILLY-NILLY.
UH, ISN'T THAT A BAD THING?
OR WILL I GET TO KEEP MY MEMORIES THIS TIME?
YEAH, YOU DO.

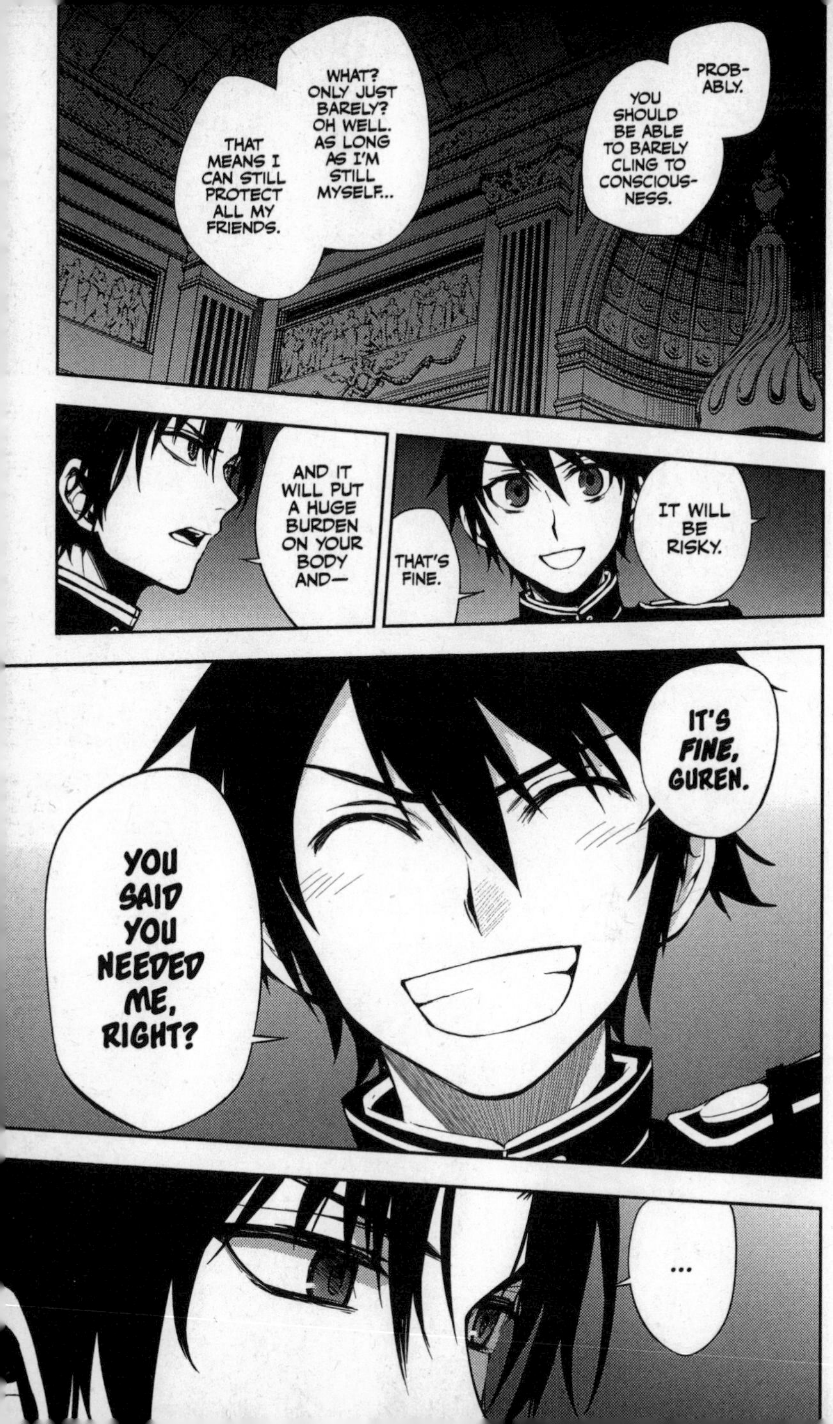
PROBABLY.
YOU SHOULD BE ABLE TO BARELY CLING TO CONSCIOUSNESS.
WHAT? ONLY JUST BARELY? OH WELL. AS LONG AS I'M STILL MYSELF...
THAT MEANS I CAN STILL PROTECT ALL MY FRIENDS.
IT WILL BE RISKY.
THAT'S FINE.
AND IT WILL PUT A HUGE BURDEN ON YOUR BODY AND—
IT'S FINE, GUREN.
YOU SAID YOU NEEDED ME, RIGHT?
...

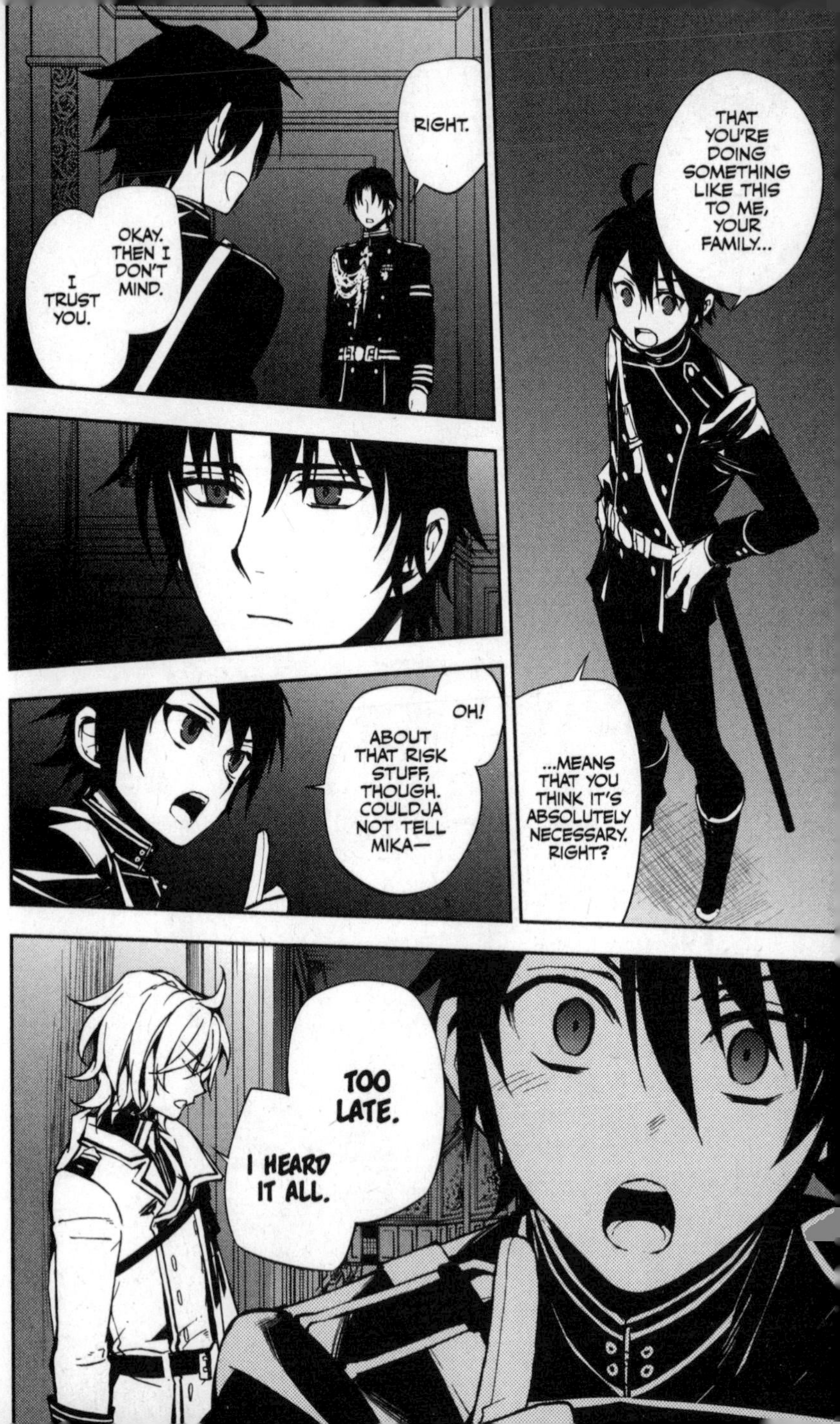
THAT YOU'RE DOING SOMETHING LIKE THIS TO ME, YOUR FAMILY...
...MEANS THAT YOU THINK IT'S ABSOLUTELY NECESSARY. RIGHT?
RIGHT.
OKAY. THEN I DON'T MIND.
I TRUST YOU.
OH!
ABOUT THAT RISK STUFF, THOUGH. COULDJA NOT TELL MIKA—
TOO LATE.
I HEARD IT ALL.

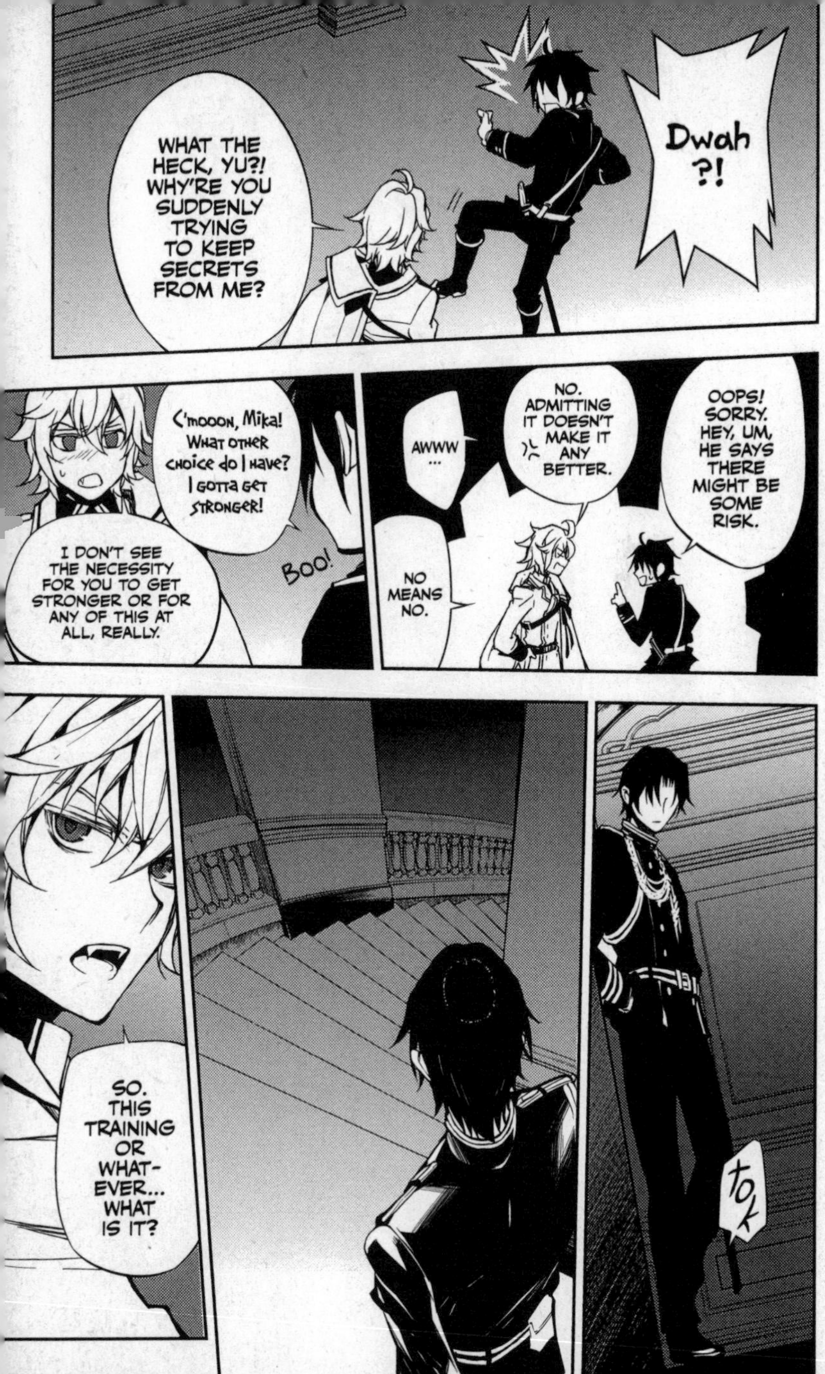
Dwah ?!
WHAT THE HECK, YU?! WHY'RE YOU SUDDENLY TRYING TO KEEP SECRETS FROM ME?
OOPS! SORRY. HEY, UM, HE SAYS THERE MIGHT BE SOME RISK.
NO. ADMITTING IT DOESN'T MAKE IT ANY BETTER.
AWWW...
NO MEANS NO.
C'mooon, Mika! What other choice do I have? I gotta get stronger!
BOO!
I DON'T SEE THE NECESSITY FOR YOU TO GET STRONGER OR FOR ANY OF THIS AT ALL, REALLY.
TOK
SO. THIS TRAINING OR WHAT-EVER... WHAT IS IT?

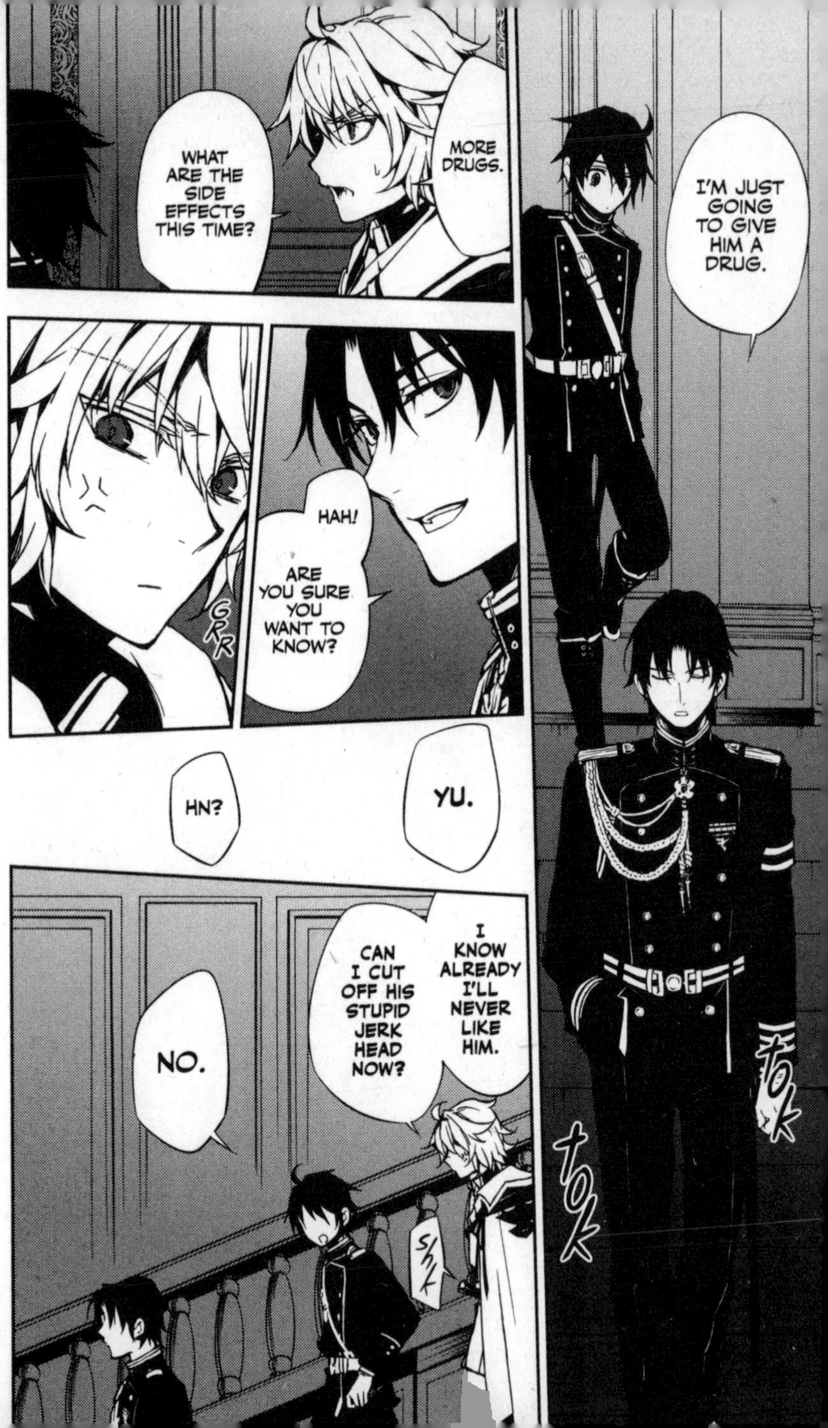

I'M JUST GOING TO GIVE HIM A DRUG.
TOK
TOK
MORE DRUGS.
WHAT ARE THE SIDE EFFECTS THIS TIME?
HAH!
ARE YOU SURE YOU WANT TO KNOW?
GRR
YU.
HN?
I KNOW ALREADY I'LL NEVER LIKE HIM.
CAN I CUT OFF HIS STUPID JERK HEAD NOW?
NO.

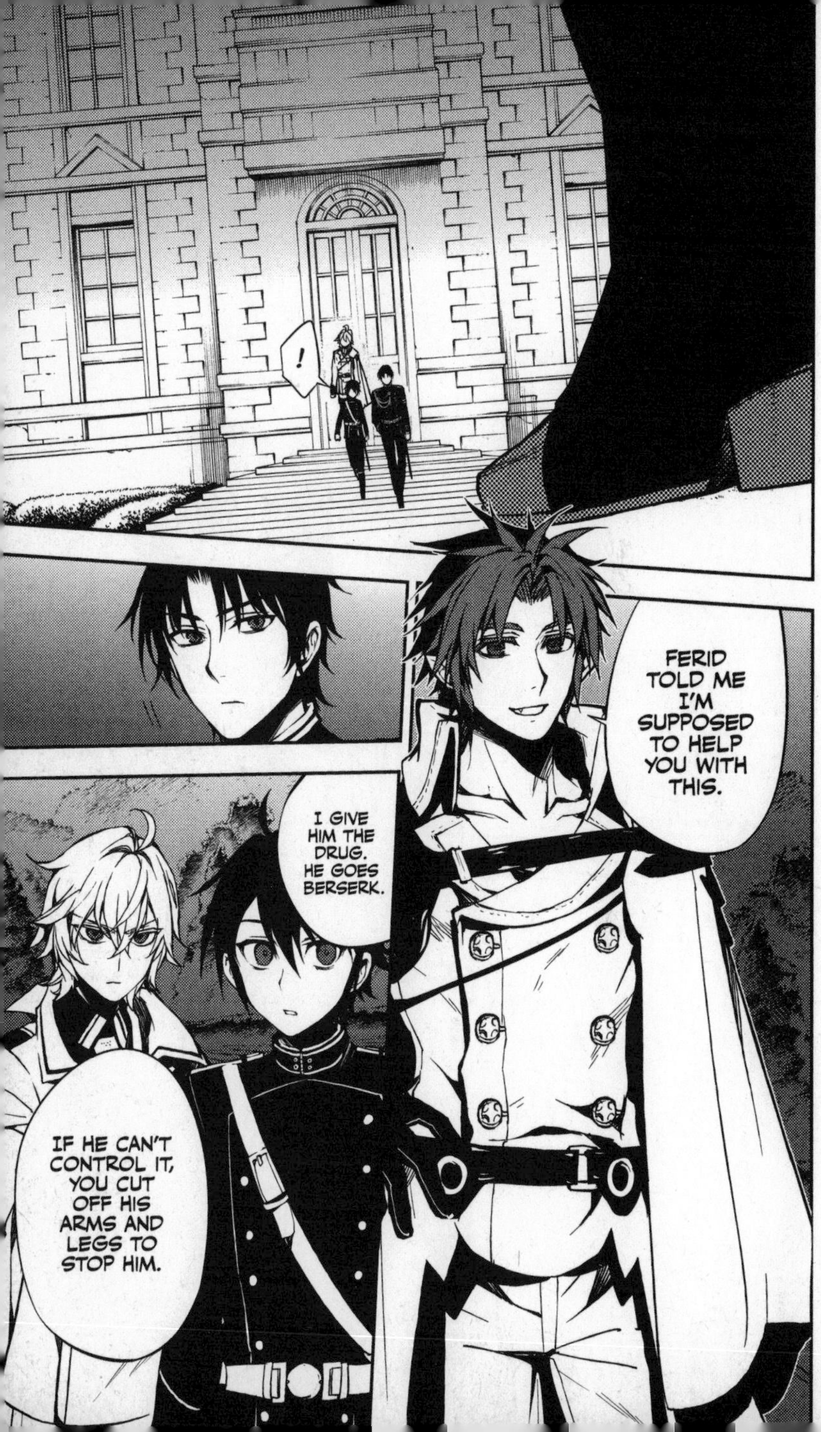
!
FERID TOLD ME I'M SUPPOSED TO HELP YOU WITH THIS.
I GIVE HIM THE DRUG. HE GOES BERSERK.
IF HE CAN'T CONTROL IT, YOU CUT OFF HIS ARMS AND LEGS TO STOP HIM.

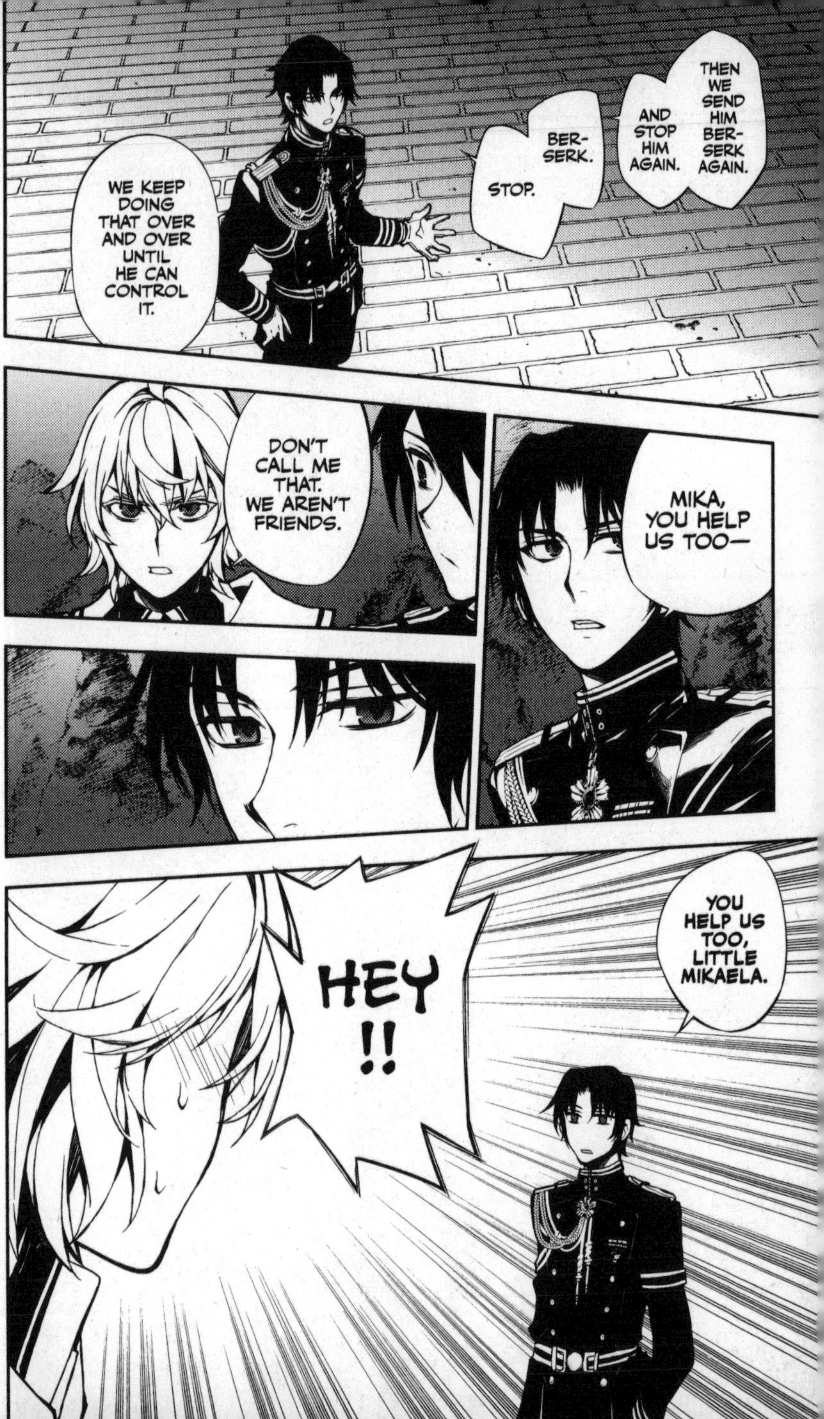
BER-SERK.
STOP.
THEN WE SEND HIM BER-SERK AGAIN.
AND STOP HIM AGAIN.
WE KEEP DOING THAT OVER AND OVER UNTIL HE CAN CONTROL IT.
MIKA, YOU HELP US TOO—
DON'T CALL ME THAT. WE AREN'T FRIENDS.
YOU HELP US TOO, LITTLE MIKAELA.
HEY!!

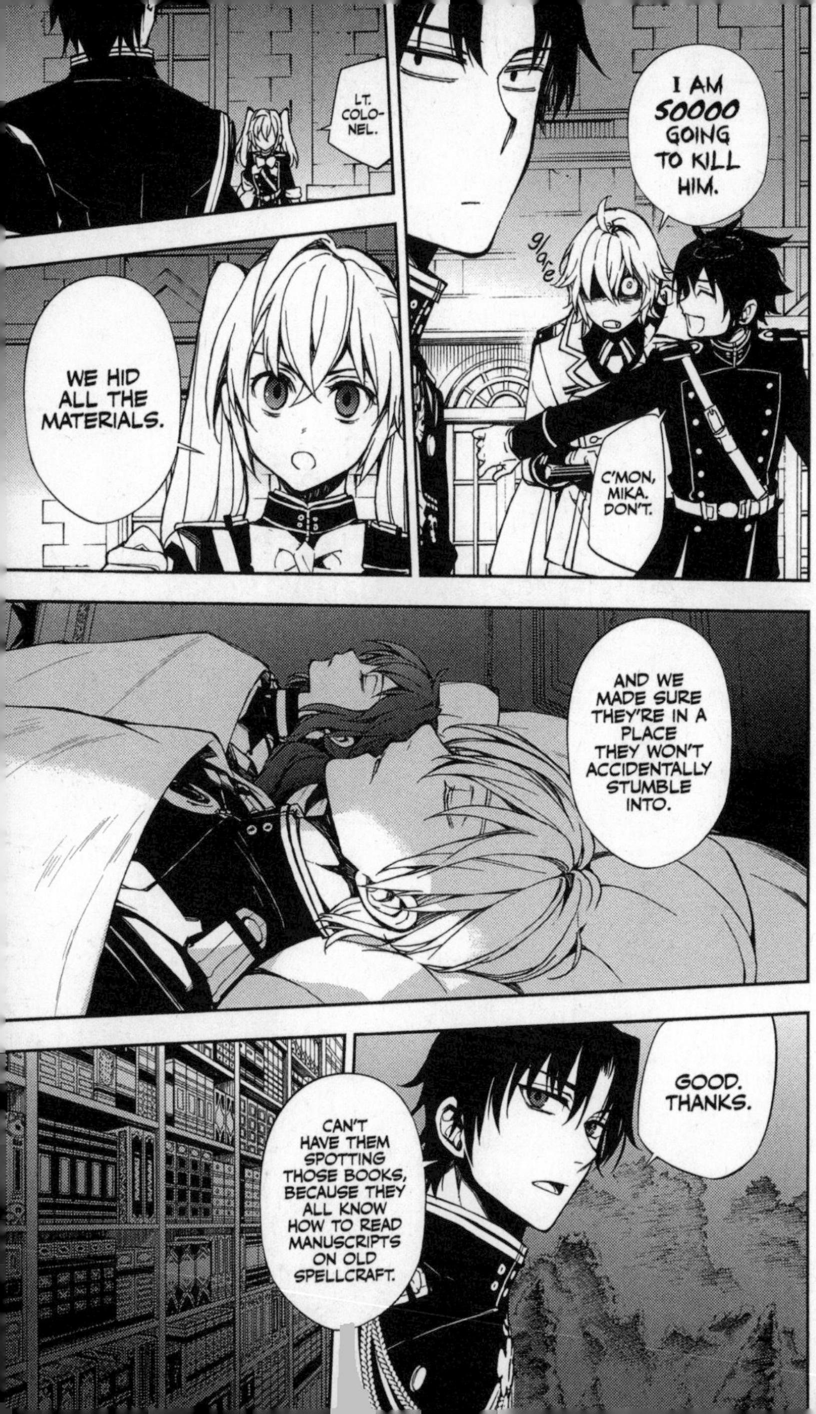

I AM SOOOO GOING TO KILL HIM.
glare
C'MON, MIKA. DON'T.
LT. COLONEL.
WE HID ALL THE MATERIALS.
AND WE MADE SURE THEY'RE IN A PLACE THEY WON'T ACCIDENTALLY STUMBLE INTO.
GOOD. THANKS.
CAN'T HAVE THEM SPOTTING THOSE BOOKS, BECAUSE THEY ALL KNOW HOW TO READ MANUSCRIPTS ON OLD SPELLCRAFT.

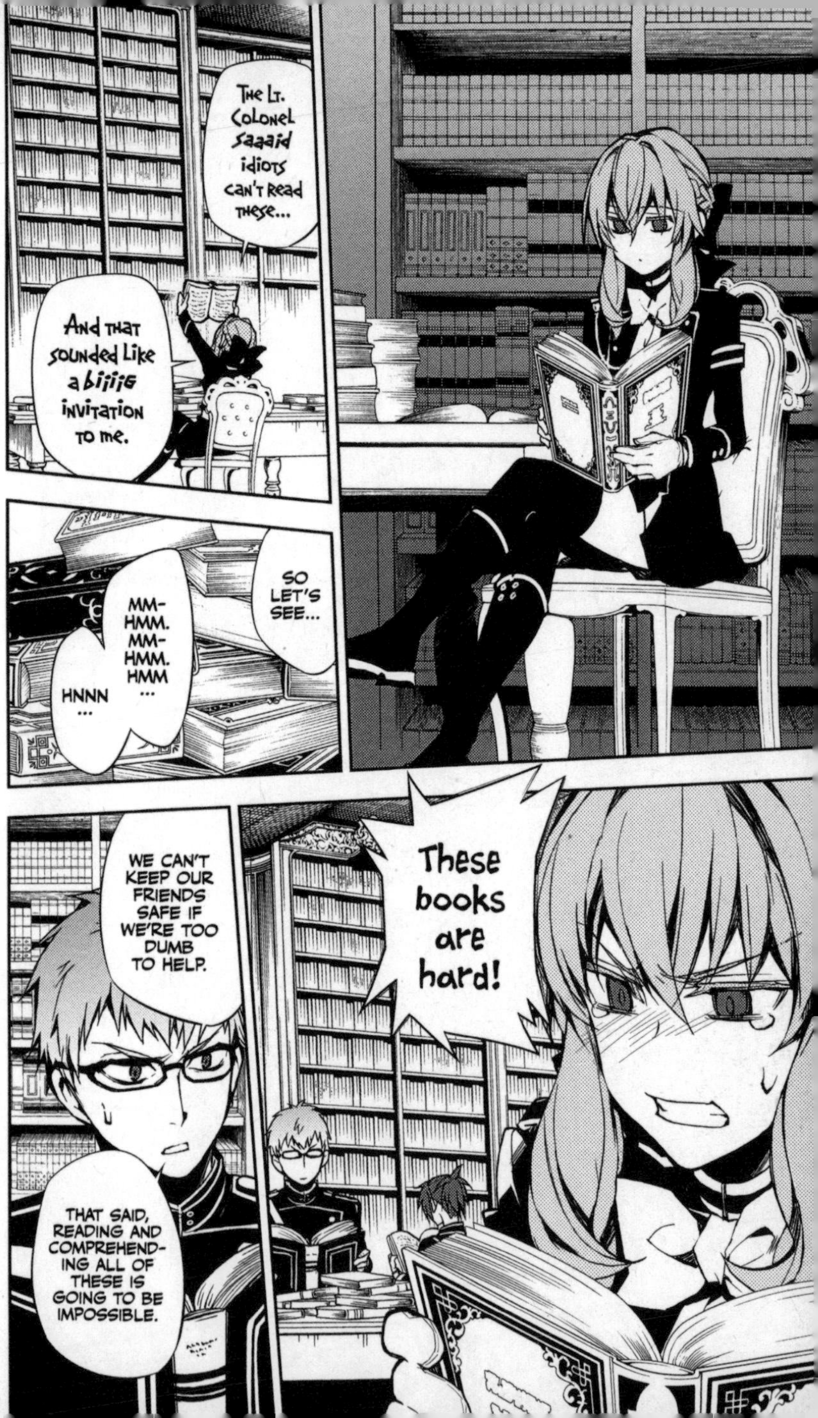

The Lt. Colonel saaaid idiots can't read these...
And that sounded like a biiiig invitation to me.
SO LET'S SEE...
MM-HMM. MM-HMM. HMM...
HNNN...
These books are hard!
WE CAN'T KEEP OUR FRIENDS SAFE IF WE'RE TOO DUMB TO HELP.
THAT SAID, READING AND COMPREHENDING ALL OF THESE IS GOING TO BE IMPOSSIBLE.

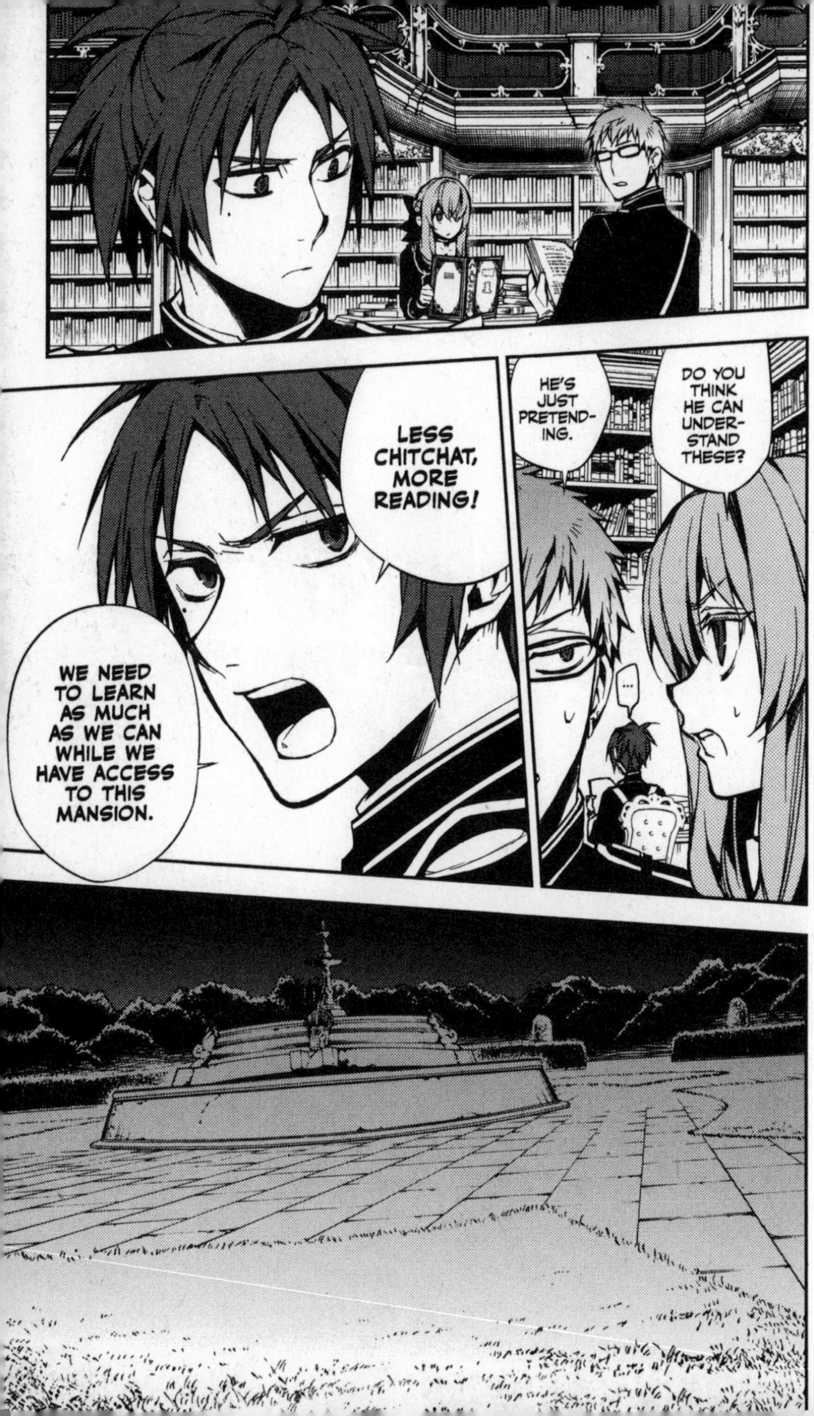
DO YOU THINK HE CAN UNDER-STAND THESE?
HE'S JUST PRETEND-ING.
...
LESS CHITCHAT, MORE READING!
WE NEED TO LEARN AS MUCH AS WE CAN WHILE WE HAVE ACCESS TO THIS MANSION.

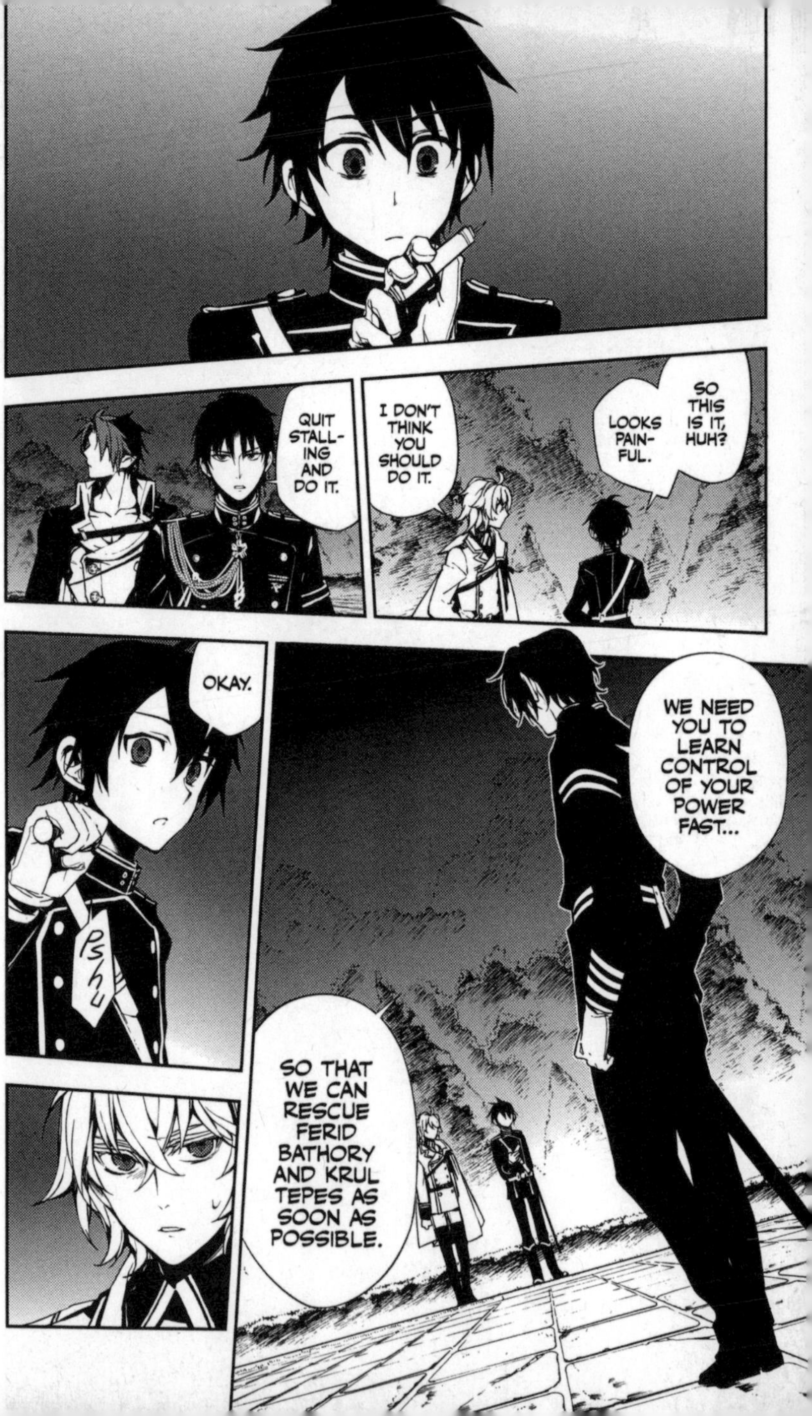
SO THIS IS IT, HUH?
LOOKS PAIN-FUL.
I DON'T THINK YOU SHOULD DO IT.
QUIT STALL-ING AND DO IT.
WE NEED YOU TO LEARN CONTROL OF YOUR POWER FAST...
SO THAT WE CAN RESCUE FERID BATHORY AND KRUL TEPES AS SOON AS POSSIBLE.
OKAY.
PSHU

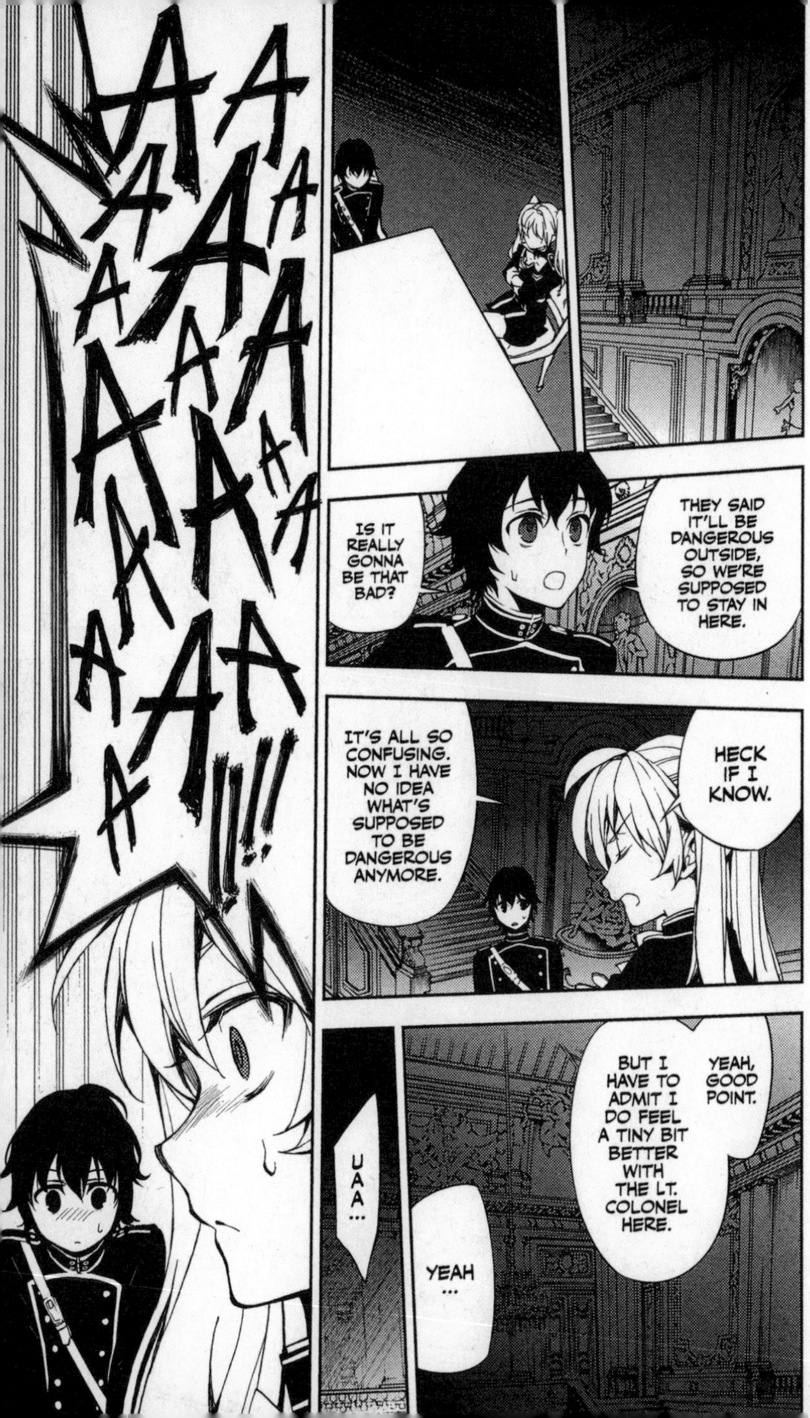
THEY SAID IT'LL BE DANGEROUS OUTSIDE, SO WE'RE SUPPOSED TO STAY IN HERE.
IS IT REALLY GONNA BE THAT BAD?
HECK IF I KNOW.
IT'S ALL SO CONFUSING. NOW I HAVE NO IDEA WHAT'S SUPPOSED TO BE DANGEROUS ANYMORE.
YEAH, GOOD POINT.
BUT I HAVE TO ADMIT I DO FEEL A TINY BIT BETTER WITH THE LT. COLONEL HERE.
YEAH...
UAA...
AAAAAAAAAAAAAAAAAAAAAA!!!

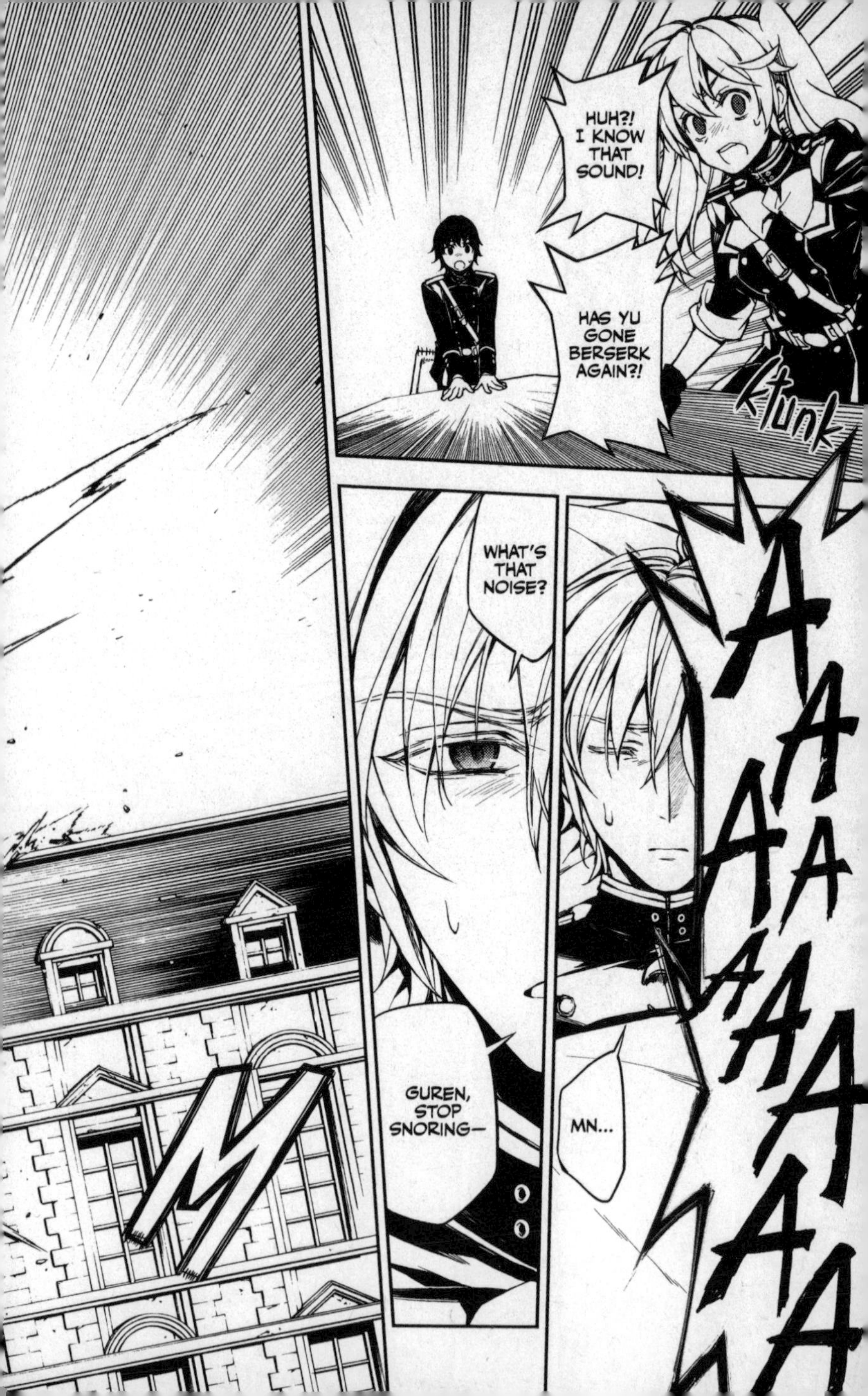
HUH?! I KNOW THAT SOUND!
HAS YU GONE BERSERK AGAIN?!
ktunk
AAAAAAAAAAAA
MN...
WHAT'S THAT NOISE?
GUREN, STOP SNORING—
M

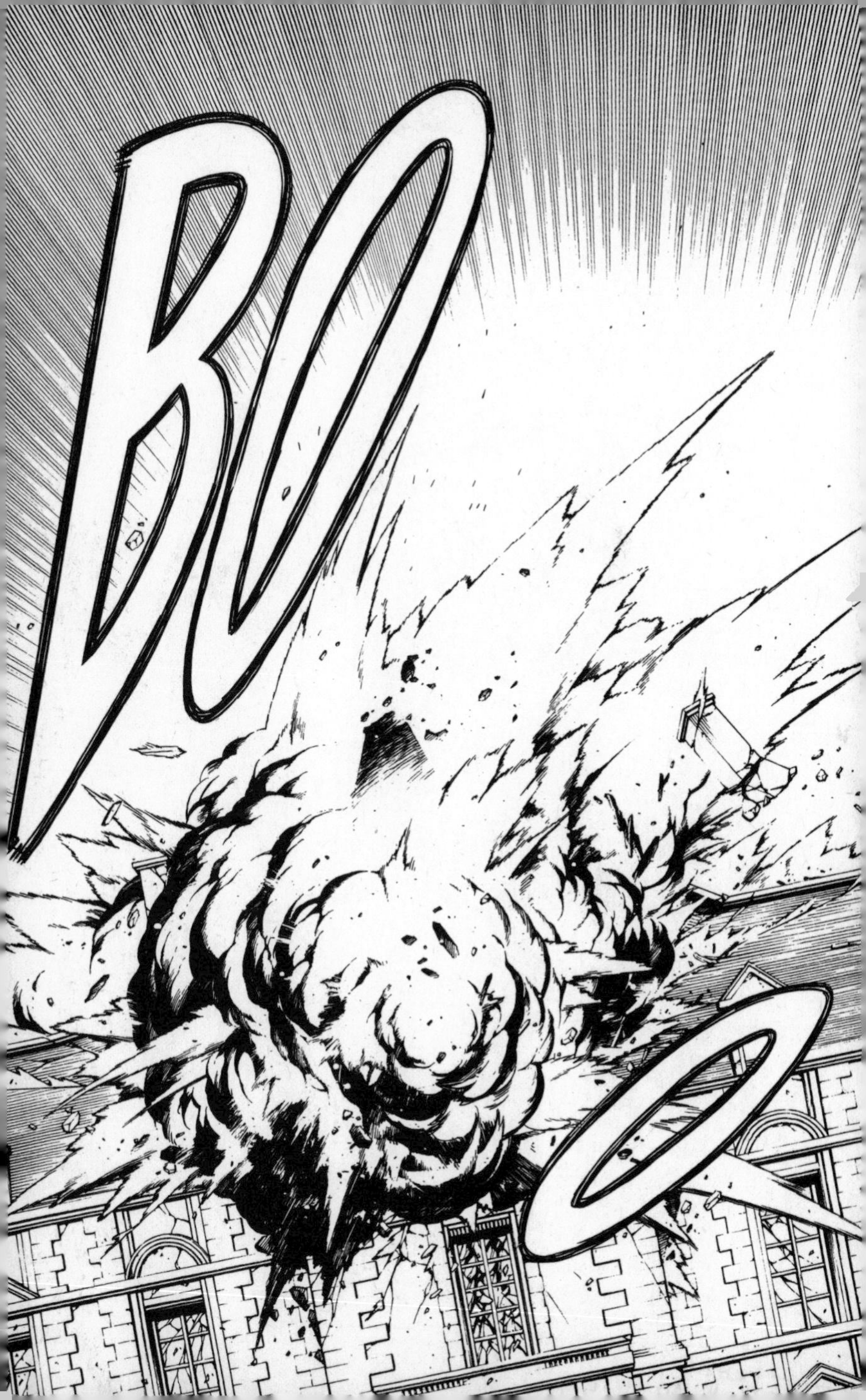
BOOO

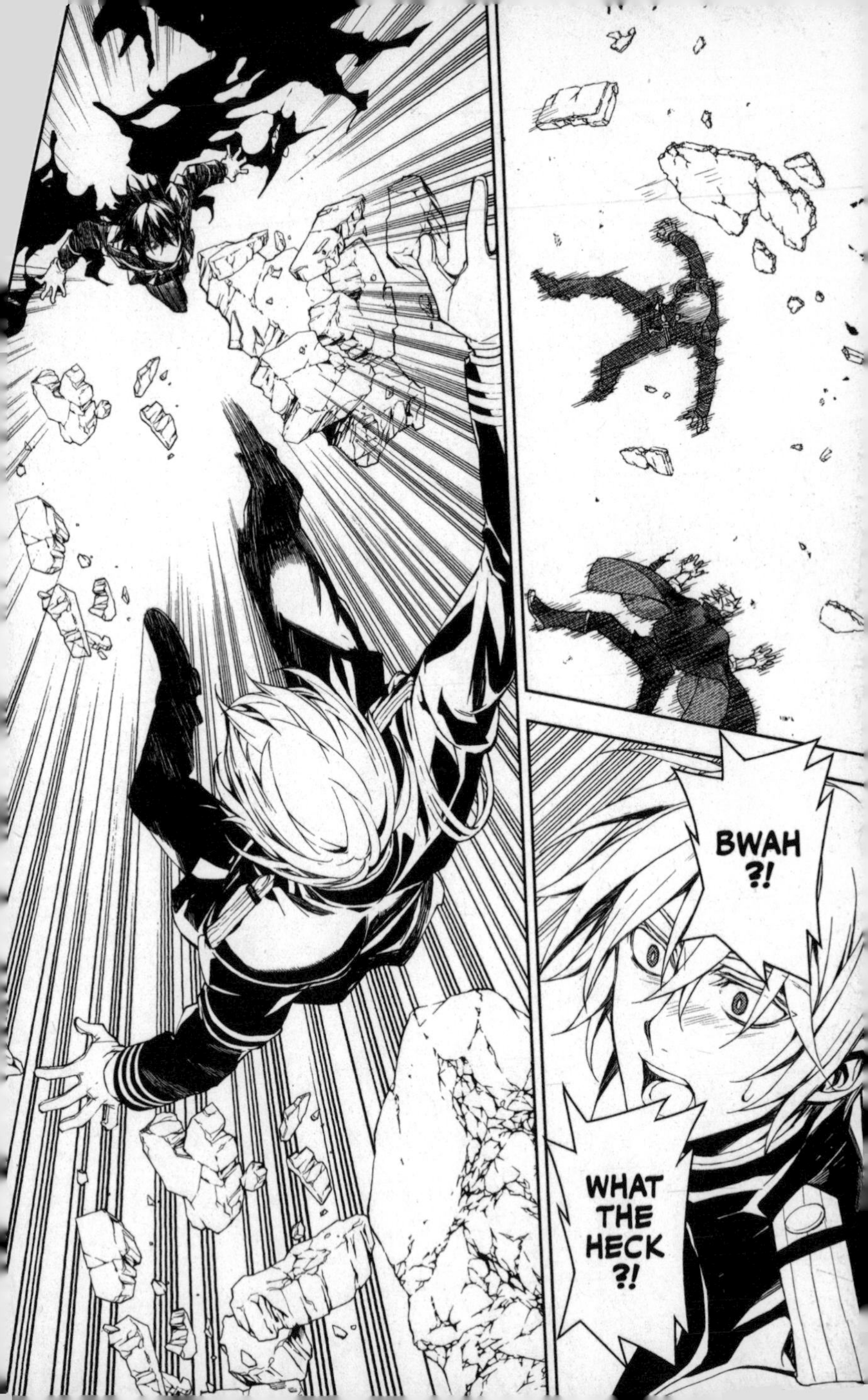
BWAH ?!
WHAT THE HECK ?!

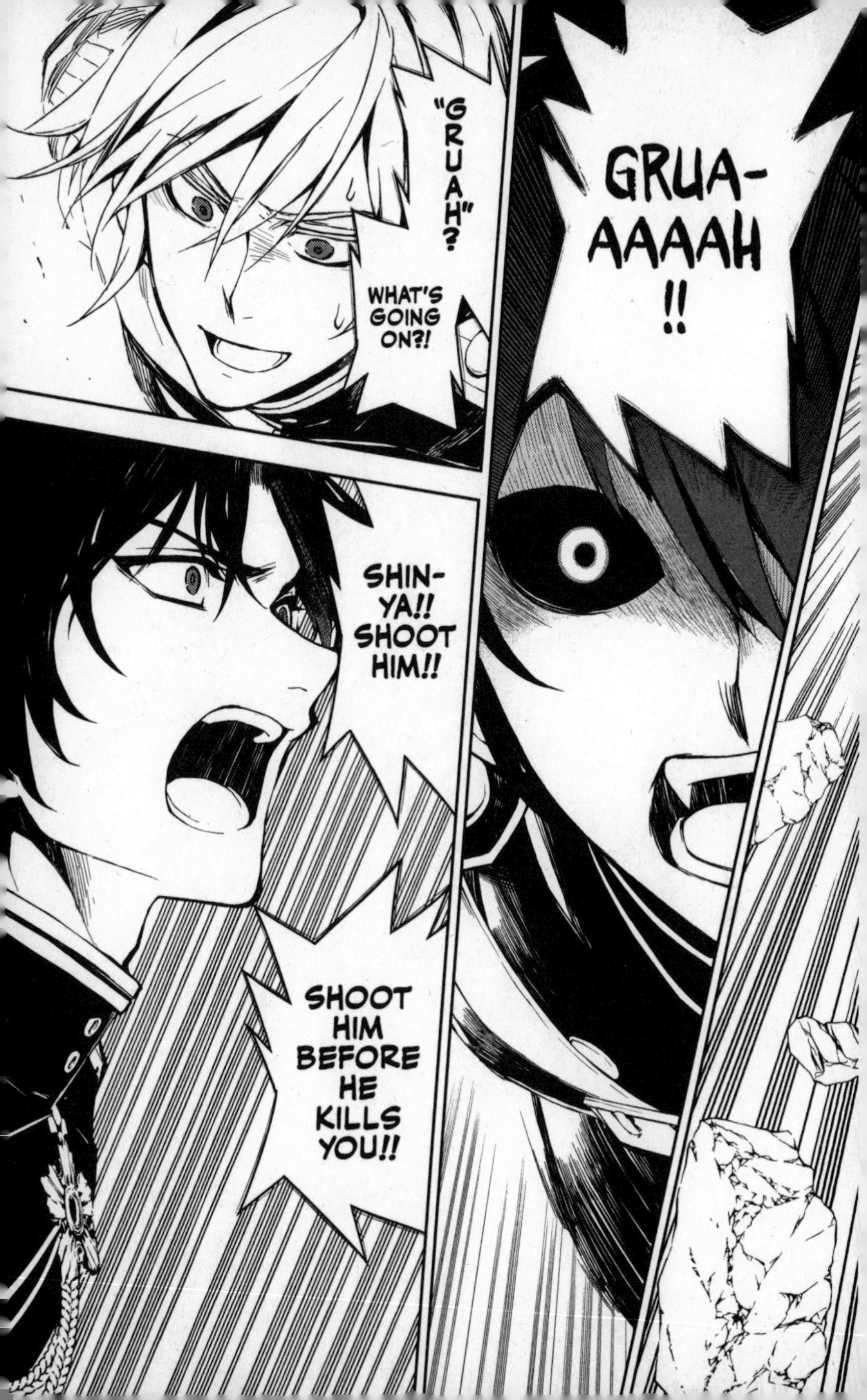
GRUA-AAAAH!!
"GRUAH"?
WHAT'S GOING ON?!
SHIN-YA!! SHOOT HIM!!
SHOOT HIM BEFORE HE KILLS YOU!!

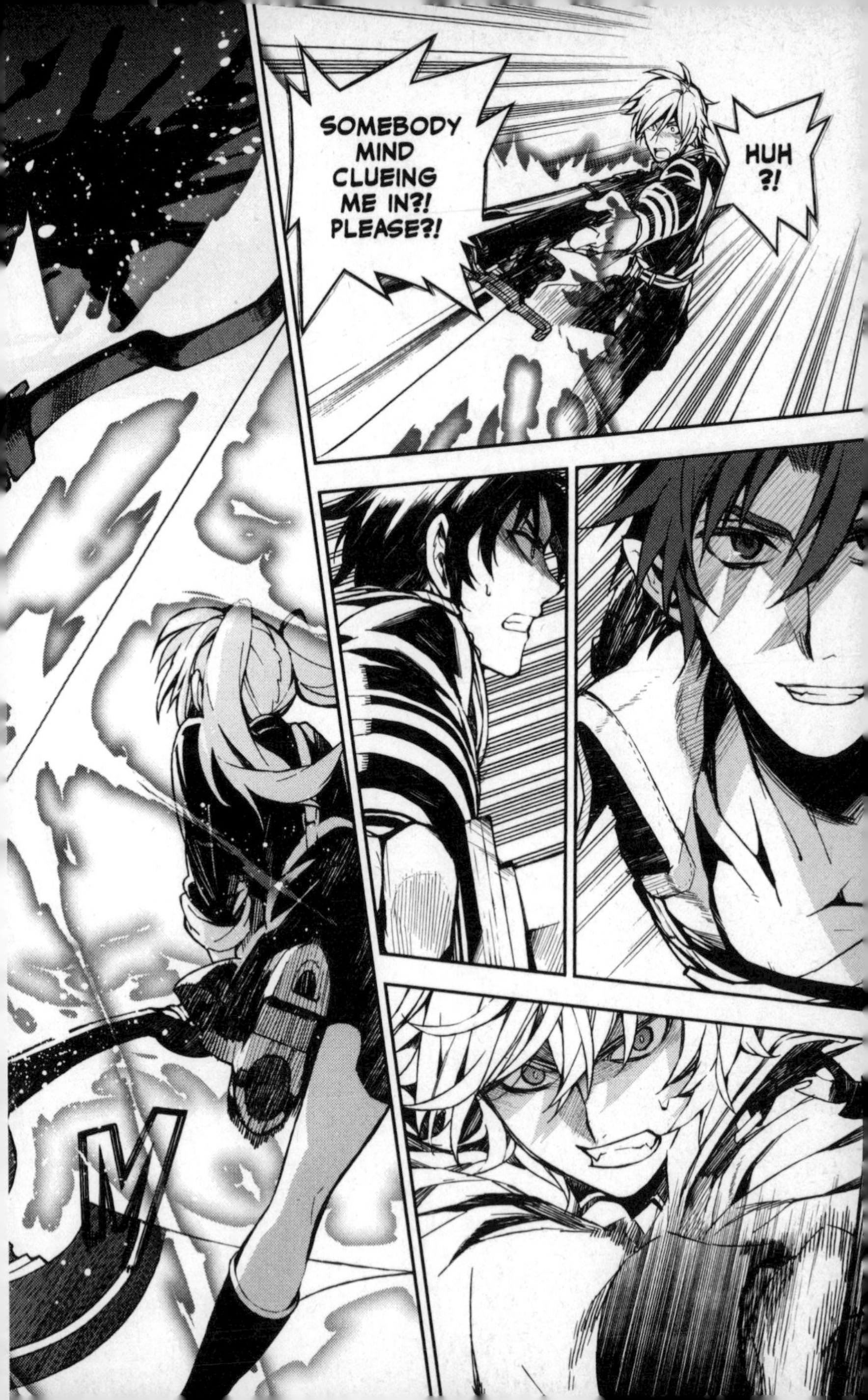
HUH ?!
SOMEBODY MIND CLUEING ME IN?! PLEASE?!

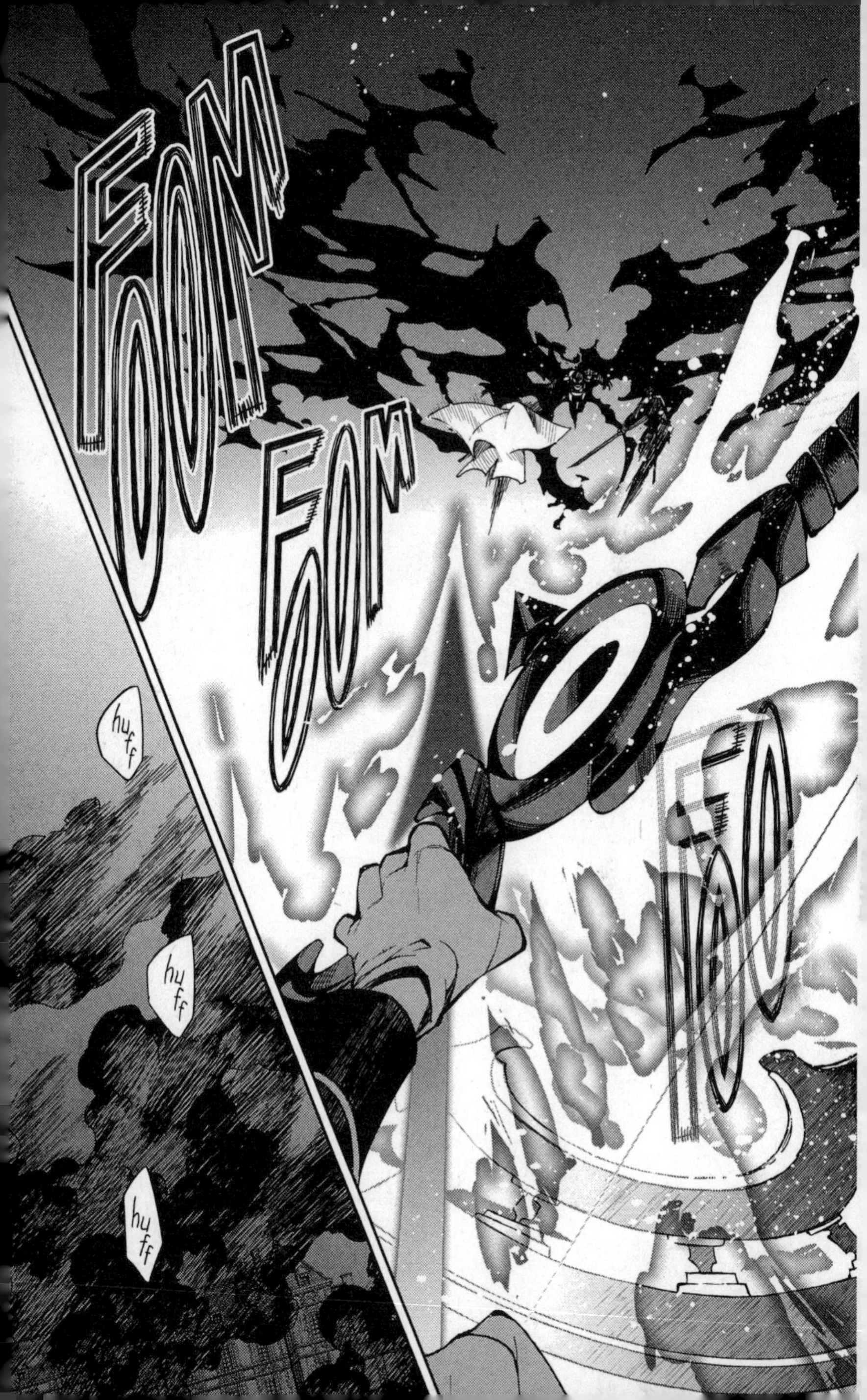
FOOM
FOOM
huff
huff
huff

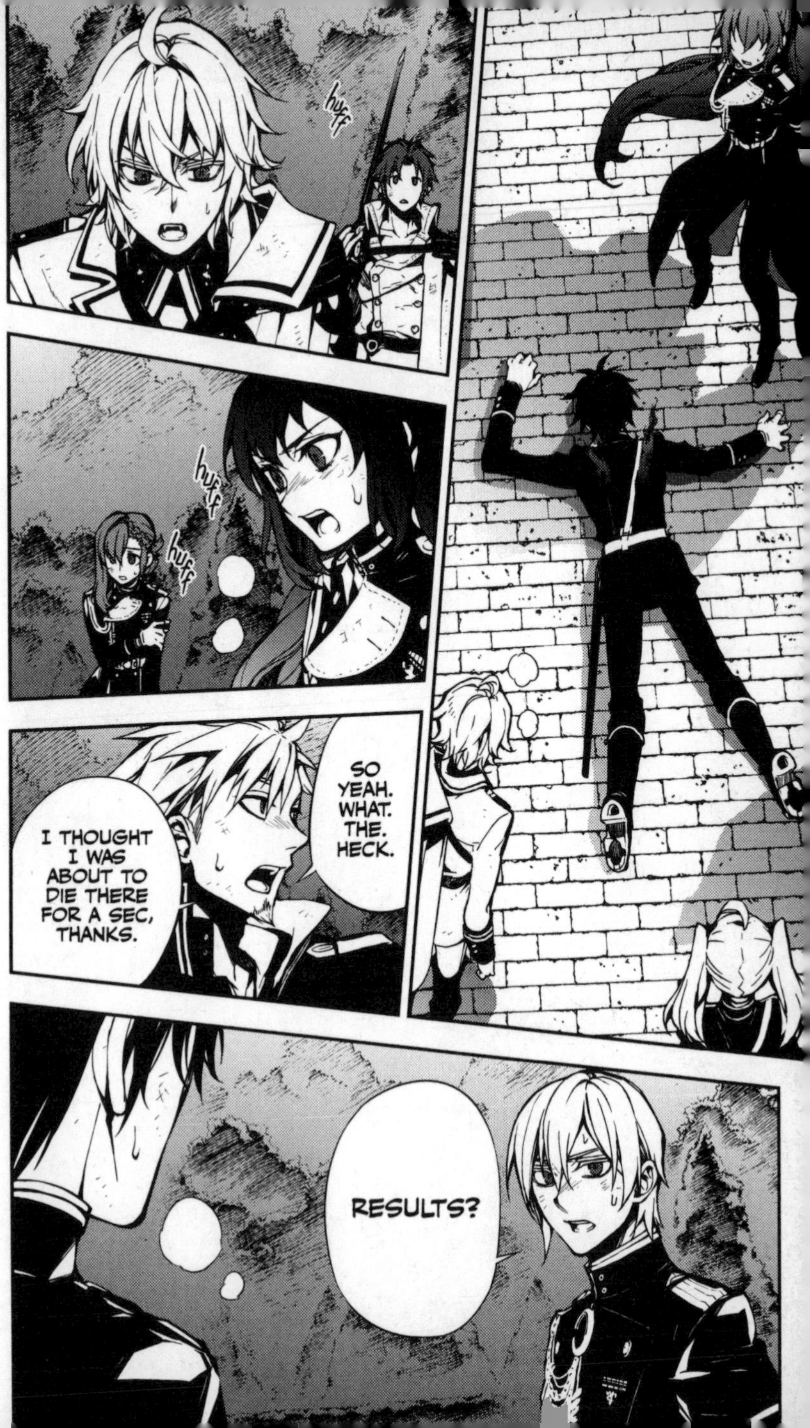
huff
huff
huff
SO YEAH. WHAT. THE. HECK.
I THOUGHT I WAS ABOUT TO DIE THERE FOR A SEC, THANKS.
RESULTS?

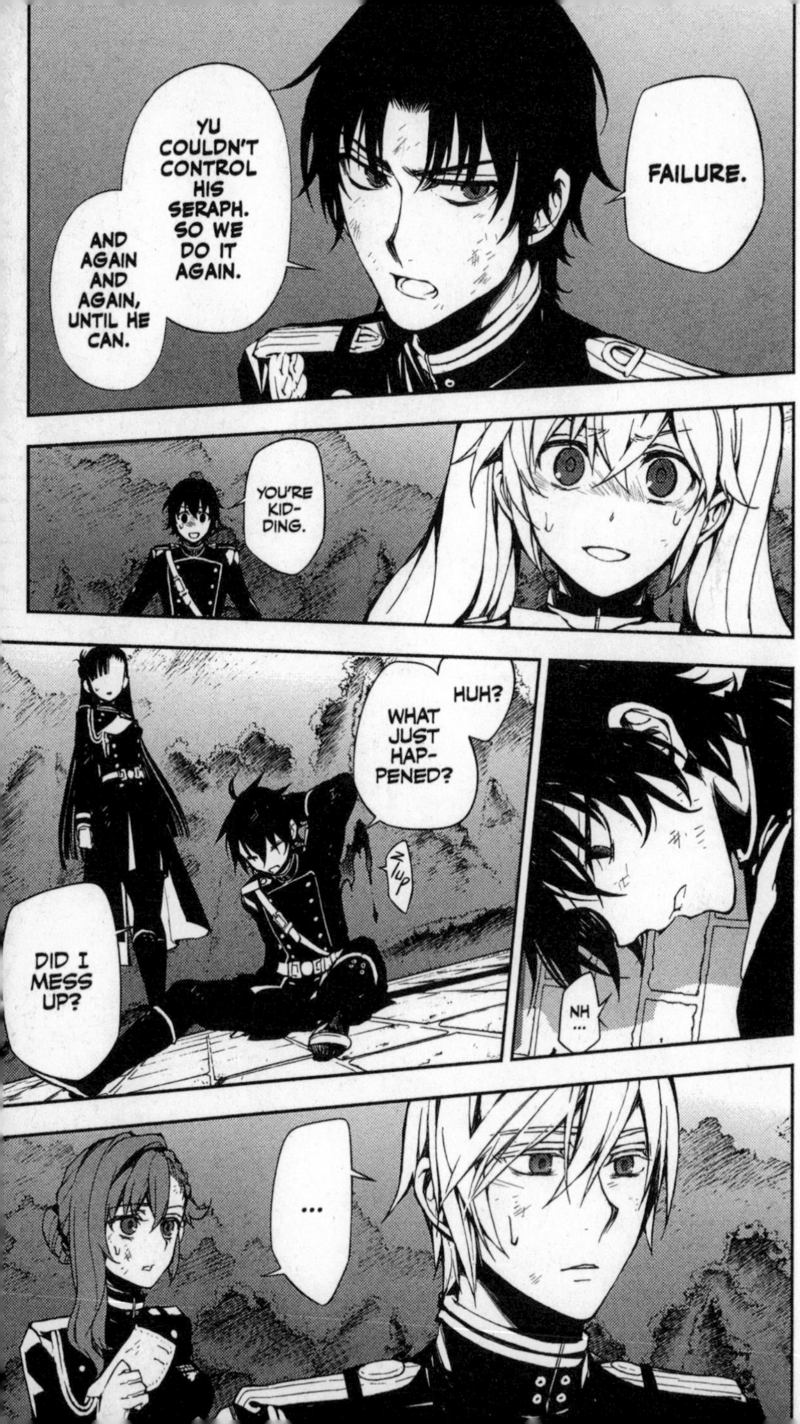
FAILURE.
YU COULDN'T CONTROL HIS SERAPH. SO WE DO IT AGAIN.
AND AGAIN AND AGAIN, UNTIL HE CAN.
YOU'RE KID-DING.
NH...
HUH?
WHAT JUST HAP-PENED?
DID I MESS UP?
...

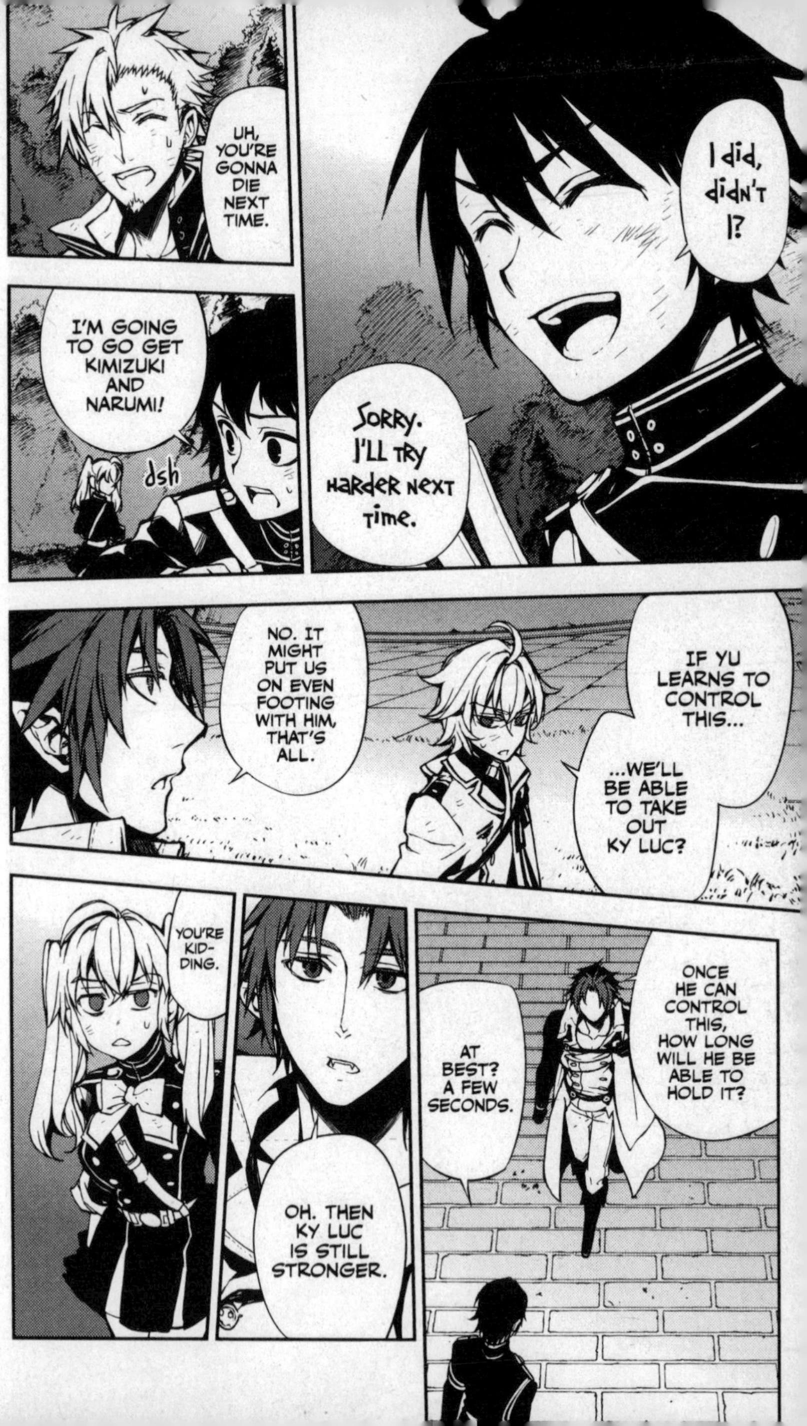
I did, didn't I?
Sorry. I'll try harder next time.
UH, YOU'RE GONNA DIE NEXT TIME.
I'M GOING TO GO GET KIMIZUKI AND NARUMI!
dsh
IF YU LEARNS TO CONTROL THIS...
...WE'LL BE ABLE TO TAKE OUT KY LUC?
NO. IT MIGHT PUT US ON EVEN FOOTING WITH HIM, THAT'S ALL.
ONCE HE CAN CONTROL THIS, HOW LONG WILL HE BE ABLE TO HOLD IT?
AT BEST? A FEW SECONDS.
OH. THEN KY LUC IS STILL STRONGER.
YOU'RE KID-DING.

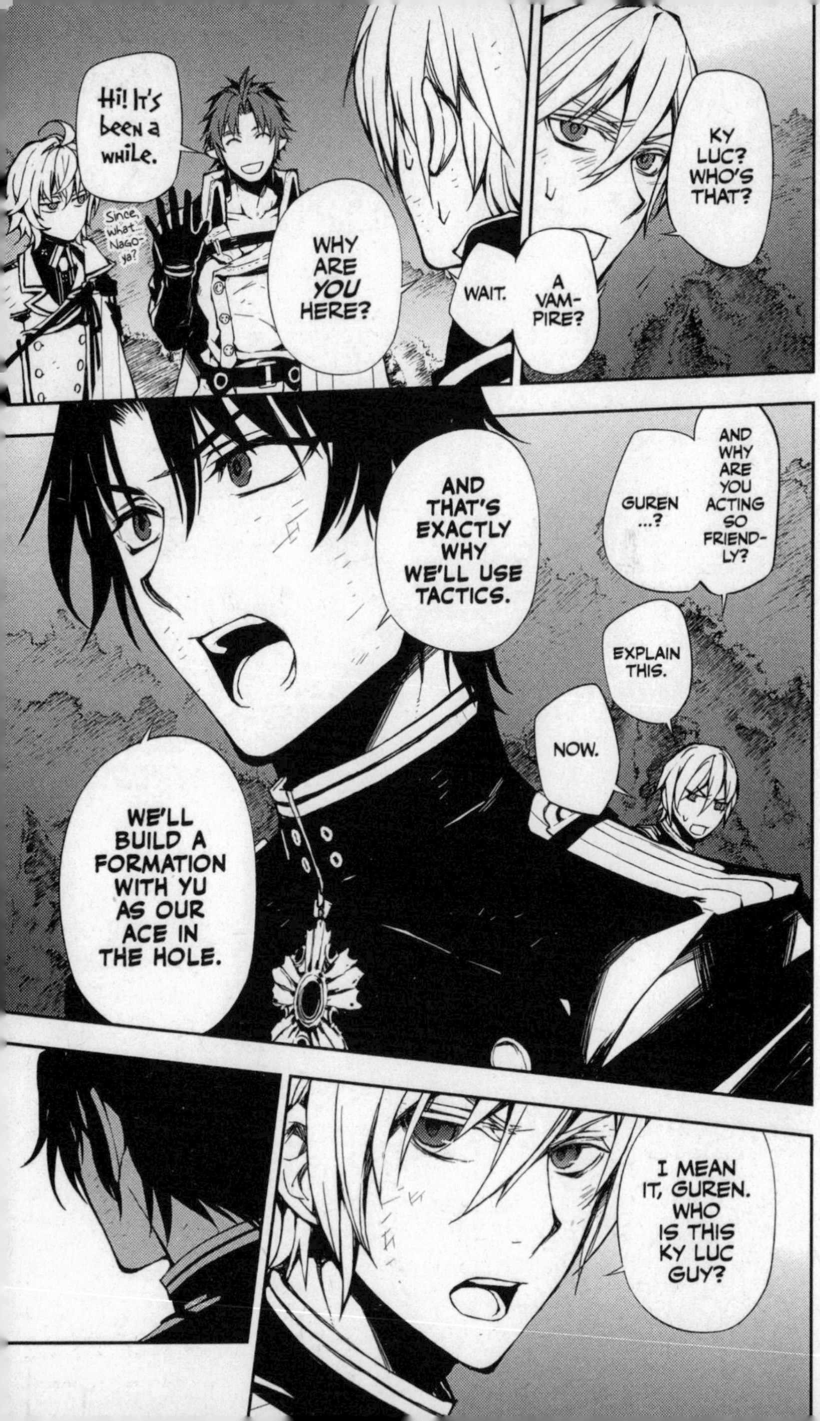
KY LUC? WHO'S THAT?
A VAMPIRE?
WAIT.
WHY ARE YOU HERE?
Hi! It's been a while.
Since, what... Nagoya?
AND WHY ARE YOU ACTING SO FRIENDLY?
GUREN ...?
AND THAT'S EXACTLY WHY WE'LL USE TACTICS.
EXPLAIN THIS.
NOW.
WE'LL BUILD A FORMATION WITH YU AS OUR ACE IN THE HOLE.
I MEAN IT, GUREN. WHO IS THIS KY LUC GUY?

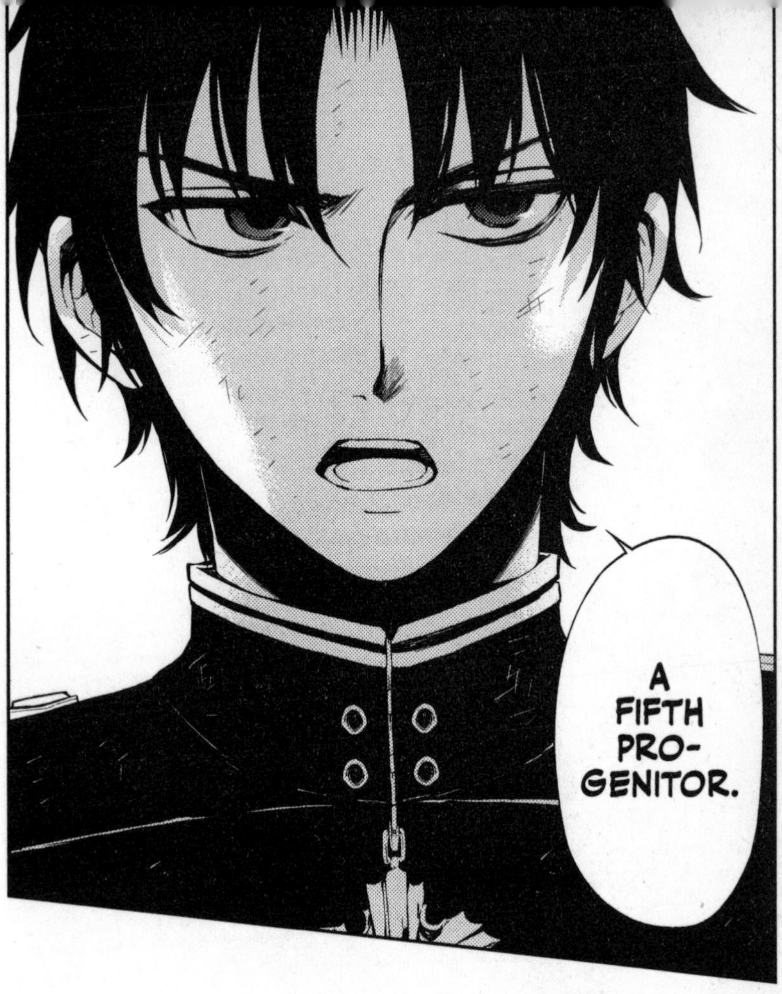
A FIFTH PRO-GENITOR.

Three Days Later

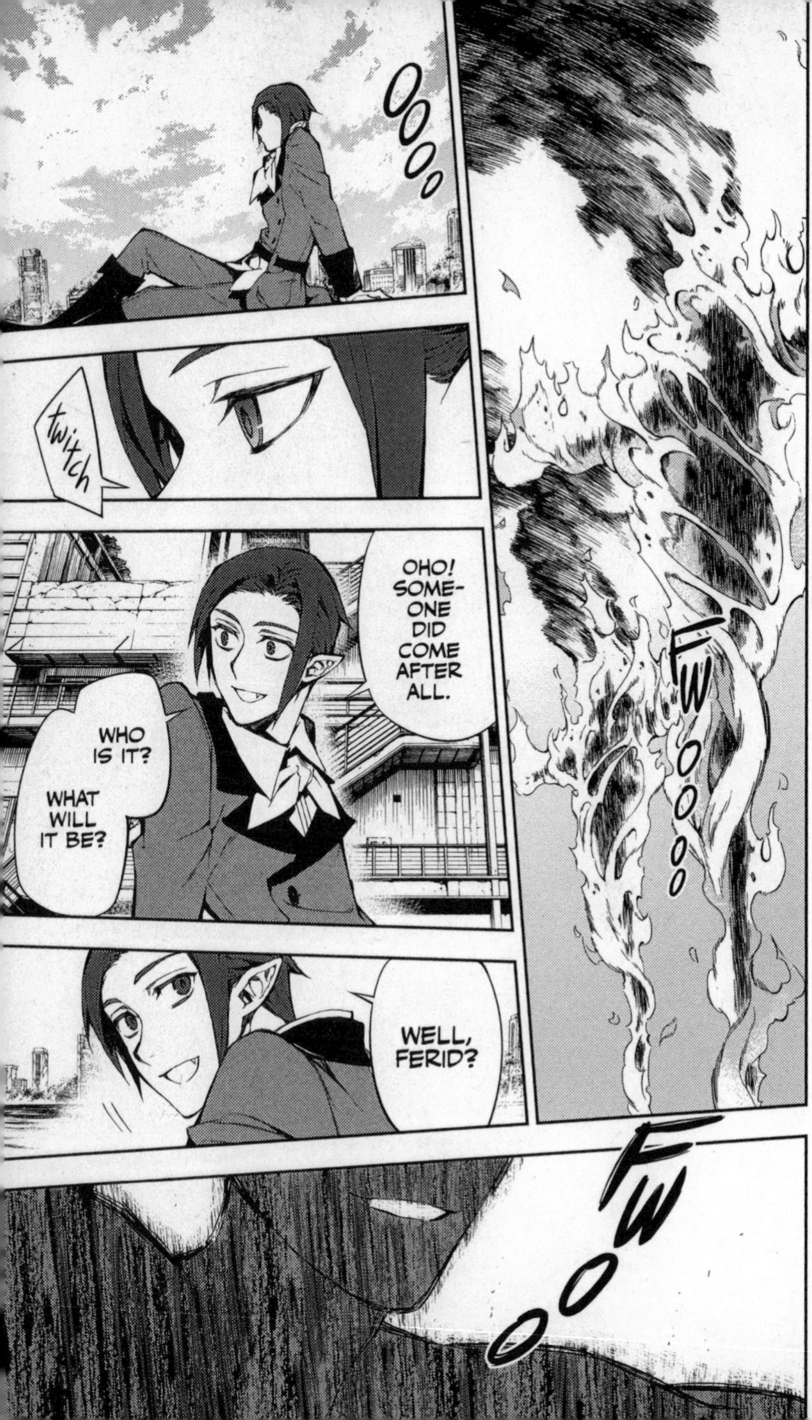
FWOOOOOO
OOOOO
twitch
OHO! SOME-ONE DID COME AFTER ALL.
WHO IS IT?
WHAT WILL IT BE?
WELL, FERID?
FWOOOO

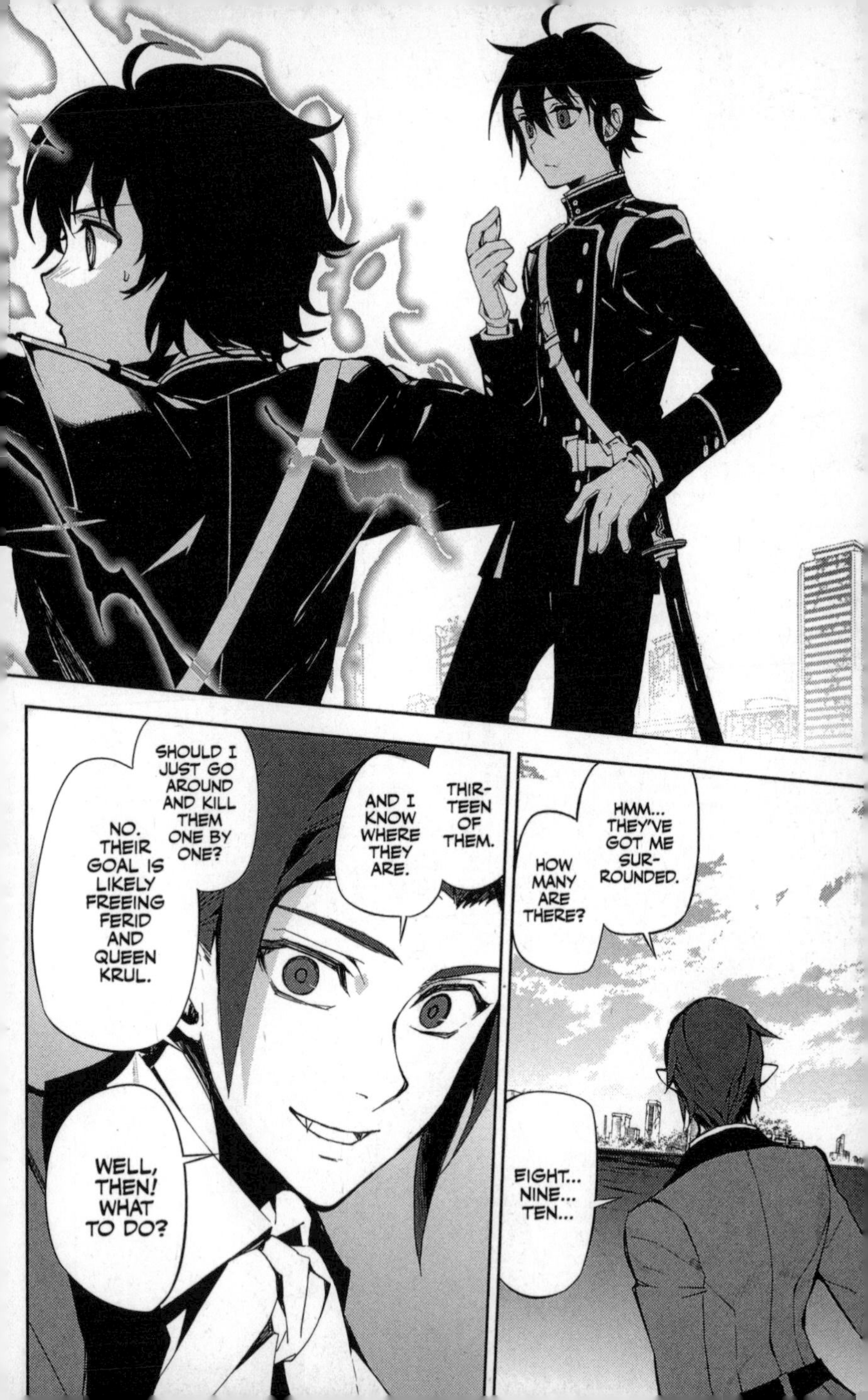
HMM... THEY'VE GOT ME SUR-ROUNDED.
HOW MANY ARE THERE?
EIGHT... NINE... TEN...
THIR-TEEN OF THEM.
AND I KNOW WHERE THEY ARE.
SHOULD I JUST GO AROUND AND KILL THEM ONE BY ONE?
NO. THEIR GOAL IS LIKELY FREEING FERID AND QUEEN KRUL.
WELL, THEN! WHAT TO DO?

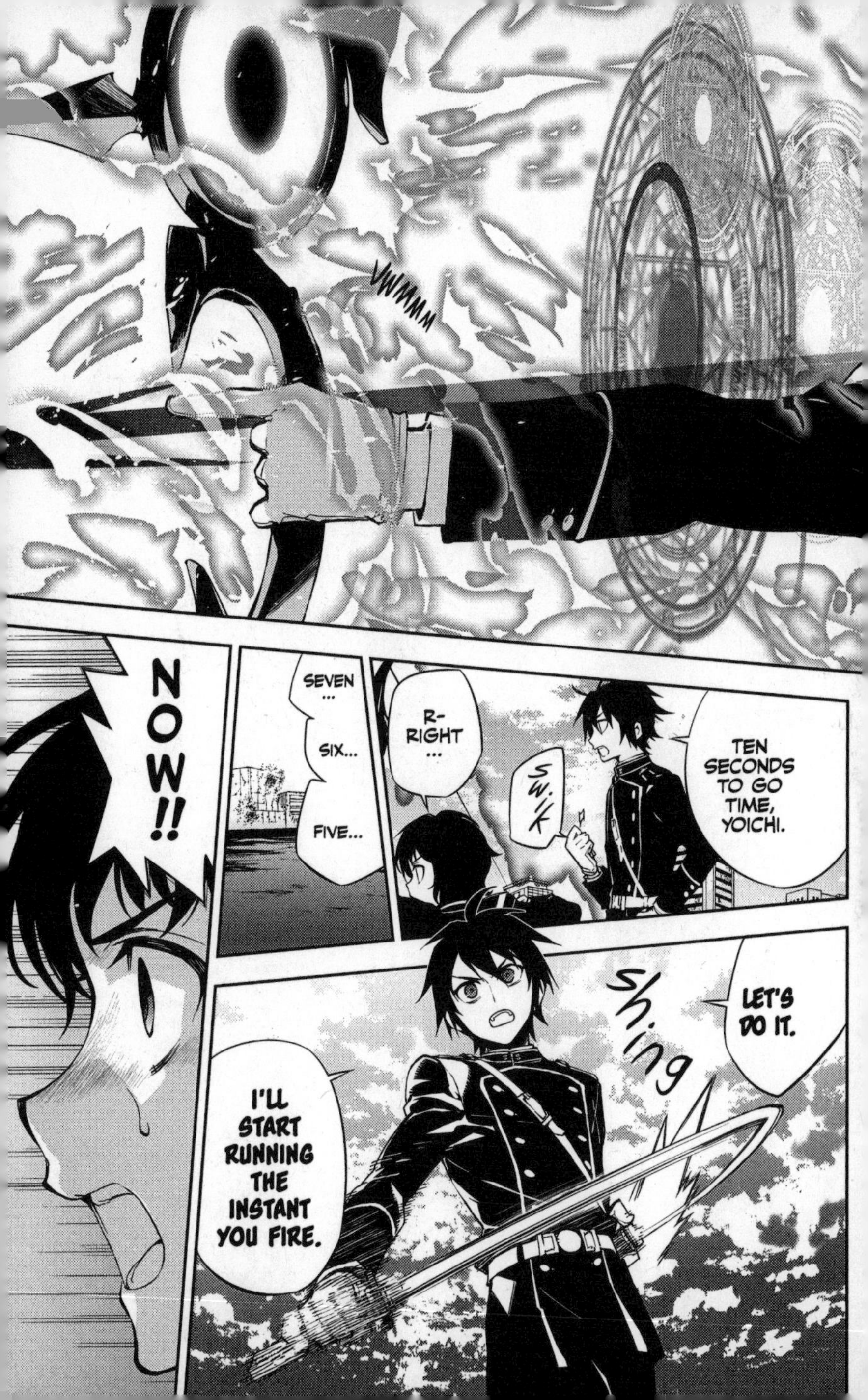
VWMMMM
TEN SECONDS TO GO TIME, YOICHI.
SWIK
R-RIGHT...
SEVEN...
SIX...
FIVE...
LET'S DO IT.
shing
I'LL START RUNNING THE INSTANT YOU FIRE.
NOW!!

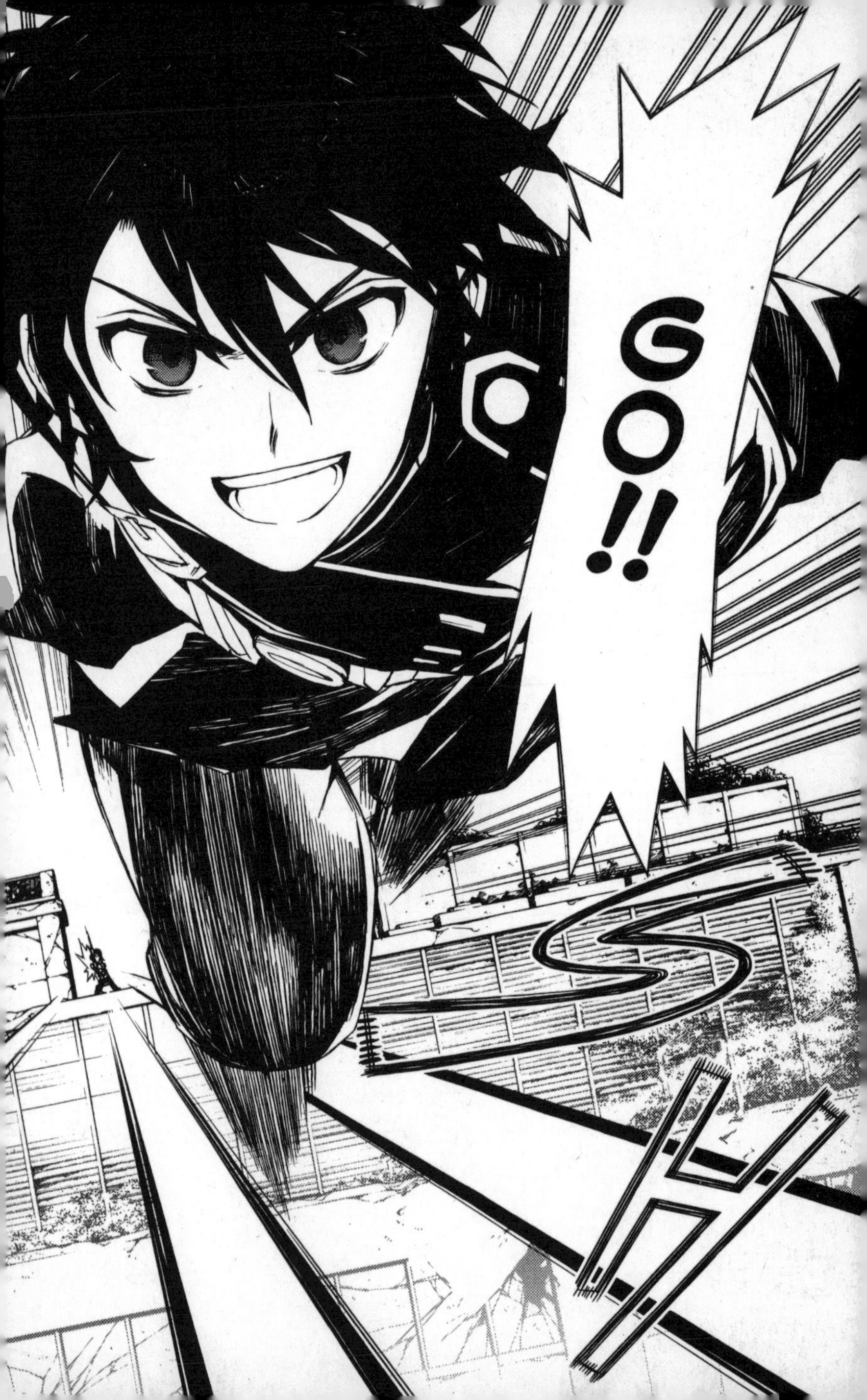
GO!!

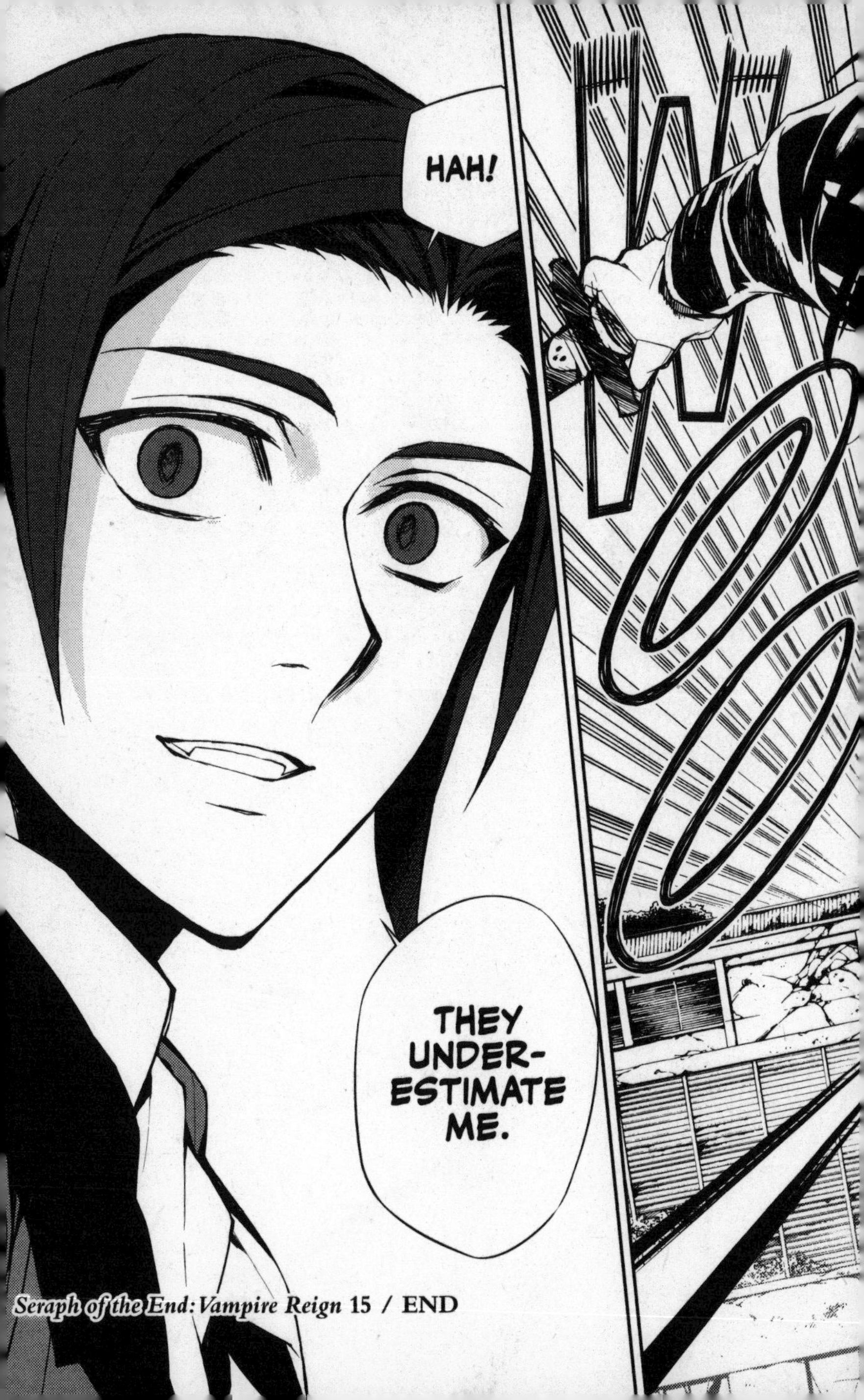
HAH!
THEY UNDER-ESTIMATE ME.
Seraph of the End: Vampire Reign 15 / END

AFTERWORD

HELLO. IT'S BEEN A WHILE. I'M TAKAYA KAGAMI.

THE NEW VOLUME IS FINALLY OUT. I'M SORRY IT TOOK SO MUCH LONGER THAN USUAL, BUT IT HAPPENED TO BE COMING OUT AT THE SAME TIME AS KODANSHA'S MANGA VERSION OF *GUREN ICHINOSE: CATASTROPHE AT 16*! WOW, WHAT AN AMAZING COINCIDENCE! OH, TO EXPLAIN THINGS FOR THOSE WHO MAY NOT YET BE IN THE KNOW, A MANGA ADAPTATION OF *GUREN ICHINOSE: CATASTROPHE AT 16* IS BEING SERIALIZED IN KODANSHA'S *MONTHLY SHONEN MAGAZINE* IN JAPAN.

WHEN I FIRST HEARD THAT A MANGA WAS ACTUALLY BEING SERIALIZED, I WAS SHOCKED. I MEAN, *SERAPH OF THE END* IS PUBLISHED IN SHUEISHA'S *JUMP SQUARE*. NOW *GUREN ICHINOSE: CATASTROPHE! AT 16* IS RUNNING IN KODANSHA'S *SHONEN MAGAZINE*? CAN THAT EVEN HAPPEN?! JUST THE THOUGHT HAD ME SHAKING WITH EXCITEMENT. THEN IT REALLY DID HAPPEN. BEFORE THE CATASTROPHE AND AFTER...BOTH STORIES ARE BEING PUBLISHED AT THE SAME TIME, SPLIT ACROSS TWO OF THE BIGGEST MONTHLY SHONEN MANGA ANTHOLOGIES OUT THERE.

AND, THANKS TO ALL YOU READERS OUT THERE, IT'S SUDDENLY SUPER POPULAR IN THE POLLS TOO!

THE MANGA IS EXTREMELY FAITHFUL TO THE NOVELS...
NO, IT'S TELLING THE SAME STORY IN AN EVEN MORE
INTERESTING WAY, SO I REALLY HOPE YOU WILL PICK UP
THE COLLECTED VOLUMES WHEN THEY COME OUT. WILL WE
SEE THIS CHARACTER OR THAT, YOU SAY? THEY'VE ALREADY
APPEARED! IT COVERS THE EVENTS THAT LED UP TO THE
CATASTROPHE, SO FOR THOSE OF YOU WHO HAVEN'T READ
THE NOVELS, I REALLY SUGGEST YOU PICK IT UP! TO THOSE
OF YOU WHO HAVE READ THE NOVELS, THE MANGA IS REALLY,
REALLY, *REEEALLY* GOOD, SO GIVE IT A SHOT TOO! I WROTE
THE ORIGINAL STORY, SO YOU KNOW I'M TELLING THE TRUTH.

SPEAKING OF ME WRITING, IF EVERYTHING GOES AS IT
SHOULD, NEXT MONTH (DEC, 2017) THE NEXT *SERAPH OF THE
END: GUREN ICHINOSE* NOVEL VOLUME WILL GO ON SALE,
THOUGH THE LAST BIT OF THAT TITLE ISN'T CATASTROPHE
AT 16.

IT'S CALLED *SERAPH OF THE END: GUREN ICHINOSE RESURRECTION
AT 19*. THE CATASTROPHE HAS FINALLY HAPPENED. HOW DID
GUREN AND SHINYA, KURETO AND THE OTHERS GET BACK ON
THEIR FEET? THE FOCUS OF THE STORY SHIFTS OVER TO HOW
HUMANITY STARTED TO REBUILD.

THEN IN JANUARY OF NEXT YEAR THE ART BOOK COMES OUT!
BOTH THE END OF 2017 AND THE BEGINNING OF 2018 WILL
HAVE AN AVALANCHE OF NEW *SERAPH OF THE END!* I HOPE
YOU ALL WILL ENJOY IT!

—TAKAYA KAGAMI

A brilliant sketch of Yuichiro by the author!

TAKAYA KAGAMI is a prolific light novelist whose works include the action and fantasy series *The Legend of the Legendary Heroes*, which has been adapted into manga, anime and a video game. His previous series, *A Dark Rabbit Has Seven Lives*, also spawned a manga and anime series.

❝ A lot of things have been going on as of late and I've been wearing a lot more suits. Growing up, I adored the movie *The Godfather* and I dreamed of having a life where I got to wear nice suits. That's why I always wear one to autograph sessions. Now I get to wear them even more during my everyday life! ❞

YAMATO YAMAMOTO, born 1983, is an artist and illustrator whose works include the *Kure-nai* manga and the light novels *Kure-nai*, *9S -Nine S-* and *Denpa Teki na Kanojo*. Both *Denpa Teki na Kanojo* and *Kure-nai* have been adapted into anime.

❝ *Seraph of the End* has reached volume 15. It has novels, fan books and a spin-off manga series. Now even Kodansha is publishing a manga series for it! The world of *Seraph of the End* is ever expanding. I hope you continue enjoying it! ❞

DAISUKE FURUYA previously assisted Yamato Yamamoto with storyboards for *Kure-nai*.

Seraph of the End

—VAMPIRE REIGN—

VOLUME 15
SHONEN JUMP ADVANCED MANGA EDITION

STORY BY **TAKAYA KAGAMI**
ART BY **YAMATO YAMAMOTO**
STORYBOARDS BY **DAISUKE FURUYA**

TRANSLATION **Adrienne Beck**
TOUCH-UP ART & LETTERING **Sabrina Heep**
DESIGN **Shawn Carrico**
EDITOR **Marlene First**

OWARI NO SERAPH © 2012 by Takaya Kagami,
Yamato Yamamoto, Daisuke Furuya
All rights reserved. First published in Japan in 2012 by SHUEISHA Inc., Tokyo.
English translation rights arranged by SHUEISHA Inc.

The stories, characters and incidents mentioned in this
publication are entirely fictional.

Printed in the U.S.A.

Published by VIZ Media, LLC
P.O. Box 77010
San Francisco, CA 94107

10 9 8 7 6 5 4 3 2 1
First printing, September 2018

viz.com

shonenjump.com

PARENTAL ADVISORY
SERAPH OF THE END is rated T+ for Older Teen
and is recommended for ages 16 and up. This
volume contains violence and some adult themes.

  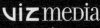

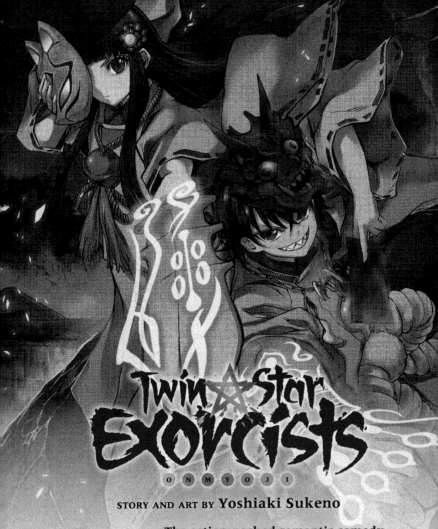

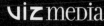